PUBLIC SECTOR FINANCIAL MANAGEMENT

Third Edition

H.M. Coombs and D.E. Jenkins

THOMSON

LEARNING

Australia • Canada • Mexico • Singapore • Spain • United Kingdom • United States

THOMSON

Public Sector Financial Management

Copyright © H.M. Coombs and D.E. Jenkins 2002

For more information, contact Thomson Learning, High Holborn House, 50-51 Bedford Row, London WC1R 4LR or visit us on the World Wide Web at:
http://www.thomsonlearning.co.uk

British Library Cataloguing-in-Publication Data
A catalogue record for this book is available from the British Library

ISBN-13: 978-1-86152-675-5
ISBN-10: 1-86152-675-X

First edition published by Chapman & Hall 1991
Second edition published by Chapman & Hall 1994
Reprinted 1995
Reprinted by International Thomson Business Press 1997 and 1999

Third edition 2002 by Thomson Learning
Reprinted 2005 and 2006 (twice) by Thomson Learning

Typeset by Saxon Graphics Ltd, Derby
Printed in the UK by TJ Digital, Padstow Cornwall

Contents

List of exhibits

List of figures

List of tables

Preface to first edition

In the period since 1979 the public sector has faced significant challenges caused by the rapid pace of change enshrined in a welter of new legislation and government directives and exhortations. As significant, however, is a change in general attitudes both towards and within the public sector which has resulted in the emergence of a new managerial culture. This culture places greater emphasis on economy, efficiency and effectiveness in all spheres of the public sector where services are delivered. As greater pressure is placed on the public sector to provide services in this new environment increased demands are being put on the financial management skills of service managers. These service managers are also frequently asked to exercise these skills with financial management information systems which were often designed more to produce the financial accounts than to provide them with the information they need to run their services.

A demand thus exists for financial information which is directly relevant to decision making. There is also a need for the service manager to become more actively involved in financial management than he or she has been previously and to develop interpretative skills. This problem is further compounded by a lack of financial training for many service managers who have traditionally relied on a central finance department for financial advice but are now expected to make their own financial decisions. Finally, students training for both financial and general managerial positions in the public sector also must be aware of the increased need for financial management skills in order to manage adequately the resources that will be within their control.

It seemed to us that in writing this book we should attempt to address these problems by examining the financial management techniques that are considered appropriate to the public sector manager, using these as a base to develop interpretative skills. In undertaking this task it might be thought that the natural starting point would be the existing literature. There was, however, no obvious place to begin as the area of financial management in the public sector has been substantially ignored by previous writers. This situation was not exactly unexpected as we have taught public sector financial management for a number of years and developed our own examples and illustrations based on our professional training and experience. This approach is, therefore, adopted in this book with substantial discussion of the practices undertaken in public sector financial management. This approach is complemented with exhibits and examples to show the techniques in practice and discussion of the non-financial factors which affect any service operating in a political environment. Importantly, it must be remembered that a technique only provides a financial result; particular emphasis must be given to the interpretation of that result, especially where non-financial factors are important. This clearly is the case with the public sector.

It is obviously not possible to cover every area of the public sector due to its size and variability. It is hoped, however, that the exhibits, examples and general text will enable the reader to see direct applications to any area of the public sector with which he or she is directly familiar. It will be noted by readers that many of the financial management techniques discussed are directly related to those currently used in the private sector. It is thought that this is particularly important given the increased emphasis on private sector management techniques that the public sector needs to develop if it is to compete successfully in a competitive tender situation. We believe that these techniques will play an increasingly important role in public sector financial management, but also that they must be used in the correct context while bearing in mind special factors that affect policy decisions in the public sector.

Each chapter concludes with a number of questions. The objects of those which are of a computational nature are, first, the calculation of the accounting solution to the problem and, second, but as important, the consideration of the wider implications of the results of the calculations. This combination of the provision of financial results and the subsequent interpretation of those results together with relevant advice on a course of action to be followed are the true financial management challenges. These challenges have been created by the changing times faced in the field of public sector financial management for trained accountants, service managers and students.

Finally, we are grateful to the Polytechnic of Wales and the Chartered Institute of Public Finance and Accountancy for permission to reproduce examination questions.

Preface to second edition

Since the first edition of this book was published the speed of changes affecting the public sector show no sign of slowing down. Indeed, it might be argued that the only constant in the environment of the public sector manager is change. Certainly, the need for all managers, potential managers and students of public sector management to be equipped with the skills of financial management can be seen no longer as a virtue but as a necessity. We have, therefore, updated and expanded the original text in line with this objective while attempting to retain much of the style of the first edition, which attracted many favourable comments from readers and reviewers.

A major new feature in this second edition is the inclusion of a number of short case studies which pull together the themes of financial management developed in the individual chapters. These case studies are based on our experiences in acting as consultants to various public sector organizations and thus represent 'real world' financial problems faced by public sector managers. In these problems we have kept the main features of each scenario without overwhelming the reader with complex financial calculations. This is to allow the reader to understand the principles of financial management and to develop skills of interpretation. More complex financial calculations, as in the first edition, are contained within the questions at the end of each chapter. In this respect an accompanying teacher's guide has been prepared with solutions to all these problems and to provide guidance with respect to the case studies as there are, in many of these cases, no unique solutions. This is as would be expected in the real world.

Finally, we would like to thank all those who spent time commenting on the first edition of this text and whose constructive ideas have been most helpful in undertaking this revision.

Preface to third edition

In writing this third edition, as with the first and second editions, the speed of change affecting the world of the public sector manager shows no sign of slowing down. In this edition we cover such issues as resource accounting, best value, public service agreements and the private finance initiative. These issues place pressure on public sector managers to improve performance frequently within an increasingly constrained budget. This is in a context where clients for the services provided by these managers, whether they be internal to the organization or external members of the public, are subjecting those services to increasing scrutiny particularly over the level and quality of performance being delivered for the 'price' being charged.

In terms of financial management, public sector accountants can no longer rely on the basic ability to process accounting entries (termed basic knowing – see Coombs, Hobbs and Jenkins, 2000, pp. 152–167). They now need to be able to provide advice and interpretation in the context of the service being delivered to improve it. We are also seeing a need increasingly to control and measure outputs and not just to achieve financial targets. Performance is increasingly related to the quality of output achieved for the resources devoted to a particular service. It could be argued that accountability in the public sector has now evolved from the traditional probity measures, as epitomized by the publication of audited financial accounts, to include performance reporting although such performance reports may largely be used and understood internally. In local government, for example, the extent to which the general public may understand, or even be interested in, the intricacies of the revised capital accounting system and the asset management revenue account is possibly debatable.

These responsibilities to deliver and demonstrate that results are being achieved are increasingly being devolved to lower and lower levels of operational management. At the same time these individuals are having to wrestle with increasingly complex accounting issues such as depreciation and cost of capital charges charged on the current value of assets in use. These are areas in which they have not necessarily been adequately trained and, in the case of resource accounting in central government, are dealing with for the first time. It is inevitable, therefore, that they want financial advice, with that advice to be delivered in a format which they can understand and in a time frame relevant to the decisions required. These changes present both a challenge and an opportunity for financial managers to provide that advice which can improve the delivery of service objectives.

In addition to updating the material within the chapters a number of new case studies have been added to this edition to pull together the themes of financial management developed in these individual chapters. Users of the second edition welcomed the addition of case studies and we trust they will find the additional cases equally helpful.

Finally, we would like to thank all those who commented on earlier editions and we have attempted to take on board points raised in writing this edition.

1 Introduction

Key learning objectives

After reading this chapter you should be able to:

1. Appreciate the importance of sound financial management techniques to the public sector.
2. Distinguish between the different definitions of public expenditure and understand the mechanisms for deciding the overall levels of public expenditure.
3. Recognize the elements of the major initiatives in the public sector which contribute to the need for public sector managers to exercise sound financial management skills.

The Conservative Government (1979 to 1997) had as one of its major policy objectives the restoration of market forces as far as possible throughout the economy. In his budget speech of 9 March 1982 Sir Geoffrey Howe stated: 'It remains our purpose, wherever possible to transfer to the private sector assets which can be better managed there.' From 1982 significant assets that were in the public sector were transferred into private ownership, for example, British Telecom, British Steel (now Corus), British Gas, the electricity boards, the water authorities and the railways. There still, however, remains a significant public sector, as will be discussed throughout this chapter.

In those areas of the economy that remained in the public sector during the time of the Conservative administration the object was to introduce the concept of the 'bottom line'. This is comparable with the profit and loss concept of the private sector and the private sector management techniques that go along with this concept. This took the form of:

- a set return to be earned on assets from contracts won under conditions of competitive tendering;
- the reorganization of management along private sector lines;
- the development of an internal market for services coupled with an increased emphasis on management's responsibility to achieve a balanced cash limited budget often under severe financial constraints due to inadequate allowances for inflationary pressures.

In addition, these objectives did not necessarily operate in isolation thus increasing the pressure on managers to perform.

The then government was also determined to introduce private sector capital into public sector projects either independently of the public sector or in partnership. In such joint ventures it was expected that the private sector would take the lead ('Autumn Statement', 1992 paras 2.111–2.117, HM Government, 1992). These partnerships were in further support of injecting private sector ideals into public sector attitudes although there was obvious potential for conflict.

The Labour government was returned to power in 1997 and initially adopted the spending plans of the government it had replaced. On coming into office, however, it introduced a new framework for monetary and fiscal policy aimed at ensuring and promoting economic stability. This policy might be described as 'Prudent for a Purpose' (Cm. 4807) and was based around the concept of the comprehensive review of public services which was aimed at directing money to key areas within the government's priorities.

This policy was to operate within:

1. a new monetary framework with the Bank of England given operational independence to determine interest rates to deliver the government's inflation target figures;
2. a new fiscal framework based on two rules:
   the so-called golden rule where, on average over the economic cycle, the government would only borrow to invest and not to fund current (revenue) expenditure; and
   the sustainable investment rule under which public sector debt would be held over the economic cycle at what was regarded as a stable and prudent level;
3. a new public expenditure regime the objective of which is to provide greater certainty and encourage long-term planning.

(*Source:* HM Government, 1999a)

While it is perhaps early days to assess the success of this framework there seems no sign that the pressures on managers in the public sector to perform are being reduced.

These pressures mean delivering value for money (VFM) which can be defined as the achievement of:

Economy	The practice of management of sound housekeeping and the virtue of thrift. An economical operation acquires resources of appropriate quality and quantity at the least cost.
Efficiency	Making sure that the maximum useful output is gained from the resources devoted to each activity or, alternatively, only the minimum level of energy and work necessary is used for a given level of output.
Effectiveness	Ensuring that output from any given activity is achieving the desired result.

It should be stressed that VFM is only achieved when all three elements are combined and can no longer be seen as a virtue but a necessity for public sector managers to achieve. Value for money has been a constant theme of all governments since 1979. In 1992 the Conservative government stated that public expenditure 'should take a declining share of national income over time, while value for money is constantly improved' (HM Government, 1992, para 2.14). In 2000 the present government stated 'the government is making sure that both existing and new spending is targeted to deliver value for money and achieve the outcomes the public wants to see' (HM Government, 2000a, para. 2.21). It will be noted that the second quotation also places emphasis on outcomes and as will be discussed later in this text this issue raises many problems for public sector managers.

The present government has also established public service agreements covering the whole of the public sector setting explicit aims, objectives and targets to be achieved with any funding provided to government departments. Throughout this process and running alongside it is a system of output and performance analysis attempting to measure how successfully any funding provided is delivering the original aims and objectives of programmes.

Such individual or, indeed, combinations of factors have placed all managers in the public sector under increased pressure to perform and deliver both individually and collectively. This is often with financial systems, which are, even today, based on the desire to produce published accounts, rather than on the operational manager's needs for financial information. Further, the manager's decision-making environment in many areas of the public sector is one in which objectives are difficult to state or are ambiguous, market prices are inappropriate and the ability to pay irrelevant to consumption. Additionally, the political consequences of certain decisions may seriously undermine the electoral chances of the party in power whether nationally or locally. Clearly all these factors represent challenges to be overcome but the role of the management accountant is to provide information to service managers in the form they require, in sufficient detail and with sufficient accuracy for decisions to be made. In addition, these tasks have to be performed in an appropriate time scale to enable the decision-making process to be activated and the decisions reached to be relevant to the circumstances facing service managers as they arise. In the chapters that follow examples of management accounting techniques applied to the public sector are examined and discussed. Management accounting is not, however, seen as synonymous with financial management.

Financial management is seen in this text as being proactive in the use of financial and other information actively to manage the public sector enterprise to achieve laid down objectives and not merely the provision of financial information. It is also becoming increasingly important for management accountants (and indeed managers in general) that they are able to interpret financial information to assist operational personnel who may need support when dealing with the complexities of public sector financial management.

The remainder of this introduction takes an overview of the public sector spending decision-making process and then examines a number of the major initiatives that have taken place over the last 20 years by governments of both political persuasions. These initiatives were undertaken in the belief that the public sector needs to operate more economically, efficiently and effectively to deliver improved services to clients. The delivery of this desire by governments to improve services depends on public sector managers having skills of interpretation of data, being in receipt of sound financial advice and guidance and on having good financial and non-financial information to hand.

1.1 The public sector planning process

The proper planning of public expenditure is clearly an important mechanism in the government's overall control of the levels of public sector spending. The Plowden

Committee, reporting in 1961, recommended that: 'Regular surveys should be made of public expenditure as a whole, over a period of years ahead, and in relation to prospective resources; decisions involving substantial future expenditure should be taken in the light of those surveys' (Plowden Report, 1961).

Since the May 1997 election the Chancellor of the Exchequer, in accordance with tradition, has restored the budget statement to the Spring but presents a pre-budget report in the Autumn. This report in effect is aimed at providing a progress report on government plans to date, reviews the state of the economy and the government's finances and gives an indication of the future direction of government policy.

The expenditure planning process introduced by the Labour government aims to provide a clear distinction between current and capital expenditure. Two categories of expenditure are used in this process. These are:

■ departmental expenditure limits (DELs) which are multi-year plans where planning is up to three years ahead;
■ annually managed expenditure (AME) which covers those items which cannot be subject to firm multi-year limits. It is not published by departments but by category of expenditure.

Until the 1960s the budget was the time when the government presented both its tax and expenditure plans to parliament although the detailed estimates and financial secretary's memorandum on public spending were normally presented to parliament a little earlier. Following the Plowden Report mentioned earlier the publication gap between the expenditure plans and the financing of those plans began to grow. The results of the public expenditure survey process were published in January and contained the results of past plans (out-turns) and further projections. Following the acceptance of the recommendations of the Treasury and Civil Service Select Committee in the early 1990s an Autumn Statement was introduced which contained more and detailed information on public expenditure and plans for three years ahead. This further emphasized the division between expenditure and financing with the budget taking place in the Spring. The last Conservative government moved the budget statement to November to coincide with the Autumn Statement. The advantages claimed for this approach were that:

1. Ministers would be better placed to judge expenditure plans in the light of the overall fiscal and tax position.
2. Presentation would be improved in that policy would appear more consistent and coherent.
3. A more informed debate could take place.
4. The early announcement of tax proposals would enable taxpayers to better plan their affairs and reduce the administrative burden on employers of changes in tax and National Insurance contributions.

(*Source:* Budget Reform, 1992)

Table 1.1 shows the budget process adopted as a result of these reforms and allows a comparison to be made with the changes introduced from 1997.

As outlined the present government has moved the annual budget statement back to March and has ended the practice of the annual public sector expenditure round. The present position is that:

1. Departments are set multi-year spending limits when the outcome of the spending review is announced.

Table 1.1   Public expenditure planning process adopted and used by the Conservative administration

1992	
November	1992 Autumn Statement. Expenditure plans 1993–4 to 1995–6
1993	
January–February	Examination of results of previous plans
March	Budget 1993 (financial year 1993–94)
April–June	Government departments prepare bids based on Treasury guidelines. Treasury analyze bids
July	Cabinet decides overall expenditure totals
September–November	Bilateral negotiations between departments and Treasury. In the event of a dispute a 'Star Chamber' adjudicates. This is made up of senior ministers independent of the dispute. Final appeal is to the Cabinet. Consideration of financing of expenditure and public sector borrowing requirement
November	Budget for next financial year and expenditure plans for future years
1994	
January	Finance Bill published
February	Departmental reports and statistical supplement to Budget published
March	Detailed estimates to parliament

2. These departmental limits are drawn together in the departmental expenditure limit.
3. Resources are allocated and monitored on the basis of agreed outcomes and departments are set quality standards for service delivery.
4. Departments have extended powers to carry budgets from year to year.
5. Firm multi-year limits are not thought practical for large demand-led programmes and are brought together under the title annually managed expenditure.
6. Annual managed expenditure is subject to annual scrutiny as part of the budget process.

The extent to which these multi-year spending plans are firmly in place is open to question. It has been commented that in his 2000 budget the Chancellor 'undermined his own hard-won credibility with the financial community by ripping up the first three-year spending programme before the first year was even over' and, in addition, that 'Brown's cavalier attitude to his own "firm" spending plans calls into question his commitment to run fiscal policy on a long-term basis' (*Public Finance*, July 2000, p.19).

Total managed expenditure

Total managed expenditure is a figure drawn from the national accounts and includes the current and capital expenditure of the public sector. Current expenditure is that expenditure which is incurred on day-to-day expenses such as salaries and wages and capital expenditure is expenditure on long-term assets such as buildings.

Total managed expenditure includes the expenditure of central government, local government and public corporations. It does not include financial transactions and is the expenditure side of public sector net borrowing. It is the government's preferred measure of the fiscal stance. DEL and AME have been defined so that they sum to total managed expenditure.

Public expenditure budgeting and control aggregates

The previous system of public expenditure planning and control had established a control total and was cash limited. Table 1.2 illustrates differences between the previous control total and the current system of DELs and AMEs for a selection of public expenditure programmes. Planned and actual expenditure for both DELs and AMEs are set out in Tables 1.3, 1.4 and 1.5. It will be noted that taken together they add to total managed expenditure.

A further change from the 2000 spending review is the introduction of resource budgeting. Until the adoption of the new system, public spending in general had been controlled by the use of cash limits although there were some exceptions, such as credit approvals for local authorities. Under the move to resource accounting what will be relevant is when the resources are consumed and not when payments are made or cash received. Therefore, under resource budgeting and accounting costs such as the

Table 1.2 Selected service comparison

Programme	Old system		New system				
Name	In control Total	Not in control Total	DEL	Main departmental programmes in AME	Locally financed expenditure (AME)	Other AME	Not in DEL or AME
Most programmes	X		X				
Controllable social security	X			X			
Cyclical social security		X		X			
Welfare to work		X	X				
LASFE					X		
Student loans Net lending	X						X
Payments to EC	X				X		

(*Source:* HM Government, 1999a)

Table 1.3 Public expenditure 1997/98–2001/02: Summary

	1997–98 out-turn	1998–99 out-turn	1999–00 estimated out-turn	2000–01 plans	2001–02 plans– resource basis	2002–03 plans– resource basis	2003–4 plans– resource basis
Departmental expenditure limits							
Current budget	149.7	155.3	165.1	177.3	185.1	197.3	209.1
Capital budget	12.6	12.1	13.8	16.4	27.0	31.9	36.6
Departmental expenditure limits	162.3	167.4	178.9	193.7	212.1	229.3	245.7
Annually managed expenditure							
Main departmental programmes	104.0	105.8	112.5	114.4	140.5	144.3	149.9
Locally financed expenditure	15.6	16.1	17.2	18.1	18.9	19.8	20.6
Other	40.8	41.7	36.7	44.7	21.4	20.0	64.9
Annually managed expenditure	160.4	163.6	166.3	177.2	180.8	186.1	193.9
Total managed expenditure	322.7	331.0	345.2	370.9	392.9	415.4	439.6

(*Source:* HM Government, 2000a,b)

consumption of stocks, provisions to meet financial payments and the costs of using capital assets (depreciation and cost of capital) will be relevant in decision making.

It is claimed that resource budgeting at the strategic level will allow:

■ a clear view of the true costs of providing individual services;
■ a more accurate reflection of capital consumption;
■ a clearer distinction between current and capital expenditure;
■ a better measure of the total value of government assets.

At the operational level, it should provide managers with information which allows them to:

■ manage more effectively capital assets by properly planning investment and disinvestment;
■ manage working capital (debtors, creditors, stocks and cash) more efficiently;
■ identify more clearly the distinction between loans and grants.

Table 1.4 Departmental expenditure limits 1994/95–2003/04

	£m								
	1995–96 out-turn	1996–97 out-turn	1997–98 out-turn	1998–99 out-turn	1999–00 estimated out-turn	2000–01 plans	2001–02 resource plans	2002–03 resource plans	2003–04 resource plans
Education and Employment	14 181	14 235	14 777	14 326	15 870	18 356	21 300	23 500	25 700
Health	32 951	33 763	35 297	37 376	40 759	45 030	49 500	54 400	59 000
DETR – main programme	9 626	9 664	9 606	8 998	10 310	10 838	13 200	15 500	17 900
DETR – local government etc.	30 294	31 315	31 372	32 737	34 199	35 353	36 800	39 200	41 900
Home Office	6 382	6 436	6 730	7 104	7 774	8 090	9 600	10 300	10 600
Legal departments	2 638	2 627	2 641	2 680	2 764	2 867	3 100	3 200	3 200
Defence	21 517	21 383	20 910	22 475	22 863	22 820	23 600	24 200	25 000
Foreign Office	1 333	1 053	1 076	1 094	1 179	1 116	1 200	1 300	1 300
International Development	2 197	2 096	1 999	2 319	2 511	2 751	3 100	3 300	3 600
Trade and Industry	3 432	3 333	3 084	2 916	3 363	3 658	4 600	4 300	4 300
Agriculture, Fisheries and Food	892	2 174	1 692	1 362	1 415	1 215	1 300	1 300	1 400
Culture, Media and Sport	1 014	955	903	917	1 022	1 015	1 100	1 200	1 200
Social Security Administration	3 289	3 401	3 229	2 944	3 294	3 208	3 900	4 300	4 200
Scotland	13 130	13 100	12 946	12 894	14 039	14 876	16 200	17 400	18 400
Wales	6 346	6 474	6 499	6 675	7 225	7 694	8 400	9 100	9 800
Northern Ireland	5 246	5 356	5 462	5 595	5 976	6 277	6 800	7 100	7 300
Chancellor's Department	2 799	2 750	2 751	3 141	3 606	3 521	4 100	4 300	4 300
Cabinet Office	1 475	1 424	1 210	1 248	1 391	1 343	1 500	1 500	1 600
Welfare to Work			144	536	850	1 420	900	900	1 400
Invest to Save							100	100	100
Capital Modernization Fund						176	400	900	1 200
Policy Innovation Fund							100	100	100
Reserve						2 100	1 500	2 000	2 500
Allowance for shortfall					−1500				
DEL	158 744	161 538	162 329	167 428	178 900	193 700	212 100	229 300	245 700
of which									
NHS	31 985	32 997	34 664	36 612	40 065	44 234	48 200	52 300	56 700

(*Source:* HM Government, 2000a,b)

Table 1.5 Total managed expenditure limits 1994/95–2003/04

	£m								
	1995–96 out-turn	1996–97 out-turn	1997–98 out-turn	1998–99 out-turn	1999–00 estimated out-turn	2000–01 plans	2001–02 resource basis	2002–03 resource basis	2003–04 resource basis
Departmental expenditure limits	158 744	161 538	162 329	167 428	178 900	193 700	212 100	229 300	245 700
Annually managed expenditure									
Social Security benefits	86 077	89 750	91 007	93 360	97 079	99 552	104 400	107 300	111 900
Housing Revenue account subsidies	4 238	4 184	3 980	3 521	3 376	3 344	3 300	3 200	3 100
Common Agricultural Policy	2 640	2 928	2 473	2 718	2 552	2 489	2 900	2 800	2 800
Export Credit Guarantee Dept.	–22	71	94	–170	931	302	300	200	0
Net payment to EC	3 355	1 802	2 153	3 572	2 579	2 690	2 500	2 600	2 900
Self-financing public corporations	–243	60	–294	–304	201	197	1 200	1 200	1 300
Locally financed expenditure	13 923	14 277	15 605	16 122	17 166	18 077	18 900	19 800	20 500
Net public service pensions	4 271	4 979	5 353	4 663	5 629	5 719	5 500	5 700	6 000
National Lottery	170	520	1 090	1 630	2 000	2 300	2 000	2 100	2 100
Government debt interest	26 452	27 987	29 975	29 542	25 482	27 770	26 100	25 300	24 700
Accounting and other adjustments	9 497	7 868	8 970	8 919	9 332	13 749	–8 100	–7 900	–7 100
AME margin						1 000	1 000	2 000	3 000
Depreciation							7 900	8 300	8 700
Costs of capital							13 200	13 500	13 800
Provisions and other charges							–300		200
Total AME	150 357	154 425	160 406	163 574	166 300	177 200	180 800	186 100	193 900
Total managed expenditure	309 100	315 963	322 735	331 001	345 200	370 900	392 900	415 400	439 600

(*Source:* HM Government, 2000a,b)

The effect of this change is now illustrated for a fictional department:

	2001–02 cash £m	2001–02 resource £m
Current/resource DEL	25 440	23 072
Capital DEL	2 440	5 105
Total DEL	27 880	25 177

Reconciliation of current cash DEL to resource DEL (£m)

Current cash DEL	25 440
Movement in creditors, debtors and cash over the year	165
Reclassification to capital expenditure	–2 438
Full resource consumption of public corporations (profits)	–95
Total	23 072

Expression of capital DEL in resource terms (£m)

Capital DEL – starting point	2 440
Reclassification of capital expenditure	2 438
Capital expenditure of department's public corporations	227
Total	5 105

This shows that the department, after allowing for movements in its working capital in its current expenditure, has had to classify some of what it has previously regarded as cash expenditure as capital. In the case of the Ministry of Defence, for example, expenditure on fighting equipment has, in the past, been treated as current expenditure but will now be treated as capital expenditure. The profits of the department's public corporations have registered as a credit in the resource budget while losses would represent a cost. For the capital recalculation the first item is a reverse of the earlier adjustment which reclassified capital expenditure in the current budget. The final item of the capital adjustment represents the capital investment of the department's public corporations which has been financed from trading activities. Under the Government Resources and Accounts Act 2000 the resource accounts will consist of:

- a statement of out-turn (showing actual out-turn against the budget);
- an operating cost statement;
- a balance sheet;
- a cash flow statement;
- a statement relating costs to objectives.

These statements exclude public sector pensions as they will adopt a similar format to that for private pension schemes.

Finally in this section, the principle of establishing an external finance limit (EFL) was introduced in 1976 initially as a short-term measure to control the external finance raised by public corporations and nationalized industries. As with many short-term measures this system still continues to operate. The government expects public corporations, if they make a cash surplus, to repay debt after paying for new investment.

Corporations are set an EFL for the financial year immediately ahead and provisionally for the rest of the planning period. The EFL is the main in-year public expenditure control for most public corporations.

Supply expenditure

As outlined earlier the two components of total managed expenditure are departmental expenditure limits and annually managed expenditure. The main elements of DEL and AME not financed from the supply estimates are funded directly from other sources such as the national insurance fund or local authority credit approvals. The supply estimates include most of the direct spending by central government departments on the NHS, defence, departmental running costs, part of the financing costs of public corporations and grants in aid to non-departmental public bodies. In addition they include such items as central government support for local authorities, grants to the devolved administrations in Scotland, Wales and Northern Ireland and grants and subsidies to nationalized industries. They are put before parliament by the government as requests for funds, debated by MPs and voted on. Parliamentary approval allows the government to draw funds from the Consolidated Fund to meet expenditures approved. If additional money is requested a supplementary supply estimate is sought by the government. If it is too late to seek a supplementary estimate provision is sought via an excess vote and such excesses are reported to the Public Accounts Committee by the Comptroller and Auditor General.

Having voted expenditure parliament naturally is concerned that it is controlled. Departments are expected to manage their budgets within their DEL and a failure to do so will result in an investigation and a reduction in the corresponding DEL for the next year. The Treasury also controls the ability of the department to transfer funds from discretionary programmes. Discretionary programmes are those programmes under the department's direct control. Virement will be allowed where there is a clear value for money case. An example of this may be where more discretionary spending could deliver greater savings on non-discretionary expenditure.

Until the end of the financial year 1998–99 a system of annual cash limits was the major control by government over its cash spending. Under the new planning process the government claims that departments have been given firm and realistic multi-year limits in cash to provide firm incentives to control costs. They are to be reviewed only if inflation exceeds targets (HM Government, 1998c). As stated, plans are made for three years but obviously the political expediency of the day will take precedence over the political contingencies of tomorrow. In the early days of public sector financial planning figures were given in constant prices or volume terms.

Planning in volume terms did have some advantages in that, for example, constant prices directly related to the operational decisions of managers on recruitment and other physical resources and revealed the 'real' trend over time. By 1976, however, it had become apparent that the use of constant prices in times of high inflation and tight monetary control caused problems in terms of planning and monitoring expenditure as cash spending resulted in programmes costing often considerably more than was anticipated. Under the volume planning system of planning and control there was no automatic reduction in the volume of the programme; if prices rose extra cash was made available and government expenditure rose automatically, consuming more of the economy's resources. Cash limits were therefore introduced and the cash figure became the determinant of expenditure during the year. The reasons given for the introduction of cash limits in the White Paper 'Cash Limits on Public Expenditure' (HM Government, 1976) included the need to:

1. give greater financial discipline;
2. ensure that resources consumed by the public sector were related to the ability of the economy as a whole to support this level of consumption;
3. control the sum spent in the financial year so that it related directly to the plan set out in the annual budget;
4. contribute to the government's counter-inflation policy by constraining managers' ability to pay higher prices;
5. relate the budget to the cash that would be spent during the year even if inflation was considerably higher than predicted.

Cash limits have also been imposed on certain areas of the budget which are demand led. It was stated in *Regina* v *Secretary of State for the Environment, ex parte* Greenwich Borough Council that the Secretary of State's obligation to fund the Housing Revenue Account under the Local Government and Housing Act 1979 was subject to the extent of the state's available resources (*The Times*, 22 August 1990).

The reasons why a particular item makes an appearance in the spending plans of any government are obviously complex. It would also be a mistake to ignore the behavioural implications of the whole process, as, for example, when expenditure bids are offered by spending ministers as sacrificial lambs to protect the core ambitions of their departments. This process has been described as 'haggling in a Turkish Bazaar' (Thain and Wright, 1990, p.51). More conventional reasons given for the inclusion of a particular item of expenditure in government spending plans include:

1. clear political commitments as set out in the party manifesto;
2. changing departmental objectives;
3. pressures from influential bodies such as non-governmental pressure groups, members of parliament and the EC;
4. ministerial judgement and initiative;
5. commitments resulting from past expenditure decisions;
6. rational investment appraisal indicating that the planned expenditure will result in savings.

Clearly, the game is one played in an atmosphere of political intrigue in which the ministers and the civil service mandarins are involved in wheeling and dealing to protect their own interests and causes.

Finally, in order to conclude this section mention should be made of the Contingency Reserve. The object of the Reserve is to allow expenditure to be undertaken that has not been planned for specifically without upsetting budget plans. If possible, any additional spending on behalf of a programme is met by savings elsewhere in that programme. Where this is not possible increased expenditure resulting from ministerial decisions is charged to the Contingency Reserve. Examples of its use might include a decision to launch a new initiative or to meet the costs of such events as natural disasters such as severe weather. The Contingency Reserve should not be confused with the Contingency Fund. The role of the Contingency Fund is to provide money for payments which, in the public interest, cannot be postponed until the money has been voted by parliament. The Fund is repaid as soon as possible, for example, if expenditure has to be incurred before a Supplementary Estimate can be passed by parliament then the Fund is repaid as soon as provision in Supplementary Estimates becomes available.

1.2 Allocating public expenditure within the UK

Devolved governments now exist in the UK for Scotland, Wales and Northern Ireland with assemblies in Wales and Northern Ireland and a parliament in Scotland. The UK central government allocates funds to these bodies. It is for them to decide where they wish to spend their budgets based on identified local priorities. The devolved administrations are fully accountable for the proper control and management of their individual allocations and for securing economy, efficiency and value for money through scrutiny. Each of the three bodies receives money under the so-called Barnett Formula which was first used in 1978. Under the formula three factors are taken into account in determining changes to each devolved administration's spending allocation in a spending review:

1. the quantity of the change in planned spending in central government departments;
2. the extent to which the central government's departmental programme is comparable with the service provided by the devolved administration;
3. each country's populations as a proportion of England, England and Wales or Great Britain as appropriate.

This calculation is made for each of the central government's departmental programmes within DEL. It should be remembered that the Scottish parliament has the power to levy its own variable rate of income tax.

1.3 The Citizen's Charter

The Citizen's Charter was announced by John Major in 1991. The aims of the policy were to achieve better quality in the provision of public services and to make them more responsive to public demands. The key to this was seen as 'to listen to what people say' within the motto of the 'customer comes first' (Citizen's Charter, 1992, p.1). In addition the then government again stated that resources to fund public services were limited and that taxpayers had a right to expect that money was spent to maximum effect. In its first report on the Citizen's Charter initiative it was pointed out that new management structures were developed, competition extended and new pay structures explored, these changes being in line with 'the pursuit of a single worthwhile cause: the safeguarding and improving of our public services for the benefit of those who use them at a cost which the nation can afford' (p.1). Charter marks were to be awarded for good service to the client.

Charters have been published in a wide variety of fields including railways, schools, tax offices and the National Health Service (NHS).

In the NHS the original Patient's Charter (now revised) set out key rights and entitlements. These included the right to:

1. receive health care on the basis of clinical need, regardless of the ability to pay;
2. enjoy respect for privacy, dignity and religious and cultural beliefs;
3. be given a clear explanation of any treatment proposed, including any risks and alternatives, before agreeing to the treatment;

4. have access to personal health records, and to know that those working for the NHS will, by law, keep those records confidential;

5. be given information on local NHS quality standards and maximum waiting times;

6. be guaranteed admission to hospital for virtually all treatments by a specific date;

7. specific times for out-patient appointments and a maximum waiting time of 30 minutes;

8. a named qualified nurse, midwife or health visitor responsible for the patient's care.

As examples of standards being set by organizations the following are some of the targets established:

1. Standards came into effect in government ministries from 1 April 1997 that defined target response times for letters sent to a ministry.

2. Parcelforce aims to respond to telephone enquiries the same day.

3. British Gas aimed to reply to letters within five working days, although in 1996 it withdrew from the Charter Mark scheme apparently fearing bad publicity should the badge be compulsorily withdrawn as a result of poor service.

4. Westminster City Council Library Service aims to provide a good quality service to its membership by a prompt response to requests.

5. Following rail privatization each of the 25 individual train companies established a passenger charter but their quality is questionable.

In local government the Audit Commission under Part 1 of the 1992 Local Government Finance Act was charged with the responsibility of drawing up a set of indicators for measuring the performance of local authority services. The Audit Commission list of indicators was first published in December 1992 and covered such services as education, social services, libraries, planning and housing benefit. The indicators were selected on the basis of:

1. the ability of the public to comprehend them without oversimplification and without creating incentives for authorities to distort them;

2. making comparability between authorities possible;

3. enabling the measurement of how effectively services meet the needs of different groups of local citizens;

4. the ability to compare the service for one authority over a period of time.

An important part of the Citizen's Charter was seen as the market testing of services provided by civil servants in terms of comparison with the private sector of quality and cost. The government aimed to market test services in, for example, the Ministry of Defence to the value of £323m involving 12 200 members of staff, the Home Office to the value of £120m involving 3850 members of staff, and the Department of the Environment to the value of £58m involving 700 staff. The total value of this market testing was estimated at £1449m and involved the jobs of 44 250 civil servants (Citizen's Charter, 1992, p.61). The type of services covered included computing services, internal audit, vehicle maintenance and professional property services.

For the policy to be successful it could be argued that there was a need to:

1. give managers greater freedom of action by allowing them to set local pay and conditions for staff;

2. give operational managers budget-holding responsibilities enabling them to negotiate such matters as cleaning; training and financial services;

3. encourage delegation to the lowest possible managerial level and provide these individuals with the necessary skills to do the job;

4. provide the rewards of enterprise to managers with clear promotion routes for those who have the capacity to do the job;
5. encourage a major cultural shift towards customer responsiveness achieving value for money, quality in service delivery and accountability;
6. provide vision as to the direction of the initiative in order to provide a focus for expectation of each service.

Over time the initiative has continued to evolve so that the programme has now been renamed 'Service First – the new charter programme'. Service First has a broader prospective than the original idea in that it will not only be awarding charters and charter marks for quality services but will also initiate new projects. The key features of the new scheme are claimed as:

1. putting users first, consulting and involving them not only in the way that services are delivered but also in *what* is delivered;
2. involving front line staff in finding ways to improve the standard of service delivery to users;
3. improving the consistency and quality of charters;
4. finding new ways to spread best practice to improve those areas not performing;
5. laying great emphasis on innovation to improve service delivery;
6. encouraging public services to work together to provide 'seamless' services.

One of the first organizations to be awarded a charter mark for good service was the Passport Agency in 1992. In 1999 the Agency was stripped of its charter mark for providing poor quality service following the installation of a new computer system.

The Citizen's Charter initiative and its new guise of Service First has had and will continue to have important implications for public sector managers in that the implementation of the measures proposed represent another call for managers to improve economy, efficiency and effectiveness in the delivery of services.

1.4 The Financial Management Initiative

In line with a general objective of improving efficiency in the Civil Service the Financial Management Initiative (FMI) was developed in 1982. The aims of the FMI were to improve the management, allocation and control of resources. In detail the White Paper 'Efficiency and Effectiveness in the Civil Service' (Treasury and Civil Service Committee 1982) states that the aims of the FMI were to give managers:

1. A clear view of their objectives; and means to assess, and wherever possible measure, outputs or performance in relation to these objectives.
2. Well-defined responsibility for making the best use of their resources, including a critical scrutiny of output and value for money.
3. The information (particularly about costs), the training and access to expert advice which they needed to exercise their responsibilities effectively.

Prior to the FMI, the Rayner scrutinies (National Audit Office, 1986b) had attempted to look at value for money in central government. The objectives of these scrutinies were:

1. To mount an eye-catching and public demonstration of how the citizen, business and industry were overburdened with forms and requests for information.
2. To examine the general practice and conventions in government that were barriers to the effective management of business resources by ministers and their officials.

3. To examine, in collaboration with ministers, selected specific activities and functions in particular departments that might be unnecessarily costly or wasteful. This examination was to question all aspects of the work normally taken for granted.

In its report 'The Rayner Scrutiny Programmes 1979–1983' the National Audit Office (1986b) recorded annual savings of £421m identified by the scrutiny programmes. In 'Learning from Experience', the report to the Minister of State for Defence Procurement (Ministry of Defence, 1988), it was reported after a scrutiny exercise that between £3bn and £4bn of the Ministry of Defence's annual expenditure related to costs that were unforeseen when projects started. The report also criticized the lack of clear responsibility, authority and accountability of the managers of major defence projects (quoted in *Public Finance and Accountancy*, 20/5/88).

At about the same time that the Rayner exercises were getting off the ground, an attempt had been made to introduce a management information system (MINIS) into central government by Michael Heseltine for the use of ministers. The idea was to enable ministers to gain information on their departments to allow better control and more informed decision making. The key features of MINIS were the preparation of annual statements summarizing performance and plans for each of the departments' activities; the examination of these by ministers, top management and the managers directly responsible for the activity; and the requirement to follow up with agreed action. Effectively, the FMI combined the relatively simple Rayner studies and MINIS into a more sophisticated financial management framework.

The National Audit Office (NAO) reported that in respect of management accounting and budgetary control systems developed under the FMI an investigation in respect of 12 departments revealed that:

1. All departments had found it necessary to develop their systems for the budgeting and control of administrative costs and for informing managers of the cost of the resources allocated to them and of their performance in using these resources particularly as regards measures of output.
2. The range of costs covered by departmental budgetary control had varied but had become more comprehensive as the systems had developed.
3. The extent to which managers could exercise control over the components of their budgets varied as did the opportunities to transfer provisions between budget heads.
4. Departments had made encouraging progress in developing budgeting as an effective control over administrative costs, although more still needed to be done to achieve the full potential benefits. In particular, the area of developing links between input costs and the value of outputs.

(*Source:* National Audit Office, 1986a)

The NAO study established that the FMI had resulted in departments identifying the need to enhance existing management systems or to introduce new ones. For this they had produced sound plans which, when fully implemented, aimed to result in systems capable of supporting managers at all levels in operating according to FMI principles.

It should be noted, however, that comments made thus far relate to the control of administration costs and say little about departmental programmes where the largest sums of government money are spent. Clearly, there will be greater difficulties here as government policy may be questioned and also there are many complex connections between programmes. These links exist not only within each department but also with other departments and agencies within the public sector.

Government agencies, as outlined in the proposal's Efficiency Unit report on the Civil Service, 'Improving Management in Government: The Next Steps' (1988) have been created. The reorganization of the Civil Service was primarily aimed at performance contracting and not necessarily at introducing competition *per se*. Each agency was required to establish quasi-contractual arrangements the objective of which was to hold the senior management of the agency accountable for its performance.

In 1992 the National Audit Office reported that the Vehicle Inspectorate (the first executive agency) had achieved a 9% increase in its efficiency and £3.5m saved (*Public Finance and Accountancy*, 21 February 1992, p.9). There had been an improvement in its service to clients. Research carried out by Dopson (Dopson, 1993, pp.17–23) in HMSO may not, however, be so encouraging as a number of staff comments were negative, although this was a small study. In contrast Kemp's comment was that 'in terms of fun, the place to be is the Agency. There the people have the opportunity to develop new service initiative and give a better service to the public' (Kemp, 1990). In 1996 HMSO was privatized as The Stationery Office (TSO) when near-insolvent and sold for £54 million, resulting in approximately 1000 job losses. As a public sector body it was claimed 'there were a lot of areas where the more that was sold the more money was lost' (*The Times*, 16 December 2000).

These broad arrangements have been retained since 1997 and the overall 'managerialist' agenda has been pushed forward. An issue that the government, however, needs to consider closely is whether, on the one hand, it can advocate freedom and initiative under the principle of agency arrangements, while, on the other, establishing rigid guidelines setting out restrictions on trading performance.

As already stated the basis of the proposals to establish agencies was to give managers increased managerial and operational freedom to meet defined targets. Each agency is required to produce a corporate plan that sets targets for the quality of productivity. Chief executives are appointed for each agency and managerial responsibilities are delegated to them. While there are implications for the staff involved in these changes it is clear that they will need sound systems for performance monitoring – again, a major role for the management accounting function and sophisticated financial management will be required. It should also be borne in mind that the achievement of agency status was originally seen as an intermediate step before privatization. This appeared to be the case with the Chessington Computer Agency with responsibility for the payment of pensions, in that a couple of years as an agency will allow it 'to develop its business on sound commercial lines' (William Waldegrave quoted in *Public Finance and Accountancy*, 11 June 1993, p.16).

1.5 The National Health Service

In the White Paper, 'Working for Patients' (1989) the then government claimed that it desired to raise the performance of all hospitals and general practitioners to that of the best. The White Paper therefore proposed seven key measures. These were:

1. To make the Health Service more responsive to the needs of patients and to transfer power and responsibility to the local level.
2. To allow hospitals to apply for the status of self-governing trusts.
3. To allow hospitals to offer their services to other health authorities and charge appropriately.
4. To reduce waiting times and improve the quality of services.

5. To enable GPs with over 11 000 patients to apply for their own National Health Service (NHS) budget to buy a defined range of hospital services from either the private sector or the NHS.
6. To improve the efficiency of NHS management by reducing it in size and reforming it along business lines.
7. To make better use of resources, improve quality of service and value for money.

(*Source:* Department of Health, 1989)

These concepts meant a significantly increased role for financial management as two of the underlying principles of the White Paper, as can be gleaned from these seven points, were achieving better financial control and monitoring along commercial lines.

This was seen as being of particular importance in such areas as:

- identifying the costs of patient care, as despite improvements in hospital financial information as a result of the Resource Management Initiative there was only a limited ability to link the diagnosis of patients to the cost of treatment;
- appraising the opportunities that may exist in joint ventures with private developers;
- managing capital assets and appraising capital investment decisions;
- an education and training role in advising staff who may have had little or no experience of financial management.

These changes were incorporated in the National Health Service Community Care Act 1990. A number of the main features of the Act are detailed in the text that follows.

National Health Service trusts

Under the 1990 Act the Secretary of State could direct regional health authorities to establish NHS trusts. These trusts assumed responsibility for ownership and management of hospitals or other facilities. The trusts, while remaining within the NHS, had to arrange contracts for services but continue to provide treatment to NHS patients free at the point of delivery. The Secretary of State set annual financing limits for each trust, taking into account the trust's capital investment plans and need for working capital. Trusts had the power to acquire, own and dispose of assets, borrow money subject to their external financing limit, build up reserves, establish pay and employment policies, enter into contracts to deliver health services, train their staff and accept gifts in trust or otherwise.

Trusts were required to earn a 6% return on assets. If unsuccessful they could be wound up. The trust was accountable to the Secretary of State via the National Health Service Management Executive (NHSME) and it was the duty of this body to monitor trusts. Its duties included reviewing business plans, annual reports and capital investment plans. Those units that did not become trusts remained under the management of the district health authority. Table 1.6 indicates how the broad manner in which trusts and directly managed units operated under the 1990 reforms.

General practitioner (GP) fund holding

As part of the Conservative government reforms of the NHS GPs were allowed to apply for recognition as a fund-holding practice. The original size of practice was a minimum of 9000 registered patients but this was later reduced to 5000. GPs had to prove that they

Table 1.6   Comparison between an NHS trust hospital and a directly managed unit

Issue	NHS trust	Directly managed unit
Management	• Each trust is managed by its own board of directors • The trust is free to determine its own management structure • Professional staff must be involved in management	• The health authority (HA) is responsible for the unit with the unit general manager being responsible for day-to-day management. Internal management arrangements are subject to HA approval
Accountability	• Each trust is directly accountable to the Secretary of State via the NHSME	• Each unit is accountable to the managing HA
Funding	• Each trust's income largely derived from contracts with authorities, GP fundholders and the private sector	• Each unit's income is largely derived from contracts with HAs, GP fund holders and the private sector
Services	• Each trust free to determine the range and extent of services it wishes to provide with limited exceptions	• Each unit provides the services it is contracted to provide
Employment of staff	• Each trust determines its own staffing structure and levels. It employs all its own staff including consultants • Each trust is free to determine pay and conditions locally (this provision abolished in 1997/98)	• Each unit determines its own staffing structure but staff are employed by the HA • Pay and other conditions of employment are subject to various review bodies

had the ability to manage a budget and have adequate administrative support (including a computer information system). The budget for each GP was received from the regional health authority although the whole year's budget was not provided up front and was based on the relative need of patients registered with the practice. The budget could then be spent on such items as drugs, payments to trusts and private hospitals and goods or services on an approved list. Overspending on the budget up to 5% in any one year was allowable although persistent overspending was investigated. Money allocated to GP fund holders was deducted from the allocation to district health authorities.

Revised NHS financial management arrangements

Stability of government policy is not something that operational and financial managers in the public sector can rely on and in this respect the NHS is no different. In the White Paper, 'The NHS, Modern and Dependable' (HM Government, 1998a) significant changes to the system just discussed were announced. These included:

1. GPs in naturally recognisable communities are to come together as primary care groups. They replace the system of GP fund holding and take responsibility for commissioning health care services for their local communities.

2. The number of health authorities will be reduced and they relinquish their commissioning role to the new primary care groups. These groups will also monitor the performance of NHS trusts. Primary care groups are funded by the health authority and their budgets cover hospital and community health services, family health prescribing and cash-limited funding for GP-related services.
3. NHS trusts are given a statutory duty for quality.
4. Health improvement programmes would be developed to deliver the 'new' NHS. The health authority's role is to lead their development and involve trusts, GPs, the voluntary sector and local authorities.
5. Local government and the NHS are expected to develop partnerships. Health action zones will be created to foster these partnerships and these zones will be expected to be innovative in their use of funding to achieve their objectives.

It is anticipated that the changes outlined in this White Paper will simplify accountability in the NHS and reduce bureaucracy. Statutory accountability is from primary care groups to health authorities to the regional offices of the NHSME and, ultimately, to the minister and parliament. Service accountability is between the trusts, the health authorities and the primary care groups.

In addition to the control of cash (defined in paragraph 2 of the Schedule 12A of the National Health Service Act 1977) the Government Resources and Accounts Act 2000 requires that every health authority, special health authority and primary care trust confine its use of resources in a financial year to the resource limit set by the Secretary of State.

Allocation of financial resources within the NHS

From 1977 money was allocated to regional health authorities in England on the basis of a complex formula known as RAWP (resource allocation working party). The RAWP formula included such elements as morbidity, size of population, population structure, cost weightings and cross-boundary flows where patients moved from one health district to another for treatment. This formula has now been replaced by the funding of health authorities on a capitation basis, weighted to reflect the health and age distribution of the population and the relative costs of providing services on a regional basis. Where cross-boundary flows exist for patient care, regions pay each other directly and in full. The report of the 'Independent Inquiry into Inequalities in Health' (1998), however, identified that priority should be given to a more equitable allocation of NHS resources. The existing formula is currently subject to review but will operate unchanged until at least 2001/02.

With regard to the funding of hospital services, each district health authority was responsible for buying the services it needed from its own hospitals, from other health authority hospitals and from the self-governing trust hospitals or the private sector. In this manner it was hoped that hospitals would deliver the best and most efficient service and that value for money would have been achieved. Those hospitals that were the most efficient would, it was claimed, attract funds, while those that were inefficient would have a major incentive to improve – the fear of closure. As can be seen, responsibility for commissioning now lies with the primary health care groups.

It has been pointed out (Masters, 1993, pp.4–5) that the changes incorporated in the 1990 Act had significant implications for the finance function. Prior to this Act the treasurer in the NHS primarily saw that function as management of the cash limit. There was thus a need for a major change of financial culture to one of being more proactive and providing financial management information and advice. Masters claims that in a little over two years the finance function moved to one which:

1. operated in a radically different revenue allocation system;
2. met the challenges of the NHS trusts;
3. implemented a completely new system of asset management;
4. created costing and settlement systems to underpin the new contracts;
5. overhauled the financial planning, monitoring and reporting systems.

Importantly: 'General managers and chief executives … started to see the crucial role that finance can and should play in the overall management team.'

External financing limits

Capital expenditure by NHS trusts forms part of the public expenditure provision in the health programme. NHS trusts can only obtain finance from income they generate themselves or from borrowing. An annual external financing limit (EFL) controls access to external finance by the trust and has been a feature of both the public sector in general and the NHS for some time and is illustrated here in the context of NHS trusts. The EFL is a net financing concept measured by new loans taken out by the trust less loans repaid adjusted for changes in deposits and other holdings of liquid assets. It is set annually by the Department of Health. The EFL can be positive or negative. If the EFL is negative this means that the trust has to repay rather than develop new capital assets.

1.6 Local government

The local government sector has had to deal with a considerable volume of legislation since 1979. Those measures of a financial nature include:

1. Local Government Planning and Land Act in 1980 which established competitive tendering for Direct Labour Organizations.
2. Local Government Finance Act in 1982 which set up the Audit Commission for Local Authorities in England and Wales.
3. Local Government Act 1988 which extended the principles of competitive tendering to a range of other services.
4. Local Government Finance Act 1988 which introduced the community charge in England and Wales.
5. Replacement of the community charge by the council tax under the Local Government Finance Act 1992.
6. Local Government Act 1999 which established best value and removed the need for compulsory competitive tendering.

Local government has been at the forefront of a desire by government of whatever political persuasion to improve value for money in the provision of public sector services.

Competitive tendering was first applied in 1980 to direct labour organizations (DLOs). A DLO is the local authority's own 'commercial' arm in which it employs its own workforce in order to provide specific services to the authority rather than employ private contractors. Under the 1980 Act authorities were required to:

1. compete for work in specified areas against the private sector (over time the original categories have been extended);
2. originally earn a rate of return of 5% on the current cost of capital employed by the DLO (later increased to 6%);
3. keep separate accounts for each category of work and to publish these accounts by 30 September in each year.

Failure by the authority to achieve the rate of return could result in the Secretary of State closing down the DLO. As a result of this power the DLO in Haringey was closed down. Similar competition provisions were then extended to other DLO activities, although the new term is direct service organization (DSO). The 1988 Act covered the collection of refuse, cleaning services, catering services, maintenance of grounds and repair and maintenance of vehicles. Appropriate targets were set in each case, for example the target for cleaning contracts was to break even.

A considerable amount of preparation was needed in order to prepare the in-house service for the process of tendering in any area, including the need for detailed business plans to be prepared and tender documents completed. Given that many local authorities often had little comprehensive information on the total workload that these functions faced it can be seen that the preparation of tender documents represented a major challenge. If the tender was successfully won there was then a need to introduce an organizational culture which required motives that were both profit and service motivated since the DSO had to earn profits to survive and achieve high standards to retain its clients' loyalty. The financial information system had also to be geared to these objectives. The areas of competitive tendering quoted earlier involved essentially blue-collar jobs. In earlier editions of this text it was suggested that there was no intrinsic reason why white-collar services, such as financial and legal, could not be put out to competitive tender and eventually this was done to include, for example, accounting and computer services. Many local authorities had, however, prepared for this action by concluding service level agreements with user departments establishing the standard of service required (and its related cost). These agreements, where in place, could effectively form the basis of competitive tenders as the majority of the preparatory work had been done in advance of the legal requirement to submit to competitive tender.

It should be noted that the government took a firm stand on any practices which were considered by central government to favour the in-house bid for the contract for the service subjected to competitive tender. Powers under Section 14 of the Local Government Act 1988 allowed the central government to intervene to negate the effect of such activities. In July 1990 the Secretary of State ordered the Knowsley Metropolitan Borough and East Lindsey District Council to retender their refuse collection contracts by July 1991 as a result of judged anti-competitive practices. In *Accountancy Age* for 23 August 1990 it was reported that, in the words of the Audit Commission, many councils in terms of compulsory competitive tendering had wasted 'their efforts trying to avoid its effects'. This stressed the need for authorities to meet the challenge of compulsory competitive tendering by sound financial management of the competition units. The powers of the Secretary of State were further enhanced under the Local Government Act 1992: Commencement (No. 2), Order 1992. This allowed, for example, intervention at any time after a contract had been awarded rather than, as previously, after work had commenced.

The Local Government Finance Act 1982 is discussed in Chapter 10. Suffice it to say here that the external auditor was given powers to investigate whether a local authority had made proper arrangements to secure value for money in its activities. In part, as a result of its activities in this field, the role of the Audit Commission was extended to the full range of organizations within the NHS. The objective of this process, as set out in 'Working for Patients', was that there should be more commitment to value for money studies, which would cover a wider range of the NHS than was previously examined, by an audit body that is demonstrably independent.

In the White Paper 'Modern Local Government in Touch with the People' and the subsequent Local Government Act 1999 the compulsory competitive tendering requirements of the 1980, 1988 and 1992 Acts were repealed. In its place, authorities will be subject to 'best value' and are required to prepare, publish and have externally audited best value performance plans. Best value is defined as 'securing continuous improvement in the exercise of all functions undertaken by an authority, whether statutory or not, having regard to the combination of economy, efficiency and effectiveness' (Notes to Local Government Act, 1999, p.2). Best value is discussed in Chapter 10. It should be noted that the government has extended the principles of best value into the NHS after some 20 years of compulsory competitive tendering (Ward, 2000, p.15). Hospitals will have to review their support services every five years with increased emphasis on quality.

On 1 April 1990 a new system of financing was introduced for local government (in England and Wales) in the form of the ill-fated community charge. This increased central control over local government financing both via the ability to cap the charge (by setting an upper limit on the charge that can be levied locally) and the control by central government of the national business rate and the level of government grant. The national business rate and the government grant account for approximately 75% of local government revenue finance. Thus, local government had an ability to control only 25% of its income and, even here, if the government felt an individual council was 'overspending' against a centrally determined notional community charge it could intervene. This intervention could reduce the level of community charge and thus make the local authority reduce its budgeted expenditure. These control principles were retained when the council tax replaced the community charge on 1 April 1993 (Local Government Finance Act 1992, s. 54) until the Local Government Act 1999. Under this Act the general capping system has been replaced by a system of reserve powers where the government can step in in what it regards as an extreme case. Capping is thus no longer universal but selective and is based on the Secretary of State (in Wales the National Assembly for Wales) judging if the budget requirement set by a local authority is excessive.

In this overview of major financial changes in the local government sector a further major initiative that took place was in the shape of the Education Reform Act 1988. This Act introduced local financial management into schools with the result that responsibility for day-to-day financial management was delegated to the lowest possible level, that is, the school. Schools are formula funding based mainly on the number of pupils on the roll. This type of delegated financial management has placed pressure on management accountants to provide appropriate information to managers delegated with responsibility to manage within the constraints of the formula-based budget. It also challenged the traditional structure of many local authority finance departments by placing budgetary control and monitoring at a much lower level than has traditionally been the case, the headteacher. In many local authorities the finance department and senior financial staff within the education department have traditionally performed this function. Under sections 45–53 of the Schools Standards and Framework Act 1998, Local Education Authority's (LEAs) were required to consult with schools on further delegation of financial powers under the concept of 'fair funding'. In principle this meant that schools could manage a greater proportion of the funds available to them and they would have greater choice in the purchasing of services required including, for example, building maintenance. The local authority is free to determine for itself the size of the local schools budget (LSB). The categories of expenditure which fall within the LSB, however, are prescribed in the Financing of Maintained Schools Regulations 1999 but included within LSB is all expenditure direct and indirect on a local authority's maintained schools. Any amounts retained by the local authority are decided by the authority, subject to any limits or conditions prescribed by the Secretary of State with the remainder being termed the individual schools budget (ISB). Budget shares allocated to schools by the formula may be spent by the governing body of the school for the purposes of their school.

The government has also taken steps to fund schools directly, announcing in the 2000 Autumn Statement extra money to go directly to schools of between £4000 and £8000 for primary schools and between £10 000 to £30 000 for secondary schools (*The Times*, 9 November 2000). This has been on the basis that, if it were not given directly to schools, such additional funding might get lost in the system (*Public Finance*, 28 April 2000, p.27) but clearly 'front line' funding can also be seen as an attack on local government. The Secondary Heads Association has, however, called for central government to fund schools directly (*Public Finance*, 4 February 2000, p.18).

This trend in wider distribution of financial management and responsibility is further emphasized by the growth of distributed computer terminals facilities in service departments with on-line budget status inquiries. The accountant will thus no longer be the keeper of the keys to the information chest and, as information is power, his/her role will inevitably be diminished unless he/she rises to the challenge to interpret the information and provide relevant financial advice. In response to such challenges many finance officers are now seconding staff to service departments to meet this new demand for interpretative skills. Only time will tell how successfully they meet these demands.

It is also relevant in dealing with education to refer to changes in further and higher education. Under the Further and Higher Education Act 1992 from 1 April 1993 colleges of further education, sixth form and tertiary colleges were removed from local authority control following the former polytechnics (now the new universities) in this respect (under the Education Reform Act 1988). These institutions are now funded by their respective funding councils (the Further Education Funding Council and the Higher Education Funding Council (HEFC) respectively). Under the Teaching and Higher Education Act 1998 the HEFC has the power to fund the provision of education and research. This has led to targets being set for the recruitment of students by institutions and a failure to recruit can have important financial consequences, especially for those institutions that rely heavily on teaching income (for example, the new universities). One consequence of this is that these bodies are attempting to diversify their income streams through consultancy and research. An increase in research income does not, however, guarantee security as through the research assessment exercise funding allocated to research can change if a university fails to perform. The universities, therefore, clearly need the necessary financial expertise to be able to respond to such changes in order to ensure financial stability. The reality of these pressures is perhaps well illustrated by a report that St Andrews University is facing a cash crisis of £2m in an annual turnover of £60m (*The Times*, 17 November 2000). In March 2000 it was reported that Thames Valley University faced cuts as funding was reduced by 11.5% after it failed to recruit to targets on student numbers (*Public Finance*, March 2000, p.10). These cuts in funding have taken place in a climate of a requirement for efficiency gains which inevitably place additional pressure on resources. Edinburgh University claimed a funding shortfall of £3m and was planning to raise £40m by bonds, staff cutbacks, property sales and a major fund raising effort (*Public Finance*, 20 October 2000, p.9).

1.7 The nationalized industries and public corporations

Nationalized industries are publicly owned bodies usually set up by their own statute and having a substantial degree of independence from government. They are usually run by boards and report to the minister responsible. The financial controls under which these industries operate were laid down in 'The Nationalized Industries' (HM Government, 1978). This framework includes:

1. Setting strategic goals and targets to provide the framework within which the industry is to operate.
2. Investment and appraisal based on a required rate of return on investment of 8% in real terms before the payment of tax and interest. This return was originally set at 5% in 1975 but 8% is seen as being comparable with private sector returns. Prices are set to cover the return demanded.
3. Financial targets and performance aims are the primary control on the industries. These are set for up to three years ahead.
4. As with NHS trusts discussed earlier, an external finance limit is set to control the level of borrowing that the trading activities need. Any expenditure on capital projects above this level has to come from the industries' own resources. Coupled with financial targets this results in price increases if the investment goes ahead unless it can be financed from efficiency savings or the sale of surplus fixed assets.

Public corporation is a term from the national accounts and the characteristics of such bodies are that they are mainly trading bodies financed largely by charges, owned or controlled by central government, local authorities or other public corporations and have substantial day-to-day independence for operational management. The Treasury has defined self-financing public corporations as those not normally dependent on subsidies and are reported in the AME rather than DEL. Nationalized industries are larger corporations that undertake functions more comparable with the private sector. The external finance of nationalized industries is identified in cash plan tables in the departmental reports and the supply estimates. Finally, trading funds are government departments that generate income by supplying goods and services. Their expenditure is controlled by using the external finance limit system which applies to most public corporations.

The present government is keen to promote public–private partnerships to improve quality and efficiency by enterprises operating in the public sector. For the London Underground the private sector is planned to be brought in to deliver a £7 billion pound investment programme and in December 1998 a reform package for the Post Office was announced aimed at giving that organization greater freedom to enter new markets.

Monitoring is carried out by the sponsoring minister and department. The industries are also subject to periodic monitoring by the Monopolies and Mergers Commission under the 1980 Competition Act. There have been numerous privatizations of public corporations and nationalized industries, one of the largest and most complex being British Rail. Even with the new Labour government privatization is not at an end with, for example, a desire by this government to part-privatize the air traffic control system. At the time of writing the plan is for the government to retain a so-called golden share thus maintaining overall control, although many MPs are concerned about safety issues (*The Times*, 16 November 2000). In addition, the present government is still considering, where appropriate, the market testing of government services. Brixton Prison had its management taken over by the private sector (*Public Finance*, July 2000, p.22). This policy is therefore in line with the statement quoted from Sir Geoffrey Howe in the opening paragraph of this chapter. Where operations could not be privatized as with, for example, the BBC, internal markets have been introduced, notably the scheme known as 'producers' choice' giving producers the option to go outside the Corporation or use 'in-house' providers. One casualty of this has been the finance department where, as part of total cuts of £750m, finance staff posts were cut (*Accountancy Age*, 27 July 2000, p.12).

In summary the controls on public corporations and nationalized industries are as follows:

- strategic objectives set in discussion with sponsoring departments;
- external finance limits are the main control over the annual operation of the public corporations;
- financial targets and performance aims are frequently set for three-year periods;
- investment appraisal at the 8% rate mentioned earlier which aims to ensure that there is a proper return on investment;
- monitoring by sponsoring departments.

The continued intention to privatize, the ongoing drive for greater efficiency and public–private partnerships, requires that financial management systems in the public corporations and nationalized industries are efficient and adaptable to meet the increased demands placed on them.

1.8 Accounting for capital assets in the public sector

Major changes in the accounting methods for capital assets are taking place within public sector organizations. These changes have potentially significant implications for both financial and operational managers in the public sector. They are broadly aimed at overcoming a perception in government that public sector managers were regarding capital assets as free goods under traditional public sector financial accounting and budgeting practices.

Traditionally, capital assets were accounted for on an historic cost basis in the public sector and, on the basis of the finance method used to acquire the asset. These finance methods could range from cash acquisition and its associated simple accounting entries to the complex financing methods used by local authorities with the positively labyrinthine accounting entries that underpinned their consolidated balance sheets and revenue accounts. Traditionally, the public sector treated any finance charges (e.g. loan charges) that resulted from the acquisition of capital assets as being outside the operational manager's control and a matter for the finance department.

Basically, the new methods of accounting for capital assets will involve the assets being valued at current valuation rather than at historic cost. This valuation will be used for balance sheet presentation purposes. Depreciation and interest charges on this valuation will be charged to services and thus become the service's responsibility. The depreciation charge represents capital consumption and matches the revenue earned in the service with the proportion of the capital asset consumed in delivering that service. The interest charge represents the opportunity cost of using the asset in its current function. The objective of these charges is to encourage managers to use assets efficiently by generating revenue equal to the capital charge or, otherwise, dispose of them. Where it is not realistic to charge for services then the service revenue account will reflect the full cost of that service provision.

Depreciation charges will depend on the valuation of the asset, estimated residual values, life of the asset and the depreciation method used. Interest charges are based on the category of asset. Basically operational assets attract interest at 6% on current cost while the more complex (and unusual) infrastructural assets of local authorities, for example, are charged at the Public Works Loans Board rate plus 1%. The actual valuation method again depends on the category of asset. Broadly speaking, operational assets are valued at their value in use in their current state and condition and are regularly revalued. The revaluation may be based on, for example, a professional valuation or indexation. Infrastructural assets, in the case of local authorities, are valued at debt outstanding on the date of the introduction of the new system less subsequent depreciation. Community assets (such as local authority statues and parks) are valued at a nominal value.

Central government plans to use resource accounting from 2001/02 while the NHS has used the current valuation of fixed assets since 1991. The 1980 Planning and Land Act effectively established the basis of the system used in the public sector with the requirement for the then DLOs to earn a positive return on the current cost of assets after allowing for depreciation. The principle of its extension to all the services of local authorities can be traced to the report by Parkes for the Chartered Institute of Public Finance and Accountancy statement on capital accounting (1988). A debate on capital accounting techniques and especially the depreciation of fixed assets can, however, be traced to at least the beginning of the twentieth century (Coombs and Edwards, 1996). The basis of the central government system can be found in the Green Paper Cm 2626 'Better Accounting for Taxpayers' Money' (HM Government, 1994) and for the NHS in its manual of accounts.

In the local authority context one of the objectives of the system is to ensure that no extra charges fall on council taxpayers. In practice, capital charges represent bookkeeping entries as their effects are reversed out in the local authority's consolidated revenue account as a result of its relationship with the asset management revenue account. The minimum revenue provision, which local authorities are required to make in order to provide for the repayment of debt, is also adjusted by the depreciation charge. In addition, there is only a requirement that capital charges are compulsory at the committee level for local authorities. It is a decision for each local authority as to whether it charges below the committee level.

1.9 Summary

Chapter 2 examines approaches to the measurement of the costs of specific services and discusses the problem of using costs in value for money studies and the apportionment and control of overhead costs. The importance of costs in the construction of service level agreements (SLAs) is considered as is the technique of full absorption costing. An examination of some of the costing problems specific to the NHS is also made.

Chapter 3 considers the use by the public sector of marginal costing and the practical limitations of the technique. It also examines the concept of relevant costing for decision-making purposes and considers it usefulness to the decision maker in the contracting process for services now found in the public sector.

Chapter 4 looks at budgeting processes in the public sector. It examines the traditional incremental approach to budget setting, considers developments and contrasts the incremental approach with more modern approaches such as planned programme budgeting and zero-based budgeting. The chapter also discusses business planning and the formula-based budget systems now becoming increasingly common in the public sector.

Chapter 5 studies the control process in budgeting by examination of expenditure profiling, variance analysis and standard costing in a competitive environment.

Chapter 6 studies the concept of sound working capital management and stresses the importance of the techniques available in generating the potential for savings to the public sector organization.

Chapter 7 examines the methods of financing capital expenditure available to public sector bodies and contains a study of four specialist areas: leasing, debt management, derivatives and public–private partnerships.

Chapter 8 examines capital budgeting in terms of the development of capital programmes in the public sector, the assessment of revenue implications and the consideration of non-financial factors in the capital budgeting decision.

Chapter 9 considers methods of investment appraisal available including discounted cash flow and cost-benefit analysis. The problems of risk and inflation are also discussed. The concept of non-financial factors in the decision process is further developed.

Chapter 10 discusses the development of the audit function in the public sector and charts its movement from a role that was primarily one of stewardship to one of examination of the arrangements made by the organization to achieve economy efficiency and effectiveness in the conduct of its financial affairs.

The book concludes with a section containing a number of case studies. This section has been included in order to allow the reader to develop an understanding of the issues raised in the text in the context of potential problems facing public sector managers. The cases themselves present a number of scenarios but the important point is not the individual scenario and the circumstances described in each case. It is that the lessons to be learnt and problems to be solved in these cases have general applicability across the public sector for public sector financial managers, operational managers and students of financial management.

Key points of chapter

This chapter examined:

1. The process of establishing the overall level of public sector spending.
2. The major initiatives that have taken place in the significant elements of the public sector, stressing their effect on financial management.
3. The importance of financial management to the public sector and the continued pressures for efficiency gains that show no signs of stopping.

1.10 Conclusion

The introduction to this book has attempted to illustrate the many challenges that are facing the public sector financial manager be he/she a trained accountant or a service manager faced with dealing with demands for achievement of economy, efficiency and effectiveness in performing the service. The new skills demanded in public sector financial management lie in interpretation of financial information and the provision of financial advice to help achieve the goals of the organization or individual service goals. This, however, adds another dimension to the problem as, frequently, the goals of public sector organizations cannot be accurately defined. The more complex the public sector organization the more difficult it is to define the goal of that organization and, in addition, its constituent elements may have conflicting goals. The historical perspective given by elements of the chapter show that the pace of change has also been rapid and currently shows no sign of slowing down. It might be claimed that the very speed of these changes makes any attempt to plan irrelevant, but herein lies the paradox: the greater the speed of change the greater the need for a planned approach in tackling it. An organization must know where it has come from in order to know where it is going and how far from any of its planned goals it is at any point in time. It is hoped that the techniques discussed in the remainder of this book will enable all public sector managers to deal with and master change by having the necessary financial skills to cope with change as it takes place.

Appendix: Summary of the supply process

Parliament approves an individual supply estimate as a 'vote'. This can be defined as a coherent area of government expenditure which is the responsibility of one government department. A single vote will then cover expenditure that can be gathered under a particular main heading relating to a single department. Where responsibility for a particular item of expenditure spreads to another department it is reflected in the vote for that department. Each department is then accountable to parliament for the expenditure detailed. A single vote is prepared in a standard format. This format is as follows, including a brief description of the component parts:

1. *The introductory note.* This is used to put the vote in context giving details on the items of expenditure, whether the expenditure is cash limited (see point 4), details on any important changes in the expenditure from the previous year and an indication of the level of service to be provided.
2. *The ambit.* This describes the purpose for which the provision is made and effectively limits the ability to spend to the ambit. The wording of the ambit may not be changed without Treasury approval.
3. *Summary and subhead details.* This section breaks down the estimated expenditure for the next financial year into its component parts. In addition, comparison is possible with the last completed year for which figures are available and with the total provision and estimated results for the current year.
4. *Receipts.* Certain receipts can be used to finance some of the gross expenditure on a vote and thus reduce the sums drawn on the Consolidated Fund (the government's bank account). These receipts are known as 'Appropriations in Aid'. Other receipts and receipts above the level of the approved Appropriations in Aid are paid into the Consolidated Fund. These other receipts and extra Appropriations in Aid are detailed

separately. Those Appropriations approved to be used to finance expenditure are related to expenditure and are given in the summary and subhead section of the supply estimates.

5. *Additional information* is usually given in the form of supplementary tables.

2 Operational and service-based costing

Key learning objectives

After reading this chapter you should be able to:

1. Prepare and interpret a unit cost statement.
2. List the strengths and weaknesses of conventional approaches to efficiency comparisons.
3. Define and apportion overheads.
4. Understand the benefits and weaknesses of different ways of charging for overheads in a public sector environment.

This chapter takes a selective and critical view of the collection and use of costs within public sector organizations. It is concerned specifically with the everyday collection and measurement of the costs of individual services. These costs include both direct costs and indirect costs (overheads) and costs which are variable and those which are fixed. They are used for purposes such as cost recovery and cost control and are used extensively in the analysis and evaluation of managerial performance.

Three distinct areas are singled out for discussion:

1. The use of costs in efficiency and value for money studies throughout the public sector.
2. The measurement, apportionment and control of overheads including charging for overheads via service level agreements.
3. A study of some of the specific problems of costing activity within the National Health Service.

Managers in any sector of the economy need to be able to assess performance in order to manage effectively the resources within their control. At the strategic level managers will be looking to formulate new policies or reformulate existing policies if a perceived need is not being met. At the operational level managers will be searching for improved administrative efficiency including the better use of resources within the existing policy framework. The problem for public sector managers is to define the output of a particular service in order to assess whether or not their service is performing within the value for money objectives of economy, efficiency and effectiveness. This chapter examines the contribution that the collection and measurement of costs makes to this process.

2.1 The use of costs in efficiency and value for money studies

Within public sector organizations there is rarely a bottom line figure such as profit which can provide a single evaluative measure of performance. This is because many services are provided out of taxation, either central or local, and do not generate sales revenue which can be the basis for calculating profit or loss. Examples include primary and secondary state education, defence and the National Health Service. Other services are provided at a 'loss' with income frequently being related to clients' ability to pay; examples include prescriptions issued by doctors and fees payable for the ophthalmic and dental services. In the absence of profit, financial measures of performance tend to be cost based. Different dimensions of 'output' are selected and cost is then related to such 'outputs' to produce a cost-based input/output ratio. Examples include the cost per patient day within a hospital, cost per vehicle operating mile for police vehicles and cost per school meal produced.

As you learnt in Chapter 1, during the past decade many services have been privatized or contracted out or at least reorganized into self-contained trading profit centres. These include the local authority direct labour organizations (DLOs) which comprise construction and maintenance activities and the direct service organizations (DSOs) such as street cleaning, refuse collection and parks. In these services there is a bottom line profit figure, but organizations must still concern themselves with the detail of costs if they are to control costs as part of securing their profit objective.

At this point, it is necessary to stress the difference between throughputs (or intermediate outputs) and outcomes. Throughputs may be defined as an indicator of the level of activity in a particular service, for example, the number of hip replacement operations carried out in a hospital, the number of children receiving education in a school. Outcomes refer to the impact that the level of activity has on the recipients of the service and which may be considered to be the whole objective of providing the service. For this reason, the ultimate measure of performance relates to outcomes rather than to units of service delivered. For example, the primary objective of providing a home for the aged would not be to provide, say, 15 000 resident bed days per year but is to improve the quality of life of those elderly people who are so accommodated. However, the measurement of outcomes presents great difficulties within the public sector. For example, how does one measure the improvement in the quality of life of residents of an old persons' home? Might their quality of life have been greater if located within the community? The services delivered by a comprehensive school are many and varied. They include the broad education of pupils, the number of GCSE grades obtained by the pupils, the attendance rate of pupils, the number staying on beyond the age of 16 or finding employment, the preparation for a world of change, the development of self-discipline and so on. Some of these are immeasurable and it is impossible to combine the others into one measure of a school's performance. The problem is aggravated because in education and health the initial intake of pupils or patients is not standardized. Pupils arrive with different abilities and come from different socio-economic backgrounds; patients may be admitted with smaller complaints but the severity of those complaints is different. These difficulties mean that, in most cases, managers will be looking at the costs of throughputs and not final outcomes.

In a situation where market prices are available, as in the private sector and, where goods and services are freely traded, then outcomes may be equated with sales revenues. Economics tells us that consumers will purchase units of output until marginal utility equates with price. In a market situation, consumers will pay no more than the perceived benefit from the service received. However, in much of the public sector in the United Kingdom, in education, health and defence, for example, such market prices are simply unavailable.

In the health sector, it is thought by many that outcomes are related to the increase in the quality of life of the patient; indeed, the concept of quality-adjusted life years (QUALY) has been developed as a measure of outcomes: a QUALY considers both the increase in life expectancy and the increased quality of life derived by the patient. This may possible represent the measurement future for the outcomes of health care. However, QUALYs are not yet in operational use within the Health Service; in place of such a measure of genuine outcome, recourse is sought in throughput measures, such as the number of beds provided or the number of patient days. The difficulty of measurement relevant to outcomes or quality of service pervades much of the public sector with the result that there is a concentration on performance measurement and control based on throughputs.

Not all activities are so bedevilled; there are some where the problem of measuring output is absent. In appraising ambulance efficiency, for example, we can readily work with cost per ambulance mile for an individual vehicle which could be compared with its past performance or with other vehicles. Such information may indicate declining efficiency or have possible audit implications if, say, fuel cost per mile showed a significant increase.

The starting point for cost-based efficiency analysis is the definition of the unit of performance to be studied; these units may be single measures such as the number of schoolchildren taught and the number of meals provided, or multiple measures such as passenger miles. Thus, one may calculate the cost per child, per passenger mile, per meal, per motorway mile and so on. These are usually referred to as unit costs.

The analysis of differences in unit costs may be assisted by the preparation of a cost statement which disaggregates total cost into the detailed cost elements and expresses throughput in terms of each of the cost elements. Table 2.1 provides an example of such a statement; it examines the costs of cleaning three offices.

An immediate problem which has to be confronted in constructing a unit cost statement is that relating to the classification of the cost elements (that is, employees, cleaning materials, equipment, and so on). One approach is to use a format that is uniform across all organizations. In the National Health Service such a format is laid down for health authorities while most local authorities follow the CIPFA-recommended standard form of accounts. The CIPFA standard form specifies in detail the classification of costs and the detailed content of each section. Both approaches adopt a subjective approach to classification in that costs are grouped according to the nature or subject of the expenditure. Thus, in the CIPFA system, the broad classification runs as follows: employees, running expenses (premises, transport, supplies and services, agency and contracted services, transfer payments, and central, departmental and technical support services) and capital financial costs. In principle, uniform approaches, such as these, allow comparison between authorities. An alternative approach is to classify costs

Table 2.1   Example of a unit cost statement

Blaenwent BC unit cost statement	Cleaning services 9 months to 31 December 2000							
	Office A		Office B		Office C			Average
Costs	Total £	Per m² P	Total £	Per m² P	Total £	Per m² P	Total £	Per m² P
Employees' pay	9 000	150.00	50 500	325.81	13 500	450.00	73 000	297.96
NI etc.	1 650	27.50	9 090	58.65	2 439	81.30	13 179	53.79
Travel	20	.33	5	.03	30	1.00	55	.22
Bonus	1 800	30.00	10 605	68.42	1 750	58.33	14 155	57.78
Employees sub-total	12 470	207.83	70 200	452.90	17 719	590.63	100 389	409.75
Cleaning materials	2 570	42.83	13 240	85.42	2 425	80.83	18 235	74.43
Equipment	430	7.17	1 270	8.19	230	7.67	1 930	7.88
Misc.	20	.33	40	.26	10	.33	70	.29
Sub-total	15 490	258.17	84 750	546.77	20 384	679.47	120 624	492.34
Contract window/ cleaning	900	15.00	3 050	19.68	750	25.00	4 700	19.18
Supervisor	3 120	52.00	3 120	20.13	3 120	104.00	9 360	38.20
Total	19 510	325.17	90 920	586.58	24 254	808.47	134 684	549.73
Statistical data								
Floor area (m²)	6 000		15 500		3 000		24 500	
Cleaners	3		17		4		24	
Floor area/cleaner	2 000		912		750		1 021	

according to their behaviour and not their subject; this requires a knowledge of cost variability and is discussed in detail in Chapter 3. The advantage of this approach is that it aids decision making and control and can give a more informed insight when carrying out performance appraisal activities and value for money (VFM) studies.

2.2 Unit cost statements

Unit cost statements have three main uses.

An indicator of relative efficiency

Unit costs serve as an indicator of efficiency relative to other establishments or organizations. The Audit Commission in England and Wales makes considerable use of unit costs for this purpose, generating batteries of comparative statistics which may act as a starting point for analysis. In Table 2.1 it is evident that the cleaning of office A is considerably more efficient in cost terms than is the cleaning of offices B or C. Its overall cost per square metre, 258p, is less than half that of B or C. Examination of the unit cost components reveals that office A's lower unit costs are largely the result of lower unit employee costs.

Efficiency over time

Unit costs serve as an indicator of efficiency over time. They allow us to compare the performance of the same organization from year to year, which can be a pointer as to whether efficiency is increasing or decreasing. The problem is that inflation will tend to increase the costs of providing a service over time. Therefore, in order to make a true comparison, the effects of inflation will need to be removed so that the 'real' trend may be observed. This may be done by using a price index, usually one which is specific to the cost element, such as the fuel cost index or the appropriate wage index. However, the Treasury guideline for all central government services in the United Kingdom, including the National Health Service, is that the GDP deflator should be used. This is a general price index and its use is said to reflect the wider economy from which central government's resources are drawn via taxation.

Cost control

Unit costs provide a basis for cost control. They can be used to set unit cost standards against which actual performance can be monitored. As is illustrated in Table 2.1, their disaggregated nature highlights the cause of high total costs in A and B: the first cost which needs to be examined is the pay of employees.

Limitations of unit cost comparisons

However, unit cost measures such as the earlier mentioned need to be used with care. Their limitations, which are discussed later, are summarized as follows:

1. They use throughputs rather than outcomes.
2. They ignore the quality of performance.
3. They may ignore differences in case mix.
4. They should make comparisons against best practice.
5. There are significant inter-authority differences.
6. Overheads may be charged in different ways.
7. Differences in delegated budgets will impair comparison.
8. Capital financing methods may affect costs.

As has been indicated, throughputs are usually taken as a proxy for outcomes; this assumes that there is a direct and linear relationship between throughputs and outcomes. It also assumes that all outcomes are proxied by the throughput indicator but this is unlikely to be the case.

They tell us nothing about the quality of performance; cleaning may be carried out to different standards of performance in the three offices and this may explain the variation. If differences in standard are laid down in the cleaning contract, the differences may be acceptable. If they are not, and differences in cleaning standards are observed, then either offices B and C are being cleaned too thoroughly or office A is not being cleaned to the required standard.

This is related to the problem of throughput mix. One cannot usefully compare the costs of two homes, one for the elderly and one for the elderly infirm. The latter will require more specialized staffing, certainly a higher staffing ratio and, quite probably, different dietary requirements. Thus, we would compare homes for the elderly with one another, and homes for the elderly infirm with others of the same type. However, the latter category includes a range of infirmities and disabilities and the differences in case mix will clearly affect costs. In this specific case, allowing for the effects of case mix is almost impossible, because the costs associated with different types of infirmity are not known. In the case of a hospital, one solution is to compare the costs of different specialities, rather than the total unit costs of activities, and then make inter-hospital and inter-temporal comparisons on a speciality-by-speciality basis.

In making inter-organizational comparisons, one is not necessarily comparing performance against defined best practice. At the very least, it is necessary to compare actual unit costs against budgeted unit costs which do represent an assumption about the level of efficiency which is being sought. Ideally, comparison would be against a predetermined standard cost which would be based upon the standard amounts of time, materials and so on required to undertake a specific task efficiently. Within the NHS there have been pilot studies of the use of diagnosis-related groups (DRGs), which are concerned with classifying acute patients (but not psychiatric, geriatric or community care services) according to their diagnostic status. These DRGs specify standardized units of workload for each diagnostic grouping and may, therefore, form a basis for establishing the standard costs of specific hospital activities; such standard costs can then provide a benchmark for the appraisal of actual unit costs. DRGs have been imported from the United States where they were originally intended as a basis on which insurers would reimburse hospitals. The aim of this was to cap the growth in health care expenditure by providing incentives for hospitals to carry out treatment as efficiently and economically as possible. However, there is some dissatisfaction with their use in the United Kingdom as it is argued that DRGs do not adequately reflect British medical practice, that classification systems for recording diagnoses and procedures are different in the UK and that DRGs must respond to local conditions. Therefore, there are moves within the NHS to measure hospital activity by grouping together sets of cases which meet specified criteria and the resources they consume. From these data it is possible to compare the work undertaken between hospitals and from year to year.

There are major differences between some local authorities. For example, labour costs in London and the South East of England may be very high compared with the North East; some local authorities are primarily rural (e.g. Dyfed in West Wales) while others are primarily industrial (e.g. Sandwell in the West Midlands); some local authorities on the south coast of England have a high proportion of retired people. The different factors impose different demands on local authorities and are likely to influence the cost of providing services. In rural areas, primary education is likely to be more expensive due to the prevalence of small schools and/or high costs of bussing pupils. In rural areas, refuse collection costs per tonne of refuse are likely to be high because of the distances that need to be covered. In industrial areas, street cleaning and road maintenance costs are likely to be high. Similar problems bedevil the Health Service where, for example, economic and social deprivation and sparsity of population will each have a significant impact on health costs. The solution to this problem is to compare like authorities with like authorities. The Audit Commission for England and Wales has identified family groups of like authorities using the Shaw Classification: this provides a focus of comparison by outside agencies but, more important, also provides service managers with specified comparator authorities with whom it may be worth establishing contact. Contact with like authorities which appear to be more efficient may yield useful lessons.

Contact may expose better systems of service delivery, differences in methods of organization, different approaches to the management of staff, different approaches to the customer, that is, the general public.

Sometimes, unit costs are compared with a national average. This practice is not particularly useful as the average figure simply conceals the wide range of performance which underpins it and makes no allowance for the factors identified in the preceding paragraphs.

Finally, three specific accountancy-related issues may weaken the usefulness of unit costs as efficiency indicators. The first of these is concerned with the charging of overhead costs to service activities. In the case of local authority homes for the elderly, there will be two sources of costs that are not directly related to individual homes: the managerial overheads of the Social Services Department, and the general overheads of the local authority (the main components of which are finance, legal, computerization and local democracy; the last of these includes members' expenses, the costs of committee meetings, the costs of elections and so on and it is not practice to apportion these costs). There is no standard method by which central and departmental overheads are apportioned, although the Chartered Institute of Public Finance and Accounting does specify recommended practice. The absence of standardization means that different apportionment methods and bases can influence the costs charged to homes or to any other managerial unit. Therefore, as far as possible, the results of such apportionments, normally included under the heading 'Central, Departmental and Technical Services', should be excluded when making inter-organizational comparisons of efficiency. However, charges based on service level agreements (SLAs) are gradually replacing arbitrary apportionment. The service providers (overhead departments) will negotiate levels of charges, volume of service, quality and timeliness with the service users. This involvement in the SLA by the management of the homes does mean that the overhead charges in these circumstances should be treated like any other cost as the expense should reflect the economic, efficient and effective management of the home.

The second point relates to the delegation of budgets to schools. Delegation is dealt with more fully in Chapter 4 but at the heart of delegated budgets is each local education authority's approved scheme of delegation. This will specify which of a number of discretionary items are to be delegated to schools and which are to be retained centrally by the authority. In one scheme a specific item may be delegated to schools; in another scheme this cost element may be treated as a discretionary exception and managed centrally. As a result of such an absence of standardization inter-authority comparisons become impossible.

The third area is concerned with measures of capital consumption such as asset rents, depreciation and capital charges. The introduction of these into public sector accounting during the last decade has improved the reporting of capital consumption. At one time the NHS split capital and revenue completely so that the revenue accounts were not required to bear the costs of capital consumption. Local authorities, by way of contrast, made a charge that reflected the method of financing the asset. Now, however, the accounting systems charge revenue accounts with an amount that is related to the value of the asset (asset rents or depreciation) and also levy a nominal capital charge of 6%, related to the cost of financing the asset. Despite the improvement in reporting, there remain issues such as the valuation of assets and policies on depreciation, including the assumed lifespan of assets, which can cause difficulties in making comparisons. CIPFA has issued recommendations about such issues to local authorities in order to improve the standardization of policies and practice.

To summarize, unit-based costs are useful indicators of efficiency and may serve as a starting point in value for money studies, as long as the caveats noted in this section are taken into consideration.

2.3 The measurement and control of overheads

Direct costs are those that can be traced directly to units of output. Furthermore, they change directly and proportionately as output changes. For example, in the production of meals, provisions costs are directly related and traceable to the number of meals produced.

Overheads are those costs that cannot be traced directly to units of activity; in the production of meals, rents and equipment costs are examples of overheads. As overheads cannot be traced directly, they are traced to units of output by a two-stage process:

1. They are first apportioned or charged to cost centres where the final output or service is produced.
2. They are then absorbed into the costs of final outputs or services by using a predetermined recovery rate.

In a hospital, the costs of nurses and clinicians, drugs, x-ray units and food, for example, are all directly traceable to patient care. However, there are other costs such as portering, maintenance, cleaning, administration and stockholding which are not directly traceable and are the overheads of the service.

Local authorities in England and Wales are required to divide their central overheads into three distinct elements (CIPFA, 1995). These are:

1. Corporate management, which comprises direction, supervision and guidance by the council, its committees and central officers. More specifically, it includes meetings of the council and other policy-making committees; the staff and accommodation required to support such meetings; chief executives, except for the time spent by them on specific services; estimating and accounting for precepts, block grants and rates.
2. Overheads from which no user benefits. This includes the back-funding of pension increase costs, the costs of computer mainframes which are unused because of a lack of work due to compulsory competitive tendering and the costs of other long-term unused but unrealizable assets.
3. Support services, which support the provision of services to the public. They include finance, information technology, payroll, personnel and administrative buildings.

The extent of apportionment

These three categories are subject to different accounting treatment and are also apportioned differently. The first category of corporate management costs are not apportioned to front line services but to a separate account. The objective of this approach is to isolate costs that would not be faced by private sector companies and not to apportion them to local authority services. This practice prevents those local authority services engaged in competitive tendering being placed at a disadvantage in the market-testing process.

The second category is not apportioned but is retained as a central cost.

The third category of costs must be charged to services. The traditional method of doing this involved no written agreement between support service providers and users. The main method of apportionment is based on a staff time analysis, which has to be completed by all staff within the support service department. Costs are then apportioned to front line departments based on the time that is claimed to be spent on each department. The costs of administrative buildings that are occupied are initially pooled and then reapportioned on the basis of floor space occupied to all departments, including support services. They are then included in the costs of support services for purposes of apportionment on a staff time basis.

2.4 The advantages of full apportionment

In the case of support services and service management it is recommended that costs be apportioned fully.

The arguments advanced in favour of making a full apportionment are as follows.

It shows the full costs of services

In this way members, officers and taxpayers may be informed of the full cost of providing services; without such apportionment, the costs of service provision would be understated and this could give incorrect signals in resource administration. However, as the following chapter indicates, the emphasis on full costs can give incorrect signals in situations that require emphasis on marginal or incremental costs.

It ensures that maximum revenue is received

It ensures the receipt of the full amount of revenue in the case of services aided by a specific percentage grant from the government (such as the police service which is funded via a 51% specific grant) or where the service is provided under an agency agreement (such as the reinstatement of road surfaces by county councils when the road has been opened by one of the utility companies such as gas or water).

Compliance with legislation

Under DLO and DSO legislation, referred to in Chapter 1, both DLOs and DSOs must compete fairly for work by submitting tenders to the client local authority in competition with the private sector. It is argued that their costs should include a share of the overheads of the 'host' local authority. Their accounts are duly charged with a share of overheads and all costs have to be covered and a 5% return on the current cost of assets earned. The requirement to earn a 5% return ensures that, in tendering for work, DLOs and DSOs must make provision for the cost of central services.

It allows true cost comparisons

It permits the true comparison of the costs of local authority provisions of a service with the costs of a contracted-out service.

Inter-authority comparisons

If all authorities follow the full apportionment policy under identical rules or guidelines it permits the confident comparison of inter-authority accounts and statistics.

Aggregation at national level

Central government makes use of the annual aggregated expenditure figures related to local authorities in its own planning. If the accounts all follow the principle of full apportionment, first there is a similarity in a major aspect of accounts preparation (which is strengthened by the use of the CIPFA Standard Form of Accounts) and, second, the service accounts all show the full cost of service delivery.

Within the Health Service, the Griffiths Report recommended that overheads should be redistributed to units (to provide a full resource budget for units) and to departments and wards. Speciality costing, another development, requires the apportioning of all costs to each separate speciality within the hospital. However, such full reapportionment, which ignores the ways in which costs behave as activity changes, may be of little use for planning and budgeting. It is possible that other developments, patient costing, charging costs to specific patients and the use of DRGs may make use of reapportioned costs but this depends on the purpose and use of the costings.

The bases for the apportionment of costs used in practice have been varied in nature but a typical pattern would be as follows:

Expenditure head	Basis of apportionment
Employees	Time spent on different activities
Administration buildings	Floor area
Printing	Number of pages
Stores	Number of cost of issues
Computer:	
Punching	Time spent, 000s key taps
System analysis	Time spent
Programming	Time spent
Special stationery	Direct to user
Operating costs	All costs, including accommodation, collected and recovered on the basis of time used

2.5 Criticisms of full apportionment

Apportionment as just described can be criticized as follows.

Cost control at the point of expenditure

If one is concerned with control of overhead items of expenditure, one cannot necessarily expect control to be exercised at the end point of the apportionment process. Hospital portering expenditure, for example, can best be controlled centrally by senior staff and by the specification of a budget which is adhered to. Indeed, there appears to be little incentive in the originating departments to control costs, if such costs are going to be apportioned elsewhere.

However, if one considers services such as photocopying, where it is possible to recover costs via a unit charge, then the charge does provide the best form of control as it appears within departmental budget and accounts.

It blunts the competitive edge

If a public sector service is competing with a private sector firm, as in the DLO case, there is evidence that DLOs are penalized by the weight of central charges which they carry in comparison with low overhead competitors. This is compounded by the 5% real rate of return which must be earned.

Timing

All apportionments of actual costs are done at the end of the financial year and are actually charged to service departments after the end of the financial year. The amount apportioned at this point can be significantly different from the estimate and can lead to apparent overspending by service departments very late in the year when they have no time to cut other costs in order to keep within their overall budgets.

The basis of apportionment

Overheads are apportioned using staff time. However, there is no guarantee that the staff time recorded is accurate. If the staff time is out of date or inaccurate, the apportionment of overheads will also be inaccurate: some service departments will gain and others will lose. In consequence, those service departments that gain will be able to spend more on services than is intended by the local authority while those that bear a higher than justified overhead will be able to spend less. The system lacks transparency and the possibility of inaccuracies has an implication for the volume of services that front line departments are able to deliver to their clients.

Opposition from service managers

The apparent imposition of high central overhead appointments can create resentment among service managers; they appear to be unjust and arbitrary, especially in those services where a rate of return has to be earned.

Antidotes to the criticisms

These criticisms can be partially countered in two, closely related, ways:

1. by workload charging;
2. by service level agreements.

Workload charging

Costs may be charged on a workload basis. To take the photocopier example: if a charge of 5p per copy is specified in advance and departments use electronic keys which provide a cumulative record of copies made, then the resulting charge appears fair and end-point departments have a role to play in controlling costs. A similar principle applies to x-ray and pathology services and a hospital laundry, where the costs can be allocated via measures of workload. Another advantage of workload charging is that it encourages the overhead units to plan in workload terms and requires them to keep within the predetermined unit costs.

Chapter 3 investigates the ways in which costs behave as activity changes and a basic distinction is made between fixed costs which do not change as activity changes and variable costs which do so. If this idea is applied to charging on a workload basis, it gives rise to a two-part tariff very similar to the system used for charging for public utility services such as gas, electricity and telecommunications. In these cases, a fixed charge is payable each quarter and represents the fixed rental for connection to the service and this fixed rental may be seen as contributing to the fixed costs of the utility. Every user must pay the same fixed element in recognition of the fact that, whatever the use made, the infrastructure, cabling and so on must be provided. On top of the quarterly fixed charge, a variable amount is payable and this is based on consumption of gas, electricity and so on. This principle of a two-part tariff may be applied to workload charging so that, in the hospital laundry example, user departments would pay a fixed annual amount related to the annual fixed costs of the laundry and a variable amount per unit laundered. The two-part tariff system contributes more information to users of the service. Indeed, in the National Health Service Resource Management Budgeting model system it is recommended that all intermediate costs (not direct costs) should be recharged in two parts, fixed and variable, so that final budget holders can readily see the net increases or decreases in expenditure that result from given changes in workload.

Service level agreements

The traditional basis of apportionment of costs of services normally provides for no written agreement between support service providers and users. The cost of all support services is simply apportioned between their users.

However, there has developed in local authorities the use of a very different approach to support services. The approach involves service level agreements.

The purpose of a service level agreement (SLA) is to define the responsibilities of a provider of support services to a client or service department. It aims to clarify expectations on the quality of support and the costs of that support activity for both sides. Coombs and Evans (2000) state that a SLA between a support service provider and the service department would include the following features:

- a clear identification of objectives of the agreement and definition of terms;
- a definition of quality standards and the setting of performance targets;
- a definition of the roles and responsibilities of both support provider and service department;
- the establishment of methods of reporting performance and the reporting cycle relating to this;
- the establishment of grievance and arbitration procedures in the event of poor service;
- the establishment of procedures in the event of either party wishing to vary the terms of the contract;
- built-in continuous improvement goals over the time period of the agreement;
- charging methods and rates at the agreed performance levels;
- the frequency of billing, payment and reporting;
- the time period over which the agreement is to operate.

To these should be added the requirement that SLAs need to demonstrate how they can deliver best value to the organization.

For example, the Treasurer may negotiate with the DLO manager a fee for the provision of payroll and invoicing services; the agreement specification will include the number of employees covered, the extent of the service, the duties required of the user in the provision of information and a statement as to the timeliness of the service. Another agreement with the Education Department may specify the number of audit hours to be deployed and also the total audit cost.

Bases for charging services must also be identified. For example, the potential charging base for internal audit services would be rate per hour, rate per day or a fixed charge plus a time-based element. Credit income collection would be charged out per invoice, per posting or per account. Finally, financial consultancy services would be charged out at a rate per person day or rate per hour.

Service level agreements have significant implications:

1. The basis of cost is clear to the service department and the amount which will be charged is known in advance, facilitating their budgeting.
2. Users and providers have to have some degree of freedom in negotiating charges.
3. They may encourage users to shop around for services which they may be able to obtain more economically from outside the organization.
4. They force careful planning and budgeting by central departments, including the necessity of operating efficiently and pricing competitively if they are to retain their customer base among the service departments, DLOs and DSOs.
5. There may be year-end balances representing under-apportionment of costs. This may be the result of poor budgeting or poor cost control by support service managers. In an apportionment system, such costs are fully apportioned to user services. However, in a service level agreement system, they remain the responsibility of the support service providers and they must make arrangements to manage such balances. Currently, the law does not permit losses to be carried forward and they would be transferred to the general accounts of the authority.
6. Within the accounts of users, support service charges replace apportioned costs. These represent a much closer approximation of the economic costs of operating the service as they arise from negotiation on costs and services in which the service user has a full part to play.
7. After the period of the SLA expires, users are under no obligation to pay for the service and this may result in losses to the providers.

Public sector organizations are now entering the post-SLA era. The next stage in the process of requiring value for money from support service providers is to be the contracting out of support services. In the NHS individual managers have applied market testing to a number of services including payroll, laundry and estates. In local authorities the contracting principles that have already been applied to DLOs and DSOs will next be applied to white-collar and professional support services.

2.6 An example of overhead recovery

Table 2.2 presents relevant data and a traditional statement in which costs are first apportioned and allocated to a print unit and, second, recovery rates (or absorption rates) are established for the purpose of achieving full cost recovery from user departments.

There are two machines and in the case of each machine, the budgeted recovery rate is obtained by dividing budgeted total costs by budgeted print hours. The budgeted recovery rates are calculated prior to the start of the financial year and user departments

Table 2.2 Print unit: Budget for year ended 31 March 2001

Cost elements	Total costs £	Machine A £	Machine B £
Materials	25 000.00	13 000.00	12 000.00
Labour	7 400.00	3 900.00	3 500.00
Electricity	2 100.00	1 300.00	800.00
Premises costs	8 400.00	4 300.00	4 100.00
Maintenance	1 800.00	890.00	910.00
Asset rents and capital charges	4 775.00	3 610.00	1 165.00
	49 475.00	27 000.00	22 475.00
Budgeted print hours	2 950.00	1 500.00	1 450.00
Budgeted recovery rate per hour		18.00	15.50

should be informed of the appropriate rates so that they may take decisions in full knowledge of the costs they will be required to bear.

It may be observed from the table that full cost recovery will only be achieved if the amounts recovered from user departments actually equal or exceed the costs of the print unit; thus, the unit must keep within its budget of £49 475, and ensure that it achieves its target usage. Alternatively, any reduction in activity should be met by reducing costs, although the absence of a two-part tariff approach means that there is no automatic link between cost reduction and a fall in income. Similarly, the absence of fixed/variable cost distinction renders difficult cost control when activity increases because the manager is unaware as to which costs may be allowed to increase, and by how much. However, the usual approach is one in which fixed and variable costs are subsumed within one recovery rate.

Three conditions are possible.

Full recovery

The unit exactly recovers all its costs. The total of costs recovered using the budgeted recovery rates exactly equals the actual costs incurred by the print unit during the period.

Under-recovery

The unit makes an under-recovery of costs. The total of costs recovered is less than the total of actual costs incurred by the print unit during the period.

			£
Let us assume that:			
Total costs incurred			50 000
Total activity	Recovered		
Machine A 1 400 hours	1 400 * £18	= 25 200	
Machine B 1 500 hours	1 500 * £15.5	= 23 250	
			48 450
	Under-recovered		£1 550

In this case, two things may be done at year end: either write off the balance to revenue or carry forward and attempt to recover the amount in next year's charge, which will be increased as a result of the carry forward. There may be a degree of inequity about the latter approach as next year's users are unlikely to utilise the services of the unit in exactly the same balance as they did in the current year.

Over-recovery

The unit makes an over-recovery of costs. The total of costs recovered is more than the total of actual costs incurred by the print unit during the period.

				£
Let us assume that:				
Total costs incurred				49 000
Total activity		Recovered		
Machine A	1 400 hours	1 500 * £18	= 27 000	
Machine B	1 500 hours	1 500 * £15.5	= 23 250	
				50 250
		Over-recovered		£1 250

The same treatment may be accorded to under-recoveries as in the previous case with the exception that, now, carrying forward the balance to next year would serve to reduce the charge for users in that period.

If overhead costs and recoveries are monitored during the year then any apparently large balances can be investigated. If it can be shown that the original budgeted overhead recovery rate was incorrect, it may be decided to revise the rate part-way through the year in order to ensure that balances are minimized at year end. Any changes must, of course, be communicated to users.

There is a further worked example illustrating the processes of overhead recovery in Exhibit 2.2 at the end of this chapter.

2.7 An application within the NHS

Central sterile supply department (CSSD) costs

One of the major practical problems, apart from forecasting usage and costs and then controlling the latter, is that of actually collecting and charging an appropriate share of overheads. An illustration of this is provided by a hospital central sterile supply department (CSSD). CSSDs are concerned with the production and issue of sterile packs. Packs usually comprise sterile soft packs of dressings, non-disposable bowls and so on and surgical instruments. Generally, the costs of raw materials and of staff are readily traced to specific packs and the CSSD respectively. However, non-CSSD expenditure, which may be charged to non-CSSD budget holders may also be involved in pack production: for example, energy to provide steam to drive the autoclave sterilizing process and linen used to cover the theatre trays. A typical situation might be as follows:

Cost element	Budget holder
Energy	Works department
Linen and laundry	Linen services
Equipment	Works department

Unless appropriate proportions of these costs can be systematically reapportioned to CSSD, the production costs of sterile packs will be understated and will reflect only raw material and CSSD employee costs.

2.8 Activity-based costing (ABC)

In order to address some of the weaknesses of the traditional approaches to the apportionment of overheads, Cooper and Kaplan (1988) developed a more sophisticated approach to tracking overheads through to products; this approach is termed activity-based costing (ABC). It is claimed that ABC provides more accurate information for budgeting, decision making (for example, pricing) and performance measurement. The key features of ABC are as follows:

- It is recognized that activities cause costs to occur.
- Cost centres are created for each activity and the costs relating to each activity are charged to each activity cost centre.
- Cost drivers are determined for each activity.
- Overheads are assigned to products using cost driver rates.

There are many more activity pools than in traditional absorption costing. Similarly, there are more cost drivers than traditional absorption bases. Therefore, a more refined product or service cost can be produced. An excellent discussion of the theoretical and technical issues underpinning ABC can be found in Drury (2000).

Although ABC originated in the manufacturing sector, attempts have been made to extend it both to the banking sector and the public sector. In the higher education sector, the Higher Education Funding Council has issued costing guidelines that are similar to the ABC approach. The following outline of an ABC costing process in a college is taken from the *Further and Higher Education Newsletter* (CIPFA, 2000, p.7).

The costing process:

- identifies the resource costs (staff, consumables, equipment etc.);
- identifies the products (courses, research papers, consultancy, catering, etc.);
- identifies the activities (course delivery, research, admissions, library);
- assigns resource costs to the activities;
- links the activities to the products using cost drivers (staff, students, space);
- analyzes and reports the results.

The *Newsletter* (ibid.) goes on to demonstrate how the ABC classification of activities can be applied to a university as shown in Table 2.3.

Key points of chapter

1. The absence of a bottom line profit measure in the public sector means that cost-based performance measures are emphasized.
2. Cost-based performance measures, such as unit costs, need to be used with great care.
3. Costs are usually related to throughputs rather than outcomes.
4. Overheads are usually fully apportioned in the public sector; this is of value but needs to be used with care.
5. Overhead apportionment is increasingly being replaced by service level agreements which define charges, volumes and quality.

Table 2.3 ABC classification of activities applied to a university

Type of activity	Definition	University activity
Unit level	Activities performed each time a product is delivered, for example, a module	Teaching and research
Batch level	Activities performed each time a batch of products is delivered, for example, a portfolio of modules	Course committees, assessment and validation events
Product level	Activities which are needed to support the provision of each type of output	Faculty administration
Facility level	Activities which sustain an organization's ability to function	General administration and provision of premises

2.9 Summary

It can be seen from the discussion in this chapter that a cost in itself may tell the decision maker little about performance. It is the manager who places an interpretation on the information in order to arrive at a decision as to the use of the information provided. It has also been pointed out that the provision of unit costs data can be seen merely as a measure of the resources devoted to an activity but says little of the quality of such output and is therefore a measure of throughput costs. Furthermore, inter-organizational comparisons are weakened by differences in location and environment and differences in accounting policies.

The apportionment of overheads is important if decision makers are concerned about the full costs of providing services. Rules and guidelines are required if such costs are to be aggregated or used as the basis of inter-organizational comparison. Increasingly, apportionment is being replaced by charging within the context of service level agreements. These have benefits for users and present a challenge to providers. They have required an examination of costs, service volumes and quality and timeliness of service.

Full cost recovery can only be obtained if costs are strictly controlled and if the use of an activity can be predicted with some degree of accuracy. Ideally, recovery should be related to the use of workload measures, and the use of a two-part tariff to reflect the distinction between fixed and variable costs would also be of benefit. The organization will need to decide how it is going to deal with over- and under-recovery of overheads at the conclusion of an accounting period.

Exhibit 2.1

This is a short case study which illustrates the preparation and interpretation of unit cost statements.

You are employed as a financial adviser to the Director of Social Services of the Glamwent County Council. The Council operates three homes for the elderly each of which has a kitchen serving as a dining room. The Director has requested that you investigate the costs of operating the three kitchens in the last financial year.

On investigation, you discover the following operating costs for the last financial year:

	Kitchen A £	Kitchen B £	Kitchen C £
Cost of provisions	32 000	35 250	12 700
Heating and lighting	3 600	4 100	2 200
Number of employees:			
Cooks	1	1	1
Assistant cooks	1	2	1
Kitchen assistants	8	9	5
Capital costs of kitchens:			
Building costs	60 000	30 000	18 000
Equipment/furniture	27 000	29 000	14 000
Number of meals produced	72 000	78 000	32 000

Notes:

1. Average annual earnings are cooks £6500, assistant cooks £5500 and kitchen assistants £4000.
2. In addition to the above staff one supervisor has overall charge of the three kitchens and is paid an annual salary of £7500. This is to be apportioned over each of the kitchens.
3. Overheads on wages and salaries amount to 10% of total salaries and wages costs.
4. Administration costs are to be apportioned to each kitchen on a basis of 1p per meal produced.
5. The totals of asset rents and capital charges for the three kitchens are as follows:

	Buildings	Equipment and furniture
Kitchen A	£5 400	£3 240
Kitchen B	£2 700	£3 480
Kitchen C	£9 720	£8 400

Required

Investigate the costs of operating the three kitchens for the Director of Social Services and draw appropriate conclusions from the costs.

Discussion

The first step is to prepare a unit cost statement as the basis for analysis. This is contained in Table 2.4 which has been prepared using the number of meals served as the denominator and the costs recorded against each item of expenditure as the numerator. Unit costs are provided for each kitchen, for each item of expenditure and a total column aggregates costs to give an average cost for each expenditure head.

Comments

1. The provisions costs vary by 5p, or 11% of the average cost of provisions. This may be caused by waste and inefficiency including over-ordering and an absence of efficient portion control. Dietary needs may also play a part in that one home may have a number of residents with special requirements. It could also be possible that kitchen C is underfeeding its residents. Finally, if there is no central purchasing, the cost differences might be attributable to different prices being paid for provisions.
2. There is some variation in lighting and heating costs and it may be appropriate as an energy conservation exercise to look at a wider sample of homes.
3. The numbers of staff vary considerably between the homes while the workload table shows that there is a particularly heavy burden on kitchen A. At the very best, kitchen C appears overstaffed and it may be possible to remove the kitchen assistant. Questions should also be raised about staffing policy in other homes.

Table 2.4 Unit cost statement: Homes for the aged (Glamwent CC)

	Kitchen A		Kitchen B		Kitchen C		Total	
	Cost £	Unit P	Cost £	Unit P	Cost £	Unit P	Cost £	Unit P
Provisions	32 000	44	32 250	45	12 700	40	79 950	44
Heat/light	3 600	5	4 100	5	2 200	7	9 900	5
Cooks	6 500	9	6 500	8	6 500	20	19 500	11
Ass. cooks	5 500	8	11 000	14	5 500	17	22 000	12
Kitchen asst	32 000	44	36 000	46	20 000	63	88 000	48
Supervisor	2 500	3	2 500	3	2 500	8	7 500	4
Overheads	4 650	6	5 600	7	3 450	11	13 700	8
Admin. costs	720	1	780	1	320	1	1 820	1
Asset rents and capital charges								
Buildings	5 400	8	2 700	3	1 620	5	9 720	5
Furn./Fit.	3 240	5	3 480	4	1 680	5	8 400	5
Totals	96 110	133	107 910	138	56 470	176	260 490	143
No. of meals	72 000		78 000		32 000		182 000	
Workload (average meals served):								
Cooks			72 000		78 000		32 000	
Assistant								
cooks			72 000		39 000		32 000	
Kitchen maids			9 000		8 667		6 400	

4. The supervisor has been apportioned to each home on the basis of one-third of the salary to each home. It would also be possible to apportion the supervisor's salary on the basis of the number of meals produced or on the basis of the number of staff employed in each kitchen. This also raises the question of the relevance of the apportionment as the supervisor is, at the kitchen level, a non-controllable overhead. Similar comments to the latter can also be made about the apportionment of overheads on salaries and wages, the administration charges and the capital costs.
5. It should be noted that no definite conclusions can be reached at this stage and no comments have been made as to the quality of care provided. However, the Director is now in a position where a problem has been identified and further work can be undertaken to seek a solution. The investigation has also enabled areas of responsibility to be identified in that, for example, the cook is responsible for the preparation of meals and the possible lack of portion control.

Exhibit 2.2

Goldstar Windows is a subsidiary company of X County Council which employs disabled workers to manufacture double-glazed UPVC windows. The process consists of cutting the delivered lengths of raw material, manufacturing the window frame and finally fitting the glass to the double-glazed units. For the year to 31 March 2001 the cost centre expenses and other relevant information is as follows:

	Total	Cutting	Manu-facture	Glass fitting	Stores	Main-tenance	Tool room
	£	£	£	£	£	£	£
Indirect materials	12 260	5 640	4 880	1 150	410	60	120
Consumable materials	5 500	1 500	2 000	1 100	—	600	300
Depreciation	70 000	35 000	13 000	12 000	1 000	8 000	1 000
Heat/light	14 250						
Insurance	12 000						
Rent/rates	19 000						
Power	48 000						
Floor area (m²)	9 500	3 000	2 500	2 500	500	500	500
Power use (%)	100	40	30	15	5	5	5
Value of building (£)	120 000	40 000	40 000	10 000	15 000	5 000	10 000
Direct labour (hrs)	20 000	5 000	8 000	7 000			
Machine hours	22 000	15 000	4 000	3 000			
Stores requisitions	8 000	1 000	3 000	3 500			500

Using the above information provided for Goldstar Windows, a three-stage process will now be undertaken which will culminate in the calculation of overhead recovery (or absorption) rates for the three production cost centres: cutting; manufacture; glass fitting.

Stage 1: This involves apportioning the total costs over the six cost centres within Goldstar Windows. In the case of indirect materials, consumable materials and depreciation, costs have already been allocated to cost centres. The remaining costs are apportioned as indicated in the following apportionment statement. The statement is termed an overhead analysis. The bases for apportioning the costs are indicated in the statement and a brief commentary on the reason for choosing the bases follows:

1. *Heat/light* expenditure is assumed to vary in relation to floor area. Other things being equal, the larger the area, the greater the heat and light required. Hence, the expenditure is apportioned to the cost centres on the basis of floor area.
2. *Insurance* is assumed to be related to the value of buildings and it is apportioned to the cost centres on this basis.
3. *Rent and rates* fall into the same category as insurance.
4. *Power costs* are apportioned to cost centres on the basis of the share of power use provided in the above data.

Stage 2: Following the initial apportionments, the total costs for all six cost centres are obtained. However, three of these cost centres are in the nature of support services and these provide services to the production cost centres. The support service cost centres are stores, maintenance, tool room. None of these produces a saleable product but without them the production cost centres, cutting, maintenance and glass fitting are unable to function.

Stage 2 involves reapportioning the support service costs to the production cost centres. The service centre costs are reapportioned as follows:

1. Stores are reapportioned to cutting, manufacturing, glass fitting and the tool room on the basis of the number of stores requisitions.
2. Maintenance costs are reapportioned on the basis of machine hours.
3. Tool room costs are also reapportioned on the basis of machine hours.

Stage 3: Overhead recovery rates are established for each production cost centre. The process involves dividing budgeted costs by budgeted activity to provide a budgeted recovery rate or budgeted absorption rate. In the case of cutting, a rate based on machine hours has been used because the cost centre appears to be very machine oriented when the labour and machine hours are prepared. With manufacture and glass fitting, the reverse applies and so the basis for the recovery rate which has been selected is labour hours.

The rates are shown in the following apportionment statement. They will be applied to all work undertaken by Goldstar Windows. The cost of work which the unit undertakes will consist of direct costs (primarily labour and materials) plus a share of overheads derived by applying the rates to the amount of time each job spends in each of the productive cost centres.

Apportionment

The first stage is to apportion the costs to the three units.
This is effected by means of an overhead analysis statement.

	Basis of apportion-ment	Total £	Cutting £	Manu-facture £	Glass fitting £	Stores £	Main-tenance £	Tool room £
Indirect materials		12 160	5 640	4 880	1 150	410	60	20
Consumables		5 500	1 500	2 000	1 100		600	300
Depreciation		70 000	35 000	13 000	12 000	1 000	8 000	1 000
Heat and light	Area (M²)	14 250	4 500	3 750	3 750	750	750	750
Insurance	Value of bldg	12 000	4 000	4 000	1 000	1 500	500	1 000
Rent and rates	Area (M²)	19 000	6 000	5 000	5 000	1 000	1 000	1 000
Power	Use %	48000	19 200	14 400	7 200	2 400	2 400	2 400
Sub-totals		180 910	75 840	47 030	31 200	7 060	13 310	6 470
Reapportionment								
Stores			883	2 647	3 089	−7 060		441
Maintenance			9 075	2 420	1 815		−13 310	
Tool room			4 712	1 257	942			−6 911
Totals		180 910	90 510	53 354	37 046	0	0	0

The next step is to calculate recovery rates.

Machine hours		15 000				
Labour hours			8 000	7 000		
Rate per machine hour		6.03				
Rate per labour hour			6.67	5.29		

Questions

2.1 You are employed as financial adviser to the Glamwent County Council. The authority operates a large comprehensive school serving three separate dining rooms. The Director of Education has requested that you carry out a financial investigation using unit cost data into the three kitchens.

On investigation you discover the following information for the last financial year (19X1/X2):

| | Kitchen | | |
	A	B	C
Cost of provisions	£80 000	£98 500	£49 000
Heating and lighting	£2 600	£2 700	£1 900
Number of employees:			
Cooks	1	1	1
Assistant cooks	1	1	—
Kitchen maids	8	6	5
Capital costs:			
Buildings	£300 000	£300 000	£180 000
Equipment	£90 000	£90 000	£60 000
Total meals produced	60 000	66 000	30 000
Income	£30 000	£31 000	£15 000

Other factors

(a) Average annual earnings are £10 000 for a cook, £9000 for an assistant and £5000 for other staff.
(b) In addition to the above staff one supervisor has overall charge of all three kitchens. She is paid an annual salary of £18 000.
(c) Wage overheads are estimated to amount to 10% of total wages and salaries.
(d) Administration costs are to be allocated to each kitchen on the basis of 2p per meal produced.
(e) Buildings and equipment are depreciated on a straight-line basis. The appropriate periods are 60 years and 15 years respectively.

Required

Prepare a cost report to the Director of Education on the costs of operating the three kitchens in 19X1/X2. The report should contain appropriate recommendations based on your conclusions about the operating costs of the three kitchens.

Note:
You may make any reasonable assumptions in preparing the report but these should be stated in the report or your working papers. (25 marks)

2.2 The Bedpan Health Authority administers three hospitals and, at each, maintains a catering service for both patients and staff.

The following information has been made available for the 9 months ended 31 December 19X2.

	North £	Hospitals South £	West £
Food stocks: 1.4.–2	3 345	16 445	1 140
31.12.–2	3 680	22 610	935
Wages: Kitchen staff			
– Patients meals	96 600	201 250	21 000
– Staff meals	47 750	263 500	10 000
Dining room staff	53 000	183 250	—
Hardware, crockery etc.	6 000	17 500	1 450
Salaries catering			
management	15 000	25 000	10 000
Income: staff meals	70 000 CR	394 090 CR	6 500 CR
sale of waste	5 500 CR	1 650 CR	250 CR
Purchase of food in the			
year	168 905	556 600	22 780
Cost of food used for			
patient meals	117 530	327 175	18 000
Patient days	96 600	241 500	15 960
Staff meals served		141 680	354 200

Notes:
1. The DHA laid down the following cost limits for the financial year to 31.3.–3:
   (a) Food cost allowance for patients was £6.70 per patient week.
   (b) Staff meals price should be set so as to recover the cost of the food used plus 60%.
2. Inflation during 19X2/X3 affected food prices at an average rate of 10%.
3. All allocations of costs between patient and staff meals have been obtained from records kept by each catering manager.
4. Menus are at the discretion of each hospital catering manager, who is also responsible for his own purchasing.
5. Increases in pay are awarded with effect from 1 April. During 19X2/X3, however, a long dispute was not settled until the middle of December, the pay award to all employees being 6.5% backdated to 1 April 19X2. The pay award did not find its way into salaries and wages paid out until the end of January 19X3.
6. Electricity and gas costs are not separately metered for the catering departments. However, based on floor area, in estimated apportionment of such costs for 19X2/X3 gives the following charges for the year:

	£
North	2 500
South	8 700
West	2 100

7. The total hospital catering budget for Bedpan HA for 19X2/X3 amounts to £1 718 000 and was apportioned as follows:

North	£435 000
South	£1 205 000
West	£78 000

Required

Prepare a report to the Senior Assistant Treasurer comparing the efficiency of the establishment and examining the probable out-turn for 19X2/X3 with reference to the budget for the year.

2.3	Oldhouse Hospital £	Newtown Hospital £	Manorcottage Hospital £
Cleaning materials	3 980	19 440	910
Equipment	300	810	160
Cleaning staff – pay	6 000	139 860	15 000
– National Insurance	600	12 150	1 320
– superannuation	480	7 830	600
– travelling expenses	—	810	—
Contract – general cleaning	31 460	2 430	240
Services – window cleaning	360	810	160
– other contract services	120	1 480	80
Miscellaneous	720	540	160
Statistics			
– Floor area	12 000 sq.m.	27 000 sq.m.	4 000 sq.m.
– Average number of available staffed beds	100 beds	300 beds	25 beds

Notes:

(i) The costs of the domestic superintendent responsible for the three hospitals are to be apportioned on the basis of floor areas. The costs for 19X6/X7 were:

	£
Pay (including National Insurance and superannuation)	4 300
Travelling expenses	430

(ii) Sundry creditors were:

	31 March 19X6 £	31 March 19X7 £
Oldhouse Hospital		
– equipment	—	600
– general cleaning	500	600
Manorcottage Hospital		
– contract services, window cleaning	50	50
Newtown hospital		
– cleaning materials	250	—

(iii) During 19X6/X7 Newtown Hospital entered into an equipment maintenance contract for £600 per annum payable annually in advance on 1 December. The payment made on 1 December 19X6 is included in the above figures under 'other contract services'.

(iv) Issues from the Central Store for cleaning materials issued during the last week of 19X6/X7 have not been included in these figures. These are: Newtown Hospital £400, Oldhouse Hospital £80, Manorcottage Hospital £10.

(v) Stocks of cleaning materials in hand were:

	31 March 19X6	31 March 19X7
	£	£
Oldhouse Hospital	250	350
Newtown Hospital	1 000	2 500
Manorcottage Hospital	50	50

These details have been extracted from the accounting records of the Somewhere Area Health Authority for the year ended 31 March 19X7. You are required to:

(a) Prepare a statement comparing the cleaning costs for each hospital for 19X6/X7.

(b) Discuss the relative cleaning costs for each hospital and the possible reasons for variances.

(c) Comment on a recent request from the domestic superintendent for an additional cleaner at Manorcottage Hospital.

2.4 You are employed as a Principal Accountant at the London Borough of Mutton. An opposition councillor is proposing to raise the question of efficiency in the library service at the next meeting of the Arts and Libraries Committee. He has information which shows that the gross costs of running Mutton's libraries is 49% higher than in Lambden (usually regarded as a high spending authority) whereas Mutton's population is only 27% higher. Your assistant has collected the following further information.

		Mutton	*Lambden*
Population (000)		247	194
Gross expenditure of library services	(£000)	3 889	2 560
including (1) recharge of management			
and administration costs	(£000)	793	615
(2) debt charges	(£000)	642	213
Income	(£000)	340	134
Number of libraries (mobile library vans)		11(1)	17(2)
Stock – books (000 items)		2 477	1 846
– other (000 items)		623	832
Issues – books (000)		8 451	6 314
– other (000)		1 937	2 865

Required

(a) Prepare a briefing note for the assistant Director of Finance who will be attending the Committee on behalf of the Director. The note should cover:

(i) the extent to which the available information supports the councillor's case;

(8 marks)

(ii) the alternative explanations which exist for any apparent differences in performance between the two boroughs. (6 marks)

(b) Why is it desirable to recharge the costs of management and administration to services? (6 marks)

(Total 20 marks)

2.5 Barkworth Health Authority is responsible for Armsworth Hospital, a purpose-built hospital for the mentally handicapped providing service for in-patients and out-patients. Callendar Health Authority provides a similar service in the Abell Wing of Delta Hospital.

The following figures are available for analysis:

	Armsworth Hospital		Delta Hospital – Abell Wing	
	Total cost £000	Out-patients share of total cost %	Total cost £000	Out-patients share of total cost %
Medical and dental	100	5	90	1
Nursing	1 800	1	1 200	3
Pharmacy and medical	130	5	80	8
Physiotherapy	50	6	—	—
Occupational therapy	90	5	150	20
Catering	300	—	310	8
Laundry and linen	80	—	80	—
Administration	200	3	50	10
Domestic and cleaning	150	3	200	12
Portering	30	—	20	—
Estate management	610	2	210	12
Energy and utilities	410	2	220	12
	3 950		2 610	

Statistics

Average no. of beds	290	210
Average no. of occupied beds	190	208
No. of in-patient days	100 000	70 000
No. of out-patient attendance	3 000	7 000

Required

(a) From the figures given calculate for each expenditure head and for total expenditure:
(i) the costs per in-patient day in each hospital;
(ii) the cost per out-patient attendance at each hospital. (6 marks)

(b) State:
(i) what conclusions you draw from your analysis of the figures; (8 marks)
(ii) the reservations, if any, you have about these conclusions. (2 marks)

(Total 16 marks)

3 Cost variability and relevant costs

Key learning objectives

After reading this chapter you should be able to:

1. Classify costs by behaviour.
2. Explain why cost behaviour is so important to managers.
3. Make use of cost behaviour in decision-making problems.
4. List the difficulties of classifying costs by behaviour in a public sector organization.
5. Understand the benefits and limitations of classifying costs by relevance to the decision under consideration.
6. Make use of incremental analysis in decision-making problems.

Chapter 2 examined traditional approaches to the collection and use of costs within public sector organizations. It was partly concerned with the traceability of costs and the apportionment of overheads to units of output. It also outlined how unit cost statements could be organized on a subjective basis leading to classification by employee costs, materials costs, premises costs and so on.

However, neither classification by traceability nor by subject makes any reference to the ways in which costs behave, for example the extent to which costs increase as one additional pupil is admitted to a school or as one additional patient is admitted to a hospital. Yet such information is clearly of value to managers concerned with decisions about increase or reductions in the services offered.

3.1 Cost classification by behaviour

To illustrate this, we will use two examples. Our first is of an infants school with 160 children in six classes; output or activity is measured by the number of children in the school. Our second example is of a large hospital of 750 beds where we shall take an extremely crude measure of activity, the number of in-patient days.

Costs may be classified into four main categories as follows:

1. variable costs;
2. fixed costs;
3. semi-variable costs;
4. step costs.

Variable costs

Variable costs (VC) are those that vary wholly and proportionally with an increase in output. Graphically, a variable cost is described in Figure 3.1. As may be seen, it commences at the origin and increases in a linear fashion.

In an infants school the only cost that can be placed in this category is that relating to consumable materials – paper, paints, and so on. These are likely to increase proportionally as the number of children in the school increases by one.

In the hospital there are a number of variable costs: drugs, x-rays and sterile packs are obvious examples of costs which increase as the number of in-patient days increase.

It should be noted that there are some costs, such as heating, which do vary from month to month. However, the observed changes are not in response to the specified measures of activity in this case and must, therefore, be excluded from the VC category.

Fixed costs

Fixed costs (FC) remain unchanged as output or activity increases or decreases. Graphically, a fixed cost is described in Figure 3.2. As may be observed, the level of cost remains constant irrespective of the level of output.

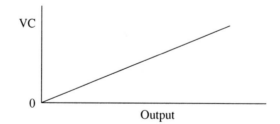

Figure 3.1 Variable costs

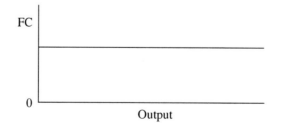

Figure 3.2 Fixed costs

Using the infants school illustration, examples of fixed costs include the costs of caretaker and security, the external maintenance of buildings and grounds, heating costs and the capital financing charges relating to the school. You will note that neither teachers' nor headteacher's salaries are included within this category. This is explained when step costs are considered later.

Within our hospital, the general manager's salary may be regarded as fixed, as will be the salaries of those senior managers immediately below that level. Building services, portering services, and equipment expenditure also come into this category.

Semi-variable costs

Semi-variable costs (SVC) contain a fixed component and a variable component which is related to output. Graphically, a semi-variable cost is described in Figure 3.3. As may be seen, it intersects the vertical axis at point A; the distance OA represents the fixed element of the cost. The linear slope to the right of point A, along the section to B, reflects the variable element of the cost.

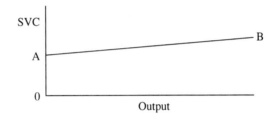

Figure 3.3   Semi-variable costs

Within an infants school, examples include a photocopier where a fixed rental is payable and then a charge related to use, which one may assume is itself related to the number of children within the school.

Within a hospital, laundry costs present such an example. There is a fixed component and a variable element related to power, water, chemicals and so on which relate to activity which is itself tied to the number of in-patient days.

In both school and hospital, the overall catering cost is a semi-variable cost made up of food costs (variable), catering assistants (step), chef (fixed), heat (variable) and so on.

Step costs

Step costs (SC) are those that are fixed for a given level of activity, but at some critical level of output, they increase to a new level. Step costs are described diagrammatically in Figure 3.4. As may be seen, the cost behaves as a fixed cost up to activity level X, but thereafter shifts to a higher level of expenditure.

Whether a cost is a step cost or a fixed cost depends, crucially, on the range of output that is being considered. Over very large ranges of output almost all costs become step costs; for example, a very large increase in the potential pupil intake may require a temporary classroom to be installed, or a wing to be added to the school and will probably require hiring new teachers on fixed salaries.

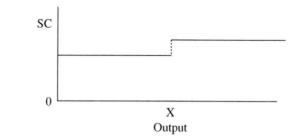

Figure 3.4   Step costs

In our infant school illustration, the school currently admits 160 pupils. If the number falls to 139, say, the headteacher may suffer a salary reduction as the school slips down to a lower group. If the number of children falls to below 150, the headteacher may have to adopt the role of a teaching head, and, in consequence, there may be some loss in staff time and a reduction in staff costs. If, however, the number of pupils increases to 175, say, the school may be entitled to an additional part-time teacher. In both of these cases, it can be seen that relatively modest changes in pupil numbers can give rise to changes in staff costs.

Consider our hospital: an increase in patients (subject to the availability of funds) may require that a ward be opened; this may well increase nursing and clinician time so that staff costs, normally regarded as fixed, step up to a new level.

3.2 Revenue and contribution

So far in this chapter our two examples have made no reference to revenue. However, in the public sector, revenue and its relationship to costs has become increasingly important.

Table 3.1 shows the relationships between revenue, variable costs and contribution. It is usual to consider each of these per unit of output; this is possible because it is assumed that each of these three variables increases in a linear fashion so that the relationship between all three is maintained with consistency.

Any fixed costs which are applicable can then be deducted in total; these are not shown on a per unit basis because to do so would represent arbitrary averaging and may suggest to a manager that such costs are also variable on a per unit basis. It should be noted that this applies specifically to the unit cost statements outlined in Chapter 2.

Table 3.1   The contribution approach

	Total £	Per unit £
Sales revenue	x	x^1
Less variable costs	y	y^1
Contribution	z	z^1
Less fixed costs	a	
Net profit	b	

There, all costs were divided by the appropriate measure of throughput. As suggested in Chapter 2, more useful for management might be the disaggregation of costs into their variable and fixed components, with detailed examination of unit costs being concentrated on the variable cost elements. To some extent, low fixed unit costs may reflect that the unit is operating near to capacity – but this information can be communicated statistically rather than via unit cost measures.

In the short term, or where there is excess capacity, an organization may tolerate its failure to cover fixed costs. As long as revenue exceeds variable costs, some contribution will be made towards fixed costs and some contribution may be better than none. Indeed, the desire to maintain the labour force or hold on to a customer (department) may result in continuing operations if revenues only cover variable cost, if this is the best that can be obtained. In the short term, the aim might be to maximize contribution. However, at the end of the day, all fixed costs must be covered. Thus, long-term considerations would require that the total contribution from operations at least equals total overheads.

If the organization's operations can, in some way, be segmented, Table 3.2 demonstrates how the layout in Table 3.1 can be expanded marginally. It is assumed that we have a refuse disposal DSO and that its disposal activities are segregated into domestic refuse and trade refuse. In this situation, each activity may have overheads specific to that activity. For example, trade refuse may have a separate chargehand and it may employ a different type of refuse vehicle – possibly a lorry as well as a refuse freighter. Such overheads are termed 'segmental fixed costs' or 'segmental overheads' and are designated by letters d and s in Table 3.2. After deducting segmental fixed costs from contribution, this gives rise to a segmental contribution (letters e and t) to the remaining overheads of the organization (letter y), resulting in the organization's net profit designated by letter z.

Table 3.2   Segmented operations and contribution

| | Domestic | | Trade | | |
| | Total | Per bin | Total | Per tonne | Total |
	£	£	£	£	£
Sales revenue	a	a^1	p	p^1	
Less: Variable costs	b	b^1	q	q^1	
Contribution	c	c^1	r	r^1	
Less: Segmental fixed costs	d		s		
Segmental contribution	e		t		
					x
Less: Organizational fixed costs					y
Net profit					z

3.3 The importance of cost behaviour

Cost behaviour becomes important whenever the level of activity is expected to increase or decrease. As activity increases, variable costs, and the variable element of semi-variable costs, increase too. Contrariwise, fixed costs will remain constant – unless, of course, they are step costs within the activity range under consideration, in which case the point at which the step occurs becomes critical.

To illustrate the importance of cost behaviour, we take two examples from an environment which is very different from that of a school or hospital, namely an employees' canteen and a grounds maintenance DSO.

An employees' canteen

A local authority runs a canteen for its workers, which must at least break even (no profit/no loss) on a year-by-year basis. During the last financial year, the costs of providing a meal in its canteen were as follows:

Variable costs per meal:
food	45p
fuel, etc.	15p

Annual fixed costs:
wages	£36 000
other overheads	£24 000
Average meal price	72p
No. of meals sold	700 000
Capacity (meals)	825 000

For the next financial year, it is anticipated that the cost of food per meal will rise to 50p, fuel, etc. to 16p, wages will increase to £38 000 and other overheads to £25 000. The catering manager wishes to know the answer to one question: How many meals must be sold to break even?

It is this kind of situation for which knowledge of cost behaviour is particularly useful, and understanding of the relationships outlined in Table 3.1 can be especially valuable. The catering manager's question can be dealt with in two stages:

Stage 1: Calculate the contribution from each meal:

$$\text{Unit contribution} = \text{average meal price} - \text{variable costs}$$
$$= 72p - (50p + 16p)$$
$$= 6p$$

Stage 2: Divide fixed costs by unit contribution to give breakeven output:

$$\text{Total fixed costs/unit contribution} = (£38\ 000 + £25\ 000)/£0.06$$
$$= 1\ 050\ 000 \text{ meals to break even}$$

The catering manager is now provided with information that gives some insight into the problems which need to be faced:

1. The breakeven output exceeds the capacity of the canteen by (1 050 000 – 825 000) 225 000 meals; quite apart from this, any increase in output would need to be sold.
2. The breakeven output level must be reduced. This can be attacked on two fronts. The first is by increasing prices. But what is the likely impact of a given price increase on demand? This can be answered only when we have some idea of the elasticity of demand for meals at the canteen. Second, the catering manager can try to find ways of reducing costs. Reducing variable costs will result in an increase in unit contribution; reducing the fixed costs will reduce the breakeven point for any given level of unit contribution.

These relationships can be illustrated diagrammatically in a breakeven chart as shown in Figure 3.5.

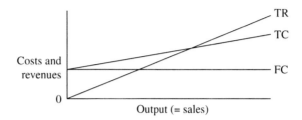

Figure 3.5 Breakeven charts

In the breakeven chart, the total fixed costs (FC) are drawn parallel to the horizontal axis. FC includes the fixed elements of semi-variable costs (SVC). Total costs (TC) are found by adding variable costs (VC) at each output level to FC. Therefore, when output is zero, TC are equal to FC because VC are also zero. The increase in TC in the range of output illustrated is wholly attributable to variable costs as there are no step costs present. The chart assumes that output is equal to sales. Total revenue (TR) from the sale of output is a straight line from the origin. As sales increase, revenues also increase.

The point of intersection of TC and TR indicates the breakeven level of sales. To the left of this point, a loss is made. To the right, a profit is made. The canteen, therefore, is currently operating below breakeven. We saw that the breakeven level of output must be reduced by increasing selling price (increasing the slope of the line TR) or by reducing TC, either by cutting VC (the line would slope less steeply) or by cutting FC (shifting down vertically both FC and TC).

A grounds maintenance DSO

Blaenwent Borough Council has set up a separate shrub-growing section within its grounds maintenance DSO. The section is to be run as a separate trading activity and its objective is to maximize profit as this will help the department subsidize grounds maintenance in the event of poor performance. It is planned that the activity will supply shrubs to the parent authority and also to other public sector organizations within the confines of the Local Authority Goods and Service Act (which limits the ability of local authorities to compete outside the public sector). A total of 20 acres of land have been set aside for this activity and the department has prepared the budget shown in Table 3.3.

Table 3.3 Budgeted costs for shrub-growing operation

	Logard Blue	Faze Yellow	Hardy Berberian	Berry Red
No. of shrub/acre	100	80	90	100
Selling price each	£4	£5	£6	£7
VC per acre:				
Seedlings	£150	£200	£225	£300
Wages	£30	£20	£25	£50
Fixed costs per annum		£3 000		

Wages may be treated as a variable cost as the shrub-growing section will buy in labour from the parent DSO on an acre-by-acre basis, as and when needed.

Discussion with the DSO manager reveals that the council, as client, has agreed to purchase 120 Logard Blues, 80 Faze Yellows, 72 Hardy Berberians and 100 Berry Reds. The manager feels, however, that such is the expertise within the department, and such the demand for the product, that it would be possible to sell up to 2000 shrubs of any type to the local and health authorities in the area. Given this, he wishes to investigate which variety represents greatest profit and, by bundling the host authority's needs along with sales of the most profitable shrub, he wishes to investigate the overall maximum profit that can be obtained.

This situation, like the last, can also be tackled in two stages. Stage 1 involves identifying the contributions per acre from the four types of shrub. The relevant calculations are shown in Table 3.4.

As may be seen, the greatest contribution per acre is provided by the variety Berry Red. Because the number of acres devoted to this activity restricts the number of seedlings that can be planted, the variety Berry Red is the most attractive financially because it makes the highest contribution per acre of this limiting factor. This suggests that any excess acreage, after meeting the authority's needs, should be devoted to this variety if the objective is to maximize contribution.

Table 3.4 Contribution per acre from the shrubs

	Logard Blue £	Faze Yellow £	Hardy Berberian £	Berry Red £
Revenue per acre	400	400	540	700
VC per acre	180	220	250	350
Contribution per acre	£220	£180	£290	£350

Stage 2 involves calculating the maximum contribution and profit that can be obtained from the operation. Relevant calculations are displayed in Table 3.5. As can be seen, after making allowance for the total of three acres which must be devoted to the first three types of shrub in order to supply the host local authority with the agreed mix of shrubs, the remaining 17 acres are used for growing the Berry Red variety.

Table 3.5 Maximum contribution and profit available

	Logard Blue	Faze Yellow	Hardy Berberian	Berry Red	Total
Sales to host	120	80	72		
Acres required	1.2	1	0.8		
Acres available for Berry Red (20–3)				17	
	£	£	£	£	£
Contribution per acre	220	180	290	350	
Total contribution	264	180	232	5 950	6 626
Fixed costs					3 000
Net profit					£3 626

By doing this, maximum contribution and profit can be obtained because the Berry Red makes the greatest contribution per acre, which is the factor of production which limits output. This produces a total contribution of £6626 and a net profit of £3626 after meeting the fixed costs of the operation.

Conclusions

The two previous examples have demonstrated that knowledge of cost behaviour is valuable to management in both planning and decision making.

In the first example, the breakeven position was established; extension of the approach would allow the prediction of required sales of any specified target profit – given by: (Fixed costs + Target profit)/Contribution per unit of output. As the assumed relationship between contribution and output is a linear one, once contribution per unit has been established, it is possible to estimate with some ease the total contribution from different levels of output. If price or variable costs are to be changed, the revised unit contribution can be assessed relatively quickly and then applied to projected levels of output.

In the second example, the concept of the limiting factor was introduced and it was demonstrated how contribution per unit of the limiting factor could be used to establish the optimum product mix.

One other valuable use of cost behaviour is found when budgeted costs are monitored against actual performance. If actual performance relates to different levels of activity than the budget, there appears little point in comparing actual variable costs with budgeted variable costs. Instead, they should be compared with what budgeted variable costs would be expected to be at that actual level of output. This point is examined within the context of flexible budgeting in Chapter 5.

3.4 Problems relating to the cost behaviour approach

As has been demonstrated, the classification of cost by behaviour is very attractive, but its practical application has to face a variety of problems.

Fluctuating nature of variable unit costs

The assumption underpinning the accountant's approach to variable costs is that they are constant per unit of output. However, increasing efficiency may result in decreasing variable costs per unit and vice versa. The likelihood of this will differ for different components of cost; variable labour costs are likely to be the most liable to change, although all unit variable costs may change as a result of modifications in equipment or methods of organization.

The prevalence of step costs

As has been indicated, many costs fall into the step category over output ranges with which we may be concerned. Within the education service, the stepped elements of salaries are fairly easy to derive. The pupil numbers bands for determining headteachers' salaries are publicized; the ground rules for relating pupil numbers to staff numbers are also well known. However, within a secondary school, changing option preferences may require relatively complex projections of the resulting costs. Within a hospital, complexity is likely to be even greater. The size of many acute hospitals (many large ones have an annual expenditure in excess of £40m) and the integrated nature of operations may mean that the step cost implications of decisions may be widespread and complex to follow through. Take, for example, a decision to treat more patients within a speciality as day patients rather than as in-patients. This may result in freeing beds and may also free nursing and clinician time (both indicating steps in a downward direction). However, the policy change is probably aimed at increasing the number of patients treated, so that drugs expenditure (a variable cost) will almost certainly increase, there may be an increase in admission costs, an increased demand on the non-emergency ambulance service and a possible rearranging of clinician and nursing hours.

Disaggregation of semi-variable costs

Rarely are costs purely variable; many costs are semi-variable. Where there exists a two-part tariff, as with telephone and photocopier charges, the standing charge is clearly the fixed element, the metered charge the variable element. However, taking a school as an example, a large part of the telephone metered charge may remain substantially fixed over significant changes in pupil numbers. The management of the school will require telephone contact – with officers of the LEA, with examining bodies, with governors and so on. On top of this, increases in pupil numbers will necessitate use of the telephone to contact parents, the LEA and so on. Thus, the apparent simplicity of the metered element of telephone charge conceals a cost which is semi-variable and may be stepped as well.

There are two distinct approaches to dealing with the problem of semi-variable costs, both are concerned with segregating the fixed and variable elements.

An engineering approach

An engineering approach attempts to build up a cost after specifying the target inputs required. For example, from what is known about cooking times, energy costs, ingredient costs and labour costs, it may be possible to build up a standard cost for a meal, segregating the costs into fixed and variable components. However, this approach may be expensive and time-consuming and requires the expertise of a variety of specialists such as organization and methods experts and energy experts.

A statistical regression approach

A statistical regression approach takes a large number of observations of costs and activity levels and uses regression analysis to derive the equations giving the fixed and variable elements of cost. Diagrammatically, Figure 3.6 indicates the approach taken. The line AB, the least squares regression line, is so constructed as to minimize the vertical deviations between the observed values and the line. Thus it is said to be the 'line of best fit'. The distance OA then represents the fixed cost element and the slope of the line AB represents the variable cost.

This approach can be carried out quickly, with a calculator or software package handling the calculations, but there are also a number of reservations, some of which are as follows. First, a number of observations are needed to give one confidence in the output of the model. Second, the line is essentially an average – it may never actually pass through any observed points. Finally, the model cannot be used as a basis for

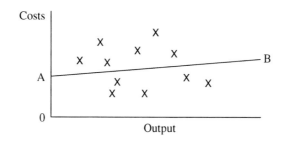

Figure 3.6 Regression analysis and semi-variable costs

extrapolating beyond the limits of the data – in either a downward or an upward direction – thus the model cannot be used to predict variable costs if it is planned to expand output beyond past levels. (Further information about regression and its limitations can be found in most statistics textbooks.)

Costs of classification

Costs are not normally classified or collected on the basis of cost behaviour. Therefore, additional time and money has to be expended to collect the necessary information. Often, little better than rough estimates of variable elements of costs and of steps may be available. However, using such estimates is better than just ignoring cost behaviour.

3.5 Incremental analysis using relevant costs

The earlier sections of this chapter have been concerned with the distinction between variable costs and fixed costs and their relationship to changes in activity. We now move on to an approach entitled incremental analysis and the concept of relevant costs – those costs which are relevant to a specific decision under consideration. This concept is much wider than that of classifying costs on the basis of behaviour; the idea of relevance/ irrelevance cuts across the variable/fixed classification.

Relevant costs and relevant revenues are those that will change as the result of a specific decision. Non-relevant costs and revenues are those that are unaffected by a specific decision. Thus the concept of relevance is distinguished by two features:

1. Relevance is decision specific: change the decision and the relevant factors change too.
2. Relevance is related to the future: a cost which has already been incurred is not relevant because it cannot be affected by the decision; we are not in a position to turn the clock back and alter a previous decision. Such past or historic costs are termed 'sunk' costs.

To expand on this idea, consider a health authority which is seeking to dispose of an obsolete ambulance in need of some repair. The ambulance originally cost £15 000 some years ago. There are two alternative ways of disposing of the vehicle and it has to decide between these alternatives:

1. to transport it, at a cost of £50, to a motor auction where its sale can be expected to net £300;

2. to obtain spare parts costing £200 and incur labour costs of £400 to render the ambulance driveable. It would then be driven to the auction, where its sale can be expected to net £1000.

In either case, return travel from the auction may be expected to cost £15.

All this information is given in Table 3.6. The relevance/non-relevance of each of the items is now examined. The following list refers to the 'notes' column in the table:

1. Revenues are relevant because they relate to the future and differ between the alternatives.
2. Original cost is irrelevant; it is a sunk cost, and it cannot be influenced by the decision. As it is a sunk cost, it is also common between the two alternatives.
3. Transport to the auction is relevant as it represents a cost of one of the alternatives only.
4. Transport from the auction is a future cost but, as it is common to both alternatives, it may be ignored as the decision is simply between those alternatives.
5. Spare parts and labour are relevant as they relate to one alternative only.

Table 3.6 Alternative methods of disposing of ambulance

	Note	Auction now £	Repair and auction £
Revenues:			
Proceeds	1	300	1 000
Costs:			
Acquisition	2	15 000	15 000
Transport to auction	3	50	
Transport from auction	4	15	15
Spare parts/labour	5		600

It follows from this that each of the following represents a sufficient condition for regarding a cost or revenue as being non-relevant:

1. All sunk costs/revenues are irrelevant.
2. All common costs/revenues are irrelevant.

The cost and revenue information has been recast in a relevant cost format in Table 3.7. As can be seen, the approach clearly identifies the relevant monetary factors with respect to a specific decision. In doing so, it strips away much confusing or irrelevant information and helps to clarify the issues for the decision maker.

Table 3.7 Relevant costs and revenues

	Auction now £	Repair and auction £
Relevant revenues:		
Proceeds	300	1 000
Relevant costs:		
Transport to auction	50	
Spare parts/labour		600
Net relevant income	250	400

Limitations of the incremental approach

There are two important limitations that need to be noted. First, a routine approach to cost collection is unlikely to provide relevant information because relevance depends on the current decision and relates to estimates of future costs and revenues rather than to past costs and revenues, which are at the core of routine costing systems. Therefore, special *ad hoc* studies will be required to establish relevant costs for each decision, necessitating the expenditure of time and money.

Second, the approach is essentially short term. Overheads may or may not be relevant to a decision. If they are judged to be non-relevant, they will not be included within the costs with which relevant revenues are compared. Yet, in the long term, all such costs must be covered if an organization is to remain viable or if it is to avoid the cross-subsidization of losses in one area, possibly from the core area of the business. This is not to say that the relevant costing approach is wrong but simply emphasizes the need to consider, when pricing, that viability eventually requires all costs to be covered.

3.6 Relevant costs and developments

Management of the public sector in the future is likely to exhibit the same trend towards embracing commercialism and competition as has occurred in the past. Indeed, in local authorities this is being reinforced by the requirement under best value that they embrace fair competition as a means of securing efficient and effective services. Against this background, we identify two illustrations of situations in which the idea of relevance can be of great value.

The preparation of competitive tenders

Direct service organizations will need to obtain business by the submission of competitive tenders. Such tenders should initially be constructed by identifying the relevant costs which must, of necessity, be covered. This would then give a minimum tender price below which no bid should be made. To this should be added an amount which makes a contribution to overheads – the amount which can be added and still provide a competitive tender depends on the judgement of the estimator. An estimate of the full cost price may provide some rough indication of the costs which may be under consideration by rivals in the field.

When tendering for the bulk of the DSO's business, overheads will become relevant; if the core contract is not obtained, the DSO may have to close and overheads will not then be incurred. Similarly, a tender for the core will require attention to the target return (breakeven point or 5%, depending on the service) as, again, failure to achieve this may result in closure.

Finally, the costing of tenders should always be carefully related to the specified standards of performance. For example, in the collection of domestic refuse, service standards will specify the number of collections weekly, the number of households, the type of refuse container (sack, dustbin, wheely bin), whether bin collected from pavement or from rear of house and so on. If any element of standard performance is inadvertently excluded from the tender cost build-up, then if successful, actual completion of the contract will reduce net income and may occasion losses.

Service level agreements

As outlined in Chapter 2, many internal local authority services are now governed by service level agreements. These can apply to internal audit, computer services, payroll services, invoice-related services, architectural services, legal services and others. They represent a movement away from the traditional apportionment of costs and offer customer departments a level of service at a set price. Consumer departments can influence the costs borne by changing their demand of the support services or, possibly, by acquiring the service from a cheaper source such as an external body. One thing is certain, it focuses the user's attention on the cost of the support services and on their perceived benefit. This is especially so when the customer department itself is subject to competitive pressure.

The next step is for each support service to run a practice account, a form of trading account. In this situation, it is in the support service's long-term interests to ensure that its charges cover its costs. This suggests that for each aspect of the service provided, it needs to consider the relevant costs of service provision, so that the charge made is related to relevant costs and not to costs that are arbitrarily apportioned. Failure to do this may well mean that users will consume services which are (incorrectly and arbitrarily) underpriced and avoid services where the reverse occurs; this would be bad business for any support service which would see costs outstripping revenues.

3.7 Costing and survival

The contribution and relevant costing approaches are both relatively under-utilized in the public sector. Variable, fixed, semi-variable and stepped costs are not normally measured or reported in routine management accounting systems. However, as the public sector becomes more competitive, markets, whether external or internal, will force organizations to look carefully at costs and prices in order to survive. Within this environment, arbitrary apportionment of overheads as the method of cost recovery and broad averaging of all costs to obtain a unit cost may prove of very limited use. Broad averaging may provide costs which are relatively meaningless if we are considering changes in the level of activity or examining specific decisions.

Of course, the decision-oriented techniques are not perfect and face significant difficulties on the cost collection side. However, even if estimated, they are related to decisions, to the future, to really examining which costs change and by how much, and are concerned with using cost information in order to earn a profit. They are also vitally important in an *ex post* capacity for VFM and performance studies whether this is carried out by management or an external monitoring body. For many of these organizations, examining the dynamics of cost behaviour may represent an important first step in ensuring survival.

> ## Key points of chapter
>
> 1. Cost behaviour is important to managers.
> 2. Variable costs, contribution and fixed costs can be used to help solve problems relating to breakeven, price, output and mix.
> 3. There are practical difficulties in classifying costs by behaviour.
> 4. Relevant costs can make an important contribution to managerial decision making.
> 5. Relevant costing has both uses and limitations when the organization must meet overheads to survive.

3.8 Summary

This chapter has examined the classification of costs by behaviour and by relevance to specific decision-making situations. It has emphasized the distinction between fixed and variable costs and introduced the concept of the contribution. Examples have indicated the power of the contribution approach, especially when changes in levels of activity, breakeven or target contribution and optimal product mix are under consideration. Additionally, the powerful technique of incremental analysis has been demonstrated, including the way in which it can be used to eliminate non-relevant data from decisions.

The difficulties involved in implementing these costing approaches have also been noted, especially the ways in which they do not match conventional approaches to cost collection. We have also highlighted the dangers of ignoring fixed costs which must be covered in the long term. However, it is argued that these techniques can yield benefits in a variety of situations, including competitive tendering, internal market pricing and purchasing and service level agreements. Indeed, in any competitive situation it is essential that an organization is aware of cost behaviour and, specifically, which costs are relevant in different situations.

Questions

3.1 Didcot County Council has a community workshop which produces picnic baskets for sale to the general public. For the financial year ending 31 March 19X9 the production details were as follows:

Units produced and sold	4 950
Selling price (per unit)	£19.00
Fixed overheads	£20 000

Variable costs per unit:

Wages	£8.00
Materials	£4.00
Variable overheads	£2.00

Estimates for the next financial year (i.e. 19–9/–0) show the following budgeted changes:

Units to be produced and sold	5 500
Fixed overheads to rise by	£7 000

Variable costs per unit:

Wage costs to rise to	£8.80
Estimated materials costs	£4.26
Variable overheads to fall by	3%
Selling price per unit	£21.00

Notes:

1. The following analysis of results is given for the three years prior to 19X8/X9.

	[19X5/X6]	[19X6/X7]	[19X7/X8]
Selling price (unit)	£14.00	£16.00	£18.00
Actual sales (units)	6 000	5 000	4 800
Fixed costs	£15 000	£18 000	£18 000
Variable costs	£72 000	£65 000	£64 800

2. The fixed overheads are allocated to the area used by picnic baskets on the basis of production floor space utilized by the department. Total fixed overheads in 19X9/X0 are estimated at £36 000.
3. Normal sales are direct to the public but a major wholesaler has approached the community workshop with an offer to purchase 800 units. There is sufficient space capacity to absorb the order but the price is only £17 per unit.

Required

Prepare a report to the workshop manager advising him:

(a) on the breakeven level of sales for 19X9/X0 (indicate the results using an appropriate graph);
(b) in the light of past sales performance, a forecast of the profit or loss if the level of sales for 19X8/X9 is achieved in 19X9/X0;
(c) whether the special order should be accepted.

Your report should draw on both financial and non-financial factors in presenting your results, including pointing out the weaknesses of breakeven analysis and the implication of the results since 19X5/X6 on the forecasted sales for 19X9/X0.

3.2 A DSO, operating on commercial principles, receives an order for work at a price suggested by the prospective customer of £1600. The customer is a public sector organization. Acceptance of the contract will not affect the progress of existing contracts. The following details emerge from an estimate of the requirements of the job.

1. Some of the materials required are in stock already as a result of a previous over-order; at present it looks as if there will be little alternative use for the materials. They originally cost £910 but can be sold for only £650.
2. Other materials will have to be purchased at a cost of £560, plus delivery costs of £10.
3. The job is estimated to need 32 labour hours and will be carried out on two successive Saturdays. The appropriate average wage rate is £2.45 per hour, and wage-related overheads amount to 55% of all wage payments. Saturday working is paid at time and a half.
4. The job will require the use of a lorry; the vehicle will be hired from the Plant DLO at a total cost of £100, driver included.

Required

(a) What is the estimated profit or loss?
(b) Should the job be accepted at the price offered?

3.3 Blaenwent Parks Department has been approached as a direct service organization to take on additional work to its existing contract. A price therefore has to be negotiated between the DSO and the client. In arriving at the contract price the following information was used:

Estimated direct labour hours p.a.	50 000
Estimated fixed overheads	£66 000
Estimated direct wages rate (hr)	£2.40

On the basis of this the direct labour rate was calculated at £3.72 per hour (i.e. a 55% oncost rate). There is still some spare capacity in the workforce and the unit aggressively seeks profitable work to fill this time. The current contract is on schedule and no problems are predicted in achieving the anticipated return.

The department has been approached by the Went Area Health Authority to undertake ground maintenance at one of its hospitals because it has cut back on its own workforce. This will involve a gang of three men plus transport working Saturday and Sunday with time and a half paid on the Saturday and double time on Sunday. Estimated hours are as follows: Saturday, 8 hrs; Sunday, 4 hrs.

Transport will be required to be hired for the weekend at at cost of £70 for the two days. In addition mileage will cost 45p per mile. Total estimated mileage is 75 miles. Direct materials will cost £140.

It is anticipated that a successful bid plus good quality work will result in the authority being invited to tender for the bulk of the health authority's work as its own DSO is closing down due to inefficiency.

Required

Calculate the minimum price the unit should tender. Why have you chosen this price?

3.4 The Getwellsoon Health Authority is responsible for eight separate establishments; a central laundry unit serves six of these and the other two have their own independent laundry facilities. The summarized final accounts for the unit for 19X3/19X4 are as follows:

	£	£
19X3–19X4		
Income:		
Recoveries		1 672 000
Expenditure:		
Staff costs – operatives	1 100 000	
– drivers	20 000	
– management	110 000	
Laundry materials used	200 000	
Repairs to premises	38 000	
Rent and rates	50 000	
Power and heat	100 000	
Vehicles – running costs	10 000	
– fixed charges	3 000	
Equipment (minor items)	20 000	
Water	25 000	1 676 000
Deficit 19X3–19X4		£4 000

You ascertain:

1. An error in the stocktaking of laundry materials at 31 March 19X4. The correct stock is £4000 less than that used in the accounts.
2. The number of articles laundered in 19X3/19X4 was:

April 19X3–September 19X3	3 000 000
October 19X3–March 19X4	4 000 000
Total	7 000 000

3. There was an increase of 15% in the charge per 100 articles laundered as from 1 October 1983.
4. No charge is made in the accounts for depreciation of laundry equipment and vehicles but the laundry is expected to return a surplus of 10% (at least) of the cost of equipment and vehicles used.
5. There are three vans in use whose cost and purchase dates are as follows:

Van	Cost	Year of purchase
	£	
A	2 500	19X4–19X5
B	4 000	19X0–19X1
C	6 000	19X2–19X3

6. Last year (19X2/19X3) the laundry made a surplus of £10 000 which was regarded by management as 'satisfactory'.

   The Authority is considering inviting tenders for its laundry requirements for 19X5/19X6 onwards which prompts the laundry manager to produce the following memorandum:

   > 'The accounts for 19X3/19X4 show the laundry producing a unit cost of less than £24 per 100 articles laundered. The major laundry plant and equipment will definitely need replacing in April 19X5 which will cost £515 000. However, the new equipment will enable us to cut the number of operatives by one-tenth.
   >
   > 'The unit supplies only four-fifths of the Authority's total laundry requirements. The new plant and machinery could cope with the other fifth without any increase in standing charges and it should be allocated to us.
   >
   > 'If this were done we should not need any additional vans or drivers; at present ours are under-employed at certain times of the week.
   >
   > 'Should the Authority agree to the above I am sure we would be below the commercial rate which I understand is around £22.00 per 100 articles laundered.'

   You are asked to produce a briefing note for the treasurer, setting out the salient points of the situation (ignore inflation).   (17 marks)

3.5 Crick CC is a widespread, rural authority which currently operates five establishments providing residential accommodation for children of school age. The total number of places provided at the establishments is 400, but recently the demand for places has fallen off, largely due to a change in population patterns within the county. The present occupancy is, consequently, 60% and this is expected to continue in 19X4/X5. The authority wishes to reduce the total number of places to 300 and it would also wish to cut its budget by at least 25%.

   The following data are available:

Establishment	No. of places	Estimated average occupancy 19X4/X5	Estimated net cost 19X4/X5 £000
A	110	80	228
B	70	40	170
C	60	30	100
D	80	40	130
E	80	50	110
	400	240	738

Estimates 19X4/X5

	A	B	C	D	E
	£000	£000	£000	£000	£000
Staffing	110	106	64	81	67
Premises	20	22	12	11	17
Food	107	44	31	40	32
Other (variable costs)	7	4	1	4	4
	244	176	108	136	120
Income*	16	6	8	6	10
	228	170	100	130	110

*based upon parental ability to pay.

Staffing and premises costs are wholly fixed costs.
  All establishments are fully financed and there are no outstanding debt charges.
  Continued use of home E beyond 19X4/X5 is dependent on major repair work being carried out which will take 15 months to complete and cost an estimated £120 000.
  Home C is only used five days per week but all other establishments are used seven days per week.

Required

With reference to financial and other considerations, analyze this information. Consider available options and make appropriate recommendations.

3.6 A division of a public sector organization operates on commercial principles and manufactures a small range of products, mainly to customers' orders. An enquiry is received for an order at a price suggested by the enquirer of £5000.
  The following details emerge from an estimate of production requirements:

1. *Materials.* These are in stock entirely because of an estimating error on an earlier order. The materials cost £750 but have a realizable value of £870.
2. *Production labour.* The division has normally sufficient orders to keep production labour occupied. Wages for production labour on the order are estimated to be £1300.
3. *Supervision.* The order would require a high degree of supervision and one supervisor would be in full-time attendance on the order for 12 weeks. Supervisors are paid £60 per week but for the high degree of attendance demanded by the order, temporary plus rates will have to be paid to other employees on other work to act as supervisors at a total cost of £360.
4. *Fixed overheads* apportioned on normal rates to the order would amount to £1500.
5. *Components* can be brought in for the order at a cost of £200 or made on otherwise idle equipment at a cost of £300 arrived at as follows:

Labour	£100
Materials	80
Fixed overheads	120
	£300

6. *Machine No. 1.* This is owned by the division and £1000 depreciation, following normal depreciation policy, would be apportioned to the order. The machine is, however, shortly due for replacement. If sold immediately, the machine is likely to realize £1200, but if used on the order would probably realize £700.

7. *Machine No. 2.* This machine is leased by the division at £100 per week on long-period agreement. Acceptance of the order would mean withholding this machine from other work and temporarily hiring a substitute machine. The only substitute machine immediately available from hirer is an older model at a price of £80 per week for 12 weeks and additional production labour to maintain output would be needed for that period at a cost of £30 per week. The estimator's report on the order is as follows:

		£
Materials		910
Production labour		1 300
Supervision		720
Overheads		1 500
Components		200
Machine No. 1 – Depreciation		1 000
No. 2		1 200
	Total cost	6 830
	Price offered	5 000
	Loss	£1 830

You are required to advise, with reasons, whether or not in your view the order should be accepted.

3.7 The budget of a profit-making contracting unit in a public sector undertaking for the year ended 31 March 1990 is as follows:

	£000	£000
Direct costs: Materials	80	
Labour	70	
		150
Contracting unit overheads		60
Total CU costs		210
General overheads		70
Total costs		280
Income		315
Budgeted profit		35

The target profit achieves a return of 8% on the current cost of assets which is in excess of the 5% target specified by the Secretary of State.

After the budget has been drawn up, the unit, which has spare capacity, is invited to tender for a construction contract by a local health authority.

The unit's internal rules lay down that the price tendered is to be found by referring to the annual budget and:

1. adding to the direct costs of the job a percentage to cover unit overheads;
2. adding a further percentage to cover general overheads;
3. adding a profit margin amounting to 12.5% of total costs.

The overhead rates are to be found from the master budget. The construction contract for the health authority would require £9500 of direct materials and £12 000 of direct labour.

Required

(a) What is the price to be tendered by the unit?
(b) The direct materials cost includes £2750, the cost of 100 units of K already in stock; these are not likely to be required for any future jobs. However, if £75 is spent on conversion, they could be used as substitutes for 100 parts of M which would otherwise have to be bought in at a cost of £22 each, or they could be sold, without conversion, for £19 each.

The direct materials costs of the contract also include £1500, the cost of the required quantity of material R which is also in stock. The material is used frequently by the company and its current cost has increased to £1800.

All other direct costs are solely attributable to the contract.

The general overhead expenditure would be the same whether the contract is accepted or not, but acceptance would increase contracting unit overheads by £3250 for additional supervision, labour, fuel and power.

What is the minimum price to be tendered for the contract?

3.8 Your public sector organization has a contracting unit which operates on a trading basis; taking one year with another it is expected to break even.

In March 19X7 the unit is asked to undertake two jobs but the unit's resources do not permit the acceptance of both. Both jobs would commence on 1 April 19X7 and take one year to complete. The following financial statement has been prepared by the cost accountant attached to the unit:

	Job A £	Job B £
Materials: in stock 20/3/X7 (at cost):		
Type A	15 000	
Type B		6 600
to be purchased	16 000	20 400
Direct labour	33 000	49 000
Depreciation of plant on site	2 400	3 200
Total of direct charges	66 400	79 200
Office and admin. oncost (6%)	3 984	4 752
	70 384	83 952
Agreed contract price	80 000	96 000
Surplus	£9 616	£12 048

Note:
1. If job A is accepted, the stock of type B materials can be sold for £12 500 (it is assumed that all stocks not required can be sold).
2. If job B is accepted, the stock of type A materials can be sold for £14 950 or, subject to the purchase of additional components for £500, can be used in place of 80% of the materials to be purchased for job B in 19X7/X8.
3. Depreciation of plant, charged in the financial accounts, is estimated to be £3200 per year (£2400 for A). The resale value at 1/4/X7 is £10 000 and this is expected to fall by £1000 for each quarter that passes.
4. In each case the fixed costs element of direct labour is £1000.
5. Tenders for each job have also been received by outside contractors; the best of these are:

Job A	£90 000
Job B	£100 000

6. The unit owns 20 units of plant of which 15 would be used on the job A contract while all 20 will be used on job B. If job A is accepted, 5 units will be hired out to other contractors at a rental of £500 each for the year 19X7/X8.

Required

A revised financial statement to show which job should be undertaken by the unit.

3.9 Tidy CC operates two landfill sites for refuse disposal and has three district councils in its area. These sites are becoming full and alternative arrangements are being considered. A large site for landfill could be made available but environmental pressures favour incineration at a more central site.

Present costs (£000):

	Refuse collection district			Refuse disposal site	
	East	West	South	A	B
Expenditure:					
Employees	400	180	670	80	120
Transport and plant	140	70	230	40	60
Other running costs	35	15	67	110	210
Debt charges	–	–	–	80	150
	575	265	967	310	540
Income	40	10	70	10	40
Net expenditure	£535	£255	£897	£300	£500
Tonnes collected/disposed (000s)	100	40	180	100	220
Proportion of time spent on:					
Collection of refuse	0.9	0.8	0.85		
Delivery to tip	0.1	0.2	0.15		

The revenue costs of the alternative arrangements now being considered are estimated as follows:

	New landfill site	Incinerator
	£000	£000
Expenditure	1 570	2 380
Income	70	120
Net expenditure	1 500	2 260

The new arrangements would affect the time spent delivering refuse to the disposal site (affecting employee and transport costs) as follows:

District	New landfill site	Incinerator
East	+300%	+50%
West	+30%	+20%
South	−15%	−50%

A transfer station could be erected on the existing site used by East DC, thus eliminating its extra costs; the station would cost £300 000 per year to operate.

Separation of waste at the incinerator site could be achieved at an additional cost of £230 000 per annum, but income would increase to £350 000 per annum.

Required

Prepare a report setting out the effect on the various authorities concerned, recommending the most appropriate course of action.

3.10 Armstrong County Council Direct Service Organization has been invited to submit a quotation for a special order of 10 000 Chalmers for the Piltdown Water Authority. The Authority requires all tenders to be supported by a breakdown of costs and profit margins to justify the prices quoted. The accountant of the DSO has prepared the following estimate of total costs for this order, based on the organization's normal costing and pricing policies:

Direct costs	£	£
Material A: 500 kgs at actual cost £3 per kg	1 500	
Material B: 250 kgs at expected cost £1 per kg	250	
Material C: 400 kgs at actual cost £1.50 per kg	600	
Material D: 100 kgs at actual cost £1.50 per kg	150	
		2 500
Labour: Grade I – 1000 hours @ £2.50 per hour	2 500	
Grade II – 500 hours @ £3.00 per hour	1 500	
Grade III – 200 hours @ £4.00 per hour	800	
		4 800
Total direct costs		7 300
Overhead: 30% of direct costs		2 190
Total cost		9 490
Add: Profit margin: 10%		949
Suggested price		10 439

The following additional information is available:

1. 600 kgs of material A have been ordered for another contract which has been cancelled; delivery is expected in a few days' time. Bloggs Ltd has no alternative use for the material. The current buying price is still £3 per kg but the material could be sold for only £2 per kg after deducting delivery costs.
2. Material B is not in stock or on order.
3. Material C is regularly used by the DSO. Because of a worldwide shortage of the material the current buying price has increased to £2.50 per kg, although the company could only realize £2 per kg from the sale of the material after deducting selling costs. The DSO's buyer foresaw the rise in price and purchased a large stock of the material six months ago; 3000 kgs are currently held by the company.
4. 50 kgs of material D are left in stock from a minimum quantity which was purchased to carry out a contract four years ago. The organization has so far found no alternative use for the material and if it is not used in the very near future it will become unusable and will have to be scrapped at a cost of £1 per kg.
5. Grade I labour is in plentiful supply but only a certain number of that type are employed. If they are used on this contract then Grade II labour will have to replace them on existing contracts. Grade I labour is paid £2.00 per hour. For Grade II labour see (6) following.
6. Grade II labour has special skills. A considerable amount of the time of these employees is unused at present because of a fall in demand for the products which they manufacture. However, the DSO expects demand to revive next year, and has therefore decided not to dismiss any employees. The current wage for Grade II labour is £120 for a 40-hour week.
7. Grade III labour is in short supply; since it is highly specialized there is no possibility of using other grades of labour as a substitute. The current rate of pay is £4 per hour. If the proposed contract is accepted, other production yielding a net profit of £480 (based on normal pricing policy) would have to be abandoned.
8. The charge for overheads is made according to a standard formula used by the DSO and is intended to cover all variable and fixed overheads, including depreciation. The DSO would have to buy a special machine for use on this contract at a cost of £8000; the duration of the contract would be around three months. It is the DSO's policy to depreciate machinery at the rate of 10% per annum. On completion of the contract the DSO would have no further use for the machine and it is anticipated that it could be sold for £7000. It is estimated that one-third of overhead costs vary directly with production; the remainder are considered as fixed.

Required

(a) Calculate the minimum price at which the contract would be worthwhile to the DSO and for each item in your estimate which differs from the estimate made by the company's accountant. Clearly explain your reasoning for making the change. (15 marks)
(b) Outline and briefly discuss the factors which the management of the DSO should take into consideration when deciding upon a price to quote for this contract.
(5 marks)
(c) Describe the problems associated with the post-audit of this contract should the tender based on your figures be accepted. (5 marks)
(Total 25 marks)

4 Budgeting

Key learning objectives

After reading this chapter you should be able to:

1. Explain the objectives of budget preparation in the public sector.
2. Discuss the strengths and weaknesses of different approaches to the budgeting process.
3. Prepare a probable out-turn statement and an estimate statement.
4. Explain the impact of the competitive environment on budgeting.
5. Prepare budgeted cash flow and budgeted profit and loss statements.

Within the public sector, the annual budgeting process has a very considerable influence on the organization concerned; it tends to be very time-consuming in preparation and gives financial effect to political decisions on the raising and distribution of resources. It also severely constrains the manner in which the organization's resources may be disbursed over the forthcoming year.

Within central government, the annual budgeting process is concerned with an amalgam of capital and revenue items; within other parts of the public sector, revenue budgeting is clearly distinguished from capital budgeting. In this book, revenue budgeting is covered in this chapter and Chapter 5 and capital budgeting is dealt with in Chapters 8 and 9.

4.1 The objectives of annual budget preparation

The objectives of the annual budgetary process within the public sector are discussed in the following section.

The establishment of required income levels

Levels of taxation, fees and charges will be established by examining current levels of income and by looking at the levels of expenditure planned for the forthcoming year. As will be seen, the desire to minimize tax increases, while increasing quality and quantity of services, provide the dynamics and stresses of the budgetary process.

Planning service expenditure levels

One of the most important objectives is to assist in the planning of service expenditure levels and the levels of service provision. The total of service expenditures has to be accommodated within the total increases in income to be raised; but within this total, choices have to be made between expenditures on different services. Such choices are at the heart of political decision making and of the democratic process. In central and local government the decisions are taken by elected representatives, not by officers; they reflect the decisions that are arrived after political debate, pressure and negotiations. Ultimately, those in power must account to the electorate for their stewardship while holding public office. Wildavsky (1974) has commented: 'If politics is regarded in part as conflict over whose preferences shall prevail in the determination of … policy, then the budget records the outcomes of this struggle.'

An illustration of the interaction of local authority members and officers within the budgetary process for 2000/01 for one local authority is contained in Figure 4.1.

In some parts of the public sector, this involvement of elected representatives does not occur at all levels. For example, once funds have been voted by parliament to the National Health Service, the distribution of health funds at regional level is determined by formulae influenced by national political considerations but at district level is determined by those appointed to management boards and by health care professionals. Public corporations and universities, for example, also take decisions in an environment in which the elected representatives are absent, although central government determines the contributions to be made from public expenditure. Yet, in all of these, the determination of the annual budget is a political process which different individuals and factions will try to influence although, in a widening range of public sector organizations, the bottom line of profit is focusing attention in the budgetary process.

Authorization of expenditure

The budget authorizes the expenditure of public funds on those services and to the total of those service expenditure levels which are agreed in the budget. Indeed, money can only be spent on what has been authorized in the annual budget; and one guideline for subsequent decisions is to enquire whether an item of expenditure is included under a budget expenditure head. For this reason, the annual budget is a very detailed and very specific document, specifying service expenditures and also the breakdown in terms of sub-service, wages, salaries, materials, transportation and so on. As will be seen in the next chapter, the opportunity for switching expenditure between budget heads (termed 'expenditure virement') is often very narrowly defined in practice. Within the National Health Service detailed budgets of the sort referred to here occur at sub-regional level only, that is at district level.

The control of expenditure

The budget provides a basis for control of expenditure. At its crudest, total annual expenditure should not exceed the budget. This philosophy can then be applied throughout the organization, to the expenditure of services and, within services, to expenditure on subservices and on detail heads. An *annual* control in itself is insufficient; the overall budget and its components need to be disaggregated into time periods, say monthly, to permit control at a much nearer point in time to when the expenditure is incurred.

June 1999
    Meeting of Special Policy Advisory
       Group
    Group Executive
    Full Labour Group

1. These meetings agreed a remit within which the Budget Advisory Group and Project Appraisal Team could begin work on a range of budget strategy options for 2000/01
2. The remit involved expenditure reductions of 3–4%
3. The additional revenue consequences of the 2000/01 capital programme were to be offset by revenue savings

June–October 1999
    The Budget Advisory Group

The Budget Advisory Group interviewed chief officers together with their Chairmen and Vice Chairmen in order to produce a budget strategy in line with the remit

October 1999
    Special Policy Advisory Group
    Group Executive
    Full Labour Group

The Budget Advisory Group reported back to members of the leading party on the range of options for meeting the reductions required. No decisions were taken at this stage

December 1999
    Special Policy Advisory Group
    Group Executive
    Full Labour Group

The Secretary of State announced provisional SSAs and capping criteria. These showed that the Authority had to reduce expenditure by £15.2m

December 1999/January 2000
    Chief Officer Team

The chief officer team met to consider the required reductions in services arising out of the report of the Budget Advisory Group. They agreed a corporate programme of reductions to put before members

January 2000
    Special Policy Advisory Group
    Group Executive
    Full Labour Group

The majority party met to consider the proposed reductions put forward by chief officers. After due deliberations over three days they finally agreed the programme of budget reductions that they could reluctantly support

January 2000
    Programme Area Committee

Met to agree reductions for their individual services

February 2000
    Finance Committee

Met to make budget recommendations to the County Council

February 2000
    County Council

Agreed 2000/01 Budget and council tax levels

Figure 4.1 2000/01 Budget exercise

A communication device

The budget serves as an excellent communication device; service managers are informed through the budget, not just of the annual expenditure allocation, but also of the service level proposed, as viewed from an input-oriented perspective.

The process focuses attention

The annual budget process focuses attention on the future; it thus forces a consideration by managers of the objectives, methods and costs of service delivery. This and the necessary consideration of inter-service and coordination issues is especially necessary within multi-service organizations. The multi-service characteristic is typical of many public sector organizations. For example, on one measure the health service provides hospital services for 472 diagnosis-related groups (DRGs) and within each group patients differ according to degree of severity of condition.

Motivation of managers

The budget is said to motivate managers. However, in a situation where outputs are difficult to quantify and in which most measurements are input oriented, this is likely to mean motivation to keep within the annual budget. As the following chapter indicates, the link between budgets and motivation is complex but it may be that managers are particularly well motivated, indeed form an attachment to the budget, when they have played a positive role in helping to formulate it.

4.2 Approaches to the budgetary process

Next we consider different models of the budgetary process within the public sector. We shall examine four models which may be regarded as paradigms and may not accord with the specific budgeting processes in any one public sector organization. These four models are shown in Figure 4.2. Before examining the different approaches, the incremental/departmental–rational/corporate continuum in Figure 4.2 needs to be explained.

Incremental/departmental

This end of the spectrum refers to budgeting systems which are incremental in nature; the budget for each year takes as its starting position the budget for the previous year and adds or subtracts marginally from that base. Budgeting processes within this grouping also tend to be dominated by the objectives of individual services and departments.

Incremental/departmental	Rational/corporate
Bid system	Programme budgeting
Financial planning	Zero-based budgeting

Figure 4.2   Continuum of models of the budget process

Rational/departmental

Towards this end of the spectrum we include budgeting systems which are rational: less concerned with the budget base and the past, but more concerned with using resources to meet currently established objectives. Additionally, it includes those systems which foster a corporate or 'wide' view, taking account of inter-service aspects, coordinating needs and giving pre-eminence to the objectives of the organization as a whole.

Next we examine two models within the incremental/departmental grouping (bid and financial planning) and two models within the rational/corporate grouping (programme budgeting and zero-based budgeting).

4.3 The bid system

This model is extremal, falling at the far left end of the spectrum. A summary of the budget cycle appropriate to this system is contained in Figure 4.3. In practice, it is infinitely varied in form but, for many organizations within the public sector, has formed the traditional approach to the budget process.

The mechanics of the bid system are as follows.

Stage 1: Separate estimate preparation

Separate departments or services prepare next year's estimate in isolation, adopting as a starting point the current year's expenditure and service levels (the 'base' budget).

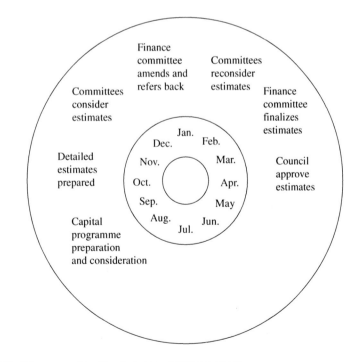

Figure 4.3 The annual cycle – incremental bid system
(*Source:* CIPFA, 1990)

Stage 2: Aggregation and comparison

The separate estimates, or bids (as within an auction system), are then aggregated and the total is compared with what can be raised via taxation and charges. Invariably, total estimated expenditures will exceed total estimated income.

Stage 3: Reductions in estimated expenditure levels

Possibly estimated income may be increased marginally by a combination of higher taxes and higher fees and charges. However, the bulk of the necessary adjustment, in order to bring into equality budgeted income and budgeted expenditure, will come via reductions in estimated expenditure levels. The bid system tends to be characterized by a fairly short time scale; as Figure 4.2 indicates, Stage 3 may occur at around December/January and the annual estimates may need to be finalized in February. In the face of time pressure, the practical guideline likely to be used to pare estimated expenditures back will be an extremely crude one such as: departments' estimates are to be cut back to the current year's estimated expenditure + x%.

Stage 4: Detailed estimate reduction

Faced by the prospect of making cuts of a possibly severe nature in a short period of time, individual departments will tend to use the following two guidelines.

1. Projected starts on capital schemes are likely to be the first to be affected. This can result in cutting out new projects, delaying progress on part-completed projects by cutting funds and postponing starts on projects to delay revenue consequences.
2. New services are likely to be cut before existing services because it may be easier to do so and because the current recipients of a service will not then object. New services may be delayed (to give six months' instead of a year's expenditure, say) or the level of service may be reduced, by recruiting fewer staff, or a service may be deferred to another year, possibly never to reappear.

Criticisms of the bid system

The bid system has been criticized extensively as follows.

Little review of the base budget
Within the bid system there is little review of the base budget which contains, possibly, 99% of the final agreed budget. The increment to the budget is based substantially on past expenditure and this reinforces the status quo. In reality, any public sector organization is faced with a complex network of changing needs and problems which the management will be struggling to anticipate and adapt to. It would not appear that the bid system outlined here would assist this practice.

A departmental orientation
The system views *departmental* estimates and allocations as the focus of the budgetary process. Of course, departments exist in order to further the objectives of the community or nation vested in their elected representatives. However, interest groups are not solely the province of any one department: old people may require the services of

health, personal social services and housing. The bid system, however, reinforces the professionalism that can exist in central and local government departments and in other public services. A clear example of professionalism at work may be seen in a county council's education department. In terms of the eventual budget document, this will be reflected in a budget that does not link the expenditures of different departments in working towards objectives.

Outcomes are ignored
The failure to specify objectives leads to a failure to establish a systematic review of the effectiveness of services in terms of their impact on the community. Emphasis is placed, instead, on the financial control of inputs with little attempt to relate these to the outputs that emanate from the expenditure. A department will be judged on its ability to keep within its expenditure limits. An increase in expenditure will be assumed to result in an increase in services to the community, although there may be no evidence to justify the assumption of a stable relationship between inputs and outcomes.

A single year emphasis
The system emphasizes the annual budget, yet one year is too short for effective planning. Present expenditure may commit the authority to future expenditures which limits the area of choice which will be available in the future. The short-term nature of the system may lead to the neglect of long-term objectives. Furthermore, as we have seen, the amount of time allowed for reconsideration of priorities, when cuts have to be made, is ridiculously short. Furthermore, in the version of the bid system that has been outlined, there has been no consideration of the impact of capital projects and their financial viability within the annual budget process.

Encourages a cynical approach
Finally, the system encourages its principal participants to behave in a cynical way; it encourages overestimating by departments in situations where estimates will be cut back by y%. The service which estimates honestly will suffer far more than one which pads out its bid in the expectation of a cut-back being required. The more services inflate their bids, the greater the cut-back required and the more the innocent suffer. A second adverse behavioural outcome is to be found in the 'year end spending spree' which all those who have worked in the public sector will recognize. The insistence that the budget must not be overspent means that, every March, there will be unspent resources. However, no department will wish to reveal an underspend at year-end as this will certainly affect future years' budgets. There may also be a strong feeling that the money will be 'lost' to the department and possibly used to bail out other overspending departments. In this situation, March will be categorized by the bringing forward of capital works, the maintenance of roads, the purchase of stationery and the recarpeting of offices. That is, the money will be spent on relatively low-priority items in order fully to consume the year's allocation and to demonstrate that the finance really was needed by the service.

4.4 Financial planning systems

The term 'financial planning' also includes a spectrum of budgeting systems but all are characterized by being placed much nearer to the centre of the continuum than the extremal bid system which has been outlined. A typical budget cycle for this system is contained in Figure 4.4. Features which distinguish financial planning systems from bid systems include:

1. their multi-year nature;
2. the issue of expenditure guidelines;
3. the joint consideration of capital and revenue budgets;
4. a more helpful specification and classification in the budget document.

The multi-year nature of financial planning systems means that medium-term, say 2–3 years, commitments and forecasts are considered together with the annual budget under consideration. The annual budget may then be seen as the first year of a multi-year rolling programme in which, each year, one additional year is added on as the past year is dropped off. Such is the format of the government's expenditure plans as published in the annual Public Expenditure White Paper.

An expenditure guideline, a target growth percentage or even an expenditure limit is established for each service prior to the preparation of detailed estimates at departmental level. This avoids the waste of effort involved in paring estimates when they are referred back to departments. Such guidelines may be given for the next two years following the budget year, thereby encouraging a longer term view of service development.

However, over the last decade, local authorities have been constrained by government-imposed limits on their council tax levels. The Local Government Act 1999 contains procedures that are very similar to the previous capping regulations. The 1999 Act gives the Secretary of State the right to decide if a specific local authority's budget requirement is excessive. If the Secretary of State decides that it *is* excessive, he is able to specify to the authority a target budget requirement and a maximum budget requirement.

There is simultaneous consideration of capital and revenue estimates. Figure 4.4 indicates that this is achieved by shifting forward the timing of the budget process. Thus, the revenue consequences of a multi-year capital programme (which is discussed in detail in Chapter 8) are considered in terms of a multi-year revenue programme. This clearly permits consideration of the future impact of current decisions and the extent to which current capital expenditure commits or frees future resources.

Much greater specificity is introduced into the budget process. In place of the bid system's base expenditure plus increment, we now find, typically:

Base expenditure + Inflation – Reductions + Committed growth + New growth

Committed growth includes the full-year effect of capital schemes which had been completed in the previous financial year, but with part of one year's revenue consequences, for example, just six months' running costs if it came on stream on 1 October. It also includes the full-year effect of employees taken on in the past year and the increments in the salaries of employees. Finally, it includes the growth resulting from a past policy decision; for example, a past decision to provide state-funded nursery education results in a pattern of future expenditure which will be significantly affected by demographic changes.

New growth includes growth in service expenditure which is at the discretion of the organization; it can mean decisions to expand existing services or to introduce new services.

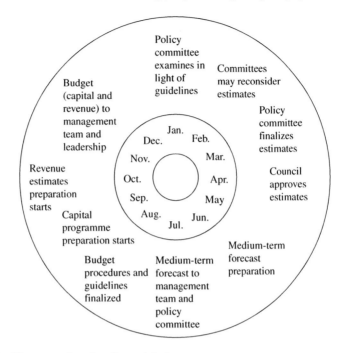

Figure 4.4 The annual cycle – financial plan
(*Source:* CIPFA 1990)

Financial planning systems have clear advantages as compared with bid systems and they do encourage the search for value for money in areas of growth and reduction. An illustration of one authority's use of this approach to examine expansion and contraction in expenditure is given by Armstrong (1992). He emphasizes the time constraint within which the budget was prepared and the benefits obtained by concentrating attention on the areas of reductions and growth.

However, financial planning systems, generally, have the following weaknesses:

1. The focus is primarily incremental and pays relatively little attention to justifying the base budget.
2. There are not explicit organizational objectives to which the budget can be reconciled; the emphasis continues to be a departmental one.
3. There is limited concern with monitoring efficiency and effectiveness; at best this is confined to the budget variations. Emphasis, as in the bid system, is on inputs, with an absence of output measures.

Financial planning systems embrace a wide variety of approaches and, as we shall see later, some of these deficiencies can be addressed by supplementary additions to the financial planning framework.

4.5 Planning programming budgeting systems (PPBS)

This system is an extremal one, being fully rational and fully corporate in nature. It attempts to link together in a systematic fashion plans, objectives, the environment in which the organization is working and the feedback of control information. In 1965,

PPBS was introduced into the Federal Government of the United States of America by President Johnson. Charles Schultze, then Director of the Bureau of the Budget, announced six goals of programme budgeting:

1. The careful identification and examination of goals and objectives in each area of government activity.
2. Analysis of the output of a given programme in terms of its objectives.
3. Measurement of the total costs of specific programmes, not just for one year but for several years into the future.
4. The formation of objectives and programmes extending beyond a single year to relate annual budgets to long-term objectives.
5. Analysis of alternatives to find the most efficient ways of reaching programme objectives for least cost.
6. The establishment of analytical procedures to serve as a systematic part of the budget review process.

Within PPBS a 'programme' is a set of activities which encompass all organizational efforts to achieve a specific objective. As was indicated earlier, a programme such as care of the elderly will cross departmental boundaries.

The multi-year aspect, with a rolling plan, is similar to the process observed in financial planning systems and serves to highlight the constant trade-off between present action and future choice.

Programme structures

Each objective and major programme area is broken down into objectives and sub-objectives and activities. This taxonomy is intended to identify the activities within the authority which contribute to each objective; it will cross departmental boundaries and, by requiring inter-service cooperation, may weaken narrow departmentalism.

Programme analysis

Programme analysis has been defined as 'the total process of':

1. systematic identification and measurement of a community's needs and the systematic appraisal of existing resource allocations;
2. identification of the alternative methods of achieving the objectives derived after consideration of the needs;
3. comparative (quantitative and qualitative) evaluation of the total social and economic costs and benefits of those alternative methods. (CIPFA, 1971)

Such analysis is an integral part of PPBS; the emphasis is on providing information which will aid government decision makers in making their choices. The analysis requires the measurement of achievement of the authority's objectives. This involves the construction of output measures which it may be difficult to make operational.

Feedback and review

The first year of the multi-stage plan lays down targets for those in the organization who must implement policies. Information on the achievements of the period must be generated and compared with the target and lessons learned. This will serve to update and extend the plans of the following period and act as a measure of the efficient and effective utilization of resources.

Limitations of PPBS approach

Despite being introduced into the United States Federal Government in 1965 and then picked up by states and by central and local government in the United Kingdom in the early 1970s, by the late 1970s its attraction had faded. The reasons for this decline, in spite of its coherent approach to budgeting and performance appraisal, are as follows.

The complexity of programme structures

Technical problems are encountered in constructing programme structures; one of the main reasons for adopting PPBS, the crossover of activities, contributed to its decline. For example, the activities associated with a particular programme, such as care of the elderly, will fall to a number of departments. On the other hand, one activity such as the provision of school meals contributes to the programmes associated with health, education and social deprivation. Thus, there is a practical problem in allocating activities to programmes. This is further complicated when the financial information requirements are examined. Joint costs (the school meals example) will need to be allocated over programmes, yet there appears no rational basis for doing this. Furthermore, accounting systems normally generate information by departments rather than by programme. It might be possible to produce data by programme structure and organization structure respectively, with a cross-walk between the two. However, this leads to duplication and a preferred system would be rooted in a multifunctional database such as the Korner accounting system in the NHS which produces data for sites and for services. Finally, progress in measuring the outputs of programmes is essential for the type of activity analysis postulated; yet this is one area where progress has been remarkably slow.

The benefits of incremental policy making

Wildavsky (1974) has indicated that the budgetary process is an integral part of the political system. It is his contention that the incremental, fragmented and sequential procedures of the traditional budgetary system aid in securing agreement between participants and thus reduces conflict. It does this in two ways. First, it commences with incremental deviations from current year base expenditure; the base is generally not challenged and it is assumed by participants that departmental activity will be carried on at a level very close to that of the base expenditure. Second, the area open to dispute is limited to the incremental changes; and, of course, it is far easier to secure agreement on an increment than on a complete programme which brings into the arena conflict due to policy differences on priorities. An essential part of the political process is the negotiated bargain; incrementalism favours the consensus-producing bargain by the trading of budgetary inducements without having to consider the ultimate desirability of programmes. Wildavsky (1974) comments: 'I am not saying that the traditional method of budgeting is good because it tends to reduce the amount of conflict ... What I am saying is that mitigation of conflict is a widely shared value in our society and we ought to realise that program budgeting is likely to affect that value.'

The pressure on participants in the process

In practice it requires its participants to adopt different roles within the organization; in the morning, a technical specialist within education, in the afternoon, playing a wider policy role in a multidisciplinary group where departmental status can count for very little. Behaviourally, then, it is a technique which may well meet resistance from those required to implement it and who may well have to accept an additional workload consequent upon the additional inter-disciplinary focus.

Limited rationality

The presence of considerable uncertainty, the paucity of relevant information and the limited cognitive ability of human beings lead to a situation where a rational approach is severely limited. In such a situation, which may characterize much of organizational life, there may be an attempt to simplify reality and this may involve the technique of incremental decision making. Due to the inability to foresee the full implications of major changes of policy, movement towards goals will be made in small sequential steps. This reduces the possibility of major error from a root and branch change in policy and permits the decision maker to learn about the environment and the consequences of action by making small changes in a series of successive decisions.

Thus a number of reasons have been advanced for the failure of PPBS. However, although it may not be installed to any great degree, the ideas it contains are valuable and can be used to help analyze the strengths and weaknesses of other budgeting systems. For example, as part of the whole central government Financial Management Initiative, the third report from the Treasury and Civil Service Committee, Session 1981–82, 'Efficiency and Effectiveness in the Civil Service' (8 March 1982), ended with recommendations which included:

1. The responsibility of ministers and top management for the setting of objectives and targets in relation to departmental programmes.
2. The management of programmes with objectives/targets/resources/out-turn statements by programmes feeding directly into the Public Expenditure White Paper.
3. Devolution of responsibility for personnel and non-personnel costs coupled with greater accountability for objectives and targets set.

4.6 Zero-based budgeting (ZBB)

Zero-based budgeting (ZBB) is a technique whereby the total cost (base plus increment) of every item included in a proposed budget must be justified and approved. No base or minimum expenditure level should be acceptable for any activity. Resources are not necessarily to be allocated in accordance with the previous year's pattern. The approach is to require a re-evaluation of all expenditure and of all activity; all activities start from a zero base. Thus, ZBB focuses on the basic purposes of an organization. In reality many government organizations may retain functions or goals which have lost their usefulness as the environment has changed. ZBB seeks to expose all such expenditure.

Its advantages may be summarized as follows:

1. It allocates resources according to priorities, between the essential and the less essential.
2. It improves decision making because budgetary allocation is related to objectives.
3. It makes managers plan ahead and defend their budgets; thereby it creates a greater feeling of ownership of those budgets.

The idea is attractive in theory. However, a major problem is related to the time which is required to complete the exercise; it is physically impossible to appraise all activities each year. In addition, many departments are locked into expenditure programmes by long-standing legislation while some policies are carried out for compelling political reasons. Finally, it is likely to generate a mass of information which cannot be adequately assimilated by decision makers.

Although it may be impractical, in the majority of cases, to subject programmes to an annual ZBB review, there can be little doubt that there is a need to expose much of government expenditure to systematic scrutiny. Three methods of scrutinizing the base, possibly within a financial planning framework involve the use of *ad hoc* efficiency studies, the use of a virement policy and the use of option budgets.

Ad hoc *efficiency and effectiveness studies*

These may be the result of internal reviews, such as will be required of schools under the delegated financial management provisions. Alternatively, they may be sparked off by the activities of external review agents such as the Audit Commission, which has done much pioneering work in local government, its ambit now widened to include the NHS. Similar work in central government has been carried out by the National Audit Office.

Virement policy

Virement policy can also be used to encourage the search for savings in the base budget. This would involve allowing discretionary savings to be switched by service managers to expenditure heads according with departmental priorities. The big attraction of this approach is that there is an inducement for those closest to service delivery, who are most likely to be able to deliver efficiency savings, to search out those savings. If any savings are lost to the department there may be little incentive to search for them. It may be argued that the incentive increases as the total of 100% of savings retained by departments is reached. One could go further and introduce incentive schemes where employees share directly in the savings generated.

Where savings are accidental and not planned, it is doubtful whether the savings should remain with the department. For example, a fall in interest rates will feed through and reduce the charges to departments' budgets. However, it is highly unlikely that departments would be allowed to retain the savings as they are fortuitous and not planned, or worked for, by departments.

Option budgets

Systematically, organizations may test the priorities of departments by the use of option budgets. To illustrate their use, a specific service may be required to identify its response to a:

10% cut in expenditure
5% cut in expenditure
1% cut in expenditure
1% growth in expenditure
5% growth in expenditure.

Such options force a service to consider policies and operating procedures. This can be made more acute by asking service managers to rank their responses to, say, a 10% cut in expenditure. If this is carried out over a period of time, cynicism (especially advancing of politically unacceptable options in response to cuts) can be squeezed out by the cumulative experience of a team of second-ranking officers who manage the options exercise, termed in a large Welsh local authority, the Budget Advisory Group (BAG). Pendlebury (1985) reports a readiness within local authorities to carry out systematic review of the base budget through the use of similar techniques. Morgan and Weaver (1993) report a recent approach to option budgets which emphasizes member/officer workshops and the use of facilitators and analysts to assist decision makers. They comment: 'There was a commitment to a fundamental review of services. Muddling through via creeping incrementalism would not do. There was no sympathy for concepts of budgeting based on rough justice, across the board cuts or equal misery.' They emphasize the value for money aspects of the exercise and the enhanced understanding, commitment and ownership felt by participants in the process.

In summary, ZBB may be regarded as an essentially short-term and tactical technique whereas PPBS emphasizes long-term strategic and corporate planning. Some of the techniques of ZBB can usefully be allied with practically based budgeting approaches within the annual budget cycle to reveal information that may be used to formulate the budget and to provide an input of information into medium-term and long-term plans.

4.7 Formula funding

The 1988 Education Reform Act started the process whereby local education authorities (LEAs) delegated budgets to schools. Initially budgets were to be delegated to all secondary schools and primary schools with more than 200 pupils but now the legislation has extended delegation to all LEA schools. Schools which have 'opted out' of LEA control (grant-maintained schools) are funded directly by the Department of Education.

LEAs have been required to develop schemes for the delegation of the majority of the schools budget including:

1. the salary costs of staff employed to work in the schools;
2. schools' day-to-day premises costs including rent and rates;
3. books, equipment and other goods and services used by the schools concerned.

The current framework for delegation contains a mandatory exception to delegation. This relates to the LEAs' need to retain sufficient and appropriate resources to enable them to fulfil their legal obligations as the employer of most school-based staff and as the landlord in relation to school sites and buildings, including their health and safety responsibilities. It follows from this that the LEA retains all expenditure for capital purposes; national guidance is provided on those elements of repairs and maintenance that may be delegated.

An LEA has the discretion not to delegate to schools funding for the following:

- insurance;
- expenditure supported by external grants or the LEAs' contribution to such grants;
- cover for maternity leave (but supply cover for absent teachers must be delegated);
- cover for certain staff absences, such as those of trade union officials;
- establishing and maintaining electronic computer networks;
- aspects of direct support to school governors.

Details of retention will be contained within each LEA's scheme of delegation that has to be approved by the Secretary of State. The funding framework distinguishes between delegated funding and devolved funding. The latter category applies when an LEA chooses to provide to schools an element of its centrally retained resources on the basis that such funding cannot be used for purposes other than those specified by the LEA.

The delegation budget

The amount appropriated by LEAs for the cost of school activities is termed the local schools budget (LSB). After taking account of mandatory and discretionary retentions, as just outlined, the balance of the LSB is delegated by means of a formula to create the individual school budget (ISB). The aim is to make the formula transparent to schools and it will normally contain the following elements:

- *Pupil-led elements.* The most significant element in each formula will be based on pupil numbers. This will distribute approximately 80% of the ISBs.
- *Sixth form funding.* This will be related to the type of qualification or subject studied and may be related to the skills needs of the local labour market and the planned increase in staying-on rates.
- *School meals* responsibilities.
- *Nursery education.* This is driven by the search for increasing places for pupils below statutory school age.

The framework for delegation recognizes the potential benefits of schools having their own bank accounts and cheque books to increase their ownership and control of their delegated budgets.

LEAs have a responsibility to monitor school expenditure, including the level and use of any balances. The LEA will need to have an audit framework in place to assist in carrying out this responsibility. Schools are required to submit detailed budget plans to the LEA by a stipulated date and must provide any revisions of these throughout the year. As part of this overall framework, governing bodies will be required to indicate what steps they intend to take to secure 'best value', both in relation to the services they purchase and their own processes for raising education standards year on year.

The effect of delegation on the role of LEAs is significant. It results in a more strategic role. They are no longer able to exercise direct or detailed control over the bulk of spending in schools with delegated budgets. However, they have responsibility for schemes of delegation and for the quality of education which LEA schools deliver. LEAs lose control over schools which opt out; as already seen, such schools are funded directly by central government.

The financial link with local government is weakened considerably. Total exceptions (mandatory and discretionary) have an upper ceiling as percentage of the aggregate schools budget and this has been increasingly squeezed, forcing LEAs to delegate to schools an increasing percentage of the aggregate schools budget. LEA central staff must then make their services and the cost of those services sufficiently attractive for schools to purchase them from the LEA and local authority. This itself implies the use of service level agreements in the relationship between the authority and its schools. With the extension of competitive tendering to professional activities such as finance and information technology, the link between local authority employees and the LEA's schools is likely to be further weakened. The effect will be that LEA schools will behave increasingly like grant-maintained schools, holding a budget which is almost fully delegated and purchasing services from a range of possible providers.

4.8 A practical approach to budgeting

This section considers the practical preparation of a budget for the financial year ended 31 March 2002; it will assume that we are now in October 2000. There are two practical steps with which we are concerned:

Step 1: To determine the 'probable' or 'estimated out-turn' for the current year: the year ended 31 March 2001. This provides the budgetary base for the construction of the budget for the next year.

Step 2: To determine the estimate for the year ended 31 March 2001.

Determining the probable out-turn for the current financial year

Broadly, the process involved in calculating the probable for the current year is to:

take: *Actual* expenditure to date;
add: *Estimated* expenditure for the remainder of the year.

In estimating the expenditure for the remainder of the year, we will need to take account of: the proportion of the year remaining; the anticipated inflation for the remainder of the year; the impact of pay awards on the employees expenditure for the rest of the year; the timing or phasing of expenditure on heating, employees and central administrative charges; and the start-up of any new activities authorized to commence during the year.

The scenario depicted in Table 4.1, relating to an old people's home, has been included so as to demonstrate this. It relates to the nine months to 31 December 2000.

Table 4.1   Home for the elderly: Expenditure for 9 months to 31 December 2000

	£
Income	18 900
Expenditures:	
Employee	18 360
Running expenses	54 500
Asset rents and capital charges	7 500
Total expenditure	80 360
Net expenditure	£61 460

In order to convert the information contained in Table 4.1 to the estimated out-turn figure for the year ended 31 March 2001, the income and expenditure figures need to be uprated, taking into account the information from the budget file, outlined as follows.

Income
Inflation will not affect this; income per resident will depend in part on the weekly charge and the application of the assessment scales. Information on both of these is absent, so the annual income can be estimated at: income per month £18 900/0 = £2100. Income for 12 months = £2100 * 12 = £25 200.

Employees

Expenditure to date is £18 360 over nine months. However, not all the months are of equal weight because employees received a pay increase of 4% with effect from the start of the third quarter. Thus, if an employee had received £100 for the first quarter's pay, then total pay to date would have been as follows:

Quarter 1	£100
Quarter 2	£100
Quarter 3	£104
Total	£304

The wage bill for the first three quarters amounts to £18 360 and it is now clear that the figure of £18 360 was incurred in the proportions 100:100:104 over the three quarters. Our individual employee would receive £104 for the fourth quarter as this is after the pay award. Therefore, because the first three quarters cost a total of £18 360 (and our individual employee received 304), then the pay for the last quarter must amount to £18 360/304 * 104. This amounts to £6280 and gives a probable out-turn for the year of £18 360 plus £6280, amounting to £24 640.

Running expenses

First, it is necessary to disaggregate the figure:

		£
Non-heating: £54 500 – £9 000 =		45 500
Non-heating per quarter: (£45 500 – £500)/3 = £15 000		
Remaining non-heating expenditure		15 000
Annual non-heating expenditure		60 500
Heating: first 3 quarters		9 000
Heating per quarter	£3 000	
Heating final quarter	£3 000 * 2	6 000
Price increase for March: £2 000 * 6%		120
Annual heating expenditure		£15 120

Asset rents and capital charges

	£
Paid 30 September	7 500
Payable 31 March	7 500
	15 000

The statement of the estimated out-turn for the financial year is shown in Table 4.2.

Determining the estimate for next year

The process involved in calculating the estimate for the next year is as follows:

1. Take the probable expenditure for the current year (Step 1).
2. Add the following:
  (a) The full-year effect of any expenditure, notably employee costs, where a part-year effect in the current year is to be converted into a full year effect for next year; for

Table 4.2 Home for the elderly: Estimated out-turn expenditure for year ended 31 March 2001

	£	£	£
Income			25 200
Expenditure			
Employees		24 640	
Running expenses:			
Non-heating	60 500		
Heating	15 120		
		75 620	
Asset rents and capital charges		15 000	115 260
Net expenditure			£90 060

example, the pay award in the Step 1 example for the last six months of 2000/01 will have to be paid for the whole of 2001/02 as it becomes consolidated into wages.

(b) The part-year effect of next year's estimated pay award. Estimated price inflation for consumables, energy, transport, etc.

(c) Any committed growth for next year, whether this be due to salary increments, the full year effect of completed schemes, and so on.

(d) Finally, add in new or discretionary growth.

3. Deduct the following:

(a) Any non-recurring expenditure in the current year which will not be repeated next year.

(b) Any savings which are estimated to accrue in the next year.

With reference to the old people's home referred to in these examples, the following items, referring to 2001/02, have also been extracted from the budget file.

Charges

Charges to residents are to increase by 10% with effect from 1 April 2001; after taking account of assessment scales, this is likely to result in additional income of 6% overall for the year.

Employees

It is expected that a wage award of 6% will be made with effect from 1 October 2001.

Running expenses

Non-heating costs are expected to increase by 7% year on year, with the exception of the non-recurring item of £500 incurred in 2000/01.

Heating costs are expected to increase by 7.5% with effect from 1 March 2002.

Asset rents and capital charges

For 2001/02 these are expected to amount to £12 000 for the year as a whole.

Using the information from the budget file, this can now be used to prepare the budget for next year.

	£
Income: £25 200 * 106%	26 712

Employees:	20X0/X1 Pay award, full-year effect £6 280 * 4	25 120
	20X1/X2 Pay award, six months only £25 120/2 * 6%	754
		25 874

Non-heating: (£60 500 – £500) * 107%	64 200

Heating:
Quarterly cost for the first three quarters:

£3 000 * 106% (6% increase on 1 March 2001) * 3	9 540

Final quarter:

Twice the average £3 180 * 2	6 360
Increase from 1 March 20X2 £2 120 * 7.5%	159
	16 059

In practice it is usual to round estimates to the nearest £5 or £10; rounding to the nearest £10 will be followed as can be seen in the estimates for 2001/02 shown in Table 4.3.

Table 4.3   Home for the elderly: Estimated expenditure for year ended 31 March 2002

	£	£	£
Income			26 710
Expenditure			
Employees		25 870	
Running expenses:			
Non-heating	64 200		
Heating	16 060		
		80 260	
Asset rents and capital charges		12 000	118 130
Net expenditure			£91 420

Re-pricing budgets and contingencies

In practice, an organization may make use of a November price base in assessing the probable expenditure for the year and also in preparing the estimate for next year. The reason for doing this is to allow a comparison in real terms (that is, at a constant price base between one year and another). If this is the case, then the following processes may be adopted:

1. The probable expenditure is stated at price levels extant at November and any known wage awards in 2000 in this case; a contingency to out-turn prices is then stated, that is, a provision for estimated price increases over the period 31 November to 31 March. This provision is applied on a line-by-line basis, to permit control and on a total basis to ensure that overall net expenditure lies within the total finance available.
2. The budget for the year 2001/02 is also stated at November 2000 price levels. This permits comparison with the probable for the previous year which is shown on the same price basis. In this case, however, the provision for estimated price increases

must cover the period from 31 November 2000 to 31 March 2002. The out-turn net expenditure is that which has to be financed from tax revenues.

4.9 Budgeting in a competitive environment

Business planning may be summed up as follows:

- It takes a long-term view of the business and its environment.
- It focuses on the strengths and weaknesses of the proposed ventures.
- It conveys the sincerity of purpose and credibility of the proposer.

The business planning process runs through the following stages:

1. The objectives of the organization are reviewed.
2. A position audit is undertaken; this identifies the strengths and weaknesses of the organization.
3. An environmental analysis establishes the opportunities and threats facing the organization.
4. This stage deals with the strategy of the organization. It identifies the range of corporate strategies, it follows this by evaluating the different strategies and finally leads to strategy selection and plans for its implementation.
5. In order to meet the strategic objectives, the organization develops plans for the medium and short term.
6. Finally, there is monitoring and review of the progress made to achieving the plans and objectives of the organization.

The position audit examines the organization's strengths and weaknesses in four key areas: products (or services), finances, personnel and fixed assets. The examination of its services and products will consider the quality levels, the price levels and their market position. The assessment of finances will examine the amount of debt, the profitability, the cost levels and the sources of funding for the organization. The assessment of personnel will establish whether gaps exist, the distinctive competencies, the level and quality of training and the levels of remuneration. The assessment of fixed assets will consider the age and location of assets, the appropriateness of assets, their efficiency and potential duration.

The environmental analysis will consider issues such as customers, technology, economy, competition and legislation. The examination of customers will look at trends in population and in demands on different services. Technology will focus on the changes that are taking place and the speed of change. The consideration of the economy will look at economic growth, future government funding and future price levels. Competition is invariably of concern from a range of alternative providers. Last, the public sector is always open to threats and opportunities from changes in legislation that is, say, designed to improve the delivery or standards of specific services.

Business planning

A business plan is a written statement setting out how the unit intends to organize itself and its resources to meet the demands of its clients and thereby develop the business. Business plans were first used in the private sector, often in support of applications for loans or grants. In the public sector, the production of business plans has been a reaction to the pressure being placed on organizations, pressure which comes through a competitive environment and the necessity to win contracts, and constant pressure to cut costs and become increasingly efficient. In both of these situations, the plan demonstrates to the client or to higher authority the capacity of the unit to organize itself to deliver the planned service at a specified cost level. In the case of NHS trusts, for example, each trust is required to submit a business plan to the NHS Management Executive (NHSME) in March each year.

The plan would include:

1. an executive summary;
2. description of the main products and services provided by the unit;
3. an analysis of the current environment facing the unit and the unit's strengths, weaknesses, opportunities and threats;
4. details of the main markets available to the unit and the evidence of market analysis and research which has been carried out;
5. details of the planned changes to the business whether these are concerned with growth or product differentiation;
6. an overview of the management and employees available to the unit, including any planned growth or reduction;
7. a list of key quality targets and indicators that will be used to measure performance against those targets. There should also be a description of plans to improve quality including arrangements for guaranteeing quality;
8. finance:
    (a) projected cash flow statements and profit and loss accounts over a three-year period;
    (b) projected balance sheets over the same three-year period;
    (c) an explanation of the unit's financial strategy including capital expenditure, borrowing/investment strategy and the payments of any dividends;
    (d) description of the approach to unplanned cost increases;
    (e) description of plans for improving efficiency;
    (f) description of plans for income generation;
    (g) an analysis of the sensitivity of the plan to changes in some of the key assumptions such as cost levels and income generation.

Projected profit and loss accounts

These will usually be required for a three-year period. Organizations now will need to produce private sector-type accounting statements, taking full account of the realization principle in recognising income and, for expenses,, using the accruals basis. Some public sector organizations have used depreciation for many years, for example, the Post Office and the BBC. However, for the first time, many organizations will need to account for depreciation.

As well as producing an annual budgeted profit and loss account, monthly budgeted profit and loss accounts should also be produced. The monthly budgets will indicate the monthly income levels and maximum monthly expense levels that can be tolerated in order to achieve the target return for the year.

The monthly income levels will be derived from the terms of contracted services and the volumes of work specified to be carried out by the contract. The monthly costs will be related to workload and should be based on standard costs for labour, transport, materials, overheads and so on. A full discussion of standard costs is contained in the next chapter. For the purposes of this chapter they can be regarded as costs that are held to represent efficient operation. In some services work study has calculated standard times for specific operations (for example, refuse collection) but in others average costs, or costs derived from regression analysis, will need to be used (for example, speciality costs). Such standards should, of course, be those that underpin the costing and pricing exercises used to formulate the tenders used to win the contracts.

The monthly budget is indispensable for control, permitting early detection of deviations from plans and allowing time for management to take corrective action.

Projected cash flow statements

A cash budget for the year will be indispensable as it can be used to discover whether the organization's activities can be financed. As with the budgeted profit and loss account, the cash budget should be presented in a monthly format. This is especially important as the effects of terms related to the timing of the receipt of contract money and the payment of creditors can be seen in overall cash terms. For an organization that must have cash in order to pay wages and creditors it provides an opportunity to anticipate problems and make provision for loans, renegotiation with creditors and so on.

Projected balance sheets

There is no reason to produce these on a monthly basis but the annual balance sheet (requiring asset valuations and depreciation) will be required. Aside from the legal requirement, it provides valuable information on liquidity, on gearing and provides a basis for the calculation of the organization's return on capital employed.

The contract specification

The competitive environment is one in which the organization gets paid for the work which it completes up to the contract specification. The organization must ensure that it completes this work to the required standard by the required date. However, any work which is not in the contract will not be paid for by the client and should not be undertaken. This will require discipline among employees who may well see themselves as operating professionally by fulfilling more than a set role. It also creates a major difficulty within the health service.

This also highlights the importance of accurate costing systems. They assist accurate pricing of a tender and the preparation of more accurate budgets and, therefore, better decision making. They also allow managers to be far more confident in cost control when they know that the reported figures are accurate. In short, a good, accurate costing system gives a competitive advantage.

A refuse collection DSO

In order to examine these issues further, specimen budget statements for a competitive refuse collection DSO are presented.

Budgeted profit and loss accounts, and budgeted cash flow statements are shown in Table 4.4 and Table 4.5 respectively. The DSO has to achieve a return on assets employed of 5% for the year as a whole. The following notes refer to the numbers in the first column of both Table 4.4 and Table 4.5.

Note (i) refers to the contract value for refuse collection agreed with the local authority. The contract specifies standards of service, amounts to be paid, and dates of payment. In this case, as Table 4.5 shows, the payments are made one month in arrears.

Note (ii) refers to sales of refuse sacks and is based on the DSO's estimates, which, in turn, are based on past experience.

Note (iii) refers to wages figures which are based on the same standard times used to prepare the tender and are based on experience of what can be achieved. They also take account of the size of the labour force and of current wage rates.

Note (iv), wages oncost, refers to specific wage-related costs borne by the employer, such as employers' National Insurance and superannuation contributions; it also refers to employee-related overheads such as supervision.

Note (v) refers to depreciation: all competitive legislation requires that depreciation be charged in the profit and loss account.

Note (vi) refers to the payment to the central departments for their services; these include financial services, computer services and legal services. As outlined in Chapter 3, such payments must now be negotiated and related to a level of service provision.

As Table 4.4 shows, a profit of £8088 is budgeted; this results in a return of 8.99% on the assets employed of £90 000. This is well in excess of the required return of 5%. However, turning to the cash flow statement in Table 4.5, it is evident that in the first year of operation there will be need for substantial loan or overdraft facilities. The revised cash flow statement in Table 4.6 includes under Note (vii) a charge for interest on the overdrawn cash balances. The rate of interest which has been used is 12%. Table 4.7 shows that when interest is taken into account in the budgeted profit and loss account, the return falls below the required 5%.

Therefore, management should seek some means of reducing the interest figure, or certain other costs, to give a return of 5% (or 6% if we were discussing the National Health Service, for example). One option which might be examined is the renegotiation of the timing of the payment of central support services to one month in arrears. The effect of this is shown in Tables 4.8 and 4.9. As can be seen, this has the effect of increasing the return to above 5%.

The budgeted figures included in Tables 4.4 to 4.9 were all prepared using a spreadsheet model. As can be seen, this is particularly suited to budget preparation as management can test the overall effect of changes in the underlying variables. In short, management can carry out 'what if' sensitivity analysis while paying particular attention to bottom line and financing issues.

Table 4.4 Budgeted monthly profit and loss accounts 2001/02

Notes	Month	Apr. £	May £	Jun. £	Jul. £	Aug. £	Sep. £	Oct. £	Nov. £	Dec. £	Jan. £	Feb. £	Mar. £	Year £
	Budgeted income:													
(i)	Contract value	46 250	46 250	46 250	46 250	46 250	46 250	46 250	46 250	46 250	46 250	46 250	46 250	555 000
(ii)	Sale sacks	800	800	800	800	800	800	800	800	800	800	800	800	9 600
	Total income	47 050	47 050	47 050	47 050	47 050	47 050	47 050	47 050	47 050	47 050	47 050	47 050	564 600
	Budgeted expenses:													
(iii)	Wages – normal	11 267	11 267	11 267	11 267	11 267	11 267	11 267	11 267	11 267	11 267	11 267	11 267	135 200
	Wages – overtime	3 167	3 167	3 166	3 900	3 900	3 900	3 167	3 167	3 166	3 167	3 167	3 166	40 200
(iv)	Wages – oncost	5 847	5 847	5 847	5 847	5 847	5 847	5 847	5 847	5 847	5 847	5 847	5 847	70 160
	Salaries	1 251	1 251	1 251	1 251	1 251	1 251	1 251	1 251	1 251	1 251	1 251	1 251	15 012
	Transport related	13 272	13 272	13 272	13 272	13 272	13 272	13 272	13 272	13 272	13 272	13 272	13 272	159 260
	Materials	1 078	1 078	1 078	1 078	1 078	1 078	1 078	1 078	1 078	1 078	1 078	1 078	12 940
(v)	Depreciation	1 125	1 125	1 125	1 125	1 125	1 125	1 125	1 125	1 125	1 125	1 125	1 125	13 500
(vi)	Central support services	9 187	9 187	9 187	9 187	9 187	9 187	9 187	9 187	9 187	9 187	9 187	9 187	110 240
	Total expenditure	46 193	46 193	46 192	46 926	46 926	46 926	46 193	46 193	46 192	46 193	46 193	46 192	556 512
	Net profit/loss	857	857	858	124	124	124	857	857	858	857	857	858	8 088
	Assets employed													90 000
	Return on assets (%)													8.9

Table 4.5 Budgeted monthly cash flow statements 2001/02

Notes	Month	Apr. £	May £	Jun. £	Jul. £	Aug. £	Sep. £	Oct. £	Nov. £	Dec. £	Jan. £	Feb. £	Mar. £	Year £
	Budgeted inflows:													
(i)	Contract value	0	46 250	46 250	46 250	46 250	46 250	46 250	46 250	46 250	46 250	46 250	46 250	508 750
(ii)	Sale sacks	800	800	800	800	800	800	800	800	800	800	800	800	9 600
	Total income	800	47 050	47 050	47 050	47 050	47 050	47 050	47 050	47 050	47 050	47 050	47 050	518 350
	Budgeted outflows:													
(iii)	Wages – normal	11 267	11 267	11 267	11 267	11 267	11 267	11 267	11 267	11 267	11 267	11 267	11 267	135 200
	Wages – overtime	3 167	3 167	3 166	3 900	3 900	3 900	3 167	3 167	3 166	3 167	3 167	3 166	40 200
(iv)	Wages – oncost	5 847	5 847	5 847	5 847	5 847	5 847	5 847	5 847	5 847	5 847	5 847	5 847	70 160
	Salaries	1 251	1 251	1 251	1 251	1 251	1 251	1 251	1 251	1 251	1 251	1 251	1 251	15 012
	Transport related	13 272	13 272	13 272	13 272	13 272	13 272	13 272	13 272	13 272	13 272	13 272	13 272	159 260
	Materials	0	1 078	1 078	1 078	1 078	1 078	1 078	1 078	1 078	1 078	1 078	1 078	11 862
(vi)	Central support services	9 187	9 187	9 187	9 187	9 187	9 187	9 187	9 187	9 187	9 187	9 187	9 187	110 240
	Total expenditure	43 990	45 068	45 067	45 801	45 801	45 801	45 068	45 068	45 067	45 068	45 068	45 067	541 934
	Net cash flow	–43 190	1 982	1 983	1 249	1 249	1 249	1 982	1 982	1 983	1 982	1 982	1 983	–23 584
	Cumulative cash balance	–43 190	–41 208	–39 225	–37 976	–36 727	–35 478	–33 496	–31 514	–29 531	–27 549	–25 567	–23 584	

Table 4.6 Charge for overdraft: Budgeted monthly cash flow statements 2001/02

Notes	Month	Apr. £	May £	Jun. £	Jul. £	Aug. £	Sep. £	Oct. £	Nov. £	Dec. £	Jan. £	Feb. £	Mar. £	Year £
	Budgeted inflows:													
(i)	Contract value	0	46 250	46 250	46 250	46 250	46 250	46 250	46 250	46 250	46 250	46 250	46 250	508 750
(ii)	Sale sacks	800	800	800	800	800	800	800	800	800	800	800	800	9 600
	Total income	800	47 050	47 050	47 050	47 050	47 050	47 050	47 050	47 050	47 050	47 050	47 050	518 350
	Budgeted outflows:													
(iii)	Wages – normal	11 267	11 267	11 267	11 267	11 267	11 267	11 267	11 267	11 267	11 267	11 267	11 267	135 200
	Wages – overtime	3 167	3 167	3 166	3 900	3 900	3 900	3 167	3 167	3 166	3 167	3 167	3 166	40 200
(iv)	Wages – oncost	5 847	5 847	5 847	5 847	5 847	5 847	5 847	5 847	5 847	5 847	5 847	5 847	70 160
	Salaries	1 251	1 251	1 251	1 251	1 251	1 251	1 251	1 251	1 251	1 251	1 251	1 251	15 012
	Transport related	13 272	13 272	13 272	13 272	13 272	13 272	13 272	13 272	13 272	13 272	13 272	13 272	159 260
	Materials	0	1 078	1 078	1 078	1 078	1 078	1 078	1 078	1 078	1 078	1 078	1 078	11 862
(vi)	Central support services	9 187	9 187	9 187	9 187	9 187	9 187	9 187	9 187	9 187	9 187	9 187	9 187	110 240
(vii)	Interest	216	434	419	403	394	386	377	361	345	329	312	296	4 272
	Total expenditure	44 206	45 502	45 486	46 204	46 196	46 187	45 445	45 429	45 412	45 397	45 380	45 362	546 206
	Net cash flow	–43 406	1 548	1 564	846	854	863	1 605	1 621	1 638	1 653	1 670	1 688	–27 856
	Cumulative cash balance	–43 406	–41 858	–40 293	–39 447	–38 593	–37 730	–36 125	–34 504	–32 866	–31 213	–29 543	–27 856	

Table 4.7 Accounting for interest: Budgeted monthly profit and loss accounts 2001/02

Notes	Month	Apr. £	May £	Jun. £	Jul. £	Aug. £	Sep. £	Oct. £	Nov. £	Dec. £	Jan. £	Feb. £	Mar. £	Year £
	Budgeted income:													
(i)	Contract value	46 250	46 250	46 250	46 250	46 250	46 250	46 250	46 250	46 250	46 250	46 250	46 250	555 000
(ii)	Sale sacks	800	800	800	800	800	800	800	800	800	800	800	800	9 600
	Total income	47 050	47 050	47 050	47 050	47 050	47 050	47 050	47 050	47 050	47 050	47 050	47 050	564 600
	Budgeted expenses:													
(iii)	Wages – normal	11 267	11 267	11 267	11 267	11 267	11 267	11 267	11 267	11 267	11 267	11 267	11 267	135 200
	Wages – overtime	3 167	3 167	3 166	3 900	3 900	3 900	3 167	3 167	3 166	3 167	3 167	3 166	40 200
(iv)	Wages – oncost	5 847	5 847	5 847	5 847	5 847	5 847	5 847	5 847	5 847	5 847	5 847	5 847	70 160
	Salaries	1 251	1 251	1 251	1 251	1 251	1 251	1 251	1 251	1 251	1 251	1 251	1 251	15 012
	Transport related	13 272	13 272	13 272	13 272	13 272	13 272	13 272	13 272	13 272	13 272	13 272	13 272	159 260
	Materials	1 078	1 078	1 078	1 078	1 078	1 078	1 078	1 078	1 078	1 078	1 078	1 078	12 940
(v)	Depreciation	1 125	1 125	1 125	1 125	1 125	1 125	1 125	1 125	1 125	1 125	1 125	1 125	13 500
(vi)	Central support services	9 187	9 187	9 187	9 187	9 187	9 187	9 187	9 187	9 187	9 187	9 187	9 187	110 240
(vii)	Interest	216	434	419	403	394	386	377	361	345	329	312	296	4 272
	Total expenditure	46 409	46 627	46 611	47 329	47 320	47 312	46 570	46 554	46 537	46 522	46 505	46 488	560 784
	Net profit/loss	641	423	439	–279	–270	–262	480	496	513	528	545	562	3 816
	Assets employed													90 000
	Return on assets (%)													4.24

Table 4.8 Interest rate reduction: Budgeted monthly cash flow statements 2001/02

Notes	Month	Apr. £	May £	Jun. £	Jul. £	Aug. £	Sep. £	Oct. £	Nov. £	Dec. £	Jan. £	Feb. £	Mar. £	Year £
	Budgeted inflows:													
(i)	Contract value	0	46 250	46 250	46 250	46 250	46 250	46 250	46 250	46 250	46 250	46 250	46 250	508 750
(ii)	Sale sacks	800	800	800	800	800	800	800	800	800	800	800	800	9 600
	Total income	800	47 050	47 050	47 050	47 050	47 050	47 050	47 050	47 050	47 050	47 050	47 050	518 350
	Budgeted outflows:													
(iii)	Wages – normal	11 267	11 267	11 267	11 267	11 267	11 267	11 267	11 267	11 267	11 267	11 267	11 267	135 200
	Wages – overtime	3 167	3 167	3 166	3 900	3 900	3 900	3 167	3 167	3 166	3 167	3 167	3 166	40 200
(iv)	Wages – on-cost	5 847	5 847	5 847	5 847	5 847	5 847	5 847	5 847	5 847	5 847	5 847	5 847	70 160
	Salaries	1 251	1 251	1 251	1 251	1 251	1 251	1 251	1 251	1 251	1 251	1 251	1 251	15 012
	Transport related	13 272	13 272	13 272	13 272	13 272	13 272	13 272	13 272	13 272	13 272	13 272	13 272	159 260
	Materials	0	1 078	1 078	1 078	1 078	1 078	1 078	1 078	1 078	1 078	1 078	1 078	11 862
(vi)	Central support services	0	9 187	9 187	9 187	9 187	9 187	9 187	9 187	9 187	9 187	9 187	9 187	101 057
(vii)	Interest	170	342	325	309	299	290	280	263	246	229	211	193	3 158
	Total expenditure	34 973	45 410	45 393	46 110	46 101	46 091	45 349	45 332	45 313	45 297	45 280	45 261	535 909
	Net cash flow	–34 173	1 640	1 657	940	949	959	1 701	1 718	1 737	1 753	1 770	1 789	–17 559
	Cumulative cash balance	–34 173	–32 533	–30 876	–29 936	–28 987	–28 028	–26 327	–24 608	–22 872	–21 119	–19 348	–17 559	

Table 4.9 Interest rate reduction: Budgeted monthly profit and loss accounts 2001/02

Notes	Month	Apr. £	May £	Jun. £	Jul. £	Aug. £	Sep. £	Oct. £	Nov. £	Dec. £	Jan. £	Feb. £	Mar. £	Year £
	Budgeted income:													
(i)	Contract value	46 250	46 250	46 250	46 250	46 250	46 250	46 250	46 250	46 250	46 250	46 250	46 250	555 000
(ii)	Sale sacks	800	800	800	800	800	800	800	800	800	800	800	800	9 600
	Total income	47 050	47 050	47 050	47 050	47 050	47 050	47 050	47 050	47 050	47 050	47 050	47 050	564 600
	Budgeted expenses:													
(iii)	Wages – normal	11 267	11 267	11 267	11 267	11 267	11 267	11 267	11 267	11 267	11 267	11 267	11 267	135 200
	Wages – overtime	3 167	3 167	3 166	3 900	3 900	3 900	3 167	3 167	3 166	3 167	3 167	3 166	40 200
(iv)	Wages – oncost	5 847	5 847	5 847	5 847	5 847	5 847	5 847	5 847	5 847	5 847	5 847	5 847	70 160
	Salaries	1 251	1 251	1 251	1 251	1 251	1 251	1 251	1 251	1 251	1 251	1 251	1 251	15 012
	Transport related	13 272	13 272	13 272	13 272	13 272	13 272	13 272	13 272	13 272	13 272	13 272	13 272	159 260
	Materials	1 078	1 078	1 078	1 078	1 078	1 078	1 078	1 078	1 078	1 078	1 078	1 078	12 940
(v)	Depreciation	1 125	1 125	1 125	1 125	1 125	1 125	1 125	1 125	1 125	1 125	1 125	1 125	13 500
(vi)	Central support services	9 187	9 187	9 187	9 187	9 187	9 187	9 187	9 187	9 187	9 187	9 187	9 187	110 240
(vii)	Interest	170	342	325	309	299	290	280	263	246	229	211	194	3 158
	Total expenditure	46 363	46 535	46 517	47 235	47 225	47 216	46 473	46 456	46 438	46 422	46 404	46 386	559 670
	Net profit/loss	687	515	533	–185	–175	–166	577	594	612	628	646	664	4 930
	Assets employed													90 000
	Return on assets (%)													5.48

Key points of chapter

1. There are many reasons why the budgeting process is so important in the public sector.
2. There is a range of budgeting systems ranging from the bid system to programme budgeting, with different strengths and weaknesses. Operational systems lie within these extremes.
3. The annual budget statement is prepared in two stages: the probable out-turn for the current year and the estimate for next year.
4. The competitive environment will require a business planning approach with budgeted monthly cash flow statements and budgeted monthly profit and loss accounts.

4.10 Summary

Traditionally, the budgeting process in the public sector has been of crucial importance in planning and in allocating resources to different services. The crudest models are the incremental bid models which have a short time horizon and are limited by other weaknesses. The most sophisticated is programme budgeting but this appears to be non-operational. Financial planning allied with some of the more pragmatic versions of ZBB seems to offer an acceptable, operational middle way.

The mechanics of the budgeting process requires the involvement of service departments and is a two-stage process with the first stage being concerned with estimating the current year's out-turn. This exercise requires the combination of estimated and of actual figures. The estimate for next year takes the current year as a base and then allows for changes in the levels of service and in price and wage inflation.

Finally, the competitive environment shifts attention away from levels of service to income, to profits and to rates of return. Knowledge of costs is important in order to tender correctly and to budget effectively. Monthly budgets should be prepared; any apparent difficulties can then be dealt with at an early stage. Two important factors mentioned in the chapter were the importance of a clear understanding of the terms of the contract by all service deliverers and the specific impact of the cash flow statement on the profit and loss account via overdraft interest.

Questions

4.1 The following information relates to a police authority for the six months to 30 September 19X9:

Eastern Criminal Records Office:	£
Employees	235 500
Premises	48 000
Supplies and services	29 750
Transport	7 600
Central departmental and technical support services	35 300
Miscellaneous expenses	27 500
Asset rents and capital charges	15 000
	398 650

Note:
(a) Employees received a pay award of 5% during the first half of the year and payable with effect from 30 June 19X9.
(b) Half of premises costs for the first half-year comprises space heating costs; space heating costs in the last 4 months of the year are expected to equal total costs for the first 8 months of the year.
(c) Asset rents and capital charges are payable on 30 September and 31 March.
(d) Due to increase in the price of fuel, transport costs will be 2.5% higher in the second half than the first half of the year.
(e) Supplies and services includes a non-recurring payment of £5000 made in June 19X9.

Required

Prepare a statement giving the estimated out-turn for the year ended 31 March 19X0.

4.2 Your local authority has agreed upon a policy of zero growth in real terms for the year 19X6/X7 and has instructed its Parks Committee that, provided their annual estimates for 19X6/X7 are prepared within a 'ceiling' calculated in accordance with this policy, they will be free to regulate their own spending on services within that 'ceiling'.

The following is a subjective analysis of the approved estimates for 19X5/X6 and the draft estimates for 19X6/X7 which have been received from the Director of Parks.

	19X5/X6 Approved estimates £	19X6/X7 Draft estimates £
Wages (inc. 50% oncost)	2 808 000	3 132 000
Premises expenses	480 000	660 000
Supplies and services	300 000	408 000
Transport	98 000	126 000
Central charges	420 000	576 000
	£	£
Asset rents and capital charges	274 560	309 200
	4 380 960	5 201 200
Less: Income – fees and charges	120 960	121 200
	4 260 000	5 080 000
No. of full time staff	330	342

Notes:

(i) Estimates are prepared using prices etc. current at 31 October except that the Wages estimates provide for known or anticipated national awards. Provision for other inflation is made centrally within a general contingency provision, which will also allow for price rises from October 19X5 to March 19X7.

(ii) The Wages estimate for 19X5/X6 assumed that wages would rise by 20% per annum from 1 November 19X5 but a national award caused a rise of £14.40 per employee per week from that date (assume 20 weeks to year end). It has been assumed that wages will rise by a further 10% per annum from 1 November 19X6.

(iii) An index of average prices is maintained which will rise from 130 in October 19X4 to 175.5 in October 19X5.

(iv) The increase in the Asset Rents and Capital Charges from 19X5/X6 to 19X6/X7 wholly reflects the planned cost of a new depot; it is planned to construct the depot in the first half of 19X6/X7 and to relocate to the depot with effect from 1 October 19X6.

(v) Central charges are allocated from the general services account, any variations in cost being reflected in the 'ceiling' of that account. The revised allocation for 19X5/X6 shows an overall increase of 15% on the original estimate.

Required

You are required to prepare the Parks Committee revised estimates for 19X5/X6 and a report indicating how their estimates for 19X6/X7 may be contained within the zero growth 'ceiling'.

Indicate how you have interpreted 'zero growth' in real terms and make whatever other assumptions you think reasonable.

4.3 The following information relates to the Careers Guidance Service of the Downshire Education Authority.

1. *Employees* (details at 1/10/X7)

Name	Salary scale	Incr. point	Car engine	Monthly miles
M. Jones*	PO1	36	1600cc	300
H. Evans*	SO1–2	33	1215cc	400
E. Davies*	5	27	950cc	250
P. Brown	4	19		
L. Williams	4	21		
R. Lewis	3	15		
P. Smith	2	12		
J. Blake	1	5		
J. Edwards	1	1		
P. Jenkins	1	1		

Note: * signifies that travelling allowances are payable as detailed in Section 2 below.

Incremental progression takes place on 1 April for those staff who have been in post for more than six months.

A wage award of 4% for all staff is expected from 1 July 19X8.

Staffing is normally very stable; however, L. Williams is to leave the service on 31 December 19X7 and R. Lewis will be promoted to take her place on 1 January 19X8. He will be paid, initially, at salary point 20. His present job will be advertised and it is expected that a replacement member of staff will be in post by 1 April 19X8 at the bottom of Scale 3.

The Education Authority has recently decided to make an additional appointment at the bottom of scale 3 with effect from 1 June 19X8.

Employers' NI and superannuation amounting to 11% and 12% of salaries should also be taken into account.

2. *Travelling expenses*

Employees are reimbursed for using their cars on official business in accordance with the following scales which will become effective on 1 January 19X8:

Car engine size (cc):	–999	1000–1199	1200+
Allowances payable:			
Annual lump sum	£342	£400	£430
Mileage allowances:			
<1100 miles per annum	–16.1p	–17.8p	–19.9p
11 000+ miles per annum	8.2p	9.2p	10.1p

When scales are revised next on 1 January 19X9, it is anticipated that allowances and mileage rates will be increased by 5%.

3. *Computerization*

In 19X8/X9 the records of the CGS will be computerized and a microcomputer will be purchased for this purpose. Quotations for the necessary software and hardware have been in the region of £5000 but county supplies expect to obtain a discount of 25% on this figure due to the fierce competition in this field.

In order to transcribe the records onto floppy disks, a temporary part-time clerk will be employed for 25 hours per week at £2.40 per hour for 20 weeks. Employers' National Insurance contributions will be payable at 11%, but the post is not subject to superannuation contributions. The rate of pay will not be affected by the pay award on 1 July 19X8.

4. *Other expenditure*

The cost of printing brochures in 19X7/X8 amounted to £3000. In 19X8/X9 the volume of brochures to be printed will increase by 12%. In addition the printer has announced a 6% increase in his charges with effect from 1 April 19X8. A further increase of 5% is forecast with effect from 1 January 19X9.

Required

Prepare the budget for the service for 19X8/X9.

Salary points with effect from 1 July 19X7

	Salary scale point	1/7/X6 salary £	1/7/X7 salary £
Scale 1	A1	2 703	2 856
	A2	2 859	3 021
	1	2 976	3 144
	2	3 162	3 342
	3	3 414	3 606
	4	3 603	3 807
	5	3 849	4 065
	6	4 200	4 437
	7	4 365	4 611
	8	4 485	4 737
	9	4 659	4 920
	10	4 788	5 058
	11	4 959	5 238
Scale 2	12	5 139	5 397
	13	5 307	5 574
	14	5 493	5 769
Scale 3	15	5 640	5 922
	16	5 811	6 081
	17	5 973	6 249
	18	6 135	6 420
Scale 4	19	6 264	6 555
	20	6 510	6 810
	21	6 753	7 065
	22/23	7 005	7 329

		Salary scale point	1/7/X6 salary £	1/7/X7 salary £
	Scale 5 {	24	7 191	7 524
		25	7 404	7 746
		26	7 650	8 004
		27	7 896	8 262
	Scale 6 {	28	8 154	8 532
		29	8 430	8 820
		30	8 712	9 114
	SO1 {	31	9 060	9 477
		32	9 363	9 795
		33	9 660	10 107
	SO2 {	34	9 945	10 404
		35	10 242	10 716
PO1 35–38 {		36	10 539	11 025
		37	10 761	11 259
PO2 37–40 {		38	11 052	11 562
		39	11 364	11 889
	PO3 40–43 {	40	11 703	12 243
		41	12 087	12 645
		42	12 408	12 981
		43	12 738	13 326
	PO4 43–46 {	44	13 065	13 668
		45	13 395	14 013
		46	13 725	14 358
	PO5 46–49 {	47	14 034	14 682
		48	14 379	15 042
PO6 48–51 {		49	14 709	15 387
		50	15 033	15 726
		51	15 357	16 065

4.4 Glyn District Council maintains a leisure centre which is used jointly by the general public and the schools of Mega-Glynn County Council. For such use, the county council contributes 30% of agreed estimated gross expenditure at November prices, plus an increase for inflation to out-turn prices measured by the retail price index (RPI).

The budget is formulated in November prices, largely based upon the probable for the current year and then a contingency for inflation to out-turn prices is calculated.

(i) The original estimate for the leisure centre for 19X9/X0 (November 19X8 prices) is as follows:

	£000s	£000s
Employees		204.4
Premises		110.6
Supplies and services		53.5
Vehicles		1.5
Establishment		50.0
Asset rents and capital charges		115.0
		535.0
Income	295.0	
Sales and charges	160.5	
Estimated deficit		455.5
		79.5

The agreed contingency for inflation for 19X9/X0 is to be calculated by applying the following percentage increases to original estimates:

Employees 3%, Premises, supplies and services, establishment 4%, Vehicles 5%.

(ii) Most recent evidence and estimates of inflation are as follows:

Employees: a 4% pay award w.e.f. 1 September 19X9.
a further 4.5% w.e.f. 1 September 19X0.

Price indices:

	PRI	Premises, supplies/services, and establishment	Vehicles
Nov. 19X8	109.6	108	125
Mar. 19X9	112.3	110.6	127
Nov. 19X9	116.4	114.5	135
(Est.) Mar. 19X0	121.3	119	140
(Est.) Nov. 19X0	124.5	123	143
(Est.) Mar. 19X1	127.1	126	145

(iii) Estimated asset rents and capital charges for 19X9/X0 and 19X0/X1 are as follows:

19X9/X0	19X0/X1
£115 000	£120 000

The loan was taken out in 19X7/X8 and is being repaid over six years on the basis of equal instalments of principal.

Expenditure of £25 000 for upgrade of the heating system is to be incurred in August 19X0; it is expected to be financed by loan, repayable over five years.

The estimated loans fund rate for 19X9/X0 was 11%: it increased to 11.5% w.e.f. 1 October 19X9 and is expected to increase by a further 0.5% w.e.f. 1 October 19X0.

(iv) Actual expenditure and the usual expenditure profiles for the six months 1 April to 30 September are as follows:

	£	%
Employees	105 270	50
Premises	52 911	45
Supplies and services	27 265	50
Vehicles	790	50
Establishment	23 660	45
Income: Fees and charges	165 200	55

(v) As compared with the 19X9/X0 estimates, use is likely to increase by 4% in 19X0/X1 despite proposed price increases of 10% w.e.f. April 19X0. This will result in a volume-related increase of 1% in supplies and services and 6% in employees. The improvements in the heating system are likely to reduce consumption in the second half of 19X0/X1 to 92% of consumption in the second half of 19X9/X0. Heating constitutes 70% of premises expenditure in 19X9/X0.

(vi) The district is aiming that the leisure centre should break even by the end of the financial year 19X1/X2.

Required

(a) Calculate the probable out-turn for 19X9/X0, compare the probably out-turn with the original estimate plus contingency and comment on the implication of the variations for future budgeting. (10 marks)

(b) Calculate the 19X0/X1 original estimate and contingency. (10 marks)

(c) Comment upon the progress being made towards the objective laid down in note (vi) and identify the additional information which would assist financial planning to achieve that objective. (4 marks)

4.5 The following expenditure relates to a district laundry maintained by the Usk-Afan Health Authority for the nine months to 31 December 19X7:

	£
Section manager	10 089
Assistant section manager	7 920
Superintendents	9 240
Laundry operatives	36 720
Administration and clerical	5 730
Engineering – pay	4 680
– parts and materials	3 930
Materials – washing	18 350
– drycleaning	1 040
Water	4 230
Steam generation	8 160
Electricity	6 470
Rates	3 600
Transport	6 420
Miscellaneous	990
Domestic/cleaning staff	5 340

The laundry is organized into three flowlines. Statistics for the nine months to 31 December 19X7 are as follows:

Flowline processed	Articles standard		Productive water usage	Steam and consumption	Electricity
	No. 000s	Weight %	Hours	%	%
Large flatwork	1 869	63	12 000	60	60
Small flatwork	453	31	9 000	40	35
Drycleaning	195	6	6 000	—	5

Expenditure is apportioned across the flowlines and, unless otherwise indicated, the pattern of expenditure and activity to 31 December 19X7 is expected to be typical of the pattern for the year as a whole.

The following information is available:

(a) Managers and superintendents received a pay award of 5% with effect from 1 November 19X7.
(b) All other employees were awarded an increase in pay of 6% with effect from 1 September 19X7.
(c) Rates are payable on 1 April and 1 October.
(d) Washing materials are expected to increase in price by 6% for the financial year as a whole; the increase in price of drycleaning materials over the same period is expected to be 8%.
(e) An electricity bill of £2500 is estimated for the quarter to 31 December 19X7; it is not included in the balances listed. The bill for the January–March quarter is normally 50% higher than the average for the remainder of the year and the electricity board has also indicated an increase of 5% in prices with effect from 1 January 19X8.
(f) All labour, managerial, administrative and transport costs are apportioned in proportion to productive standard hours.
(g) Engineering material costs are apportioned on the same basis as engineering pay.
(h) Washing materials, other than drycleaning materials, are related to processing activity by weight of articles processed.
(i) Rates and miscellaneous expenses are apportioned equally over all flowlines.
(j) The laundry is expected fully to recover costs. To this end, the following rates for recovering costs were established in December 19X6 for the financial year 31 March 19X8:

	Pence per article
Large flatwork	4.5
Small flatwork	14.0
Drycleaning	16.0

Required

(i) Prepare a statement showing estimated expenditure for the year to 31 March 19X8. (16 marks)
(ii) Comment on the laundry's operating performance for the year to 31 March 19X8. (4 marks)

4.6 Supplies arrangements for several health authorities in the region are channelled through a central stores administered by your authority. The following information is given for 19X9/X0 at out-turn prices:

	X9/X0 original estimate £000	X9/X0 revised estimate £000
Issues	3 600	3 400
Opening stock	960	950
Purchases	2 700	2 800
	3 660	3 750
Closing stock	810	1 060
Cost of issues	2 850	2 690
Surplus	750	710
Overheads:		
Salaries and wages	490	495
Running expenses	230	235
Surplus	30	–20

Investigations reveal the following:

(i) Stores issue prices are to be updated on 1 April 19X0 for 12 months by an average of 11.5%.

(ii) It is anticipated that in 19X0/X1 the volume of issues will be 1% lower in volume terms than the latest forecast for 19X9/X0.

(iii) In 19X0/X1 it is planned to cash limit the sum available for purchases to that shown in the original 19X9/X0 budget. However, despite keen contract negotiation by the purchasing departments, the anticipated year-on-year increase in purchase prices will amount to 5%.

(iv) Past experience shows that levels of stock at the year end normally amount to 30% of total purchases during the year.

(v) In 19X0/X1 it is estimated that salaries and wages of stores staff will increase by 13% on the revised out-turn for 19X9/X0. Running expenses are expected to increase year on year by 15%.

(vi) Discussions reveal that a large public authority in the area is interested in entering into the present supplies arrangement. If this new authority participates, issues are estimated to be 10% higher than currently predicted after taking into account known factors affecting 19X0/X1. There would also be a corresponding increase in purchases. Initial calculations show that, based on the present year's revised estimates, overheads would increase by £40 000 for salaries and wages and £8000 for running expenses. This is before the effect of any 19X0/X1 pay or price changes.

A sample investigation based on existing members has shown that a system of direct supply contracts would result in average prices some 10% less than the set stores issue prices at 1 April 19X0. Under these arrangements, prices would be held constant for three months and updated by 6% at the beginning of each quarter. Past records show that 40% of the issues take place in the first quarter and the balance is spread evenly over the rest of the year. You estimate that there would need to be additional administrative and transport costs in the existing authorities amounting to £250 000 at 19X0/X1 out-turn prices.

Required

(a) Estimate the financial position of the central stores in 19X0/X1 from the information given and consider separately the possibility of additional membership and the alternative offered by direct supply contract arrangements.
(b) Comment briefly on the position revealed by your findings.

4.7 The following information relates to the Department of Business Studies in a new university.

1. *Academic salary scales* (w.e.f. 1.4.X2)

Incremental points	LII/SL Amount	LII/SL No. of staff	PL Amount	PL No. of staff	HOD Amount	HOD No. of staff
	£		£		£	
1	16 600	–	21 400	–	25 000	–
2	17 200	5	22 000	–	25 600	–
3	17 800	–	22 600	–	26 200	1
4	18 400	–	23 200	–	26 800	–
5	19 000	–	23 800	6		
6	19 600	5	24 400	3		
7	20 200	–				
8	20 800	7				
9	21 400	8				
10	22 000	10				
No. of staff		35		9		1

Staff progress to the next incremental point on 1 September each year (unless at maximum of scale).

The following staff changes will take place during the year 1.4.X2–31.3.X3

(a) 1 SL retires on 31.8.X2 (currently on maximum of scale)
(b) 1 PL retires on 31.12.X2 (currently on maximum of scale)
(c) 1 SL (currently on maximum of scale) promoted to PL (salary point 3) on 1.1.X3
(d) 1 LII appointed on minimum of scale on 1.9.X2
(e) 1 SL appointed on incremental point no. 6 on 1.1.X3
(f) 1 new SL appointed to assist in teaching accounting on incremental point no. 7 on 1.9.X2

A pay award of 3% p.a. is to be implemented with effect from 1.4.X2.

2. *Clerical/administrative staff salary scale* (w.e.f. 1.7.X1)

	Incremental point (as at 1.4.X2)	Amount £
	1	8 200
	2	8 500
1 clerk/typist	3	8 800
	4	9 100
	5	9 400
1 clerk/typist	6	9 700
	7	10 000
	8	10 300
Departmental secretary	9	10 600
	10	10 900
Administrative assistant	11	11 200

A pay award of 1.5% with effect from 1.7.X2 is anticipated. Incremental progressive takes place on 1st April each year.

3. Provide for employers' National Insurance contribution of 9.5% of staff salaries and superannuation contribution of 11.5% of staff salaries.

4. *Student numbers* (19X2/X3)
   Full-time   850 (including 3rd year students on industrial training: 50 degree students and 150 HND students)
   Part-time   760

5. *Teaching materials*
   Current allowance is £10 per full-time student (part-time students' allowance is 80% of full-time allowance).

6. *Travelling expenses* (staff)
   Training: £80 per degree student (full-time students only)
                 £40 per HND student
   Other: £70 per member of academic staff in post on 1.4.X2.

7. *Printing and stationery*
   Current allowance is £24 per full-time student
   (part-time students' allowance is 75% of full-time allowance).

8. *Furniture and equipment*
   £12 000 allowances for 19X2/X3

9. *Inflation*
   Provide for the following price increases in 19X2–X3 (where appropriate allowances will be increased in line with inflation).

	% p.a.
Teaching materials	4
Travelling expenses	2
Printing and stationery	2
Furniture and equipment	1

Required

You are required to estimate the total cost of the Department for the year ended 31.3.X3.

5 Budgetary control

Key learning objectives

After reading this chapter you should be able to:

1. Understand the importance of timely, relevant and accurate budgetary control information in a form suitable for managers.
2. Recognize the various techniques of budgetary control in respect of both capital and revenue expenditure.
3. Recognize the need to consider human aspects of budgetary control.
4. Recognize the growing importance of performance objectives and the need to monitor and control results against these targets.

The previous chapter examined the process of budget preparation and also illustrated one measure of budgetary control by its reference to the calculation of the probable out-turn for the year prior to that which the new budget relates. Clearly, once a budget has been established, it is necessary to set up controls and procedures which enable the budget to be monitored and for warnings of budget drift to be sounded as soon as possible. The calculation of a probable out-turn for the year at budget preparation time is but one element of this process. In many public sector organizations, also, the practice of holding a central contingency fund for unforeseen inflation or circumstance has been abandoned in favour of placing a cash limit on the appropriate managers thus restricting the ability to spend to the cash-limited figure. In the competitive tendering services this luxury is not possible in any case as all contracts must be completed in budget if the relevant profit is to be made. Any overspending in these circumstances will thus impact, in the first instance, on the resource available to the service manager and, in the second instance, on the overall profitability of the competitive unit. Failure to contain items within service department budgets will reduce the organization's working balances and could, depending on the circumstances of the public sector organization, result in government penalties being imposed, as with local government under the block grant system. These factors tend to place a premium on timely, accurate and relevant information. Control may be centred on detailed regulation as under Standing Orders and Financial Regulations, both of which place emphasis on the regularity of the budgetary control process without measuring the performance of the budget holder in carrying out the service function. This chapter examines the traditional methods of control in the public sector in the budgetary process and then considers how techniques developed in the private sector can have application to areas of the public sector.

5.1 Essentials of a system of budgetary control

Budgetary control can be defined as 'the establishment of budgets relating the responsibilities of executives to the requirements of a policy and the continuous comparison of actual with budgeted results either to secure by individual action the objective of that policy or to provide a basis for its revision' (CIMA). It should be pointed out that there is no significant difference between the principles of budgetary control in either the public or private sector. The statement implies that, as budgets are established for various elements of the organization, managers are given responsibility for the management of budget resources in those areas. This has in part been illustrated by the earlier mention of the cash limit system but a recent example would include the changes made as a result of the introduction of local management in schools where the headteacher and governors assume responsibility for the delegated budget and its management. Clearly such a system requires information which has to be related to the delegated responsibilities within the organization. Thus the cost centres established to monitor and control expenditure must be related to responsibility centres and be sufficiently disaggregated to provide the information that is needed. Within these cost centres the financial coding system must not only provide maximum flexibility for the analysis of expenditure and income at the cost centre level, but must also provide the chief financial officer with information at the strategic level to take the overall global view on actual performance of the budget against estimate. An illustration of what can go wrong where control is not properly exercised is shown in Exhibit 5.1.

The basic principles underlying the budgetary control system should be as follows.

Timely, relevant, and accurate information

Line managers should not be reduced to maintaining 'little black books' to enable them to ascertain their budget position. The information system should be designed to meet the needs of the line manager and not just the convenience of the chief financial officer. Many public sector computer systems were designed around the need to produce the financial accounts and management information was almost a by-product of this process. Information needs to be accurate, but, by the same token, it is no use providing 100% accurate information if the time for action has passed. There is also a need to avoid the provision of large computer tabulations which are beyond the ability of managers to assimilate. Information by exception is required. Increasingly, use is being made of on-line enquiry as in LAFIS (Local Authority Financial Information System) operated by local authorities. This system allows short programs to produce answers to straightforward preset questions under its AIDA (programming language developed by ICL for on-line enquiry) system with more complex requests being processed usually overnight under a MERIT (modelling, enquiry, reporting interactive technique) program.

Clear divisions of responsibility

Levels of responsibility must be identified and set out in the appropriate regulations to avoid confusion and to speed up action. The basic rule is that the person certifying the expenditure for payment should be responsible for the budget, i.e. that expenditure being certified can be contained within his or her budget provision.

Consistency

It is essential that a consistent basis is used for comparison purposes. Thus if the budget is cash limited it will include an allowance for inflation. As expenditure is processed and appears in monitoring statements this will allow direct comparison with the original budget. This may be more difficult if a central contingency fund is maintained to cover inflation as, until it is allocated to individual budget heads, uncertainty will surround the sums of money that managers actually control.

5.2 Commitment accounting

One of the problems facing managers in trying to control expenditure and monitor income is to know, for example, what level of expenditure has been committed but, as yet, has not been reflected in the financial information that is available. This problem has resulted in the phenomenon of the 'little black book' (referred to earlier in this chapter) for recording this expenditure. A more formal method of recording this information is by way of a system of commitment accounting where the financial information system recognizes a transaction and its impact on the budget as soon as a purchase or other financial commitments are entered into. This clearly means that the information is more up to date and, as such, should be more meaningful to the manager, thus facilitating budgetary control.

A number or problems are, however, associated with the system and these include:

1. The difficulty of measuring the size of the commitment as an order may only be an estimate. If the commitment is entered on receipt of the invoice in the service department there can be duplication of effort if it is later submitted to the finance department for payment. This may even lead to a suggestion of distributed payment processing to save time in information processing rather than a commitment system.
2. There can be audit implications of allowing distributed data processing and direct access to the financial information system by departments outside the finance function.
3. The most significant areas of expenditure are salaries and wages in the public sector and these do not require a commitment system to aid control. Expenditure on central departmental support may be controlled by a service level agreement which will specify the terms of payment and the total level of liability. Debt charges and debt management fees will be controlled by the finance department. Significant areas of expenditure can thus be controlled effectively without a commitment accounting system.
4. Additional complications are introduced as orders are cancelled or amended. There will be a need to adjust commitments at the year end in order to close the accounts to reflect the accruals position.

An alternative to a full commitment system developed by many public sector organizations is a memorandum note within the financial information system which records the commitment but does not amend the financial records.

5.3 Expenditure profiling

It is obvious that some expenditure that occurs during the year is highly predictable, the most obvious example being salaries and wages. This raises the concept of expenditure profiling (this idea is further developed when cash flow management is discussed in Chapter 6). The concept need not only be applied to expenditure as items of income are predictable, for example the receipt of government grants. Despite the difficulties, profiling should not be restricted only to the easier items like salaries and wages and should be extended to the remaining budget heads. These can be built up by an historical analysis of expenditure and income or through predictable payment as, for example, under a maintenance contract. Fuel bills can be studied and will indicate higher bills in the winter months. Income for a swimming pool is likely to be higher in the summer than the winter months. For an open-air swimming pool income is likely to be concentrated in June, July and August. The objective is not 100% accuracy but to provide managers with information on which to take decisions. At the end of each budget period the manager is able to compare actual with projected and calculate the variance. The key point is that the more significant the variance the greater the need for investigation. A projected out-turn for the year can also be calculated on the basis of actual expenditure to date and the consequent necessary action can be triggered. Such action may include reduction in planned expenditure on other heads to absorb any overspend predicted as a result of the profile analysis. There is an obvious need for the manager to be concerned with the overall picture and not just the results on individual heads. Table 5.1 indicates a profiling exercise which has been carried out on fuel costs for a public sector organization. It also allows for inflation and changes as the result of virement, inflation and a supplementary estimate. The supplementary estimate illustrates the impact that the completion of a capital scheme can have on the revenue budget.

5.4 Virement

Virement is the transfer of funds from one budget head to another although the exact rules of virement will depend on the individual organization. One object of virement is to prevent the need for a supplementary estimate as an underspending from one head may be transferred to another head which has an overspending. A virement would not normally be allowed where, if it occurred, the organization would be involved in recurrent expenditure as this would represent a commitment of future resources.

It can be seen that virement allows some element of flexibility in the budgetary control process. One problem with unrestricted virement is that managers would inevitably spend all their budget allocation for fear of a budget reduction in the subsequent year. This is also linked to the problem of carryover into the next financial year as treasurers may attempt to claw back underspending. There is some evidence, however, of a more flexible attitude by some public sector organizations in allowing the carry forward of underspendings on certain heads as an addition to the following year's budget. The converse, of course, is that any carry forward of overspendings will result in a reduction in the following year's budget. Virement and carry-forward may be allowed in an organization where the saving in the current year is a result of a conscious decision by the manager concerned. The percentage of the saving retained by the department will vary between organizations, but clearly it has to be sufficiently large to encourage

Table 5.1 Energy profile

	Apr.	May	Jun.	Jul.	Aug.	Sep.	Oct.	Nov.	Dec.	Jan.	Feb.	Mar.	Year
Profile % expenditure	6	5	4	3	3	5	8	10	14	16	16	10	100
Cumulative % profile	6	11	15	18	21	26	34	44	58	74	90	100	100
Original estimate £	12 000	22 000	30 000	36 000	42 000	52 000	68 000	88 000	116 000	148 000	180 000	200 000	200 000
Inflation £						1 000	2 600	4 600	7 400	10 600	13 800	15 800	15 800
Virement £												3 000	3 000
Supplementary estimate* £										1 000	2 500	3 500	3 500
Control total £	12 000	22 000	30 000	36 000	42 000	53 000	70 600	92 600	123 400	159 600	196 300	222 300	222 300

*Capital scheme completed and operating ahead of schedule.

such action. Savings arising as a result of good fortune will normally be prime candidates for return to central balances. It should be noted that the Health Service has the ability to vire automatically between capital and revenue, up to 1% from revenue to capital and up to 10% from capital to revenue. In addition carry-forward is allowed of unspent monies from one year to the next of up to 1% of the combined capital and revenue allocation.

5.5 Supplementary estimates

Normally the budget process will be completed prior to the year to which the budget relates. During the year, however, items of income or expenditure may arise which are so large they may require a supplementary estimate. In local government it was possible to levy a supplementary rate for unforeseen expenditure but this is now no longer possible. Clearly, if it is impossible for an item to be contained within an original budget, then action is required. This may take the form of providing a supplementary estimate by reducing balances and transferring them to the required budget head or virement from within the overall department's budget, or even reducing another department's estimate to make funds available for transfer. The better the level of control and intelligence available the earlier this situation can be detected and more drastic action may be avoided. If it is decided that the budget is to be amended all changes should be built into the financial information system as soon as possible.

5.6 Reports

It has already been stated that reports should be timely, accurate and relevant. Simon (1953, 1959) has commented that: 'Administrative man satisfices as he has not the wits to maximise', indicating that the cognitive ability of man is restricted. Thus reports should be restricted to the essential information appropriate to the level of the managers receiving the information. Exceptions should be reported and clearly flagged, ideally under a priority system. To relate to this discussion to the earlier profiling, any significant over- or underspendings would receive priority indicators. This requires tolerance levels to be set for individual items of expenditure and income.

The monitoring cycle needs to be related to the needs of managers, although the normal reporting cycle is monthly. The competitive units may require weekly information on crucial contracts. Also, it should not be forgotten that on-line facilities may exist for day-to-day problems. In addition, it may be desirable that the computer information system contains both financial and non-financial information, including, for example, staff numbers and other physical units such as metres of road to be cleaned and patient bed days. A form of budget report is shown for a theoretical new university in Table 5.2.

This illustrates the use of memorandum notes and the relationship between items within the budget, as, for example, the overspending on lecturers has resulted in extra consultancy fees. Items of major significance have a marker attached.

5.7 Controlling central government expenditure

Within central government the Treasury monitors all expenditure by departments. As would be expected departments also monitor expenditure centrally with individual managers responsible for controlling their own expenditure programmes to the agreed level of spending on their own programme area. The way in which this has traditionally been done in central government is now explored in some detail in order to provide readers with an example of budgetary control in practice. The implications of the change to resource budgeting in central government are discussed at the end of this section.

The main elements of the control of cash by central government are:

1. *Reporting blocks.* The Treasury and departments agree early in the financial year the breakdown of the vote into reporting blocks of expenditure of a manageable size. These then form the basic control units. Reporting blocks generally follow the subheads of the vote although where such subheads are too large they can be subdivided for better control. Subheads of minor items of expenditure are normally brought together into a single *de minimis* reporting block.

2. *Profiles* as discussed earlier in this chapter are then prepared for each reporting block to provide a planned flow of expenditure and income against which performance can be monitored. The forthcoming financial year is divided into quarters reflecting such factors as seasonal variation. These profiles are discussed and agreed between the Treasury and the departments to ensure realism as they represent the key control function in that they provide the bottom line. The Treasury must also be satisfied that when all blocks are combined they will not exceed the cash limit. As the year proceeds actual out-turn data can then be compared with the profile. A mid-year expenditure return showing likely results for the year is prepared showing the likely out-turn on each block for the year in question. This is discussed between the Treasury and the departments. If a department becomes aware that it will overspend at any time during the year it must notify the Treasury immediately. Supplementary estimates may be granted if considered appropriate by the Treasury and parliament.

3. Receipts and expenditures are recorded by the APEX (Analysis of Public Expenditure) system controlled by the Paymaster General. Expenditure is included from departmental returns with receipts and adjustments notified separately. APEX data are sent to the Treasury weekly where they are transferred to the Treasury's financial information system which then provides the analysis as required for departmental monitoring.

4. Departmental monitoring is monthly with the computer system projecting the likely out-turn for the year based on the expenditure and income recorded to date. This highlights potential problem areas to enable cost centre managers to take remedial action if judged necessary. Clearly, as the year progresses and more information becomes available the ability to predict the likely outcome for the year in question is more accurate.

5. Towards the end of the financial year as the chancellor needs to prepare his budget departments need to prepare a forecast of their most accurate estimate of likely out-turn. This is particularly important for the demand-led expenditures such as unemployment benefit due to the fact that they are not cash limited and have a major impact on the government's demand for finance. When the budget was in March this exercise was carried out in February, but with the move to a December budget this exercise will need to be done earlier.

6. At the end of the financial year the department must account for the sums spent. The final stage is the preparation of an appropriation account which shows for each vote the sums authorized and the sums spent and for ease of understanding normally

Table 5.2 Budget monitoring report (extract): A new university out-turn to month 8

Subjective	Position to date			Projection to year end			Exception report and memorandum note
	Planned Expenditure £000	Expenditure to date £000	Variance £000	Approved budget £000	Projected out-turn £000	Variance £000	
Employee costs:							
Management staff	1 750	1 745	−5	2 800	2 820	20	Award higher than expected*
Principal lecturers	2 000	2 120	120	3 250	3 275	25	As above*
Lecturers	3 500	3 750	250	5 300	6 000	700	Vacant posts filled early – see income***
Administrative staff	2 300	2 300	0	3 500	3 500	0	
Manual workers	1 200	1 250	50	1 800	1 800	0	
Total salaries and wages	10 750	11 165	415	16 650	17 395	745	
Premises:							
Maintenance	800	800	0	1 200	1 200	0	
Energy	1 000	1 050	50	1 500	1 475	−25	Energy conservation scheme starts January
Rent and rates	750	750	0	1 125	1 125	0	
Cleaning	900	850	−50	1 350	1 100	−250	Cleaning made subject to competitive tender
Misc.	50	50	0	100	100	0	
Total premises	3 500	3 500	0	5 275	5 000	−275	Repair bills down**

Transport (detail)	904	975	71	1 356	1 300	−56	
Supplies and services (detail)	400	200	−200	800	450	−350	Savings on books***
Total university expenditure	15 554	15 840	286	24 081	24 145	64	
Income:							
Student fees	−18 000	−17 750	250	−22 000	−22 000	0	
Consultancy	−1 000	−1 050	−50	−2 000	−2 120	−120	Extra consultancy due to fewer vacancies**
Other	−50	−50	0	−100	−110	−10	Extra interest on investments
Total income	−19 050	−18 850	200	−24 100	−24 230	−130	
Net position	−3 496	−3 010	486	−19	−85	−66	

Note:
Capital expenditure charges and central administration controlled centrally.

Key:
*** Major variation from budget requires close monitoring.
** Keep under review.
* Minor overspending predicted.

follows the format of the supply estimates. Budget holders are responsible to line managers, who are responsible to the accounting officer (the permanent head of the department concerned). The individual in signing the appropriation account accepts responsibility for the propriety of expenditure and the accuracy of the account. Accounting officers are accountable to their minister but may be called by the Public Accounts Committee to give evidence. The accounts are audited by the Comptroller and Auditor General (CAG). The minister, the Public Accounts Committee and the CAG all report to parliament. The control is thus complete in that parliament voted the funds and has now received reports on how the money was spent.

This reporting cycle has concentrated on the more traditional methods of budgetary control in central government. This is because it has been concerned with the monitoring of supply expenditure. For the new agencies there is a need to control not only cash but accruals as well. Under the 1990 Government Trading Act agencies operate in a trading fund environment. The trading fund gives powers to exist outside the normal votes system providing a financial framework which covers operating costs and receipts, the power to borrow and to establish reserves. The accounts will be published on the same basis as companies controlled by the Companies Acts and consequently the agencies will require budgetary control systems which relate to their published profit and loss accounts and take account therefore of accruals based transactions. The 1990 Act also gave the Treasury the power to extend these provisions to any suitable activities of departments irrespective of whether they are agencies or not (Hardcastle, 1990, p.28).

The change to resource accounting is effectively an extension of these arrangements from agencies to the whole of the departments of state. Under resource budgeting what matters is when the resources are consumed and systems will need to be adapted to control the consumption of resources. Departmental expenditure limits are split into capital and revenue allocations while expenditure that cannot be reasonably controlled is allocated to annually managed expenditure.

As the process is a complicated one in the initial phase, depreciation, cost of capital charges and provisions will be allocated by the 2000 spending review into the annually managed expenditure figures. This decision was based on the inexperience of service managers in forecasting in these areas. From the 2002 spending review, however, it is planned to allocate these charges to departmental expenditure resource limits. In controlling these items it will be necessary that managers recognise timing differences in that prepayments will not be a charge on the current year's budget but will include accruals where assets have been acquired but paid for later. Stock consumption will also be a charge to be controlled. In future they will need to control capital expenditure closely as the depreciation charges and cost of capital charges will be an additional expense falling on their budgets. The requirement to produce balance sheets will place an incentive on managers not only to manage capital assets given capital charges but also to manage stocks, debtors and creditors (see Chapter 6). Proper management of these items can produce savings to revenue budgets. Motivational effects are relevant as there will be a need for appropriate incentives if maximum efficiencies are to be achieved.

5.8 Flexible budgeting and performance measurement

Having given an overview of the reporting framework and budgetary control process it is now necessary to examine the mechanism of control in action, and at this stage, to attempt to couple the concept of budget performance in terms of outputs achieved with control. It is clearly nonsensical to suggest that because a budget has been controlled to achieve the planned spend that the objectives of that budget as originally perceived have been successfully met. There is a need therefore to relate the budget to some measure of outputs as these will identify the objectives that the spending pattern is meant to achieve. This reintroduces the concept of non-financial measures mentioned earlier in this chapter.

If we take, for example, a creditors' payments team, the majority of any expenditure will be on those employed to deal with the payment of invoices received. This is a budget which is relatively easy to achieve and control, especially if there is the minimum of staff turnover. Without some measure of performance the control process is almost meaningless as a budget spend may be achieved with little regard to the stated objectives. Financial control can be built into the process in that, when the budget is being set, target creditor processing figures should be built in. These could then be monitored alongside the actual spend. This process is effectively happening in terms of the service level agreements currently being negotiated with service departments by some finance departments. The estimated creditor payments will form the basis of the contract. It is therefore only a small step to introduce monitoring of the performance of the individual components of the service level agreement. This type of simple performance budgeting can be extended to such areas as the number of home help applications processed, the number of driving licence applications dealt with and so on. Effectively, it is attempting to measure and control against a performance standard those costs which are essentially fixed as, for example, the bulk of salaries and wages in the public sector normally are.

This concept is obviously related to unit cost as the figures used invariably lend themselves to this type of analysis, but the important difference is that the budget has been based on target performance. If we now extend this concept of performance measurement to the catering budget for a hospital ward given in Table 5.3 its application to a variable cost can then be considered.

Clearly, the first thing to note is that the catering cost is within budget in total but that the unit cost of catering is 80p above the estimate. If the estimated cost had been achieved then the total catering cost should have been £74 200 (a saving of £3180 on the final cost or 4% of the original budget). The control question is not therefore did we achieve our budget but why did things go wrong and where? There are now a number of avenues of investigation opened up, including, first, did we pay more for food than anticipated or, second, was there a high level of waste and other inefficiencies in the

Table 5.3 Catering budget for a hospital ward

Performance measurement – catering costs ward 10
Estimated patient days: 3 650
Estimated catering costs per patient day: £21.20
Estimated catering costs for year: £77 380
Actual patient days: 3 500
Actual cost per patient day: £22.00
Actual catering costs for year: £77 000
Estimated patient days based on ten beds in an 11-bed ward occupied for 365 days (i.e. 90.9% occupancy rate)

preparation of the food? (It is obviously also possible to have a combination of the two.) At this stage we have identified a financial variance, and while further analysis may also question items such as quality at least questions are now being raised. In addition we might question the low bed occupancy rate achieved or, alternatively, the realism of the projected 90.9% occupancy rate. The skill lies in the interpretation of the data, not merely in their provision.

The key concepts to grasp at this stage are, first, that we have attempted to relate budget performance to the level of workload in that the budget was 'flexed' to compare with the actual results and, second, that we have introduced the idea of standard setting in terms of the workload required and the anticipated delivery of service (i.e. standard catering costs). The standard cost of the catering function used in the estimating process would be arrived at after suitable discussion with the appropriate staff. In addition the traditional approach of budgeting in the public sector would be to include in the analysis only those costs for which the catering manager would be directly responsible. The below-the-line costs such as central departmental support would be excluded.

Following on from this introduction into the principle of flexibility in budgeting it can be seen that we are attempting to measure output by comparison with the level of inputs that should have been committed to achieve the operation as it was actually performed. Table 5.4 illustrates this concept for a street sweeping and cleaning operation.

It can be seen from that the organization has cleaned more miles than intended under this contract in the first month of the financial year. If costs and income had been to budget net profit for April would have been £238. Under the actual result the organization appears to have made £362. However, it can be seen that when the budget is flexed the profit made on the actual road mileage cleaned is only £35. The reasons for the poor performance can be seen in the variance column. These areas could be further investigated as clearly this type of enterprise needs to perform efficiently if it is to achieve the required rate of return. Is should also be pointed out that the control of additional work is essential to the survival of the organization. Traditionally, public sector workers have undertaken extra work if requested by clients. This work will now only be paid for if a variation order is obtained.

Flexible budgeting is based on an adequate knowledge of cost patterns. In the last example costs have been assumed to be directly variable with mileage unless otherwise specified. The concept of a semi-variable cost was introduced in respect of the administration charge. This was because it was assumed that the basic monthly charge was fixed but that the extra wages costs triggered extra charges, possibly due to the need for more processing in the finance section. These terms would be stated in the service level agreement. The fixed cost of depreciation has not been flexed.

5.9 Control by standards

The concept of standard costs was introduced in the previous chapter and referred to in the previous section. It will now be examined in greater detail. The concept was originally developed in industry but has application in the public sector as this section will show. The most obvious direct application is in the competitive sections of public sector organizations but it has implications in other areas of the public sector, as will also be demonstrated. To establish the standard costs of an operation it is necessary to identify those costs which will be incurred as a result of the operation – labour, materials and overheads. These can only be established after detailed study.

Table 5.4 Street sweeping and cleaning operation flexible budget exercise

	Contract 19X0/X1 £	Actual Apr. £	Flexed Apr. £	Variance £
Revenue billed:				
Contract fees	205 000	17 288	17 083	205
Misc. income	1 500	125	125	0
Total	206 500	17 413	17 208	205
Expenditure:				
Wages – ordinary	58 660	4 888	4 947	59
Wages – overtime	19 550	1 658	1 649	–9
Wages – oncost	39 105	3 273	3 298	25
Salaries	6 520	543	550	7
Transport costs	41 220	3 480	3 476	–4
Materials	1 450	115	122	7
Depreciation – fixed	2 500	208	208	0
Administration – semi-variable	34 635	2 886	2 921	35
Total expenditure	203 640	17 051	17 171	120
Net profit	2 860	362	37	325
Assets at current cost	£31 000			
Return on current cost %	9.23	14.01	1.43	
Miles cleaned to standard	41.60	42.10	42.10	

Notes:

1. All revenue due was billed in April.
2. Additions to the contract mileage authorized for April were £205. (Anticipated income for April was £205 000/12. Actual is = £205 000/12 + £205 = £17 288.)

The types of standard that can be developed are:

1. *Historic cost standards.* These are standards that remain unchanged over long periods and can be used as a base for comparison purposes, but often they do not represent currently achievable standards and thus have limited use.
2. *Ideal standards.* These costs would only be achieved under perfect conditions and clearly will have the potential to affect adversely the motivation of managers if it is perceived that the impossible is being asked.
3. *Currently achievable standards.* These are costs that can be achieved in an efficient organization. These targets provide a fair basis to measure performance against. These costs can be used in the planning process as they represent standards which should be achieved. In Table 5.3 the catering cost estimate should relate to an achievable standard.

Standard costing can ideally be applied where there is an activity which is primarily repetitive. In the public sector, for example, refuse collection is a standard function with repetitive runs and a measure of work in that the number of bins emptied is reasonably consistent. Street sweeping and cleaning activities fall into the same category. To apply the principle to these operations it is necessary to identify responsibility centres as it is pointless to establish standards and not hold individual managers to account.

Standard costs and results do not stand by themselves. It is necessary to undertake further analysis of the results to identify clear responsibilities and to take corrective action if required. It has already been indicated in discussing Table 5.3 that, having shown a variation between planned and actual catering costs, a number of avenues are open for exploration. The financial information system should indicate to managers where the problem lies. The fact that this process will take place may also work as an incentive to the individual to perform better within the area of his or her responsibility. The analysis of events after they have occurred should also indicate ways in which performance might be improved in the future irrespective of whether or not problems exist at present.

The concept of standard costs and variance analysis is now developed by way of Table 5.5 which applies the technique to a street sweeping and cleaning contract.

As street cleaning has been subject to competitive tendering the contract price is fixed for any street cleaning undertaken.

Table 5.5   Blaenwent street sweeping and cleaning contract: Budget period 1

	£	£
Budget for period 1		
Income: 10 000 miles of cleaning at £6 per mile		60 000
Direct materials: 500 kg at £10 per kg	5 000	
Direct labour: 3000 hrs at £8 per hr	24 000	
Variable overheads: 3000 hrs at £2 per DL hr	6 000	
Fixed overheads	15 000	
		50 000
Budgeted profits		£10 000
	£	£
Actual results for period 1		
Income: 9000 miles at £6		54 000
Direct materials: 510 kg at £9.90 per kg	5 049	
Direct labour: 2950 hrs at £8.10	23 895	
Variable overheads	5 750	
Fixed overheads	14 500	
		49 194
Actual profit		£4 806

Note:
Budgeted fixed overheads are charged on the basis of direct labour hours. This gives a fixed overhead rate of £5 per direct labour hour (£15 000/3000).

From Table 5.5 it is possible to calculate the following variances:

Materials

Total cost variance	= (Actual production × Standard cost per unit of production) – Actual materials cost
Price variance	= (Standard price per unit of material – Actual price) × Quantity purchased
Usage variance	= (Standard quantity of materials for Actual consumption – Actual quantity utilized) × Standard price

Labour

Total cost variance = (Standard quantity of labour hours for actual production – Actual labour hours worked) × Standard hourly rate

Rate variance = (Standard wage rate per hour – Actual wage rate) × Actual hours worked

Efficiency variance = (Standard quantity of labour hours for actual production – Actual hours worked) × Standard wage rate per hour

Variable overhead

Expenditure variance = Budgeted variable overheads for actual input volume – Actual variable overheads

Efficiency variance = (Standard quantity of input hours for actual production – Actual input hours) × Standard variable overhead rate

Total variable overhead variance = (Actual production × Standard variable overhead rate) – Actual variable overhead cost

Fixed overhead

Expenditure variance = Budgeted fixed overhead – Actual fixed overhead

Volume variance = (Actual output – Budgeted output) × Standard fixed overhead rate

Efficiency variance = (Standard quantity of input hours for actual production – Actual input hours) × Standard fixed overhead rate

Capacity variance = (Actual hours of input – Budgeted hours of input) × Standard fixed overhead rate

Total fixed overhead variance = (Actual production × Standard fixed overhead rate) – Actual fixed overhead

Income

Total margin variance = Total actual profit – Budgeted profit

Income margin price variance = (Actual unit profit margin – Standard unit profit margin) × Actual sales volume

Income margin volume variance = (Actual sales volume – Budgeted sales volume) × Standard profit margin

The relationship between these variances is shown in Figure 5.1, together with the results of the calculations given. Before we analyze the variances, Table 5.6 (p.141) reconciles the budgeted figures with the actual profit.

5.10 Examination of variances

Materials

Price variances

The purchase price of materials is clearly beyond the control of the operating department and will probably be based on a contract price negotiated by a central purchasing department. Price levels are thus the responsibility of this department unless an unauthorized supplier has been used. Quality should be borne in mind if the

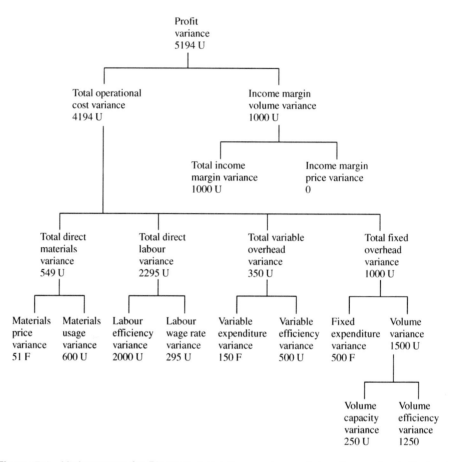

Figure 5.1 Variance tree for Blaenwent street sweeping and cleaning contract: Budget period 1

price variance is favourable, as should the effect of market forces beyond the control of the central supplies department.

Usage variances
Obvious causes of poor performance are excessive waste, poor quality and theft.

Labour

Rate variance
Clearly the cost of labour is determined by the wage rate and, in the public sector, the rate is normally set nationally, although the recent trend is for local agreements. Wage rates will be beyond the control of the unit manager, although the use of higher skilled workers than necessary will raise the actual rate.

Efficiency variance
This factor is controlled by the unit manager and reasons should be sought from him or

Table 5.6 Reconciliation of budget statement with actual results: Budget period 1

	£	£
Budgeted net profit		10 000
Income variances:		
Income margin	0	
Income margin volume	1 000 U	
Materials variances:		
Price	51 F	
Usage	600 U	
Labour variances:		
Rate	295 U	
Efficiency	2 000 U	
Variable overhead variances:		
Efficiency	500 U	
Expenditure	150 F	
Fixed overhead variances:		
Expenditure variance	500 F	
Volume capacity	250 U	
Volume efficiency	1 250 U	5 194 U
Actual net profit		£4 806

Key:
F = favourable variance
U = unfavourable variance

her for this variance. Factors may include breakdowns, inefficient working practices being allowed to develop or poor quality labour.

Overheads

When we examine overhead variances what is happening is that we are examining the difference between the actual amount of operational overhead incurred and the amount charged to operations through previously determined overhead absorption rates.

Fixed overheads

The fixed overhead expenditure variance is attempting to identify what proportion of the total fixed overhead variance is due to actual fixed overhead being different from budgeted fixed overhead. The volume variance seeks to identify the balance of the total fixed overhead variance which results from actual production differing from budgeted production. The volume variance can be further divided into the volume efficiency variance and the volume capacity variance which attempt to identify why actual operational performance was different from budgeted operational performance. The volume efficiency variance shows an inability to use capacity efficiently while the volume capacity variance indicates a failure to use capacity effectively (e.g. due to mechanical breakdowns).

Variable overheads

The total variable overhead variance is, as with the fixed overhead variance, broken down into two elements. The variable overhead expenditure variance measures the change between actual expenditure and the allowed overhead for actual labour hours (i.e. it allows for the current level of (in)efficiency). The variable overhead efficiency variance effectively in this case duplicates the labour efficiency variance and the reasons for this variance are the same.

Income variances

In this example the contract price was fixed and therefore there was no income margin price variance. The income margin volume variance arose due to the difference between budgeted operational mileage to be cleaned as against actual mileage cleaned.

Conclusions

This example of standard costing coupled with variance analysis and flexible budgeting has shown that a powerful tool is available to help service managers cope with the challenges of competition. The use of a computer would reduce the burden of calculation and the significant variances could be highlighted for managers by means of an exception report. This technique presents one of the challenges of change to the public sector manager.

In order to conclude this discussion of the technique of variance analysis and to show its versatility the example outlined in Table 5.7 looks at a typical grounds maintenance operation without the complication of the earlier overhead analysis.

The information Table 5.7 is quite straightforward to calculate and would provide the manager with more information than is probably currently available. Reasons for the variances can now be investigated. The table has also concentrated on the costs and income which are directly under the control of the service manager. Variations in fixed overheads – for example, a variation in any central support charges – are not directly within the service manager's control. Any change in these charges, while relevant to the service department as a whole, are not directly relevant to this individual contract at this stage. The overall control of these costs lies at a higher level, though reasons for changes may be related to this individual contract, e.g. if a protracted legal dispute took place. Costs such as central support must be monitored at the higher level as they cross all internal boundaries in the service departments. Service managers need to be concerned with the costs they directly control.

5.11 Control of fixed overheads

One of the major fixed overheads incurred by service departments in the public sector is for the provision of central departmental support services such as legal and financial services. The allocation of central departmental support costs to service departments has been largely arbitrary leading to major fluctuations between the original estimate and the actual charge. This no longer acceptable for the following reasons:

1. Compulsory competitive tendering for many services has meant central support must be easily, accurately and readily identifiable.
2. The emphasis on value for money requires central departments to be accountable for their costs and charges.
3. During the year service departments require accurate, timely and relevant information on charges. The year-end allocation of central support costs is inadequate for these purposes.

Table 5.7   Ground improvement budget

	£
Estimated costs:	
Labour: 30 hrs at £3.85 (incl. overheads)	115.50
Materials: Soil – 24 sq. m. at £21.5 per sq. m.	516.00
Peat – 21 bags at £7.40 per bag	155.40
Transport	35.00
	821.90
Recharge to Service Dept.	900.00
Surplus	78.10

Actuals:
Labour: 32 hrs at a total cost of £126.40
Soil: 25 sq. m at a total cost of £525 (incl. delivery)
Peat: 20 bags at £7.45 bag
Transport: £35

Analysis of variances

Costs	Actual	Flexed	Variance	Price of rate	Use or eff.
	£	£	£	£	£
Labour	126.4	115.5	10.9 U	3.20 U	7.70 U
Soil	525.0	516.0	9.0 U	12.50 F	21.50 U
Peat	149.0	155.4	6.4 F	1.00 U	7.40 F
Transport	35.0	35.0	0.0		
	835.4	821.9	13.5 U	8.30 F	21.80 U

4. The accounting profession recommends full allocation which will only be correct if charges are made on a rotational basis.
5. The concept of devolved budgets requires the direct matching of all costs and revenues.
6. Arbitrary allocation of central support services effectively results in subsidies by some departments to others. Some services departments thus gain apparently 'free' services which distorts priorities.

These problems have led to the development of the concept of service level agreements where a contract is negotiated between the central department and the service department. This contract specifies the nature of the charges to be made for services in considerable detail and thus makes both sides fully aware of the implications of undertaking any activity. Any variations in the contract have to be agreed. The contract price effectively makes the central department a 'profit' centre with any non-approved overspendings on the contract 'losses'. This arrangement gives the service department better control over one of its major fixed overheads both in terms of cost and the quality of service it can demand for the price that it is paying.

5.12 Control of capital programmes

The appraisal of capital schemes is discussed in subsequent chapters, but due to the relationship with the revenue account the control of capital expenditure is best dealt with here. Delayed completion in a capital scheme should result in savings on the revenue budget as provision for a scheme to come on-stream should have been made in the revenue budgeting process. The opportunity for a virement would therefore exist. If the reverse situation applies then consideration will need to be made as to whether or not the scheme should go ahead early. Such a decision will depend on whether sufficient underspendings already exist to absorb the running costs (i.e. the revenue consequences) of the capital scheme or if a supplementary estimate is to be provided. The change in the phasing of the capital programme as a result of the early or delayed completion of a capital scheme can have 'knock-on' effects on the revenue profile. Cost over-runs on capital schemes will also have revenue effects as other schemes, with planned revenue consequences, are deleted from the capital programme to stay within the overall capital budget. Reserve schemes may also be introduced to prevent any underspending. Thus a complex web of interrelationships exist between the capital and revenue budgets. These interrelationships do not always result in increased revenue costs as some capital schemes such as energy conservation will result in reduced spending.

Slippage in capital programmes is always a major problem for public sector organizations so tight control needs to be kept of those factors which can cause delay. Detailed cash estimates with regular monitoring will indicate the build-up of slippage and any possible implications of rising inflation. Actual techniques of monitoring progress normally centre around network analysis with the critical path(s) identified. Any delay in critical activities will affect the overall completion time of the project. The network will also be used to provide an analysis of future cash flows as activities are either completed early or delayed.

While this chapter has concentrated on the single-period revenue statement and its control, the existence of capital programmes stresses the importance of the need for a long-term revenue plan of three to five years, despite the difficulties to be faced and the assumptions needed to prepare it. This plan would range more widely than just the implications of the capital programme of the particular public sector organization, to include anticipated trends in revenue income and revenue costs. Control of the corporate revenue and capital programmes lies with senior management.

5.13 Human aspects of budgetary control

It is not possible to leave any discussion on budgets without considering the behavioural implications of accounting information. It can be argued that while budgets are about control they should also be about motivating people. Motivation can be defined as 'the need to achieve some selected goal and the resulting drive that influences action towards that goal' (Horngren, 1987). Argyris (1953) identified the budget as creating four areas for potential human conflict. These are now discussed in a public sector context.

The pressure device

The budget can be seen by managers and subordinates as a pressure device in an attempt to get individuals to work harder and more efficiently. Many public sector organizations are being forced to constrain budgets due to financial pressures. This creates additional pressure on staff as demand for the service may not be correspondingly reduced or it could even possibly increase. Pressure is imposed by management to achieve, say, higher caseload levels per member of staff, resulting possibly in success from management's point of view but at the expense of increased resentment by staff and resistance to any further change.

Poor relationship with the finance department

The finance section is seen as the 'budget policeman', finding success in reporting poor performance. This effect is probably compounded in local government by the Treasurer having the section 151 responsibility for internal audit under the Local Government Act 1972. Success for the finance department in an adverse budget or audit report is the failure of the service manager. This can lead to loss of interest in budget reports and poor internal relationships. This effect may be enhanced where the service concerned is the subject of competitive tendering and jobs are at risk while the finance department has not been subject to the rigours of competition.

Avoiding of responsibility

Poor managers are able to blame the budget for failure to achieve, especially if participation was absent in the budget setting process, by stating that the budget was totally unrealistic. Subordinates, resentful of the managerial style adopted, also blame the budget for creating undue managerial pressure.

Departmentalism

The budget sets targets which in the public sector largely relate to the requirement for managers to spend only within strictly defined cash limits. Departments spend to the cash-limited figure for fear of losing funds next year. The needs of the department are thus put before the needs of the organization as a whole.

The way in which performance is reported would also appear to have an effect on aspiration levels and the cohesiveness of individuals and groups. This can be either positive or negative. Similarly, the setting of standards for monitoring may have the same effect. It is suggested that one means of helping to create identification with the budget process is by participation both in the initial budget-setting process and in subsequent revisions. This participation should, however, be real participation to be effective. Equally important is the receipt of adequate feedback as no one can maintain adequate motivation if they are kept in the dark on the results of their efforts.

Much of the work done on the human aspects of budgeting relates to the private sector but it is claimed that one aspect of the zero-based budgeting process (discussed in the previous chapter) is that managers feel more closely involved in the decision-making process. Clearly, there is more work to be done but the increasing demand by managers for financial management information means that any barriers which exist must be broken down if that information is to be used effectively. This implies an educational role for the accountant.

5.14 Control through performance

This chapter has emphasised the control of performance via financial measures but increasingly the setting of non-financial performance indicators and targets is influencing control systems in the public sector.

In central government, for example, these targets are expressed through public service agreements (PSAs) and the principles are set out in Cm 4181, 'Public Services for the Future: Modernisation, Reform, Accountability'. These PSAs set targets via aims and objectives for the improvement in a range of key service indicators over time. They are an attempt to measure what the government (and the public) receives in return for its investment in public services and are thus an attempt to focus on outcomes for resources consumed. They are aimed at adding a different dimension to public accountability by representing a planned outcome from a particular course (or courses) of action and, as such, need to be controlled, measured and reported on. The government will need to establish systems that enable reports to be prepared which clearly identify the target to be achieved by putting appropriate and measurable performance indicators in place for each service. These reports will then need to give timely information clearly where performance is being achieved or falling short. Only then will managers be able to act in an appropriate manner to redirect resources. It will be noted that the principles for reporting on non-financial information are the same as those for financial information. It could also be argued that the behavioural implications of setting targets in this area again significantly overlap with the principles of financial targets given the potential motivational implications. That is, timely, relevant and accurate information with clear divisions of responsibility consistently reported. This represents a considerable challenge to any organization, let alone one operating in the public sector.

An extract from the performance targets for the Department of Social Security following the July 2000 spending review is set out in Exhibit 5.2 to illustrate for readers the type of targets being set in PSAs. It will be noted that a number of targets are interrelated with other departments of government stressing the principle of joined-up government. This inevitably complicates the ability to achieve laid-down goals and time will tell how successful this strategy will be.

Key points of chapter

1. The importance of monitoring performance of the budget against the physical achievements of the budget was stressed.
2. The concepts of flexible budgeting, standard costing and variance analysis were introduced.
3. Emphasis was placed on the complex relationship between capital and revenue budgets and the need for a long-term revenue budget was stated.
4. The importance of budgets as a motivating factor was discussed.
5. The linking of performance criteria with the allocation of financial resources represents a major new challenge to public sector managers.

5.15 Summary

This chapter has examined the process of control in the annual budget cycle but has also stressed the need for long-term planning and control of the long-term revenue and capital projections. Examination was made of the traditional method of budgetary control where expenditure is simply compared with estimate and the conclusion reached that this was inadequate and that some measure of workload needs to be built into the budget-setting exercise. These measures should be related to the objectives of the budget and then be monitored as out-turn figures become available. It was stated that monitoring reports should be timely, accurate and relevant to the needs of the managers, with the computer system being used to highlight exceptions rather than produce bulky financial data beyond the cognitive ability of the individual manager to handle. Consideration was given to the part that standard costing could play, particularly in the competition services and an illustration was given of the technique together with explanations of variances. Examination was also made of the relationship between the capital programme and the revenue budget. Finally, human aspects of budgetary control were considered.

Overall, it was felt that the budgetary control process and the demands that it places on financial management skills represent a major challenge of change for public sector managers, particularly the need to interpret and act on information. It was also pointed out that the setting of performance challenges such as public service agreements would add considerably to these challenges.

Exhibit 5.1   Hackney Borough Council

An example of what can go wrong if adequate financial and managerial controls are not properly exercised is illustrated in the case of Hackney Borough Council. On 17 October 2000 the Borough Treasurer issued a report under section 114 of the Local Government and Finance Act 1988 identifying a possible budget shortfall of up to £15m by the end of the financial year 1999/2000. The report questioned the financial viability of the authority and is suggestive of circumstances where the authority is bankrupt. The Treasurer, however, indicated in his report that due to a lack of adequate financial controls this prediction could not be taken as reliable and the eventual shortfall might reach £40m. The Chief Executive in his response drew up a financial recovery plan and at the same time accused some managers of ignoring or subverting attempts to control expenditure. He also pointed to expenditure being omitted from projections, not being known about or misrepresented in documentation presented to members. The recovery plan included a need to make savings of £4.5m in the current financial year and £18m in the following. It was estimated that 250 jobs would be lost and the authority placed an embargo on temporary and agency workers other than in key areas such as education. The Chief Executive also wanted to change the terms and conditions of the staff with inevitable union reaction that the authority was a financial shambles and that the workers were paying the price for this financial ineptitude. Other measures included contracting out waste management services and bringing the housing benefits service in-house. The Chief Executive was also attempting to convince the District Auditor that by cutting expenditure and raiding reserves the authority could balance the budget by March 2000.

The package of cuts suggested by the Chief Executive was approved by members, although it is reported that police in riot gear were required to control crowds outside the town hall during the meeting. Officials were hoping that, subject to the District Auditor accepting the financial recovery plan as realistic, the Department of the Environment, Transport and the Regions would allow them to borrow money against future capital receipts to fund specific projects. The Audit Commission issued a report claiming that essential services were failing residents with over 17 000 housing benefit applications waiting to be processed and only 50% of council tax collected. The Audit Commission was also demanding a root and branch review of management and financial systems and would continue to monitor the authority closely.

To consider the effect on services of these financial and management problems a brief examination is made of events in the education service of the borough. In July 1998 the School Standards and Framework Act was passed which allowed central government extensive powers where local education authorities were found to be failing. Various education inspections (carried out by Ofsted) were critical of the management of schools by the authority. The School Standards Minister announced that while there had been improvements in Hackney there were areas of concern particularly in the council's management and financial control. In March 1999 Hackney was told that it would become the first education authority to have some of its powers taken away by central government after an Ofsted reinspection found insufficient improvements in the services it provided to its schools.

(*Sources:* McHugh, 2000, pp.6, 14. BBC Online Education 'Hackney's troubled past' and 'Hackney still failing to support its schools', 19 March 1999 and 21 July 1998)

Exhibit 5.2   Public service agreements – Department of Social Security

Aim
The Department of Social Security will actively contribute to the government's overall aims of:
• tackling poverty;
• promoting opportunity;
• modernising government.

Objectives and performance targets
Objective I: Ensuring the best start for all children and ending child poverty in 20 years.

1. Make substantial progress towards eradicating child poverty by reducing the number of children in poverty by at least a quarter by 2004. Joint target with HM Treasury.
2. Introduce the reformed Child Support scheme for new cases by April 2002 so that, by April 2003, for such cases:
   • the accuracy rate for assessments and reviews is not less than 90%;
   • payment arrangements will have been established on average within six weeks;
   • the level of compliance will be at least 75%.

Objective II: Promoting work as the best form of welfare for people of working age, while protecting the position of those in greatest need.

3. Increase employment over the economic cycle. Target contributes to Welfare to Work PSA.
4 Reduce the number of children in households with no one in work over the three years to 2004. Target contributes to Welfare to Work PSA.

5. Over the three years to 2004 increase the employment rates of disadvantaged areas and groups, taking account of the economic cycle – people with disabilities, lone parents, ethnic minorities and the over-50s, the 30 local authority districts with the poorest initial labour market position – and reduce the difference between their employment rates and the overall rate. Target contributes to Welfare to Work PSA.

Objective III: Combating poverty and promoting security and independence in retirement for today's and tomorrow's pensioners.

6. Reform second-tier pension provision, working with pension providers and employers, so that by 2004:
   - stakeholder pensions have given more people access to good value, funded second pensions;
   - two million carers and two million disabled people with broken work records have, for the first time, started to build up a second pension;
   - 14 million low and moderate earners have started to build up a better second pension than would be possible under SERPS.

7. Introduce an improved, integrated modern service for delivering benefits and information to pensioners. This service will by 2004:
   - reduce the average cost of processing retirement pension claims and maintaining the caseload by 20%;
   - reduce the average cost of processing minimum income guarantee (MIG) claims and maintaining the caseload by 15%;
   - ensure that 90% of MIG claims are processed within 13 days once evidence requirements are met;
   - reduce by 20% the amount of MIG that is incorrectly paid.
   (Target also contributes to Objective IV.)

Objective IV: Modernizing welfare delivery so as to improve the accessibility and accuracy of services.

8. Make significant progress towards modernizing welfare delivery so that:
   - by 2004, 85% of customers have their benefits paid into their bank account;
   - by 2004, 60% of the computer systems which support the delivery of pensions and income support have been replaced;
   - by 2004, to have made available an electronic claims facility, for Income Support, Jobseeker's Allowance and Incapacity Benefit;
   - from 2001, to commence the rollout of new IT equipment to all staff dealing with customers so as to improve the services provided.

9. Reduce by 50% losses from fraud and error in Income Support and Jobseeker's Allowance by 2006, with a 25% reduction by 2004.

Value for money

10. Increase the efficiency of social security administration through:
    - improving the performance of the Child Support Agency in line with target 2;
    - improving the efficiency of services to pensioners in line with target 7;
    - improving the efficiency of services to working age claimants in line with target 8 and through the new working age agency;
    - reducing error and fraud in line with target 9.

(*Source*: HM Government, 2000c)

Questions

5.1 As a newly appointed management accountant at the Rossborough Health District you have been given the job of setting up and implementing a budgetary control/management accounting service for the Catering Department in the District's largest hospital. No system exists at present though the financial accounts record all expenditure and income subjectively for the hospital. The catering manager has been asking for some financial management information to be provided for him. Your terms of reference give you three months to set up the system and to put it into operation.

The following data are available to you:

(1) Name of hospital – Getuwell General Hospital.
(2) Number of available beds – 700.
(3) Average bed occupancy – 90%.
(4) Number of catering staff employed – 100 (including management, clerical, cooks, kitchen and dining room staff).
(5) A bonus scheme was introduced for catering staff three years ago.
(6) Total staff employed in the hospital – 3500 of which 1000 live on the site in accommodation that provides no facilities for self-catering.
(7) Number of staff meals provided – it is estimated that the numbers have stayed constant over the past two years. There is a requirement to provide three main meals a day for staff. Meal prices are altered periodically at the discretion of the catering manager in line with inflation.
(8) All meals (both for patients and staff) are provided from one central kitchen in the hospital and raw materials (food) are drawn in bulk weekly from the central store.
(9) The DHS has laid down the following cost limits:
    (a) The weekly allowable food cost per patient is £8.50.
    (b) Staff meal prices should be set so as to recover the cost of the food used plus 60%.

Outline the steps you would take to set up the system, indicating the type of information you would provide in order to assist the catering manager to control his expenditure.

5.2 'In the present economic climate, traditional negative financial control – primarily ensuring budgets are not overspent – is of great importance, but this should not devalue the need for developing positive financial control – the examination, review and re-direction of limited resources' (*Public Finance and Accountancy*).

In the light of this quotation critically examine the arguments for, and possible methods of, achieving flexibility in budgetary procedures and control.

5.3 Blaenwent BC own and runs a leisure centre and is currently monitoring the likely expenditure on the complex to 31/3/X9. On the basis of expenditure to the end of November 19X8 the following position has been revealed:

Projected income and expenditure to 31/3/X9:

	Pool £	Hall £	Squash £	Catering £	Total £
Income:					
Charges	75 600	14 160	12 000	22 200	123 960
Expenditure:					
Employees:					
General	25 200	3 465	3 465	5 040	37 170
Man./admin.	8 000	5 000	2 000	1 200	16 200
Cleaners	1 600	1 000	400	240	3 240
Premises:					
SP supplies	13 800				13 800
Telephone	200	200	200	200	800
Printing	250	250	250		750
Sports mats		1 125	1 125		2 250
Catering				4 500	4 500
Debt charges	60 000	44 000	36 000	10 000	150 000
	109 050	55 040	43 440	21 180	228 710
Net expenditure	(33 450)	(40 880)	(31 440)	1 020	(104 750)

The Authority has set the following targets for 19X8/X9:

	£
Swimming pool	(33 000)
Sports hall	(33 650)
Squash courts	(30 000)
Catering (surplus)	3 000
	£93 650

Under the Welsh Office Circular *Competition in the Management of Local Authority Sport and Leisure Facilities* the target set for the management of sport and leisure facilities is that expenditure should at least equal income. The authority having in mind this target for the future have agreed that the leisure centre be set this as a target for future years.

Required

Examine these figures and with the target that has been set for 19X8/X9 consider what course of action can be taken and what further information is needed (if any).

What effect does the longer term goal have on your strategy?

5.4 It has been agreed by Curem Health Authority that, overall, the price of meals sold to staff and at functions should be based on a 50% mark-up on the cost of provisions.

The following information refers to the out-turn for the year to 31 March 19X1 of two hospitals within the area, Hospital A, a large multi-specialist unit and Hospital B, a small neighbouring convalescent unit.

As Management Accountant, you are required to:

(a) calculate whether the required target is being achieved at each hospital;

(b) comment briefly on any reason which you consider might affect the results.

		Hospital A	*Hospital B*
		£	£
(i)	The following figures are extracted from the accounts for the year:		
	Provisions purchased (zero rated)	223 347	7 110
	Provisions purchased (inc. VAT at standard rate)	65 626	2 133
	Income from meals served	147 080	18 407
	Hospitality and other income	2 445	600

In addition the following points require to be taken into account:

(ii)	Stock of provisions as at 1/4/X0	34 205	1 315
	Stock of provisions as at 31/3/X1	29 874	734
(iii)	Outstanding invoices not yet paid (all zero rated)	4 915	308
(iv)	Meals vouchers sold during the year	520	370
(v)	Hospital A provides meals for a local Meals on Wheels Service for which no bill has yet been charged	10 300	–
(vi)	There is outstanding income for hospitality provided	490	–
(vii)	Assume that all income figures are inclusive of VAT at the standard rate, except Meals on Wheels which is zero rated		
(viii)	At Hospital A, it is not possible to separately identify the cost of provisions for patients. For the purpose of this calculation this is assumed to be £8.15 per patient per week. In 19X0/X1 there were 21 340 such patient weeks.		

5.5 The following details have been extracted from the records of the Property Services Agency for the nine months ended 31 December 19–9. The information relates to the cleaning of three offices operated by the Agency. Details of the offices are as follows:

Office A is a medium-sized office complex built in the 1960s with a variety of administrative functions. The building was modified in the 1970s to operate on an open-plan basis within each administrative function.

Office B is a large office complex in the South East which houses the central functions of a main government ministry and has a major conference centre attached.

Office C is a small office based in a provincial town.

	Office A	Office B	Office C
	£	£	£
Cleaning materials	2 900	14 440	3 590
Equipment	890	1 780	453
Cleaning staff pay	9 500	48 300	14 000
NI, etc.	950	490	1 400
travel	30	20	30
bonus	2 000	5 000	3 600
Contract services:			
Window cleaning	950	3 500	850
Supervisor (cont.)	4 000	4 000	4 000
Misc.	20	65	15
	21 240	77 595	27 938
Floor area	6 000 sq. m.	16 000 sq. m.	3 000 sq. m.
Number of cleaners	3	18	4

Notes:
(a) The supervisor is responsible for the three offices and is paid an annual salary of £16 000.
(b) Stocks of cleaning materials at the following dates were:

	31/3/X9	12/12/X9
	£	£
A	230	500
B	900	3 000
C	90	80

(c) Wages owed to cleaning staff at Office C were £200 at 31 December 19X9.
(d) The budgeted cleaning costs for the year are £180 000.
(e) The window cleaning contract for the year is for £5800.

Required

Prepare a report for the director of cleaning services on the comparative costs of the service to 31 December 19X9 and the projected outcome to 31 March 19X0.

5.6 Derwent District Council owns and runs a leisure centre and is currently monitoring the likely expenditure on the complex for the year to 31 March 19X9.

The following information relates to the eight-month period 1 April 19X8 to 30 November 19X8:

Employees	£
Swimming pool staff	16 000
Sports hall and squash courts	4 400
Catering staff	3 200
Cleaning staff (private contractors)	2 160
Manager and administration staff	10 800

Premises
Running costs:

Swimming pool supplies	9 200
Telephone (one quarterly account paid)	200
Printing tickets and stationery	500
Sports materials	1 500
Catering supplies	3 000

Income:

Squash courts	8 000
Sports hall lettings	9 440
Catering	14 800
Swimming pool	50 400
Debt charges (estimated annual charge)	150 000

Notes:

(a) Assume income expenditure fall evenly throughout the year unless otherwise stated.

(b) Expenditure is allocated to facilities as follows:

In proportion to floor area	Cleaning staff
	Manager and administrative staff
	Premises
In proportion to capital costs	Debt charges
Equally to all facilities	Telephone
Equally to all facilities (except catering)	Tickets/stationery
Equally to sports hall and squash courts	Sports materials and equipment
	Sports hall and squash court staff

(c) All employees except cleaners and the manager and administrative staff will receive a pay award in December backdated to 1 October. This will increase by 10% the cost of employees entitled to the award.

(d) Floor areas are:

Swimming pool	800 square metres
Sports hall	500 square metres
Squash courts	200 square metres
Catering area	120 square metres

(e) Capital costs are:

	£
Swimming pool	300 000
Sports hall	220 000
Squash courts	180 000
Catering area	50 000

(f) Anticipated deficits for the year are:

	£
Swimming pool	(33 000)
Sports hall	(33 650)
Squash courts	(30 000)
Catering (surplus)	1 000
	£95 650

Required

Prepare a statement showing the probable out-turn for 19X8/X9 together with a brief report on the results obtained.

5.7 The Northern District Health Authority operates a pharmacy that produces drugs which are sold to other districts within the region. The standard direct mix for a quantity of 1000 litres of the drug 'Keep Calm' is as follows:

			Standard price per litre
Chemical	A	500 litres	£0.50
	B	250 litres	£1.00
	C	300 litres	£0.75

The drug passes through three sections of the pharmacy and the following is the standard labour cost of 1000 litres of 'Keep Calm':

Section	X	1.2 man hours @ £2.00 per hour
	Y	4 man hours @ £1.50 per hour
	Z	2 man hours @ £1.30 per hour

In the month of October 19X8, 20 200 litres of 'Keep Calm' were produced and the following costs were incurred:

Section	X	128 hours at a total cost of £259
	Y	360 hours at a total cost of £576
	Z	220 hours at a total cost of £264

	Materials consumed during October 19–8	Actual price per litre
A	11 800 litres	£0.45
B	4 900 litres	£1.10
C	6 100 litres	£0.70

As the management accountant responsible for the pharmacy **you are required to**:

(a) Prepare a statement that analyzes the appropriate variances for the month.

(13 marks)

(b) Briefly outline possible reasons for the variances you have calculated in (a) above.

(3 marks)

(c) Outline the steps that are involved in calculating a standard cost and what the role of a management accountant is in this process. (4 marks)

(Total 20 marks)

5.8 The following memorandum has been received from the Director of Social Services:

'I have been notified by each of the six Divisional Offices that their quarterly expenditure tabulations appear to indicate overspendings on the home help employees (Code 483/711). The total of their expenditure on head at month 6 is £600 000; the annual budget is £1 000 000, presumably their expenditure should be only £500 000. Projected to the year end this gives an overspend of £200 000.

'(I say "appear to indicate" because in fact the manual records of number of hours' service provided, which is the record we use for determining how many home helps to employ, is, in the case of 3 Divisions, below the budgeted figure.)

'We plan growth of £200 000 in our draft expenditure plans for next year, so this should cause no problems then. In the current year, fortunately, present expenditure trends indicate that we are likely to underspend by an equivalent amount on the Elderly Persons Homes budget, and I suggest that we finance the home help overspend by virement from this head.

'I thought I should bring this to your attention in view of your responsibility for budgetary control.'

As principal accountant you examine the monthly expenditure tabulations in your department and note that expenditure to month 3 was £200 000, which you see from past years' tabulations was normal at this stage, but that there has been a sharp rise since.

Your Chief Financial Officer asks you:

(a) To outline the points you would make in reply to the memorandum.

(b) As part of imminent reviews of both the authority's computerized accounting system and its budgetary policies:

(i) to outline the main requirements for computerized budgetary control information in respect of home help expenditure;

(ii) to list the main issues to be considered in a review of the authority's policy on virement.

5.9 Managers are concerned to motivate staff yet budgets are concerned with controlling staff. How would you reconcile this conflict?

5.10 Discuss the extent to which the behavioural impact of financial information needs to be considered by those involved in the budgeting process in the public sector.

6 The management of working capital

Key learning objectives

After reading this chapter you should be able to:

1. Understand the importance of the management of working capital to the public sector.
2. Discuss the individual elements of working capital and the importance of each element in the overall working capital equation.
3. Understand the techniques available to manage working capital.

All businesses should be concerned to maximize the efficiency with which they manage both current assets and current liabilities. This is particularly important in the public sector because of the size of the organizations and the consequent value of these figures. To illustrate this point extracts from the published consolidated balance sheets of two local authorities showing the position with regard to current assets and current liabilities for the year ended the 31/3/00 are reproduced in Table 6.1.

Clearly these are large figures which require attention if they are to be managed effectively. In addition, Cardiff City Council acts as the pension fund-managing body for both its own employees and those of the Vale of Glamorgan Borough Council. At 31 March 2000 the balance on this fund stood at a market value of £632 490 000 compared with £545 336 000 at the previous year end. It should be remembered that, in the case of local authorities, a funded scheme is operated for pension liabilities and an appropriate deduction is made from the salaries and wages of employees in addition to a contribution by the employing authority. As these contribution are made to ensure the fund can meet its future liabilities, it is obviously important that the fund is actively managed. Good management has the potential to reduce the costs to the organization as any deficit has to be made up. In fact the Cardiff pension fund had assets which at its last actuarial valuation in 1998 only represent 82% of accrued liabilities allowing for future pay increases. It is normal for the pension funds of local authorities to be managed externally and in the case of Cardiff the fund managers are Jupiter Asset Management. Finally, in the case of Cardiff, it had trust funds at 31 March 2000 valued at £8 669 041 and, again, these require good financial management if funds are to maximize returns.

Table 6.1   Extracts from consolidated balance sheets as at 31 March 2000

	Cardiff City Council					Monmouthshire County Council		
		1998/1999		1999/2000		1998/1999		1999/2000
	£000	£000	£000	£000	£000	£000	£000	£000
Current assets								
Stock	1 419		1 389			1 193	473	
Debtors	58 946		49 887			11 862	11 139	
Temporary investments	24 000		18 001			17 239	13 382	
Cash in hands of officials	463		603					
		84 828		69 880		30 294		24 994
Current liabilities								
Creditors	54 007		47 722			16 580	12 252	
Loans due within one year	17 097		25 288				500	
Cash overdrawn	16 921		16 006			2 296	3 192	
		88 025		89 016		18 876		15 944
Working capital 31 March 2000		–3 197		–19 136		11 418		9 050

(Sources: Cardiff City Council, 2000. Monmouthshire County Council, 2000.)

The need to manage working capital is not confined to local authorities. An additional examination of the accounts of the Queen Victoria NHS Trust revealed income of £18 640 000, current assets of £1 764 000 and current liabilities of £1 414 000 at 31 March 1998. The cash flow statement shows that there was an overall increase in cash in the year of £736 000 before financing charges of £289 000. To turn to the Post Office turnover in 1999/2000 was £7522m (£7010m 1998/99) with current assets of £3979m (£4432m) and current liabilities of £2256 (£2724m) at the balance sheet date.

Considerable attention in the public sector tends to be given to the management of capital expenditure but the thrust of this chapter is to argue that greater attention needs to be given to the management of working capital. This approach is one which includes concentrating on those resources which management outside the finance function come into contact with most often and one which possibly may get overlooked in the financial planning process. The benefits of this approach are that proper management of these resources will generate additional revenue or reduce costs so that more funds will be available for services which are often under pressure. It may also make reduced bills possible for the taxpayer by the more efficient use of resources. It must also be pointed out that an overall policy on working capital management needs to be developed as, clearly, all items within the definition of working capital impact on each other.

6.1 Treasury management

The function of Treasury management received considerable publicity following the collapse of the Bank of Credit and Commerce International (BCCI) and its closure on 5 July 1990. The Western Isle Council held over £20m with the bank at the date of collapse with a number of other local authorities also losing money. Other banks used by public sector bodies have also created problems for those organizations – Chancery Bank and Edington Bank among others. In addition the hearings and report of the Treasury and Civil Service Committee into the collapse of BCCI were highly critical of the role of local authority finance officers in investment management (Treasury and Civil Service Committee, 1992).

In the light of this, and before examining in detail the mechanics of the control of the components of working capital, a number of principles for the investment of cash balances are first examined. Lenders should:

1. Determine investment strategy in conjunction and parallel with their borrowing strategy. Cash balances should be invested where they achieve the best return commensurate with security.
2. Delegate legal authority to the investment manager to invest funds on behalf of the organization. This authority should clearly set out the duties and responsibilities of the investing officer acting under delegated powers.
3. Create separate responsibilities for deciding investment strategy, and supervising and controlling the day-to-day management of investments.
4. Regularly review the risks associated with particular investments and the range of investment opportunities. Risks should be spread by diversifying the portfolio.
5. Hold a list of authorized investments and regularly update it. This is particularly important with regard to the credit risks associated with all investments. Recourse should be made to credit rating agencies as appropriate although it must be remembered that at all times responsibility lies with the investor and not the agency.
6. Determine the maximum amount of cash (or percentage of available resources) that can be held in any particular investment and do not exceed any limits set.
7. Fully document all procedures and transactions.
8. Regularly report on performance at the appropriate level within the organization.

The Bank of England publishes the London Code by which the conduct of banks, building societies and other financial institutions is governed. This code takes account of the recommendations made by the Treasury and Civil Service Committee and stresses that principals (the investors) have the responsibility to assess the creditworthiness of the counter-party whether dealing directly or via an agent when investing funds. It is also the decision of the principal as to what reliance is placed on statements made by brokers and other parties. The role of the brokers is to act as arrangers. The code even recommends that participants in the wholesale money market tape conversations which can be then used to resolve trading disputes.

6.2 Cash management

The cash management function will be undertaken in the finance department and is clearly concerned with forecasting the demands by the organization for such facilities as a bank overdraft with the objective of minimizing charges. The finance department will also attempt to maximize returns on any balances in hand. Where it is necessary to borrow to finance a capital programme then a strategy has to be devised which achieves this objective at minimum cost. In this context it is essential to at least develop an annual cash flow forecast, within the overall budget process, which can be continually rolled forward. It should, however, not be forgotten that where competitive units exist within the overall framework of an organization individual cash profiles should be prepared for them. This is because they will normally bear a charge for any overdraft facility they may require. Equally where they are in cash surplus they should receive an interest credit as a contribution to profit. It is also essential that such a cash flow forecast should take place within an overall business plan to enable the competition unit to manage its total resources to maximum effect in its attempts to achieve its profit targets.

Table 6.2 illustrates a cash flow forecast for 12 months for Cashshire County Council. The detail of this model may at first sight appear only to apply to those public sector bodies which have powers to raise overdrafts or make investments, for example local authorities and the public corporations. All organizations, however, need to plan their cash flow and with the increased emphasis being placed on business planning in the public sector greater emphasis is given to this aspect of working capital management.

It can be seen that a detailed breakdown of expenditure has been attempted but clearly in practice more information will be needed. This will include the preparation of separate cash flow projections for revenue and capital expenditure and income. These overall plans will represent the framework in which monthly, weekly and daily forecasting should take place.

Using Table 6.2 the following points may be made:

1. *Employee costs.* Employee costs will be available from the normal budget processes and will normally be incurred evenly over the year, although it is obviously possible to build in seasonal variations. In addition there will be a need to consider the impact of pay awards at the appropriate award date, although delays in settlement will affect day-to-day management and will be noted for the appropriate action.
2. *Premises expenses.* Premises costs such as those for repair and maintenance can be based either on a planned maintenance programme or, if these costs are consistent from year to year, on past performance. Many public sector organizations have agreements with the energy suppliers on payment and clearly the terms of these agreements can be built into the forward plan. Rates payments again should be known in advance.
3. *Agency payments.* Agency payments are the payments that Cashshire makes to agents such as district councils for services carried out on its behalf. These payments would normally be set out in the terms of the agency agreement.
4. *Precept dates.* Precept dates for those authorities precepting on the County Council would be known in advance and from past experience.
5. *Grants.* Grants from central government and precept income from district councils would be known before the year began and can thus be fed into the plan with a considerable degree of confidence.
6. *Capital cash flows.* Capital cash flows can be forecast from the capital programme with any major changes – for example, as a result of action by the capital contracts auditor – which affect payment modifying the forecast as it occurs. The forecast would obviously only include payments to outside contractors as many in-house direct service organizations are paid by internal transfer.

A detailed analysis needs to be made of all the items in the forecast to establish as far as possible any trends. Clearly, however, there will be some items where it will be necessary to make assumptions if no set pattern can be identified. The key point is that the 12 months rolling forecast provides the framework for the organization to manage its cash resources effectively. Proper monitoring of actual receipts and payments is essential to maintain the detailed control necessary for the ongoing monthly, weekly and daily forecasting on which management decisions will be made.

Table 6.2 Cashshire County Council cash flow forecast

	Apr. £000	May £000	Jun. £000	Jul. £000	Aug. £000	Sep. £000	Oct. £000	Nov. £000	Dec. £000	Jan. £000	Feb. £000	Mar. £000	Total £000
Expenditure:													
Employees:													
Teachers	15 124	15 124	15 124	15 124	15 124	15 124	15 124	15 124	15 124	15 124	15 124	15 124	181 488
APT & C	4 600	4 600	4 600	4 600	4 600	4 600	4 600	4 600	4 600	4 600	4 600	4 600	55 200
Manual workers	3 800	3 800	3 800	3 800	3 800	3 800	3 800	3 800	3 800	3 800	3 800	3 800	45 600
Premises:													
Repairs and maintenance	1 200	1 200	1 200	1 200	1 200	1 200	1 200	1 200	1 200	1 200	1 200	1 200	14 400
Fuel and light	500	490	300	300	300	475	475	550	750	800	800	800	6 540
Rent and rates	90	90	90	90	90	90	90	90	90	90	90	90	1 080
Miscellaneous	45	45	45	45	45	45	45	45	45	45	45	45	540
Transport	980	980	980	980	980	980	1 090	1 090	1 090	1 090	1 090	1 090	12 420
Supplies and services	4 000	4 000	4 000	4 000	4 000	4 000	4 000	4 000	4 000	4 000	4 000	4 000	48 000
Agency services	1 200	450	650	1 200	450	650	1 200	450	650	1 200	450	650	9 200
Precepts	1 200	1 200	1 850	1 200	1 200	1 850	1 200	1 200	1 850	1 200	1 200	1 850	17 000
Pay awards	850	850	850	1 210	1 210	1 410	1 410	1 410	1 410	1 410	1 410	1 410	14 840
Net capital payments	2 540	–510	–80	2 300	500	–100	1 950	2 000	2 250	3 700	4 100	14 950	33 600
Total expenditure	36 129	32 319	33 409	36 049	33 499	34 124	36 184	35 559	36 859	38 259	37 909	49 609	439 908
Income:													
Sales and services	7 500	7 690	5 000	8 300	3 500	3 500	3 500	7 500	9 000	9 000	8 500	7 300	80 290
Revenue support grant	22 000	22 000	22 000	22 000	22 000	22 000	22 000	22 000	22 000	22 000	22 000	22 000	264 000
Precepts	0	9 750	9 750	9 750	9 750	9 750	0	9 750	9 750	9 750	9 750	9 750	97 500
Total income	29 500	39 440	36 750	40 050	35 250	35 250	25 500	39 250	40 750	40 750	40 250	39 050	441 790
Total net expenditure	–6 629	7 121	3 341	4 001	1 751	1 126	–10 684	3 691	3 891	2 491	2 341	–10 559	1 882
Balance b/f	10 500	3 871	10 992	14 333	18 334	20 085	21 211	10 527	14 218	18 109	20 600	22 941	10 500
Balance c/f	3 871	10 992	14 333	18 334	20 085	21 211	10 527	14 218	18 109	20 600	22 941	12 382	12 382

Daily cash forecasting

It has just been stated that the yearly forecast provides the framework within which monthly, weekly and daily forecasting takes place. A brief examination now follows of a possible procedure for daily cash forecasting for a typical public sector organization:

1. obtain actual balance for previous day from the bank;
2. estimate cheques clearing and credits due for the day;
3. check direct debits;
4. contact cashier for any income still held;
5. calculate investments or borrowings to be repaid including principal and interest and any loans and interest due;
6. calculate estimated balance at the end of the day deducting any likely uncleared income leaving the cleared balance available for investment or the borrowing needs identified.

On completion of this process a decision can be made on the size, and period, of any loan (borrowing) that it will be possible to make (to arrange). In taking the decision it will be necessary to consider the following factors:

1. future availability or otherwise of cash as indicated by the weekly, monthly and amended long-term cash flow forecasts;
2. interest rates on loans and borrowings;
3. predicted interest movements;
4. borrowing/lending instruments.

Clearly, it is necessary to consider making arrangements to ensure that there are always sufficient funds available to meet any future demands. It may be sensible, therefore, to establish call accounts into which cash may be deposited pending demands but which still earn interest. Interest rates and their relationship are obviously important and will be a major factor in deciding on the size and period of any investment. The rates for overnight money, call accounts and longer term investments will vary between the type of investment, the length of the investment and as relative rates change between investment opportunities. It is also important to consider predicted movements in interest rates as the organization would clearly not wish to tie itself into long-term lending if interest rates were anticipated to rise. An extra ¼% on a loan of £3 000 000 would produce additional interest of £3750 over six months.

6.3 Bank reconciliation

A complement to the process of cash flow planning is the need to reconcile the organization's cleared bank balance with the balance shown in the cash book. This process is known as bank reconciliation and acts both as a check against fraud and error and as a check on the assumptions regarding cheque clearance and income receipts built into the cash flow projection. The primary task is to perform an analysis of the cheques presented and the cheques outstanding with the balance at the bank and the cash book balance. In theory the exercise is relatively simple but the complexity of the exercise in practice will depend on the extent to which the organization has computerized the system.

6.4 Transfer of money

The traditional method for payment of sums due has been by cheque and cash. Today, however, numerous methods of payment exist and each method will have an impact on the cash flow management of the organization. These methods of payment are therefore now examined.

Standing orders

Under this system a debtor will instruct the bank to pay a set sum on a specific day at regular intervals to the organization to which the sum is due. Any alteration to the sum due and the date payable must receive the authorization of the debtor. Payment details are provided by the organization and this reduces the possibility of error.

Direct debits

As with standing orders the debtors will authorize the organization to remove an agreed sum from the debtor's account. The main advantage is that for changes in the amount due no further authorization is needed.

Credit transfers

The debtor gives full details of the bank account numbers and sort codes of each of any numbers of creditors to be paid and can thus effect transfers to those creditors' banks of the payments due by means of a single cheque if the relevant information is attached. This method might be used by a public sector organization to pay its monthly salaries bill.

Bankers automated clearing services (BACS)

The main purpose of this system is to process payments quickly by transferring payment details using electronic communication devices such as magnetic tapes and direct communication links.

Bank giro credits

The bank giro system operates by providing the debtor with the necessary payment details on a giro form. This is then taken to an appropriate payment point with the cash or cheque needed to pay the account. The amount is then credited to the organization's bank account. Examples of its use in the public sector include where there are regular weekly or monthly sums due, as for community charge payers and council house tenants, and for which pre-printed payment forms are provided.

In any organization it is likely that all these payment methods may be used. It will be essential therefore that the most appropriate method is used in relation to the sums collected. All methods have a cost of collection and this must be balanced against the advantages gained. Under a housing rents collection system, for example, it may be decided to employ rent collectors. This will have the direct costs of employment plus overheads but it might be considered that the rent collector maintains contact with the tenant and may be in the best position to identify and chase up arrears.

6.5 Alternative investment instruments

Having identified the cash that is available for investment it is necessary to consider the types of alternative investment instrument that are available. With public sector bodies it may not be possible to invest in the full range of instruments that are available to the private sector. In the case of local government, for example, regulations under the Local Government Act 1989 restrict the approved investments open to a local authority. Superannuation funds, operated by county councils, are also controlled separately, their operations being covered by the Local Government Superannuation Regulations 1986.

Government bonds

These are stocks issued by the government and are default free. This can be seen as a major attraction. The yield may, however, not be viewed as being particularly attractive unless an investment is made at the peak of an interest rate cycle, in which case there is the opportunity for the capital gain. With government stocks a rise in price effectively means a fall in the interest rate while the reverse applies when the price falls.

Local authority debt

This is similar to government bonds and can take a variety of forms. While some writers argue that it is not as secure as government debt it is secured on the council tax and, as such, the risk of default is low.

Certificates of deposit

These are certificates issued by banks and building societies for deposits received. They can be held long term but the period is decided by the investor. There is the additional advantage that they can be sold in the money market. The investor is therefore able to realize funds if unforeseen problems arise. In return for this advantage interest rates can be lower than available elsewhere. The advantage to the bank is that the deposit period is fixed and the funds deposited are not refundable until the term matures.

Call and notice money

Call money is money invested with no fixed date of repayment in contrast to notice money which, as the title suggests, requires due notice of withdrawal.

Eligible bank bills

Eligible bank bills are certificates for debt issued by private companies but which are guaranteed by an eligible accepting house (i.e. merchant bank). The process of accepting means that in exchange for a commission the merchant bank guarantees repayment on maturity. Eligible bank bills can be sold on the market.

Treasury bills

Treasury bills are pure discount instruments and are issued by the government and local authorities. They are a marketable and safe investment for the investing organization but the yield may be low due to their high creditworthiness.

In summary, a wide range of potential investment opportunities exist varying from overnight lending to Eurodollar deposits denominated in sterling or a foreign currency. The ability of a public sector organization to invest will depend on government controls, alternative interest rates, brokerage and commission charges and the amount of money available. Finally, targets should be set for returns on investments which should be closely monitored to measure success. (A more detailed analysis of the type of investments open to public sector organizations can be acquired from the Financial Information Service of the Chartered Institute of Public Finance and Accountancy, 3 Robert Street, London WC2N 6BH.)

6.6 Borrowing

Clearly, the opposite to the ability to lend is the need to borrow. This may take the form of a bank overdraft or a long-term loan to finance capital expenditure. The need to enter this area of cash management will again be indicated by the cash projection that the organization has prepared. In the case of some public sector organizations such as the Health Service there is no borrowing. Local authorities, however, are heavily involved in these transactions and in very specialized areas such as the interest rate swaps (see Chapter 7). The financing of capital expenditure is dealt with in Chapter 7 where such interest rate swaps are also examined.

6.7 The practice of investment management

In order to set this discussion in a practical context the investment practices of a number of public sector bodies are examined. The procedures adopted by each body clearly depend on the circumstances facing those bodies. The more funds there are available to invest the more sophisticated the procedures necessary to ensure the proper management of surplus funds.

The overall objective of the Severn Trent plc in investing surplus funds is 'to secure adequate operating funds at least cost, to invest surplus funds to best advantage (subject to an acceptable level of risk) and maintain a good financial reputation for the Company at all times'. Treasury policy is approved by the board of directors and there is a strong reporting chain with the treasury set up as a separate cost centre. Investments are diversified to minimize risk and a monetary limit is set for each investment. Investments are concentrated in areas in which the investment team has expertise and specialist investments such as foreign exchange are avoided. The counter-party list is regularly updated and contains, for example, the major UK clearing banks, Swiss banks and sterling commercial paper. Dealing procedures are clearly laid down in a detailed written manual. Appropriate targets are set and performance monitored (Cargill, 1991, pp.10–12).

Local authority investment is constrained, as mentioned earlier, by regulations issued under the Local Government Act 1989 (the Local Authorities (Capital Finance) (Approved Investments) Regulations 1990). At Kingston Local Borough Council the effect of these regulations was to bring cash management in-house and restrict investments. The Council was able in 1989/90 to borrow £23.5m from the Public Works Loan Board at fixed rates and given its large internal cash balances was able to lend this money at higher rates. The Authority has a small team under the Treasurer which meets regularly to plan investment strategy which is to maximize returns at minimum risk.

This is within the context of maintaining short-term liquidity and the Council's need to borrow funds. Performance is measured by comparing actual results against the returns which could have been earned from the seven-day rate of interest. The Authority uses brokers who are members of the Sterling Brokers Association as well as dealing directly with a limited number of borrowers (Knights, 1991, pp.12–14).

Smaller bodies may well adopt a more passive approach to investment management, investing only in the major clearing banks or a limited number of building societies. Others have appointed external advisers. Test Valley District Council has used the services of external companies offering a cash management service. The primary objective of this strategy was to provide secure longer term returns than could otherwise be achieved by investing internally. Investment was restricted to high quality longer dated securities in the narrow range of investments as defined under the Trustee (Investment) Act 1961. The composition of the portfolio was to be the subject of discussion but the movements of securities within a particular market was left to the external consultants. The treasurer comments that the authority has achieved a higher return than if the investment policy had been decided in-house, although it is recognized that ultimate responsibility for the creditworthiness of borrowers lies with the authority (Giddings, 1991, pp.14–15).

6.8 Management of debtors

Any public sector organization must be concerned with the proper control of its debtors. This applies not only to those services which are provided to clients on a voluntary basis and may be withdrawn if a bad payment record exists, but also to clients who are already in possession of a service such as council housing. As the Audit Commission points out: 'The prevention of arrears is by far the most effective strategy.' A significant problem which has been created under the community charge system for financing local government is the difficulty of collecting income from debtors. This creates extra pressure on cash flow and may result in a need to borrow resulting in extra interest charges on the revenue account.

In its debt collection system a public sector organization needs:

1. a close working relationship between the service departments and the recovery department or section to ensure that problem cases are identified as soon as possible;
2. accurate, complete and timely information available to all staff involved in the arrears process;
3. a standard recovery procedure to be in place which is an automatic system and is regularly reviewed. Due to the politically sensitive nature of some of its services and its public image it needs to have provision to identify special cases;
4. to ensure that any action should be quick and effective;
5. firm action to be taken against poor payers (subject to point 3) to demonstrate that the organization is prepared to apply sanctions;
6. consideration to be taken of the costs of recovery as once legal action is started the process is expensive;
7. to avoid giving credit if the service is one where cash can be collected on delivery.

The granting of credit involves the organization in a cost as interest could be earned on the outstanding balances or interest could be saved on any overdraft which finances the credit granted. Some public sector organizations offer incentives for lump sum payments of due amounts or for specific payment methods. Exhibit 6.1 illustrates the cost of credit granted for a competitive arm of a public sector organization where there is a choice in respect of its client base and trading terms.

While it is assumed that in dealing with other public sector tax-financed bodies they will be financially secure, where legislation allows trading with private sector organizations this is not necessarily the case and the possibility of bad debts must be considered. It may be felt that by offering a discount for prompt payment this risk may be reduced. Similarly credit references may be taken up and this would certainly apply with large contracts. (In the case of capital contracts public sector organizations operate an approved list of contractors. In order to be placed on this list it would be normal for the accounts of an applicant for inclusion on the list to be appraised.) As trade credit is an institution in the market place the allowance of credit is almost a prerequisite to increasing business and profitability. Risk is thus inevitable, but as with all risks it must be managed.

Exhibit 6.1

Transplant is a public sector organization which undertakes vehicle maintenance for other public sector organizations. It has been approached by a potential customer for a vehicle repair which it estimates will cost £1500. The standard mark-up on this type of contract is 15%, but Transplant is considering offering 30 days credit or, alternatively, a 5% discount for payment within 15 days. The cost of borrowing to the organization is 10%. The cash implications of these methods of payment are set out in the table below.

Transplant is now in a position to examine the cost of these alternative strategies and decide which may prove most attractive to winning the business. As the organization is a new customer the incremental cost of the transaction is the £1500 cost price and this has been used as the basis of the transaction.

Where the table indicates that the profit is £132.59 Transplant now has the use of these funds for an additional 15 days and as such is in a position to consider either investing them or reducing its borrowing. Assuming that borrowing is at the higher rate then this would increase the profit to £139.33 (10% × 1638.75 for 15 days).

Clearly, both parties have to weight up the costs and opportunities of the transaction as any saving Transplant makes will represent costs to the other organization. In a competitive situation, Transplant must also consider the likely terms and conditions of contracts on offer by its competitors.

Cost and credit to Transplant

Payment strategy	Cost price £	Contract price £	Profit £	Profit %
Cash sale	1 500	1 725	225	15
30-day credit (cost of credit £1500 at 10% = £12.33)	1 500	1 725	212.67	14.2
5% discount (cost of credit 15 days at 10% = £6.16)	1 500	1 638.75	132.59	8.8

Alternative methods of debt collection

It has been assumed up to now that the organization is undertaking its own debt recovery procedures but possible alternatives include the following:

1. A debt collection agency could be employed which would charge a commission on the value of debts successfully recovered. The organization inevitably loses some control of the recovery process and would have to specify the terms of the contract carefully.
2. Debts could be factored which will generate cash flow but there will obviously be a charge. In addition a factor would only be interested in 'good' debts and it is difficult to imagine factoring the individual debts that many public sector organizations have.
3. Credit insurance involves the insurer in covering risks which cause a significant loss to the organization if the client becomes insolvent. Normally, there is a risk limit with the insured bearing the balance. Clearly, this method is unsuitable for covering the many small debts that, for example, a district council may build up in terms of rent arrears.

In terms of the collection of debt the universities are claiming a success in the management of the collection of tuition fees from students in the first year of the new system. A survey of vice chancellors and principals (CVCP) reported that 97% of students had paid. And that the universities had collected £146.5m and that only £3.5m remained outstanding. The government had expected a higher level of non-payment and had set aside £5m to cover the expected shortfall (*Public Finance*, 11 February 2000, p.16). It should be remembered that these are global figures and individual university figures may be worse.

One area of concern for many local authorities and bodies such as housing associations is the housing benefits system which has been described by housing professionals as 'a shambles'. It has been suggested that the time taken to process a housing benefit claim can be 18 weeks and in certain London boroughs longer. Administrative errors can also lead to the overpayment of housing benefit and this is clawed back from, for example, the housing association which has little or no chance of recovering these sums from tenants given their economic and social circumstances in many instances. One association's arrears are reported as having risen from £862 078 to £1 891 481 over a three-year period (Jacobs and Smith Bowers, 2000, p.25) with obvious financial costs to the association concerned. In addition, there are proposals that the current system of housing benefit which is directly payable to the landlord be paid directly to tenants via income support. The tenant would be responsible for payments of rent to the landlord. While this may be welcomed on empowerment grounds the implementation of such a proposal in practice is probably open to question given its probable effect on rent levels. Finally, with regard to property, landlords in the public sector need to be aware of the problem with voids. These can occur where a tenant is decanted for, say, essential repairs. It is obviously vital that any property be empty for the minimum period otherwise substantial additional rent loss will occur. In addition there is obviously the possibility of vandalism.

Finally, as new sources of income are sought by public sector organizations it is important that systems are developed to ensure that income is collected. British Waterways, for example, reports that self-generated income jumped by 24% in 1998/99 and outside funding of schemes had increased by 62% on the previous year.

6.9 Management of creditors

It was reported in Hansard (February 1990) in the debate on the Interest on Debt Bill that certain government departments do not consider for payment any account unless it is at least 30 days late. In the same debate it was also pointed out that a health board in Scotland had gone on public record as saying that due to a cash crisis it would not get to the end of the financial year unless it did not pay any bills. Clearly, this type of action could place suppliers in severe difficulties and could present major difficulties over future supply. Politically, this exploitation of credit has not proved acceptable and many organizations in the public sector and notably government departments and agencies have signed up to the CBI's Prompt Payment Practice Code. The Queen Victoria NHS Trust, for example, in its Annual Report for 1997/98 reports that 99% of invoices were paid within 30 days from the receipt of goods or a valid invoice in accordance with the CBI code and government accounting rules. In 1998, however, the government passed the Late Payment of Commercial Debts (Interest) Act that allowed interest to be charged for late payment of any qualifying debt. A qualifying debt is a debt under a contract where the supplier and purchaser are acting in the course of their businesses. The statutory interest rate outlined on the DTI's web site is base rate plus 8%. There may, however, be a reluctance by small businesses to enforce the legislation because of the fear of losing clients.

In Liverpool City Council an investigation was launched into late payments following an Audit Commission report that showed that the council was failing to meet payment targets. On investigation, it was discovered that this was due to disputed accounts, copy invoices in the system, slow certification procedures and failures by suppliers to address invoices to the correct departments (Kelly, 2000, p.34). Changes have now been introduced into the creditor-processing system to ensure prompt payment although there is, of course, the danger to the council that it is now paying early and as such losing interest on cash balances as a result.

In many ways this process is the reverse of that considered earlier in relation to debtors. Now the 'boot is on the other foot' and the public sector organization is consequently in the position of judging whether or not it is to its advantage to pay early and claim any discounts. If there are no discounts then there is no advantage to paying early unless there is a desire to impress creditors with speed of payment. This is illustrated in Exhibit 6.2.

Exhibit 6.2

A public sector organization has received a bill for £10 000 with the receipt of goods. Payment is to be with the supplier in 30 days. The cost of capital to the organization is 15%. If payment is delayed the supplier charges a penalty of 3% monthly on the uncleared balance.

It can be seen from the table below that for up to 50 days the public sector organization still has an advantage in delaying payment. This is a financial advantage only and could result in the loss of supplier goodwill. Moreover, if it is a call-off contract negotiated by a central supplies department, it could result in the loss of discounts. It is the possibility of gaining a poor reputation for payment that is the major control on delaying payment as interest charges for delay can be difficult to sustain.

Financial implications of delaying payment

Time period	Credit	Cost	Saving
	£		£
30 days	10 000	0%	123.29
40 days (no penalty)	10 000	0%	164.38
40 days (with penalty)	10 000	36% p.a.	65.74
50 days (no penalty)	10 000	0%	205.47
50 days (with penalty)	10 000	36% p.a.	8.21

Note:
This example assumes that the cheque has been cleared by the end of the credit period.

Most public sector organizations are normally large bodies with centralized payment functions. The delay in processing that this involves may result in the loss of discounts (if these are considered desirable) and – equally significantly from the manager's point of view – the loss of flexibility which results from the financial information provided for them to control cost centres, especially if a commitment system of accounting (Chapter 5) is not in operation.

There is a need to assess the impact that the creditor system has on the financial information available. It is suggested that a 'typical' system might be:

1. invoice received in service department, matched with goods received note and original order, arithmetically checked, contract price examined, certified for payment, coded and checked for possible discounts;
2. batched for payment with other invoices and forwarded to finance department for payment on appropriate dates as per notification from finance department;
3. received in finance department batched for computer input and control totals recorded;
4. keyed into computer for subsequent preparation of cheques and update of financial information system and bank reconciliation;
5. rejected invoices will be subsequently resubmitted;
6. distribute financial information to service departments (on-line enquiry may be possible).

While special procedures will exist for urgent payments and capital contracts it can be seen that this system inevitably builds in delay, especially if an invoice misses a deadline. Similarly, the system may not be flexible enough to cope with discount deadlines. An alternative is decentralized payment procedures where departments enter invoices directly leaving the finance department to process the cheques and concentrate on internal controls and audit trails. The main advantage is that the financial information is updated more quickly which should lead to improvements in budgetary control. In addition the service departments will be aware of discounts and prompt processing can lead to these being claimed. In this case the policy of discounts against the cost of early payment will need to be considered.

6.10 Management of stock

The application of inventory control is of particular importance to those units of the public sector that are subject to competitive tendering. This is particularly true for those businesses that are required to make a return calculated on the current cost of assets as the stock adjustment under current cost accounting (CCA) affects the profit and loss account and also the level of capital employed. It is obvious that any loss of stock from whatever cause will be a charge to the profit and loss account. To this end, many direct service organizations have made a conscious effort to reduce or remove stocks and stores (buildings are also part of capital employed). Stock holding is important, however, in normal service activities as the traditional end-of-year spending spree to utilize the remainder of the budget can lead to large increases in stocks of materials which would not otherwise be ordered. Cash is thus tied up in materials and not earning interest. There is also a danger of deterioration if stocks are not kept in adequate storage conditions.

There is a need in any activity for adequate sources of supply to complete the task in hand. In the case of the competition activities this may take the form of holding items in stock as this will reduce the uncertainty of supply. The holding of stocks in sufficient quantity may also result in attracting discounts. Clearly, this strategy has to be set against the cost of operating stores. The alternative is to direct purchase supplies to the site on the just-in-time (JIT) principle but then there is the danger of late delivery and the costs of idle time and so on. In any case the public sector may require emergency stocks to be held and a stores building will need to be maintained. Thus only the marginal costs will be relevant to the organization. It is probably true to say that for a DSO activity that a balance of combining direct purchase and a stores system will achieve the optimum policy. This will require a detailed study to tailor need to the individual organization but the following factors would need to be considered:

1. transportation costs;
2. idle time in waiting for materials;
3. price differentials between stores items and contracted direct suppliers;
4. stores running costs;
5. levels of emergency items;
6. stock-holding costs;
7. capital costs of buildings;
8. the general nature of the work, e.g. construction contracts would involve forward planning to enable materials to be pre-ordered for delivery direct to site.

In respect of emergency items it might be possible to operate an imprest system with vehicles carrying a basic stock of materials regularly used, which is reimbursed after any use either from stores or direct suppliers.

Once a decision has been taken to operate a store it is necessary to ensure that it is operated efficiently in terms of the levels of stock carried. Maximum and minimum stock levels should thus be set and regularly reviewed. In terms of ordering stock the following formula has been devised for economic order quantities.

$$\text{Economic order quantity} = \sqrt{\frac{2 \times AD}{S}}$$

where:

A is the cost of placing an order;
D is the annual demand;
S is the annual cost of holding one unit of stock.

The reorder point is the quantity level of the stock that triggers a new order to be placed and is simplest to calculate when there is certainty about demand and lead time (i.e. time for delivery). This is given be the formula:

$$\text{Reorder point} = \text{Demand per unit of time} \times \text{Lead time}$$

Where, however, there is uncertainty about demand or supply there is a need to provide a safety stock which will be the minimum level necessary to meet unexpected demand. The computation of safety stocks hinges on the ability to forecast demand which is based on past experience. The major relevant costs will be the costs of holding stock and the stock-out costs. The optimum exists where the costs of carrying an extra unit are exactly counterbalanced by the expected stock-out costs. Exhibit 6.3 provides a brief example of the calculations required.

Key points of chapter

1. The importance of the management of working capital in the public sector has been stressed.
2. The need to develop policies for each element of working capital is important.
3. It is an area in which managers in service departments are able to play a vital role.

6.11 Summary

Working capital management has a key role to play in the public sector but its importance may be overlooked due to the distributed management of financial resources operated in public sector organizations. Substantial policy benefits are available if this importance is recognized and communicated within the organization. By the creation of a stated policy and objectives for the management of working capital the organization has the opportunity to speed up or slow down the flow of cash. This will have major implications, due to the size of working capital balances, for the returns available to the organization and its ability to maintain services.

Exhibit 6.3

Transplant, the competitive vehicle repair workshop of a public sector organization, competes with other public sector organizations for work. One fleet that it services regularly has just replaced its 3-ton lorries with a new vehicle specification and these lorries will require a new type of brakeshoe. The daily demand for brakeshoes is estimated to be 10 pairs and the purchase price of each set is £25.

The cost associated with placing orders and maintaining a stock of brakeshoes is estimated as follows:

1. The total costs incurred in the purchasing department over the last year are £18 800 and the number of orders placed were 4000. It is expected that costs will rise by 5% over the next year.

2. Shipping costs are £10 per order.
3. A storeman will receive and inspect the brakeshoes as they arrive and it is estimated that this will require one hour per order. The storeman is paid £3.50 per hour and variable overheads are allocated at the rate of £5 per hour in this department.
4. The desired rate of return on stock is 20%.
5. The management operate the workshops on a 260-day year.
6. Six working days are required to receive delivery from when the order is placed.

Required

Calculate the economic order point and the reorder point in units together with the minimum annual cost at the economic order point.

The first step is to calculate the cost of placing an order:

	£
Estimated order costs (£18 000 1.05%) ÷ 4000	4 935
Shipping costs	10 000
Labour costs per order	8 500
	23 435

Estimated cost of placing an order

The value of the carrying cost is composed of the required rate of return on stock which is £25 × 20% or £5. The annual quantity required is 260 working days multiplied by the number per day which is 10:

$$EOQ = \sqrt{\frac{2(260 \times 10) \times 23.435}{5}}$$

$$= 156 \text{ pairs per order}$$

$$\text{Reorder point} = \text{Usage per day} \times \text{Lead time}$$
$$= 10 \times 6$$
$$= 60$$

Reorder point is when 60 pairs of brakeshoes are in stock.

Minimum annual cost is calculated by:

$$C = \frac{A \times P}{E} + \frac{E \times S}{2}$$

$$= \frac{2600 \times 23.435}{156} + \frac{156 \times 5}{2}$$

$$= £780.58$$

Questions

6.1 A local authority DSO uses 5000 units of raw materials on a continuous basis in a year. The DSO estimates that the cost of carrying one unit in inventory is £0.20 per year. Placing and processing an order for additional inventory cost an estimated £225 per order.

(a) What are the annual ordering costs, carrying costs and total costs of inventory, if the DSO orders in quantities of 1500, 2000, 2500, 3000, 3500 and 4000 units, respectively?

(b) Graph the ordering and carrying costs (y-axis) relative to order quantity (x-axis) and comment on the results achieved.

(c) Calculate the economic order quantity using the appropriate formula.

(d) Discuss the value of establishing a sound policy of inventory management to any public sector organization.

6.2 The Central Purchasing Department of a large government department places orders for various items of stationery at monthly intervals. In respect of one particular item (Code Z400) the relevant data are:

Annual wage 40 000 boxes
Minimum order quantity 2500 boxes
Cost per box £2.75

Usage of material is regular and on average 40% of the amount purchased is held in stock. The cost of storage is 60% of the value of stock held. The average cost of placing an order is £140.

A value for money exercise is currently being carried out in the purchasing department and as part of this exercise this particular item has been selected for review.

You are required to:

(a) Explain what is meant by the term 'economic order quantity', supporting your explanation with an appropriate graph.

(b) For item Z400 tabulate the costs of storage and ordering the item for each level of orders from five to 20.

(c) Calculate the economic order quantity using an appropriate formula. Compare the results achieved with (b).

(d) Discuss the advantages and disadvantages to the purchasing department of using the result of your calculations.

6.3 Transplant is a vehicle maintenance department of a public sector organization. It has been approached by a local health organization to undertake some repair work on one of its fleet of ambulances. The estimated cost of the repair work is £2000. The standard mark-up on this type of contract is 10% with Transplant considering offering 30 days credit or alternatively a 5% discount for the receipt of payment in full within 20 days. The cost of borrowing to Transplant is 13%.

(a) Calculate which option is the most appropriate for Transplant.

(b) It is understood by Transplant that the local health organization is considering contracting out all its present in-house maintenance. Assess any implications of this to Transplant in deciding its policy in (a).

(c) Discuss what is meant by an organization's credit terms and what they determine.

6.4 A public sector organization has received a bill for £15 900 with the receipt of goods. Payment can be made in three days for a 5% discount. Payment in full is due within 30 days. If payment is delayed a penalty of 4% monthly is payable under the terms of the contract to the supplier. The cost of capital to the public sector organization is 14%.

(a) Which policy on payment should the public sector organization adopt?
(b) What effect would a rise in the cost of capital to 15% have on this policy?
(c) What effect would a fall in the cost of capital to 10% have on your advice in (a)?
(d) Discuss who pays the cost of credit – the supplier or the buyer – and in what way.

6.5 A district health authority is to consider the building of a health centre in an expanding town at one end of the district. Two sites have been proposed; site A is in the centre of the town and can be developed immediately, whereas site B is on the edge of town and progress can only be made in 18 months' time when the access road is improved. The planning department has prepared the following information for the authority:

	Site A	Site B
Cost of land	£50 000	£15 000
Works contract	£240 000	£260 000
Contract start	April 19X8	August 19X9
Contract period	8 months	7 months
Fitting out costs	£25 000	£35 000
Running costs p.a.	£92 000	£94 000

You may assume that the contractor will be paid in equal monthly instalments for the contract period, except for the 5% retention which is paid 6 months after completion. You may make any other reasonable assumptions about the timing of cash flows, but they should be stated in your answer.

(a) Carry out a financial appraisal of the two options and interpret your results.

(15 marks)

(b) Comment on any other information that ought to be presented to the members at the same time as the financial appraisal in part (a).

(15 marks)

6.6 The customers of a public sector organization pay their accounts in the following ways:

	Number of annual transactions
Cheques banked centrally	1 200 000
Cash at shops (value – £40 million)	1 100 000
Bank giro credits	300 000
National Girobank credits	100 000

The following costs are incurred in processing the income:

	£000s
Shop salaries	590
Central cheque handling salaries	40
Central cash balancing and control salaries	30
Collection of cash by security firms	62

The organization pays bank charges as follows:

Cheques paid in	5p each
Cash paid in	9p per £100

Notes:

(i) 20% of shop staff time is spent on cashiering.

(ii) Employer's superannuation etc. amounts to 20% of salary.

(iii) Balancing and control of cash items costs twice as much as cheques. Giro items involve no cost.

(iv) 20% of customers using bank giro pay in cash.

(v) Customers are charged 30p by National Girobank for the payment for an account at a post office.

(vi) Cheques received in shops are banked centrally.

The bank proposes to introduce a charge to the organization of 20p for each bank giro payment. **You are required** to prepare a report for the board indicating whether the facility should continue to be offered.

6.7 A public authority is currently examining methods of payments of its weekly paid 'manual' workforce which numbers 260 employees.

Details of the current payment system are as follows:

(a) 180 employees are paid in cash. The payroll is run on Wednesday, the day before pay day; the payslips, coin analysis and a cheque for the total cash payment are collected by a security firm. The security firm cashes the cheques on the Wednesday, makes up the wages and pays out at four pay points on Thursday morning. Employees attend the pay points in work time and this takes, on average, 20 minutes per employee. Pay packets not collected are returned to the wages office which acts as a fifth pay point. In the case of employees at distant locations, the pay packets are normally collected from the wages office by the appropriate supervisors and delivered to the workforce, thereby averting 'lost time'. Total cash payments amount to £30 240 per week; of the 180 employees, on average, 135 attend the pay parades.

(b) 80 employees are paid by open cheques, sent either to homes or banks by first class mail to arrive on pay day. Open cheque payments amount to £6900 per week and analysis of the time at which these cheques are debited to the authority's bank account reveals the following pattern:

| | No. of days after pay day | | | | | |
	0	1	2	3	4	5+
% Debited	15	5	0	0	75	5

Two alternative systems have been proposed:

Alternative 1
All employees would be paid by crossed cheques sent directly to bank accounts; this would necessitate all manual employees having bank accounts. The stationery required, cheques, is expected to cost £180 per year. It is estimated that, on average, cheques would be cleared three days after pay day. The authority's bankers have indicated that the current charge of 22p per cheque cleared would apply under this option.

Alternative 2
All employees would be paid by BACS transfer. As with alternative 1, this option would require all employees to have bank accounts. Costs involved amount to:

Weekly tape delivery to BACS processing centre	£11
BACS cost per transaction	3.5 pence
Magnetic tapes (initial cost only)	£25

Under this option the total wage bill would be debited to the authority's bank account on pay day. This will necessitate some reorganization of internal payroll procedures and require the employment of one additional person in the wages office for one half-day per week, at an appropriate proportion of an annual cost of salary and overheads amounting to £5800 per year.

Other information

(a) The security firm charges £3450 per annum for its services.

(b) Manual employees work a 38-hour week.

(c) The wages office currently employs 2.5 people at an average total weekly cost of £230 per person; it has been estimated that about 2% of their total time is devoted to holding and reissuing pay packets not collected at designated pay points.

(d) Discussions with unions representing the manual workforce indicate that a one-off *ex gratia* payment of £150 per employee would be sufficient to encourage all employees to open bank accounts.

(e) Current short-term borrowing rates are 10% per annum.

Required

You are the auditor investigating this issue as part of a more general investigation of BACS. Prepare a report to the senior assistant treasurer detailing your findings and making appropriate recommendations.

Your report should concentrate on analysis and interpretation rather than description. (24 marks)

6.8 Wondershire County Council operates a workshop for the disabled which produces and sells a single product – Ali Baba linen baskets. In order to train the disabled in all aspects of commerce the workshop is run as a separate entity. The following information relates to the workshop:

(a) Each basket sells for £10 and has a variable cost element of £6.50 made up as follows:

	£
Materials	1.50
Labour	4.00
Overhead	1.00
	6.50

(b) Fixed costs of £2500 per month are paid on the 28th of each month.

(c) Anticipated credit sales are as follows:

1999			2000					
Oct.	Nov.	Dec.	Jan.	Feb.	Mar.	Apr.	May	Jun.
650	700	700	600	620	640	640	640	660

(d) Cash sales are expected to be 5% of credit sales and are at a discount of 5%.

(e) Production quantities are forecast as follows:

Oct.	Nov.	Dec.	Jan.	Feb.	Mar.	Apr.	May	Jun.
750	800	750	610	630	650	660	670	680

(f) Customers are invoiced at the end of each month and payments are received:

> 60% by the end of the month following the month of the invoice
> 35% by the end of the next subsequent month
> 5% one further month later

(g) Suppliers of material are paid one month after the material has been used in production.
(h) Wages are paid in the same month as they are incurred.
(i) 60% of the variable overhead is paid in the month of production, the remainder in the following month.
(j) The workshop manager anticipates that the workshop will be £2000 overdrawn at the bank on 31 December 1999.

Required

(i) A month by month cash budget for the first six months of 2000.   (14 marks)
(ii) The manager considers that cash flow may be improved if customers paid their bills earlier. Briefly outline the advantages and disadvantages of offering discounts.

Market research suggests that by offering a 5% discount 75% of credit sales will be received by the end of the month after the customer is invoiced. Assume the remainder pay one month later at full price. What effect would this have on cash flow?   (6 marks)

6.9 A public body expects the following cash receipts and payments in the financial year beginning 1 April 19X7:

1. Opening cash balance at 1 April 19X7 of £500 000 credit.
2. Annual revenue receipts of £13 500 000. Two-thirds is receivable bi-annually on 1 April and 1 October. Normally 50% is collected in the due month, 40% in the next month, and 10% in the third month. The remaining one-third is receivable in ten equal instalments, May to February.
3. Annual revenue grant of £13 120 000, receivable in two equal instalments in September and March.
4. Monthly employee payments of £1 600 000.
5. A pay award of 5%, operative from 1 July, although delays in the bargaining process are expected to result in actual agreement and implementation three months after the operative date.
6. Annual material purchases of £3 000 000. 40% of the purchases occur in the first six months. Creditors are paid 60% in the month of purchase, 40% in the following month. Purchases in March 19X7 total £250 000.
7. Other expenses of £204 000 incurred evenly throughout the year.
8. Capital payments of £800 000 in June and £610 000 in December.
9. Bank charges of £250 000, payable in advance. The bank has offered a further option for consideration, namely, one-half of 1% of turnover (gross annual receipts plus gross annual payments), payable in arrears.
10. Cost of capital is 10%.

You are required to:

(a) prepare the 19X7/X8 cash budget;   (12 marks)
(b) decide the best method for paying bank charges;   (4 marks)
(c) outline briefly the main functions of cash budgets in the public sector. (4 marks)

6.10 Gwent CC have been experiencing severe problems recently in the collection of
trade debts in terms of payments to Gwent DSO being delayed.

It has asked you (a representative of a public sector advisory agency) for advice
on ways to reduce the effect of these problems on its liquidity position.

One of the alternatives which you have identified for Gwent DSO is to enter an
agreement with a factor which has the following features:

1. The factor would forward 90% of Gwent DSO's invoice values on receiving a
    copy of these. Remaining amounts would be remitted to Gwent DSO, by the
    factor, as received from customers.
2. All sales invoice raising and debt collection duties would be undertaken by the
    factor for which it would charge a fee of 5% p.a. of the gross annual invoice
    value, payable in 12 equal monthly instalments.
    This will lead to a saving in fixed sales ledger costs of £4000 per month.
3. Amounts advanced to Gwent DSO would attract an interest charge, payable to
    the factor of 15% p.a. payable on a simple, monthly basis.

    Gwent DSO's sales are currently at a level of £500 000 per month, all on
    credit, and these are expected to increase at 3% per month for the next three
    months and then to remain at that level.

    Gwent DSO's credit terms are 30 days net, but most of its customers are
    currently paying after 90 days. It is estimated that the factor will reduce this
    payment period to, at most, 60 days.

    Gwent DSO's cost of short-term borrowing is 14% p.a.

Required

(i) Calculate whether it is likely to be to Gwent DSO's advantage to enter the
     factoring agreement.   (14 marks)
(ii) Identify and discuss other possible alternative methods of overcoming Gwent
     DSO's debt collection problems, if its entire sales are made within the UK.
                                                                                  (5 marks)
(iii) Explain the ways in which debt collection problems might be increased should
      Gwent DSO decide to commence exporting and describe three ways of
      reducing the effects of these problems.   (6 marks)
                                                                          (Total 25 marks)

7 The financing of capital expenditure

Key learning objectives

After reading this chapter you should be able to:

1. Discuss the relative advantages of the different methods of capital finance.
2. Distinguish between the capital finance of central government departments (including the NHS) and local authorities.
3. Explain the capital expenditure controls operating in the different parts of the public sector.
4. Identify the key issues in a borrowing strategy, a leaseback deal and the use of derivative instruments.

The strict definitions of capital expenditure within different parts of the public sector are provided in Chapter 8. This chapter will be concerned with the objectives, policies and constraints relating to the financing of such expenditure, and specifically will consider the following:

1. The different approaches to the finance of capital expenditure and the implications of these diverse approaches.
2. The impact of various controls and constraints which have been imposed by legislation or by agreement between parties.
3. An examination of the dynamics of three important and changing areas of capital finance, namely, borrowing strategy, lease finance and derivatives.

7.1 The central objective in capital financing

The central objective in the financing of capital expenditure is to ensure that all calls on the organization for money to support expenditure on fixed assets, and the refinancing of loans which fall due for repayment, can be met. Consider a simple example such as is shown in Table 7.1.

Table 7.1 Projected financing needs

Year	Current £m	Current + 1 £m	Current + 2 £m
Capital expenditure	27	29	19
Refinancing	6	11	4
Finance required	33	40	23

In the situation depicted in Table 7.1 over the three-year period the treasurer or director of finance has to ensure that a total of £96m is available to support planned capital expenditure of £75m and to refinance borrowing used to finance past capital expenditure, amounting to £21m. This finance will need to be provided in the required pattern shown in Table 7.1 with £33m in this year, £40m next year and £23m in the year after.

In looking for ways of securing this finance, the responsible officer will be seeking funds which minimize the cost to the organization; furthermore, that finance is raised only when required so as to minimize the time period over which it is held and, therefore, the time period over which it has to be paid for. We next consider, in broad terms, the approaches to the sourcing of capital finance employed in the public sector.

Approaches to the financing of capital expenditure

Broadly, there are four different approaches employed within the public sector, as follows:

1. financing from revenue;
2. financing by borrowing;
3. financing from reserves;
4. financing by leasing.

7.2 Financing from revenue

If an organization pays for capital expenditure, as it occurs, out of its recurring revenue resources, this is termed 'pay as you go'. It involves using the revenues from current taxation, fees and charges, asset sales and privatization proceeds. It avoids financing assets by borrowing. Local authorities may choose to indulge in this approach to the finance of capital expenditure, financing expenditure on assets from income from fees, local taxation and the government block grant.

There are five advantages of pay as you go. First, it saves the organization concerned interest charges, it also avoids the not inconsiderable costs associated with managing debt, as would certainly be involved with borrowing. Second, it is said to foster accountability, a decision made now to extend the town hall will be reflected in current taxation. Thus, the expenditure may be felt quite sharply by current taxpayers and the accountability link between expenditure and impact on the taxpayer made immediate. Third, it avoids committing future generations of taxpayers, who will have their own burdens to carry; and it prevents current politicians from deferring to the future the financing impact of their decisions. Fourth, in the case of direct service organizations (DSOs) the current regulations specify that revenue-financed assets are to be excluded from an organization's asset base when the return on capital employed is being calculated. This results in a doubly positive impact in the return on capital employed in the years following the acquisition of the asset: there are no annual financing charges to be borne by the revenue account and the asset base within the return on capital employed calculation is reduced. Finally, in the long run it can be shown that, with regular and recurring capital expenditure, pay as you go will eventually work out more cheaply than borrowing. This is illustrated in Table 7.2; as can be seen, in seven years' time the revenue consequences of borrowing start to exceed those of pay as you go.

Table 7.2 Pay as you go and borrowing compared

Year	Now	+1	+2	+3	+4	+5	+6	+7	+8	+9
Capital expenditure £m	10	10	10	10	10	10	10	10	10	10
Finance Pay as you go	10	10	10	10	10	10	10	10	10	10
Borrowing Annual borrowing	10	10	10	10	10	10	10	10		
Repayments Principal	1	2	3	4	5	6	7	8	9	10
Interest	.5	.95	1.35	1.7	2	2.25	2.45	2.6	2.7	2.75
Total	1.5	2.95	4.35	5.7	7	8.25	9.45	10.6	11.7	12.75

In Table 7.2 it is assumed that the loan is repaid in ten equal instalments so that in the first year the repayment is simply one-tenth of the first year borrowing. In the second year it is one-tenth of the first year borrowing plus one-tenth of the second year borrowing and so on. It is also assumed that repayments are made at the end of the year. The interest calculation is based on a rate of interest of 5%, which is estimated to remove from current interest rates the allowance for estimated inflation. It is also assumed that the annual interest is repaid annually. The calculation of the interest payment is shown in Figure 7.1.

However, the pay as you go approach can be criticized. First, given that the expenditure is being incurred for capital purposes future generations of taxpayers will have the benefit of the asset at no capital cost to them. The present generation is effectively subsidizing the future.

It may also have the major disadvantage that capital is seen as a free good by service managers. This applies particularly to a situation where there is no annual charge for capital consumption in the annual revenue accounts although such a charge does not necessarily have to relate to the method of financing. After all, it is possible to have a system of depreciation accounting which is entirely independent of the method by which an asset is financed; for evidence of this, one has to look no further than the systems in place in local authorities and the NHS. In the former, asset rents (in lieu of depreciation) and capital charges at 6% of the cost of the asset (reflecting the financing cost of the asset) are in place; in the NHS, we find depreciation and the requirement to break even after charging a 6% return on capital employed.

Year 1: 5% * 10

Year 2: 5% * (10 + 9) (10 being the second-year loan and 9 being the amount outstanding relating to the first-year loan)

Year 3: 5% * (10 + 9 + 8) (10 being the third-year loan, 9 being the second-year loan and 8 being the first-year loan)

This is then applied to the remaining years of the loan using the simple formula for the sum of an arithmetic progression:

$$\text{Sum} = \frac{(\text{first number} + \text{last number})}{2} * \text{Number of items in the series}$$

thus,

Year 4	=	(10 + 7)/2 * 4	=	34 * 5%
Year 5	=	(10 + 6)/2 * 5	=	40 * 5%
Year 6	=	(10 + 5)/2 * 6	=	45 * 5%
Year 7	=	(10 + 4)/2 * 7	=	49 * 5%
Year 8	=	(10 + 3)/2 * 8	=	52 * 5%
Year 9	=	(10 + 2)/2 * 9	=	54 * 5%
Year 10	=	(10 + 1)/2 * 10	=	55 * 5%

Figure 7.1   Calculation of interest charges in Table 7.2

Third, if a 'pay as you go' policy is adopted it may be difficult to achieve a reasonable level of stability in tax rates and council tax levels from year to year. In addition this will be further complicated by the gearing effect for local government as the central government has indicated that it will only increase grants and the uniform business rate by no more than the rate of inflation. Consequently, a 'pay as you go' policy may significantly affect council tax levels from year to year. Table 7.3 illustrates this quite clearly.

In this table inflation is assumed to be 6% and revenue expenditure and government grant are both increased in the second year in line with this. As can be seen, the increase in gross expenditure of 25% is wholly attributable to financing capital expenditure out of revenue. However, government grant is assumed to increase only in line with inflation and this results in a 37.5% increase in council tax. The assumption that government

Table 7.3   Pay as you go and council tax levels

Year	2001 £m	2002 £m
Revenue expenditure	50	53
Capital charged to revenue	2	12
Gross expenditure	52	65
Less grant	20	21
Raised from council tax	32	44
Increase in tax		37.5%

grants increase in line with inflation is likely to be overgenerous if declining levels of grant in real terms are used to squeeze increasing levels of efficiency out of the local authorities. Furthermore, the stringent capping of local authority expenditure by central government would render impractical any policy that results in such a significant potential increase in revenue expenditure.

7.3 Financing by borrowing

The advantages of using borrowing to finance capital expenditure are, obviously, a mirror image of the disadvantages to pay as you go. In practice, the main philosophical argument is that assets such as schools have long lives and, within existing legislation, borrowing serves as one method of spreading the capital cost over several generations of taxpayers; that is, relating benefits received to taxes paid in a fairly crude way. In addition there has been a strong practical argument, which is that many assets can only be afforded because payment for them is deferred via borrowing. Table 7.3 indicates that in the long term pay as you go is cheaper than debt finance. However, there can be no doubt that borrowing allows the provision of a greater volume of asset-related services in the short run than pay as you go can ever provide. Also, with pay as you go, the costs of borrowing are effectively shifted from the government to the taxpayer, who must bear higher taxes or reduced services, because of annual expenditure on fixed assets.

Inflation provides an argument in favour of borrowing. When the loan is repaid inflation reduces the real cost of the money repayments and, therefore, the real cost to the taxpayer. If the organization has a choice the balance of advantage must be decided by factors such as the interest rate, repayment periods and government controls.

There are significant differences in approaches to borrowing within the public sector and it is important to make a clear distinction between central government borrowing and local government borrowing. The case of central government borrowing is dealt with first.

Central government and the NHS

All central government departments and NHS borrowing is carried out by central government at Treasury level and it must be stressed that borrowing is not available to individual central government departments or to the NHS other than the hospital trusts.

The NHS receives from central government an allocation of capital and revenue funds each year and all capital expenditure in that year is charged against its capital allocation for that year; none is defrayed by borrowing. Thus, it may appear that the NHS is following a pay as you go policy for capital expenditure. However, as has been stated, the funds to finance that expenditure come from central government. These in turn come from either the taxpayer, the money markets, in the form of government borrowing or from sales of public sector assets under the privatization policy. No attempt is made by the Treasury to identify the specific source of finance which is tied to a specific expenditure.

The Public Sector Borrowing Requirement (PSBR) indicates the extent that the public sector borrows from other sectors of the economy and overseas and covers borrowing by central government, the nationalized industries and local authorities. It is closely related to another concept, particularly in the framework of national accounting, the public sector financial deficit (PSFD). The PSFD is the balance of public sector current and capital transactions combined and represents the net acquisition (positive or negative) of financial assets by the public sector.

PSBR forecasts are prepared by the Treasury and are built up from detailed assessments of receipts and payments provided from other sources by, for example, the Inland Revenue, Customs and Excise, and the Department of Social Security. While an attempt is made to build in all the information available the forecasts can go wrong for a number of reasons. Economic developments may be forecast incorrectly as certain elements of public sector expenditure and income are sensitive to upturns or downturns in the economy. These elements would include taxes on income, expenditure taxes and social security payments. Even if aggregate economic development may be predicted accurately there may be a failure at a lower level to translate this information correctly by sector. A changing pattern of consumption might affect VAT receipts for example. Another problem is concerned with the timing of the receipt of income and the payment of bills which can represent unpredictable variations. Finally, unforeseen receipts and payments, which may be large and are clearly unpredictable, may result in forecasting errors.

If the Health Service is taken as a specific receiver of funds the authority will receive its capital allocation and draw down funds as needed from the Department of Health. Bank balances are required to be kept to a minimum (while avoiding overdrafts). There is no question of investing money received in advance of requirements although this is permitted for self-governing trusts within the NHS.

Local authority borrowing

Here we are explicitly concerned with raising long-term loans to finance capital expenditure. As has been seen, in the case of some public sector organizations, such as the NHS, there is currently no borrowing. Local authorities, however, are heavily involved in these transactions which require fairly considerable skills in debt management.

General powers that permit local authorities to borrow for capital purposes are contained within Schedule 13 of the Local Government Act 1972. It is no exaggeration to state that the controls on borrowing by local authorities have effectively determined the accounting system employed since the ability to hold permanent debt is denied to them. Under Schedule 13 all loans are secured on the revenues of the authority and each year the authority must raise sufficient in local taxation to cover repayments of principal and interest which must then be charged to the annual revenue account.

7.4 Financing from reserves

Financing from reserves involves using sources of finance that have been built up in the past. The reserves may have been built up from a variety of sources such as contributions from revenue, the sale of assets or charitable contributions and bequests. The advantage of such reserves is that they isolate the organization from a harsh outside world which may be characterized by high interest rates. In addition, they avoid the costs associated with servicing and managing debt.

They may also be useful as a means of adding to the volume of capital required to support a capital expenditure programme. At one time local authorities used them in this fashion, although this is now barred to them. Indeed, the Local Government and Housing Act 1989 repealed the general power to set up separate funds such as a capital fund. In their place, local authorities adopted commercial practice of setting up reserves and provisions. Apart from relatively insignificant charitable trust funds, they are not currently found in the NHS or in central government generally. Capital reserves are found in the private sector. If such reserves are represented by funds, then pending investment, it is usual to invest such reserves, the interest and dividends from the investments accruing to the reserve fund, such as happens with a superannuation fund.

There is one other specific instance where reserves may be established to provide for future capital expenditure; this is where outgoings are irregular, but it is desired to regularize their impact on the organization. For example, in a programme of vehicle replacement, one way of smoothing the impact of irregular purchases of vehicles is to charge the expenditure to a designated renewals provision, the revenue account making regular transfers to the provision. Of course, there will be other ways of smoothing the expenditure, notably by a planned replacement programme which avoids peaks and troughs in replacement or via a programme of leasing vehicles.

Finally, when the reserve is an organization-wide reserve and not built up for a specific purpose, a policy has to be determined regarding repayment of advances from reserves. The advantage of repayments is that the value of reserves is maintained. Additionally, in order that no one service benefits at the expense of others, it would seem essential that interest is paid to the reserve fund. Then, it would be necessary to determine what rate of interest to prescribe; in order to preserve the neutrality of the reserve, it would seem appropriate to select a rate of interest close to that which other new non-reserve loans are paying. By doing this, the organization as a whole may benefit, as no outside borrowing takes place (although the opportunity to invest outside is lost!), but no one service benefits compared with another.

7.5 Financing by leasing

Leasing involves use of an asset, under agreed terms and with agreed payments, but without ownership. It is extensive within the private sector, having enjoyed a boom in the 1980s, initially the result of favourable tax treatment of lessors, following from a much longer term development in the United States. However, its use is significantly limited within the wider public sector within the United Kingdom; although prevalent within local authorities, until recently its use was proscribed within the National Health Service and it enjoys very limited use within central government generally. As far as local authorities are concerned, there is no specific statutory authority for leasing but these transactions are a well-established method of finance and are *intra vires*, although the government has stepped in to regulate certain aspects of leasing arrangements entered into by local authorities with particular reference to land and property.

The principal advantages of leases are twofold:

1. They can provide a source of finance, when others are limited at very competitive rates.
2. They are very flexible and can provide levels of service at the lessees specification, with low or no risk.

The basic types of lease agreement are now discussed.

Land and property leasing

There are three types of lease. The first is *lease/leaseback*. Under this type of scheme the public authority first acquires a site and then develops it with money provided by the investor. The investor leases the land from the authority at a peppercorn (minimal) rent, and then subleases the development back to the authority at an agreed economic rent.

The second type is *sale/leaseback*. Again, the public authority acquires a site, sells the site to the investor or developer who then leases the complete development back to the authority.

The third type is *deferred purchase*. In this type of transaction the organization enters into an agreement to buy a development over a period of time and reimburses the investor the funding costs. Title remains with the investor until the final payment.

In each of these cases, a public authority has access to a developer or investor who provides the required development, at the authority's specification, when the authority's ability to enter the conventional lending market may be curtailed by, for example, constraints imposed by central government. To finance from revenue would be prohibitive, in terms of the impact on local taxation, and property leasing deals offer a way forward.

They have been in use for over 20 years in the United Kingdom, but during the 1980s gained a poor reputation as they became associated with 'creative financing'. Thus, for example, one local authority sold assets such as bus shelters and public conveniences to an investor; the investor paid up-front cash for the assets, which the authority could designate as capital receipts and use to finance much needed capital development elsewhere. In return, the local authority agreed to lease back its former assets from the developer over a period of time. This was regarded as a classic piece of 'live now, pay later' financial chicanery and from 1988 the use of such financing vehicles required the approval of the Secretary of State.

Equipment leasing

There are basically three types of equipment lease available: finance leases, contract hire and operating leases.

Under a finance lease the substantial risks and rewards of ownership are transferred to the lessee for the life of the asset. The lessor covers his finance charges and capital costs in the initial primary period. The lessee bears all maintenance charges. At the end of the lease the asset is sold to a third party with any income as a lease rebate to the lessee. A secondary period may be available normally at a nominal percentage of original purchase price.

The lessee's payments are rental in nature but the purchase price of the asset counts against the government's capital controls on local authorities.

Under an operating lease the lessee pays an economic rent to the lessor who takes all the risks and benefits of ownership. Operating leases do not count against capital controls on local authorities as it is felt that they effectively represent revenue expenditure. There are, however, specific requirements for local authorities and these include:

1. The residual value does not accrue to the local authority.
2. The property of the asset does not transfer to the authority at the end of the lease.
3. A renewal or extension of the lease is not made at materially less than the market rent.

Contract hire agreements are a straightforward rental agreement whereby the user agrees to rent the asset for a fixed period at a fixed sum. Ownership and all the ongoing risks remain with the lessor and, while the terms of each agreement vary, the lessor assumes responsibility for running costs (excluding fuels and oils) and arranging replacements in the event of breakdown. If supported by an operating lease contract hire agreements do not count against capital expenditure controls on local authorities.

For direct service organizations, and for any organization within the public sector needing to obtain a specified return on capital employed within the new competitive environment, a major advantage is that leased assets do not form part of capital employed as ownership remains with the lessor.

Consider the example in Figure 7.2. The organization concerned must obtain a return of 5% on assets employed. As can be seen from the 'assets owned' column, it is highly marginal with a return of just 4.6%, which could endanger its continued existence. Faced with this problem, and encouraged by central government wishing to see sales of public sector surplus assets, the plant is leased under an operating lease, it no longer forms part of the organization's capital and return on capital increases to 27.5%.

Indeed, faced with competitive legislation, many local authorities have separated direct service organizations (DSOs) from plant ownership, locating the latter as a separate commercial unit, leasing out its vehicles and plant to those DSOs wishing to make use of them; reinforcing the commercial principle, the lessor unit is itself required to make a specified 5% return on capital employed.

In order for leases to be excluded from the balance sheet, they must be classed as operating leases. Finance leases must be capitalized, disclosed on the balance sheet and the cost of the leased asset (less amounts written off) included as an asset of the organization.

7.6 Capital expenditure controls and local authorities

It will be apparent from what has been said already that local authorities are subject to particularly tight central government controls on their capital expenditure and its financing.

Prior to April 1990 the system of control in operation had been introduced under the Local Government Planning and Land Act 1980, which came into force on 1 April 1981. These controls specified that for each authority the Secretary of State would detail 'prescribed' capital expenditure and the amount which each authority could spend on

	Assets owned £m	Assets owned and leased £m
Assets employed		
Buildings	0.2	0.2
Plant	1.0	
Totals	1.2	0.2
Operating income	2.955	2.955
Operating costs		
Operating expenditure	2.7	2.7
Depreciation (20% plant)	0.2	
Lease charge (20% plant)		0.2
	2.9	2.9
Net profit	0.055	0.055
Return on assets	0.055/1.2 = 4.6%	0.055/0.2 = 27.5%

Figure 7.2 Effect of leasing on return of assets

capital expenditure, termed its capital allocation. Capital expenditure had to be contained within the total capital allocation for each authority, subject to a tolerance of 10%; any further underspend would be lost. The capital allocation could also be enhanced by using capital receipts (cash raised by selling assets). In most cases, 50% of the capital receipt could be spent in the year of receipt with 50% of the remaining balance in each successive year – termed the 'cascade effect'.

The pre-1990 system was criticized on a variety of grounds, and to give a flavour of these, the following are included:

1. It operated on a short one-year planning cycle with no commitment to future years and fostered uncertainty when long-term planning was needed.
2. It had contributed to a decline in the quality of capital stock, especially in education, with insufficient allocations for adequate replacement and maintenance.
3. The system was extremely costly and complex to implement.

The Local Government and Housing Act 1989 introduced a revised system of control with effect from 1 April 1990. The system has the following features.

Credit approvals

Under the Act local authorities are given 'credit approvals' which limit, to the value of the credit approval, the amount of capital expenditure that can be met from borrowing or other credit arrangements such as leases.

There are two types of credit approval: a basic credit approval (BCA) which can be used at the discretion of the authority and a specified credit approval (SCA) which may be used for projects specified by the Secretary of State. There is no provision for tolerance between years; if an authority underspends, it loses that spending power.

The credit approval may be supplemented by a proportion of capital receipts, and by meeting capital expenditure from revenue. Revenue financing is limited by capping and, politically, by the amount the council tax payer will agree to pay.

Capital receipts

In determining the BCA, the Secretary of State takes into account his assessment of available capital receipts. However, a proportion of capital receipts received must be set aside for redemption of debt (currently 75% of receipts regarding the sale of council dwellings, and 50% of other capital receipts). The non-reserved part of capital receipts, for example the 25% part of the amount received from the sale of council dwellings, can be used to finance capital expenditure over and above that covered by credit approvals. The cascade interpretation applied to the previous legislation is now prohibited so that the initial discretionary 25% (say) is fixed and none of the balance can subsequently be converted to discretionary use.

It is possible that the Secretary of State may announce a temporary moratorium on the prescribed use of new capital receipts.

Leases

Operating leases relating to vehicles, plant and equipment are not charged against the credit approvals. However, new property leases will count against the credit approvals based upon the capitalized value of the payments to be made under the lease approval.

The 1989 legislation represents a change from that imposed under the Local Government Planning and Land Act 1980 when the nature of the expenditure itself was controlled rather than the source of finance.

The government is currently discussing alternatives to the current system of capital expenditure controls. A green paper issued by the Department of Environment Transport and the Regions (DETR), entitled 'Modernizing Local Government' (2000) considers that the current system's main strength is that it protects those who use and pay for local services from the risk of authorities running up unsustainable debt levels. However, it goes on to argue that the current system is considered to have three weaknesses:

- It seriously erodes local freedom and responsibility because it prevents local authorities from carrying out additional borrowing funded from their own resources.
- It has encouraged an artificial distinction between capital and current resources sometimes preventing good value 'spend to save' schemes from proceeding.
- When schemes are funded by credit approvals, the revenue costs of repayment and interest are largely supported through increased government grants, so the investment is seen as a 'free good' without long-term consequences for local taxpayers.

In view of these weaknesses, the green paper (ibid.) suggests a new approach. It is proposed that there would be a core set of prudential indicators for which local authorities would set their own ratios, for example of debt to revenue, working within a centrally agreed framework. The indicators would help make clear the impact of capital expenditure proposals on the revenue account and allow performance in managing investment to be monitored and assessed. They would be set by a local authority at the budgeting stage and would guide subsequent decision making and monitoring by members. The proposed system would be backed up by the fundamental principle of the balanced budget (specified by legislation) and accounting codes.

In the transitional period there would be a need for powers to control the rate of increase in authorities' debt. The government would have the right to reimpose this if national macro-economic conditions warranted it and would maintain a reserve power to restrict the right to borrowing of those authorities which do not act prudently, fail to deliver best value or fail to consult with local voters and stakeholders.

7.7 Capital expenditure controls and the National Health Service

Capital expenditure in the National Health Service (NHS) is a small proportion of total expenditure and it is initially distributed by central government to regional health authorities; the regions retain a proportion for the funding of regional schemes and distribute the balance to the (district) health authorities and any non-trust hospitals. Trusts are outside this system. Thus, regions and health authorities are given a capital allocation for the year; unlike the local authority case, this actually represents cash to be spent.

There are certain tolerances allowed on the capital expenditure which is allocated to regions and health authorities:

1. Up to 10% of the allocation may be carried forward from one year to the next.
2. Up to 10% of the capital allocation may be transferred to the revenue allocation and up to 1% of the revenue allocation may be transferred to capital.

In addition to these tolerances, there is one further important element of flexibility. Perrin, in Henley *et al.* (1992), explains that health authority treasurers operate a capital 'brokerage' system coordinated by the regional treasurers. An authority may be unable to use all its capital allocation because of project slippage. Alternatively, it may have to slow down capital development because it cannot cope with the revenue consequences as soon as was originally planned. In either case, it can waive part of its capital allocation back into the regional pool of capital for 'brokerage' to some other authority that can use the capital in the current year. In return, the first authority will receive favourable consideration at some later date if it needs some extra capital. In effect, this is a form of inter-authority loan scheme, interest free.

NHS trusts

The controls on trusts are fairly stringent. Every March each trust must submit a business plan to the NHS Management Executive (NHSME). The trust must include within the business plan justification for capital expenditure and include plans for its financing. Trusts must normally fund capital expenditure from their own resources or by borrowing, which is subject to constraint. Thus a trust's capital authorizations are obtained through this project appraisal process and the amount of borrowing available in total is determined by the outcome of the Public Expenditure Survey process. Until trusts have access to private capital, their capital expenditure proposals will be subject to similar constraints as operated in the pre-trust era. Additionally, the trusts are subject to two further constraints which have a connection with capital expenditure:

1. They must earn a 6% rate of return on capital employed. Depreciation is charged in their accounts and their income must cover all costs, including depreciation and earn the rate of return. The income of trusts is obtained by contracting with the purchasing health authorities and general practitioner fundholders within the competitive health environment.
2. The borrowing of each trust is subject to an external financial limit (EFL). This control sets a ceiling on the total amount of external borrowing. EFLs derive from the annual public expenditure. If EFLs for trusts become increasingly tight, they must look at their own internal resources in order to reduce calls on external borrowing. They must examine factors such as increased efficiency, reductions in inventories, the sale of surplus assets and opportunities for bringing in private sector finance under the Public Finance Initiative (PFI). It is possible to have a zero EFL implying that no borrowing is possible. A trust's ability to keep within its EFL while continuing to provide value for money is keenly monitored by the NHSME.

7.8 Special topic 1: The Private Finance Initiative (PFI)

The PFI aims to introduce private sector finance and know-how into the planning, construction and operation of public sector capital assets. The background to its introduction to the public sector is found in the long-term constraint on public sector investment; the desire by central government to keep public sector debt at less than 40% of gross domestic product; and a recognition that the public sector can obtain improved value for money by introducing private sector skills and solutions that are perceived as being different to or better than those found in the public sector. Thus PFI should result in a higher level of investment in public sector infrastructure without increased public sector borrowing. The other aim of policy is to reallocate some of the risk related to infrastructure projects from the public sector to the private sector. The PFI is part of the range of public–private partnerships.

In order to justify the use of private sector finance, the public sector organization must submit a full business case. The submission must include a comparative value for money appraisal of PFI funding and the public sector funding and management (the Public Sector Comparator). This comparison must demonstrate that PFI will demonstrate greater value for money than the Public Sector Comparator. The analysis will involve discounting the real terms options of both options at 6%.

Examples of PFI schemes are as follows:

■ PFI has been used in planning the construction and operation of a proposed new hospital in Worcester costing £90–£95m. The benefits claimed for PFI in this case include the access to capital when it is required, the reduction in financial risk associated with a private partner taking responsibility for capital cost increases and also the transfer to the private partner of any problems over the life of the project in terms of design and future defects.

■ The Ministry of Defence has been an enthusiastic user of the PFI. For example, in 2000/01 it expects to involve £405m of private investment in defence projects. PFI money has been used on a range of schemes to date including the Attack Helicopter Training Project (£165m), a Joint Services Command and Staff College (£68m) and the provision of family quarters at Lossiemouth (£24m).

A possible PFI project might relate to building a school. If this took place, the local authority would pay a series of fees to the developer to cover design, construction costs, any support services (such as caretaker, groundsmen, cleaners) and the transfer of risks to the private sector (risks such as delays in completion and cost overruns).

The process of the evaluation of a prospective PFI project would go through three stages:

Initial analysis and appraisal

There must be justification that a project meets specific needs and that the project is technically feasible before going any further. There can be investment appraisal at this stage to determine that the benefits exceed the costs of the proposed project.

Generation of alternatives

This will involve examining different methods of financing. It will involve testing the market for potential private sector providers and identifying the potential public sector financing route (the Public Sector Comparator).

Investment and option appraisal

Various investment appraisal techniques are applied in a more detailed analysis of the project and the manner of its financing. Its objective is to choose the best financing and operating alternative from a value for money perspective taking account of factors such as lifecycle costs and cash inflows over the duration of the project and levels of service.

The financial elements will be discounted at 6%.

The advantages of the PFI are as follows:

- The public sector body is not committed to a large lump-sum payment at the commencement of the project.
- Instead, the commitment is to pay out a series of cash flows over a fixed time period. This may allow for easier budgeting.
- The public sector obtains the expertise of the private sector.
- There is the opportunity for a public–private pollination of ideas and there may be secondment opportunities for staff.
- The investment does not require the public sector body to have access to borrowing or other sources of capital finance.
- The private sector body takes on the risks of financing, constructing and operating the asset.
- The public sector should obtain better value for money from the PFI.

The disadvantages are as follows:

- There may be a transfer of assets to the private sector. This implies a loss of control and accountability by the public sector organization.
- Private sector providers will need to make a profit.
- They will also have to pay higher finance charges than the public sector.
- Risk transfer to the private sector will also result in an increase in the costs to be recovered by the provider.

In isolation, each of the last three points would increase the costs of the project. However, it is anticipated that the greater efficiency of the private sector will produce savings that exceed these higher costs. One aim of the detailed option appraisal is to determine whether this occurs and whether the PFI delivers value for money for the public sector organization.

7.9 Special topic 2: Setting a borrowing strategy

In this section we examine some of the key variables in the establishment of a borrowing strategy; the organization chosen as a vehicle for demonstrating this is a local authority because, currently, it is one of the few types of public sector organizations that takes an active role in debt management.

First, we look at the types of borrowing or the range of borrowing instruments that are available to the local authority treasurer. The types of borrowing that a local authority may undertake include the following.

Short term (less than 12 months)

Short term borrowing for capital purposes is termed 'temporary borrowing' and includes the range from borrowing overnight to borrowing for up to a year. The money is usually cheaper than longer term finance because it is at risk for a shorter period of time, and provides an important source of finance when long-term interest rates are high. If interest rates are high, borrowing short term is very advantageous because it does not commit the organization to high interest rates over a long period. Regular short term borrowing provides an entrée to contacts in the money markets which will permit the lending of temporary surpluses of cash.

However, it is volatile, in that some forms of temporary money are repayable on demand and temporary borrowing may require refinancing when interest rates are high. Finally, the amount of temporary borrowing that an organization can take is limited by legislation.

Medium term (one to five years)

Local bonds

These are usually sold to the general public and the amounts involved are often relatively small in capital financing terms; they are deliberately flexible in structure with a flexibility over term, dates for interest payments and a relationship between interest rates offered and the size of the loan. A register is maintained by the local authority and, as with building societies, interest is paid net of standard rate income tax except in the case of investors on a low income to whom interest may be paid gross.

Negotiable bonds

These are concerned with larger sums than local bonds and are sold in large tranches on the money market; they offer same-day transferability and this advantage confers lower rates of interest. However, an issue is an expensive exercise.

Long term (over five years)

Public Works Loans Board

Local authorities have access to borrowing from the Public Works Loans Board (PWLB), which allows access to funds raised by central government. The money is usually very long term with a minimum period of ten years and, in theory, a marginally attractive rate of interest is available on loans that do not exceed an authority's given quota.

Stock

This is issued and traded on the London Stock Exchange, in common with government and corporate stock. The amounts involved are very substantial, as are the fixed costs of issue, which mean that organizations may form into consortia in order to secure the cost advantages of a large-scale issue. There is a queuing system for issue and a considerable amount of time is required to organize a stock issue.

Apart from these, there are a variety of other loans available from the market and among the most popular are variable or floating rate bonds; these are medium and long-term loans with the interest rate tied to underlying short-term interest rates (the London Inter-Bank Offer Rate – LIBOR) but adjusted by previous agreement. Thus, the interest rate may be adjusted annually or more frequently.

The variety of loan packages on offer means that discounted cash flow (DCF) techniques need to be employed to identify the true interest rate that a loan carries. DCF is discussed in Chapter 9.

Constraints on borrowing

As has been indicated earlier, the volume of temporary borrowing available to an authority is subject to control by legislation. We have also seen that total annual borrowing is subject to the ceiling imposed in credit approvals.

Additionally, many local authority treasurers set a floor on the average loan period of outstanding debt. The higher this floor is, the longer the average loan period and the less frequently the authority will need to refinance its debt. Of course, when interest rates are high, there may be pressure to borrow for shorter periods and then refinance the loans with longer term borrowing when rates decrease.

In summary, the position is highly complex with a range of borrowing instruments, costs of administration and rates of interest, with constant changes in overall rates of interest, with financing required for both new capital expenditure and for refinancing of debt.

We now examine the application of this to a problem of borrowing policy within a local authority.

Scenario

At 30 December 2000 the Assistant Director of Finance of the Loanshire County Council is considering the borrowing policy for the remainder of the financial year. The position on interest rates is that they have fallen by about 2% since April 2000, but are now expected to increase in view of the inflationary outlook. The composition of current outstanding debt is shown in Table 7.4. The estimated borrowing requirement, excluding the refinancing of temporary debt, is shown Table 7.5. The loans which are expected to be available during the next three months are as summarized in Figure 7.3. The authority's temporary loan debt is limited to £25m at 31 March 2001.

Table 7.4   Composition of current debt

	£m
Stock	15.00
Fixed rate bonds	24.08
Variable rate bonds	21.00
PWLB loans	73.60
Temporary loans (£28.5m repayable by 31.3.2001)	31.50
Total (average rate of interest 10.8%)	165.18

Table 7.5   Estimated borrowing requirements

Jan/March	2001	–1/–2	–2/–3	–3/–4	–4/–5	–5/–6
£m	5.4	14.5	38.7	13.4	25.9	33.0

The authority also aims for an average loan period of at least seven years on all debt raised in a financial year. It does this in order to achieve an average loan period of at least seven years on the whole amount of its outstanding borrowing. The long-term debt raised during 2000/01 to date has been as follows:

£17.5m PWLB 10-year instalment
£1.0m fixed interest rate bonds for two years
£1.0m fixed interest rate bonds for three years.

Type of loan	Amount	Terms		
PWLB	£2.5m	12% 10 year		
		12.5% 25 year		
Fixed and variable rate bonds	Unlimited	Interest rates		
		Years	Fixed	Variable 3-month + rate
			%	%
		1	11.5	
		2	11.75	.75
		3	12	1
		4	12.125	1 1/16
		5	12.25	1.124
		6	12.375	1.25
		7	12.5	1.5
		8	12.5	1.5
Temporary loans	Unlimited	< 3 months		11.25%
		3 months +		11.375%

Figure 7.3 Loans available during the next three months

Discussion

Faced with this scenario, the matters which the Assistant Director is likely to be concerned with are discussed in the following sections.

Increasing interest rates

Interest rates have been declining but are expected to increase. In itself this would lead to long-term borrowing, but this is mitigated by the fact that, at 11/12%, long-term interest rates are still relatively high. Presumably then, one would advocate borrowing for a period of, say, three years, allowing time for interest rates to rise and then fall, hopefully to below today's levels.

Future borrowing needs

The previous recommendation is reinforced by the need to borrow £38.7m in two years' time which would lead one to avoid any further borrowing for refinancing of debt during that financial year. By the same token, the estimate for 2003/04 shows a much lower level of borrowing. Later years show an increase in borrowing well above the 2003/04 level.

The next three months

Of the temporary loans £28.5m will need to be refinanced by 31 March 2001. However, the temporary loan ceiling is £25m; this means that after allowing for £3m re the loans which do not require refinancing (£31.5m–£28.5m), there is £22m of temporary loans available. This leaves £6.5m which must be found from non-temporary sources.

Non-temporary borrowing will amount to £11.9m for the next three months, made up of £6.5m from the temporary shortfall plus £5.4m of new borrowing.

The average loan period

The debt raised so far this year provides an average loan period of 9.23 years. The calculations underlying this are contained in Figure 7.4.

Loans	Amount £m	×	Duration	=	Budgeted loan years m
PWLB	17.5		10 years		175
Fixed bonds (2 years)	1.0		2 years		2
Fixed bonds (3 years)	1.0		3 years		3
Totals	19.5				180

Weighted average loan years = 180/19.5 = 9.23 loan years

In order to determine the minimum duration of the additional £11.9m of loans:

Total borrowed (19.5 + 11.9) m	£31.4m
Multiply by minimum loan years requirement	*7
	219.8m
Less loan years on lending to date:	180.0m
Loan years required on remaining debt	39.8m
Divided by amount of outstanding debt	11.9m
Minimum required duration of remaining debt	3.34 years

Figure 7.4   Calculation of the average loan period

As the authority is aiming for a minimum average of seven loan years on new debt, the additional borrowing of £11.9m must have an average loan period of at least 3.34 years. This will mean borrowing a mix of three-year and four-year bonds in the ratio of approximately £2 of three-year bonds to each £1 of four-year bonds.

Variable and fixed rate bonds

The choice between variable and fixed rate bonds is a difficult one but if the whole spectrum of interest rates is going to increase, they will probably stay above current levels for at least a year which may push the future variable rate up above the current fixed-term rate. However, if interest rates fall, the future variable rate may fall to below the current fixed rate. There is no correct answer to this problem; it depends on economic forecasts and one's attitude to risk.

Conclusion

In conclusion, the following policy represents one way forward:

1. replace 'temporary' with 'temporary up to the ceiling of £25m';
2. borrow the remaining £11.9m from a combination of three-year and four-year fixed interest loans.

7.10 Special topic 3: A property leaseback deal

The bare bones of a leaseback deal have been outlined already. In this section we look more deeply into the dynamics of such an arrangement. A summary of the steps involved in such a deal is contained in Figure 7.5.

Public body	Developer
1. Acquires site	
2. Commissions a design	3. Finances the development
4. Leases the site to the developer, at a peppercorn rent	5. Sub-leases the site back to the public body

Figure 7.5 Main steps in a lease-leaseback deal

As may be seen in Figure 7.5, it is the public authority's responsibility to acquire the site in the first place and then to commission a design for the scheme that it wants. The developer provides sufficient finance to construct the development, including the original costs of site acquisition and design, if necessary. When the site is fully developed, the public authority leases the site to the developer at a nominal rent termed a 'peppercorn'. The developer then sub-leases the scheme to the public authority at a rental which is initially related to the amount of finance advanced by the developer. This final step gives it the term lease-leaseback.

Usually, the finance required to construct the development is advanced in stages by the developer, often with floors and ceilings relating to the amounts to be advanced, so that the funding company can manage its own cash flows efficiently. Any drawings outside these limits may be subject to a penalty clause. Such advances normally accrue or 'roll up' compound interest which is added to the total of monies advanced.

The payments to the developer will commence on completion of the project and will be established, as a minimum, at x% of the total of the amount advanced plus rolled-up interest. The initial total annual payment is known as the 'finance rent'.

The finance rent is usually subject to review at regular intervals and may well be tied to the growth in rental value of the actual development. The sub-lease may specify that the developer may have a share in the equity of the development with the 'equity sharing ratio' accruing to the developer being set at:

$$\frac{\text{Finance rent}}{\text{Initial market rental value for the development}}$$

Therefore, subject to the floor set by the finance rent, the developer can expect to see income rising with rental values.

The advantages to a public sector organization of this type of agreement is that the management and control of the organization rests with them, as do any risks associated with the development. The financier is shielded by the finance rent from a downturn in returns.

Of course, if the public sector body wants to share more equally in the fruits of its own commercial management, it should strive to minimize the amounts advanced by the financier and, therefore, the equity-sharing ratio. This would require the contribution of finance from its own internal resources.

In the past, such deals have been arranged for the purpose of financing buildings such as civic and commercial centres and, in the future, could be used to finance a variety of greenfield areas such as, for example, car parking and luxury private bed provision at hospitals.

7.11 Special topic 4: Derivatives

The term 'derivatives' refers to financial instruments which derive from primary instruments such as loans. Here three types of derivative are examined:

1. interest rate swaps;
2. financial futures;
3. options.

Interest rate swaps

During the 1980s interest rate swaps were a rapidly growing activity in the United States and were used by several local authorities in the United Kingdom during the latter half of the 1980s. Swaps have largely arisen as a means by which organizations can gain access to borrowing on more favourable terms than could be achieved with direct borrowing.

Basically, a swap may be defined as a transaction in which two borrowers agree to borrow equal amounts of principal, from different lenders, and then make interest payments which are unrelated to the direct borrowing of each.

Swaps exist because different organizations can borrow at different rates of interest in different markets. They frequently involve swaps between fixed-interest rate loans and floating rate loans, where the interest is tied to an underlying short-term rate such as the London Inter-Bank Offer Rate (LIBOR).

There are many variations on the swap idea, but, for illustration, the simple or orthodox swap is as follows. Suppose that one borrower is local authority X which can borrow fixed-interest rate money fairly cheaply but wants access to floating rate loans because it feels that interest rates will fall. Borrower Y is a company which is able to raise floating rate funds very cheaply but wants to raise fixed-rate loans and secure itself to the current interest rate for a long period.

The current situation is shown in Figure 7.6. Next we shall consider how each party may benefit from the relative advantage obtained by the other.

Considering Figure 7.6, X and Y make an agreement with each other; X will borrow £10m fixed for five years at 10%, Y will borrow £10m floating five years at 8%. Each also agrees to pay the interest due on the loan raised by the other: X pays floating rate interest at 8%, Y pays fixed rate interest at 10%. Each gains as follows:

$$X: \text{annual gain } (9\% - 8\%) * £10m = £100\,000$$
$$Y; \text{annual gain } (11\% - 10\%) * £10m = £100\,000.$$

A public authority	A company
Borrower X	Borrower Y
Available:	Available:
£10m, fixed 5-year, 10%	£10m, fixed 5-year, 11%
£10m, floating 5-year, 9%	£10m, floating 5-year, 8%

Figure 7.6   Initial position

Thus, each organization borrows in the manner that it desires and in each case at 1% below the interest rate available to it.

Local authorities have used swaps as a method of reducing the interest cost of debt or in order to hedge against a fall in interest rates which also serves to reduce interest costs.

However, the case of Hammersmith and Fulham had a significant effect on the dealings of local authorities with the banks and other financial institutions in relation to interest rate swaps. The Court of Appeal decided that interest rate swap transactions were capable of being in the power of local authorities as long as they were undertaken for the purposes of interest risk management and not for trading puposes. Thus under the swap principle local authorities would be able to swap fixed-rate debt for variable rate debt as long as they are able to show that the transaction is to further normal investment management. The judgement in the Hammersmith and Fulham case was that the Council's transactions between 1983 and July 1988 were illegal in that they were entered into for trading purposes and contravened section 19 of the Local Government Act 1972. The House of Lords subsequently ruled that swaps were *ultra vires* and therefore unavailable to local authorities. This ruling meant that local authorities were precluded from getting the best out of prevailing interest rates which must increase the overall costs of borrowing. This ruling had important implications for the banks as transactions which they had entered into with local authorities were now deemed illegal and several banks made significant provisions for losses within their accounts following the House of Lords ruling.

Financial futures

Financial futures are contracts to buy or sell a standard quantity of a financial instrument at a predetermined future date but at a price agreed now. The financial instrument may be an interest rate on a five-year loan or a stock market index, for example. Within the United Kingdom the heart of the market in financial futures is the London International Financial Futures and Options Exchange (LIFFE). Local authority superannuation funds have power to use these under the Local Government Superannuation Regulations 1986.

The main function of futures is to protect the fund and reduce risk. One illustration of this is the use of futures to guarantee the purchaser of a specific interest rate at some predetermined future date. If a financial manager expects interest rates to increase but this sentiment is not shared by the market then a future can be used to ensure that funds are available in the future at current market rates of interest.

Future contracts must be completed and a pension fund, say, must be able to fulfil the contract. In practice, completion is assured by both buyer and seller depositing a small initial margin as a form of security. Then, each day the gain or loss on the futures contract is calculated within the clearing system and is settled up by whichever party needs to make the payment.

Options

These are financial instruments which give the buyer the right but not the obligation to buy or sell the underlying asset at an agreed price (termed the exercise or strike price) and within a specified time period. The underlying assets might be a quantity of shares in a company, an amount of a loan at a future interest rate or a quantity of an underlying market index such as the *Financial Times* stock exchange list of the top 100 firms on the London Stock Exchange known as (FTSE100). Thus, options differ from futures in one very important respect: with a future the buyer has to complete the deal whereas with an option the buyer is not obligated to complete the deal. However, the seller of the option does have an obligation to complete the transaction if the buyer wishes to exercise the right to complete.

Options are of two types:

1. Call options give the buyer the right to buy the underlying asset.
2. Put options give the buyer the right to sell the underlying asset.

The buyer of the option pays a small premium to the seller or writer of the option contract. This premium is retained by the writer of the option and is used to defray expenses and compensate for the risk involved in writing options.

There is a traded market for options which is regulated by LIFFE but options have existed for considerably longer than the organized market. Options which are bought and sold on the organized LIFFE market are termed traded options; they offer standardization in terms of quantity represented by one option contract (for example, 1000 shares) and in terms of duration of the contract. Standardization provides for an organized market and it is possible for the purchaser of an option to resell the option. Premium prices and exercise prices for traded options are quoted on a daily basis in the press. The risks and rewards for traded options differ as between the different parties. The risk of buyers is limited to the premium price which has been paid. The gain to writers of options is limited to the premium received but potential losses can be substantial because the writer has an obligation to complete the contract if called upon to do so by the buyer.

As with futures, call options may be purchased in order to protect the fund against anticipated price rises. A fund manager should not consider writing call options unless it holds the underlying asset so that the fund can settle the option from existing resources if the option is exercised.

It is important that fund managers have adequate understanding and experience if they are going to take advantage of the opportunities offered by options. It is also essential that there are sound control systems in place.

Key points of chapter

1. There are four main methods of financing capital expenditure.
2. Each method possesses specific advantages and disadvantages.
3. Central government control effectively constrains an organization's ability to use the four methods.
4. The PFI presents a way to input private capital and skills into the provision and operation of public sector assets.
5. A borrowing strategy aims to reduce costs but must operate within constraints.
6. A leaseback deal offers a flexible way of introducing private sector finance.
7. Derivatives can reduce borrowing costs but must be used with care.

7.12 Summary

Local authorities can finance capital expenditure in a number of ways although the use of capital funds has recently been withdrawn from them. The latest method of central government control constrains the total of annual capital expenditure via the system of credit approvals. The total can be enhanced by a defined proportion of capital receipts and by financing from revenue. In local authorities the management of loans and the use of leases are well developed.

Central government uses a combination of borrowing, revenue (taxation primarily) and the receipts from asset sales and privatizations. Leasing plays a very minor role.

The NHS currently receives a capital allocation from central government; this allocation is effectively cash for capital expenditure. No borrowing is permitted. There is some flexibility at the margin via the capital/revenue and inter-year tolerances and this is increased by the brokerage system implemented by NHS treasurers. Currently, trusts have little flexibility in the area of capital finance. However, in future we may see them looking at borrowing strategies, leaseback and derivatives. As we have seen, these represent ways of reducing the costs of borrowing while leaseback is a way of bringing private sector funds into the public sector in a joint financing approach.

Questions

7.1 You are the loans officer for a small district council responsible, under the treasurer, for managing the borrowing and lending activities of the authority. Your treasurer has recently been appointed after a career in the Health Services.

(i) Write a note to the treasurer about your job.   (13 marks)

Include in your answer:

(a) The objectives you are seeking to achieve.
(b) An outline of the constraints under which you work.
(c) A summary of the information you require at various stages to do your job.

(ii) How would you recommend that your performance should be evaluated; for example, who should receive reports on your activities and what should be the contents of these reports?   (5 marks)
                                                                (Total 18 marks)

7.2 Contrast the methods of capital finance available to a health authority and a local authority.

7.3 Prepare a reply to the following letter:

> 16 Bramble Villas
> Goodtown
> 25 September 20X0

The Treasurer
Good Health Authority

Dear Sir

Annual accounts
I have just seen a copy of your accounts for 2000/2001 and I wish to raise a question about one of the depreciations charged in the accounts.

I have examined central government accounts for many years and I understand fully the rationale for the cash-based system used there – particularly its clarity and transparency. I cannot understand why you have departed from such a tried and tested system by introducing fairly arbitrary non-cash depreciation. What can the organization possibly benefit from this practice?

I look forward to your explanation.

Yours faithfully

Ian M Expert

7.4 Set out the principal arguments for a policy of pay as you go rather than a policy of financing through borrowing.

7.5 Contrast the capital controls on health authorities with those on local authorities.

7.6 Prepare a short memorandum setting out the principal factors to be considered in establishing a borrowing policy at the current time.

7.7 A developer is financing a project via a leaseback deal. The developer makes the following advances of cash:

1 April 19X1	£500 000
1 October 19X1	£500 000

The project is completed on 31 March 19X2. It is agreed that the developer is to be credited with interest on advances at the rate of 20%, compounded each six months and added to the total advanced on 31 March 19X2.

Required

Calculate the developer's total financial interest in the project at 31 March 19X2.

7.8 Indicate how interest rate swaps may be of value to both the following parties:

Authority A	*Company B*
Funds available:	*Funds available:*
£25m fixed 10-year 11%	£25m fixed 10-year 12%
£25m floating 10-year 10.5%	£25m floating 10-year 9%
Funds required:	*Funds required:*
£25m floating	£25m fixed

7.9 Glamshire (Cars) Ltd, a subsidiary company of Glamshire Council, is considering the correct method of financing its car fleet.

Michael Morris, the Group Accountant, has narrowed the choices down to two.

1. Purchase the fleet outright.
2. Lease the fleet on contract hire (with maintenance) basis – an operating fleet.

He has spent some time gathering information that he felt was relevant to the decision in hand.

General information

(i) Cost of capital – 15%.
(ii) Corporation tax – 35%.
(iii) Capital allowances on fleet purchase to be 25% reducing balance.
(iv) Corporation tax to be payable one year from end of accounting year to which it relates.
(v) There are six major costs of acquiring and operating a fleet, finance, insurance, maintenance, fuel, incidentals and management.
(vi) The fleet of vehicles to be acquired would be 17 Ford cars ranging from the Sierra 2.0i Ghia to the Escort 1.3L fivedoor estate.
(vii) Useful life of fleet three years before replacement. Straight-line depreciation is used for the outright purchase option.
(viii) Costs relate to best quotes obtained for each option.
(ix) Cash flows deemed to arise as follows:
Initial purchase price – year 0.
Lease payments – at *beginning* of each year in which they occur. All other payments – at end of each year which they occur.
(x) Ignore inflation.

Company Method of finance	Evans Hailshaw Purchase £	Lease plan Contract hire £
Purchase price (*total*)	141 132	N/A
Monthly lease/hire payments	N/A	6 052
Residual value after three years	58 343	N/A
Insurance per *vehicle* per *year*	1 000	inclusive
Total maintenance over three years	21 219	inclusive
Total petrol over three years	47 850	inclusive
Total incidentals over three years	16 173	51 000
Total management charge over three years	9 750	1 950

Note: that the management charge is calculated as follows:

Number of hours required × fully absorbed cost per hour.

The fully absorbed cost per hour is £13, made up as follows:

	£
Wages of fleet manager(ess)	5
Pension and wages cost	2
Admin. overhead	5
Provision of car	1
	£13

*These figures are based on a manager(ess) having to spend 1/3 of their time (1/15 in the case of contract hire) managing the car fleet.

Required

(a) Evaluate the options open to management, taking taxation into account but ignoring inflation and carefully explaining your treatment of the management charge.
(b) Which would you recommend, taking into account the advantages and disadvantages of each method of financing?
(c) One advantage of contract hire is that more of your costs are certain. How would it be possible to put some sort of monetary value on this? (You are not required to do any calculations.)

8 Capital budgets and capital programmes

Key learning objectives

After reading this chapter you should be able to:

1. Identify the problems of defining capital expenditure in the public sector.
2. Prepare a capital programme and demonstrate its benefits to managers.
3. Explain, critically, how projects are screened and selected.
4. Calculate the revenue consequences of a project.
5. Explain one way in which financial and non-financial factors may be combined in project appraisal.

Capital expenditure by central government, the NHS and the local authority sector runs currently at about £35bn per annum. Within the different sectors, there must exist systems for appraising, organizing, financing and controlling such investment. It is important that the correct capital investment decision is taken as poor decisions can have the following consequences:

1. They can lead to investments in assets which give no productive benefit and, due to the large scale, and sometimes specialist nature of some projects, may have no alternative use. The resale value, if any, may bear little relationship to actual cost.
2. In those areas of the public sector subject to competitive tendering, incorrect investment will increase costs with no obvious improvements in efficiency or output, leading to reduced profits or even losses which, if sufficiently large, could ultimately close the operation down.
3. In the more traditional service areas of the public sector such as health, social services and education, the incorrect investment decision will place increased costs on the taxpayer. This could prove particularly important in local authorities given the potential impact of the council tax, in that the commitment of the government is to increase the business rate and revenue support grants by no more than the retail price index. This will inevitably place a greater burden on the local taxpayer resulting from specific local authority inflation or local authority service increases that are not in line with central government's expectations. The relationship between local increases in expenditure and the resulting disproportionate increase in local taxation is termed the gearing effect.

All capital investment decisions should be taken within a framework which identifies a specific need for a project within the stated objectives of the organization. In the private sector the objective of all projects is usually the maximization of profit. Within the competitive arms of the public sector any investment decision must contribute towards the stated target rate of return. For example, in a capital works unit of a local authority where the return is expressed as a 5% return on the current cost of capital employed the selected project must achieve at least this return. A similar requirement would apply to NHS trusts which have to achieve a return of 6%. Where the target is expressed in terms of income equalling expenditure at a minimum the project should be at least self-financing. Where no stated target exists any project should contribute to maximizing service delivery by improving economy, efficiency and effectiveness.

8.1 The definition of capital expenditure

Within the private sector, a fixed asset is defined according to the nature of the expenditure, its materiality and whether it confers benefits beyond the current accounting period. In the case of local government, a similar approach is taken, with capital expenditure being regarded as any outlay which is of value to the authority in the provision of its services beyond the end of the year of account. It is then recorded as a capital asset provided there are no legal constraints. Capital outlays which are very small in relation to the general magnitude of such outlays may be recorded in an aggregate minor capital assets account. Capital outlays which are not material to the size and nature of the local authority or which could be consumed in the following accounting period are disregarded in the asset accounts. Within the NHS and other sections of central government, rules are specified as to the type and scale of the expenditure. Thus, at the time of writing, capital expenditure in the NHS is specified as expenditure in excess of £5000 giving benefit for more than one year.

Within the private sector, fixed assets are normally depreciated, ensuring that the profit and loss account bears a charge for the use of the assets and thereby restricting distributable profit and maintaining the organization's original capital. Within local authorities, currently, fixed assets are recorded, but are not depreciated; the charge to the revenue accounts is a reflection of how the asset has been financed by the local authority: for example, if the asset is financed by loan, the Local Government Act 1972 specifies that the interest and principal repayments are charged to the revenue accounts as the loan is repaid. Other methods of financing are: by a direct charge to revenue; from earmarked provisions such as renewals provisions; by grants; and finally by the application of capital receipts. If an asset is financed by loan, the principal repayment in the service revenue account might be regarded as being equivalent to depreciation as long as the life of the asset equals the life of the loan. However, the question of depreciation is not at all irrelevant as CIPFA and local authority treasurers now implement depreciation with effect from the end of the 1994/95 financial year. A depreciation charge is currently calculated outside the main accounts for specialist direct service organizations (DSOs) and direct labour organizations (DLOs) and is directly relevant to calculating the rate of return.

Within central government, assets are currently not recorded as such in the organization's accounts and there is no charge for depreciation to the revenue accounts of the component departments. Expenditure for capital and revenue purposes is strictly segregated and serve primarily for the allocation of distinct and separate capital and revenue funding to organizations.

Within the NHS assets are now recorded within the accounts at replacement cost and depreciation is recorded within accounts. The revenue accounts of non-trust health units bear a charge for capital consumption equivalent to depreciation plus 6% interest on fixed assets which are held. The managing health authority has a duty to ensure that such health units break even after covering these capital charges. In the case of trust hospitals there is a requirement of a 6% return after allowing for depreciation.

8.2 The generation of new projects

In practice, every year new investment projects will be proposed within all these organizations. Almost inevitably, given the infinite demand for capital schemes, there is an inability to satisfy all demands because capital finance is normally restricted. There is one exception to this which is the situation of capital-led revenue. This occurs when specifically targeted capital funding is more freely available than revenue funding and can occur in organizations such as central government in which capital resources are completely separate from revenue resources. For example, there might be sufficient capital funds to acquire a body scanner, but the organization may be unable to find the annual revenue support costs. Apart from this type of situation, the classic case is one of capital rationing which means that we should only accept capital schemes which have been subject to rational processes of project selection and appraisal. A common problem of all public sector organizations is thus the prioritizing and applying of funds to specific projects. In prioritizing, account will be taken of the benefits flowing from the project, the estimated capital costs associated with the project will need to be calculated, as will the annual recurring revenue costs (or benefits) flowing from the project. Thus, a proposal for a new wing of a hospital will establish the patient-related services to be located therein, along with support services. The capital costs will be estimated from construction costs and equipment costs. Land purchase costs will be relevant if the health authority or trust does not already own the land. Before the wing can be up and running, there will need to be consideration of removal costs, the staffing levels will be carefully established and staffing costs estimated; similarly the whole range of non-staff costs will have to be estimated. Of course, the expenditure will not take place instantly but be phased over a period of time; any income will also be phased, as may the gradual transfer of patients to the wing.

Competing projects require to be prioritized or ranked in order of importance and in many organizations such ranking takes place as a result of the action of a project appraisal team (PAT). This team is usually composed of officers from various disciplines and it is their task to recommend the schemes which conform with the organization's objectives and should be included in the capital programme. In many organizations the inclusion of a scheme in the capital programme is a two-stage process:

1. An outline appraisal which gives approval in principle for a scheme to be included within a multi-year capital programme; at this stage, the need for the project is established and an estimate of costs is developed.
2. A more detailed project appraisal of those projects within the capital programme. This will establish more detailed estimates, especially of revenue costs, may attempt to measure benefits from competing projects, and examine in detail the financing of the project.

It is also essential that the PAT keeps under review schemes already in the capital programme. Given the time it takes to determine whether schemes should go ahead and to complete work, it is essential that the original justification of the scheme still exists for otherwise scarce resources will be wasted. Reserve schemes should also be available in case project delay or 'slippage' takes place. If central government operates a control on cash spending, there will be a need to introduce schemes quickly to utilize the funds available otherwise the capital allocation may be lost, especially if all opportunities for virement to revenue have already been used up. Such a reserve list might include vehicles which were part of a planned replacement programme but which it was impossible to replace due to inadequate funds. Clearly vehicles can be replaced and paid for rapidly unless there are any specialist requirements.

The planning of schemes by stressing the revenue consequences also enable service managers to identify when a project is coming on stream. In a 'no growth' revenue budget situation they will be identified sufficiently far in advance so that revenue savings may be found to absorb the operational costs of the capital scheme in order that capital assets do not lie idle. The inclusion of a scheme in the capital programme does not mean that the scheme will automatically go ahead. Before final approval is given, detailed specifications will be drawn up and put out to competitive tender. These tenders should be compared to the original estimates before a final decision on proceeding with the scheme is made.

The objectives of capital budgeting

In summary, capital budgets are devised to:

1. Express in financial terms the capital works necessary to meet the objectives expressed or implied by an organization's objectives and policies.
2. Set out agreed priorities for the commencement of capital schemes.
3. Facilitate the coordination of plans and resources by:
    (a) allocating financial resources between departments;
    (b) assisting in implementing the capital scheme;
    (c) providing a basis for forecasting capital cash flows and requirements;
    (d) providing a basis for forecasting revenue effects;
    (e) providing a basis for budgetary control;
    (f) satisfying government capital control requirements.

8.3 The multi-year capital programme

As was outlined earlier, the two major concerns in the screening of new projects are likely to be, first, the specification and financing of the capital cost involved and, second, the revenue consequences of such capital expenditure (RCCE). In practice, a number of projects may be under consideration, or in different stages of completion, and one valuable device of forecasting the financial impact is the medium-term capital programme.

Table 8.1 provides a summary indication of the form of such a programme.

In Table 8.1, it is assumed that the current year is 2000/01. The table shows, for example, that the total estimated capital expenditure in 2002/03 is £88 000, that Project 056 incurred expenditure prior to the current year, that only Project 059 is due to commence in the current year, and that Project 061 will incur capital expenditure in years beyond 2004/05. Projected start and finish date information is provided for each project, as is information about the estimated RCCE; all except Project 059 are expected to incur additional revenue expenditure, but 059 is expected to produce savings of £28 000 per year.

Table 8.1 An outline capital programme

Project	Start/end	Capital expenditure (£000)					Total	Full-year RCCE £000
		1/4/01	01/02	02/03	03/04	04/05		
056	99/01	58	43	10			111	27
059	00/01		120	78			198	28+
060	02/03				27		27	3
061	02/06				30	35	80	9
		58	163	88	57	35	416	11

Within the public sector in general, most projects *are* likely to result in additional RCCE. For example, an extension to a hospital is unlikely to reduce costs, although it may well increase the level and quality of service provided to patients. Similarly, a new motorway will generate benefits to users, but will result in additional maintenance costs for the Department of Transport. In the competitive services it will inevitably be a prerequisite that a proposed capital scheme will at the very least be self-financing. If the scheme is not self-financing it should be rejected unless the parent organization, for safety or environmental reasons possibly, is prepared to make a specific subsidy towards the new scheme.

Thus, from Table 8.1 it may be seen that the capital programme acts as a valuable planning document. It identifies the projects that will be coming on-stream in the future and provides a summary estimate of the capital costs of each project, year by year and in total. The total capital expenditure for each year is an important indicator of the amount of capital expenditure which will need to be financed. An organization's ability to finance capital expenditure will itself be a limiting factor, the bottom line for each year may be used as a ceiling and any new projects may only be accommodated if the ceiling is not breached. If it is desired to rephase the totality of capital expenditure, then the capital programme is a useful basis for examining the impact of rescheduling on the annual total expenditure. The programme tends to be of a 'rolling' nature; each year a new year is added and the previous year disappears. Projects also move into and out of the programme; when they come within the current planning horizon of the programme, in this case 2004/05, they are included and are taken out in the year after completion. Similarly, a project may be withdrawn from the programme, for example, due to changes in needs, priorities, estimated engineering problems, or because sufficient financing is unavailable possibly due to a desire by central government to cut public sector capital expenditure.

The capital programme does have one significant weakness. It is purely input oriented; the only values indicated are those of input values. It says absolutely nothing about the outputs – the service improvements, the benefits to taxpayers, that result from the expenditure.

8.4 The detailed project appraisal

Capital costs and their financing

At this stage detailed estimates of capital costs will be provided, as will information as to financing. This will clearly involve the input of a variety of professional skills; in the NHS engineers, builders and doctors will be able to specify the detailed physical requirements and possibly estimated capital costs. It may be difficult to evaluate such estimates other than by examining the *actual* costs of similar projects carried out elsewhere, suitably uprated for inflation. Experience shows that, from defence contractors to tunnel builders, the capital costs are often grossly underestimated. A comparison of previously planned completion dates with actual results may also prove rewarding. There will also be a need to provide detailed phasings, establishing key dates for the work to be carried out and this may require the use of critical path analysis. Key dates are also important so that the chief financial officer can organize finance to come on-stream when it is needed. This is true of capital finance which may be taken up as necessary and is especially true of RCCE which will typically build up in stages within and between years.

Within central government, funding will originate from the organization's capital allocation, which is fixed for the year. Within NHS trust hospitals there is no specific capital allocation. Instead, the trust must submit a detailed option appraisal, the amount of detail which has to be included is influenced by the scale of the project. For example, for schemes costing more than £1m but less than £10m the following information must be provided:

1. the objectives of the scheme;
2. description of all the options considered for meeting the objectives;
3. the criteria used to evaluate the options and explanation of why the selected option was chosen;
4. details of the selected option;
5. estimates of demand and of income generated by the scheme. This would include evidence of purchaser's intentions. It would also include an examination of the scheme on depreciation, unit costs, prices, rate of return and external financing limit;
6. the total capital and revenue costs and their timing. This would include details of any asset sales which are expected to take place and also the presentation of a discounted cash flow analysis (see Chapter 9);
7. the benefits to patients resulting from the scheme including quality benefits such as reductions in waiting lists, greater throughput or an improved environment;
8. proposals for the financing of the schemes;
9. assumptions, sensitivity analysis and contingency plans.

If the scheme is accepted by the NHS Management Executive and the Treasury, then the trust's external financing limit (EFL), which gives it power to borrow, may be increased. Any shortfall in borrowing will need to be funded from internal sources. Additionally, the trust will be required to examine the PFI option.

As you will have learned in Chapter 7, in a local authority, the treasurer will need to establish, first that 'approvals' for the project are available from the DOE, Welsh Office or Scottish Office. Such 'approvals' carry the right to borrow to finance the project. Without such permission, the project can be financed only from revenue or proceeds from the sale of assets (capital receipts). The use of these capital receipts is severely restricted by central government.

If the treasurer opts to borrow then the specific interest payable on the loan will be charged to the Loans Fund (LF) of the authority. The actual interest costs of the LF are aggregated and an average rate of interest is calculated. The departments of the local authority then pay this average rate of interest to the LF, the total annual charge being based upon the loans which the department has outstanding. However, the LF rate of interest does not reflect the true incremental cost of the project, as it is an average rate based on past as well as current borrowing. You learnt in Chapter 3 that the relevant costs of any decision are the future differential costs. Therefore, the relevant costs in this case are not the average interest costs but the interest costs specific to the project being financed by the loan. The loans fund on capital expenditure is financed by borrowing. It is possible that any competitive services could be charged the real rate of interest to bring home a more realistic cost of financing.

The service revenue accounts bear asset rents and capital charges. These are in the nature of internal transfers and one of the objectives of such transfers is to inform managers of the cost of assets. However, as indicated earlier, the real cost to the local authority is related to the cost of the specific financing method: interest in the case of a loan, a cash outflow if finance is from revenue or reserves.

After considering such issues, it will be possible to derive a payments and financing programme for a specific project. The example here is taken from a local authority. A home for the aged is to be constructed; the phasing of payments and their financing outlined in Table 8.2.

Table 8.2   Project X: Home for the aged: capital payments

Expenditure item	Financing	1999/2000 £000	2000/01 £000	Total £000
Land	Loan	120		120
Construction	Loan	110	60	170
Furnishings	Revenue		30	30
		230	90	320

The estimation of RCCE

As with capital costs, the specification of items such as staffing levels, provisions, maintenance costs, heating costs and so on will be provided to the treasurer by the social services department, the buildings maintenance unit and the energy officer. However, the treasurer has an important role in pulling together these diverse costs and providing the financial input to several key areas. The treasurer will estimate employee costs (pricing the staffing levels and adding appropriate percentages for employers' National Insurance and superannuation contributions), establishing the annual rates payment, converting the energy input into expenditure equivalents, estimating the annual charge for central and technical services and, of course, calculating the estimated capital financing charge. The estimated running cost provided to the treasurer can be compared to existing unit costs to see if they are realistic.

An annual RCCE estimate for the home for the aged would then be established and this is contained in Table 8.3.

There are some specific observations which need to be made about the statement contained in Table 8.3. The following notes correspond to those in the table:

1. *Central departments, technical and support services.* These, abbreviated in Table 8.3 as CDTSS, represent the overhead of management and administration required to provide the service. They include, for example, the costs of paying staff and creditors, appropriate legal services, and a share of the administrative costs of the social services department.

Table 8.3 Example of a statement of annual RCCE: Project X: Home for the aged: estimate of revenue consequences in first full year: 2001/02

	Note	£	£
Income: Fees and charges			
Accommodation charges			40 000
Expenditure:			
Employees: Wages		80 000	
Employers' NI and superannuation		17 600	
			97 600
Premises-related costs		18 500	
Supplies		43 400	
CDTSS	1	12 600	
Miscellaneous		7 000	81 500
Capital financing charges			
Revenue contribution to furniture		30 000	
Principal repayments of loan	2	7 250	
Interest on loan	3	43 500	80 750
Gross estimated costs			259 850
Net costs			219 850

2. *Principal repayments of loan.* It is assumed that the treasurer decides to borrow the money required over 40 years and that the money is to be repaid in equal instalments of principle (EIP). Therefore, the charge to the revenue account is £290 000/40 = £7250 per year.
3. *Interest on loan.* It is assumed that the money is borrowed at 15% giving an interest payment in the first year of 15% × 290 000 = £43 500. As the years pass, the annual interest payment will fall; in the next year, for example, it will reduce because the loan outstanding has been reduced by the first year repayment of an instalment of principal. In 2002/03 it will be 15% × (£290 000 – £7250) = £42 413.

Another feature of Table 8.3 is that it refers to the *first full year,* that is the first year following construction when the home has been in use for a whole year. The home may well accommodate residents during 2000/01, but for only a part-year. Because of the phasing in of use, normally with a part-year, such revenue estimates are normally prepared up to, and including, the first full year. The first full year is an important base for projecting future years' expenditure; the bottom line figure of £219 850 is also the amount which needs to be financed from the resources of the local authority. In future years, at current price levels, the annual net cost will fall to £189 850 because the revenue contribution to furniture will not be charged in 2001/02. Thus, at this stage, the treasurer needs to be sure that the net revenue expenditure figure can be funded from within the authority's resources. A similar consideration will weigh on central government; within the Ministry of Defence, the cost of a new jet fighter is the capital cost, but this has to be supported by an ongoing infrastructure which consumes revenue resources that have to be budgeted and provided for. Exhibit 8.1 contains a worked example relating to the estimation of capital payments and revenue consequences.

The value of this approach

The approach just described is essentially a financially based project appraisal. As such it does have specific values; it concentrates on the financial fundamentals of cost, phasing and financing; it also emphasizes the RCCE. In fact, it deals with almost everything concerned with providing financial support for a project.

However, its value in appraisal *per se* is rather limited unless we are simply comparing two projects with precisely the same output, for example the relative costs of a bridge or an underpass to provide pedestrians with means of crossing a busy road in safety. Where the benefits from projects are not expressed in cash terms, the methodology has no way of integrating these into the appraisal. To take our road crossing example one stage further, a third option might be a Pelican crossing, but this causes delays to motor vehicles and is also less safe to pedestrians than either a bridge or a subway. Such differences cannot be integrated using this approach. Similarly, difficulties occur when competing projects have different lifespans; differences in years of service provided are not readily incorporated within this framework. The difficulties outlined in the last sentence can, however, be tackled using discounted cash flow, an approach which is explained in Chapter 9.

In addition, the absence of strict output measures may lead to a situation where political muscle is the prime determinant of the projects to be selected.

In this situation the newly competitive units may well experience difficulty in promoting their schemes into the programme due to the powerful vested interests of the older established service departments.

Second, the approach is only useful for comparing projects with the same mix of financing. For example, if one project is to be wholly financed from revenue (a one-year charge), then comparison of the net RCCE of each is impossible; only by taking out the actual method of financing and imputing a notional figure, based probably on the notional debt charges, can the two projects be compared.

Finally, the separation of capital and revenue funds which is found in central government and the NHS is itself likely to produce sub-optimal decisions. This is because additional constraints are formulated, namely capital and revenue funding constraints and, furthermore, the separation means that there is a danger that if capital funds are free there will be a bias to capital projects, some of which may well have uneconomic revenue consequences. These revenue consequences may force out existing schemes which are performing satisfactorily because the prestige capital project must be seen to be operational and must be funded. Again, we find capital-led revenue, a problem identified when we considered the generation of new projects earlier in this chapter. In other words, it does not arrive at necessarily the 'best' project, but the project which best meets the funding sources which are currently most freely available.

8.5 The administrative ranking of projects

The problem of comparing projects with different patterns of service or outputs has led to an approach termed 'goals achievement matrix' or 'desiderata ranking' and is used primarily by health authorities and also by local authorities in sifting a variety of options to arrive at an optimal decision. The approach taken is as follows:

1. A small multidisciplinary team will be established to define the desirable service features that they are looking for from different projects. Such service features are known as desiderata or goals.

2. The team then attaches weights to these desiderata to reflect their relative importance. Normally the weights sum to 100.
3. The team scores the performance of each project against the identified desiderata. Different forms of scoring system may be employed but a common system employed within the NHS is as follows:

> +4 Meets the desiderata excellently.
> +2 Meets the desiderata well.
>   0 Meets the desiderata adequately.
> −2 Meets the desiderata inadequately.
> −4 Meets the desiderata not at all.

4. For each project, its specific desiderata score is multiplied by the weighting referred to in point 2.
5. The individual weighted scores are summed, thereby producing a quantified index of non-financial costs and benefits.
6. Such overall scores for each project are then taken into account jointly with the results of the financial appraisal.

For example, the methodology was used within a health authority to appraise three different options for the establishment of new central stores. A small multidisciplinary team was established made up of representatives drawn from finance, stores, transport, and end-users from hospitals and community health. In carrying out the non-financial appraisal, the team's discussions were first concerned with agreeing the desiderata and weights with which they would work. The desiderata and relevant weights are set out in Table 8.4. The team then scored the different options as laid out in Table 8.5.

Table 8.4   Desiderata and weightings resulting from team discussions

Desiderata		Weights
D1:	Improvements to stock control	30%
D2:	Improved managerial and financial information	15%
D3:	Adaptability to future changes	15%
D4:	Ease of introduction	10%
D5:	Ease of operation	15%
D6:	Total volume of storage space	10%
D7:	Reduction of the annual training requirement	5%
		100%

The desiderata rankings summarized in Table 8.5 were at variance with rankings by cost; after lengthy discussion, option 2 was selected. Although this was not the lowest cost option, it was felt to offer best overall value for money on a pound-for-pound basis ('value' being judged by reference to the desiderata ranking).

The value of this approach

Desiderata ranking does allow for the quantitative evaluation of non-financial aspects of the appraisal and does therefore bring into the appraisal a valuable dimension. It also has the merit that it can be carried out quickly by a small team. This team approach, as it is

Table 8.5 Results of desiderata scoring

Desiderata	Weights	Options					
		1		2		3	
		Score	Weighted	Score	Weighted	Score	Weighted
D1	30%	−4	−1.2	+2	+0.6	+2	+0.6
D2	15%	−4	−0.6	+2	+0.3	+2	+0.3
D3	15%	+2	+0.3	+4	+0.6	0	0
D4	10%	+4	+0.4	0	0	−1	−0.1
D5	15%	+4	+0.6	+2	+0.3	+1	+0.15
D6	10%	−2	−0.2	+3	+0.3	+1	+0.1
D7	5%	+4	+0.2	+1	+0.5	−2	−0.1
Grand total	100%		−0.5		+2.15		+0.65
Project ranking			3		1		2

intrinsically multidisciplinary, also has the advantage of creating identity with the scheme across departmental boundaries. The costs of implementation are relatively low, but the speed of appraisal is relatively high; these twin advantages explain its popularity in practice.

However, the technique may be criticized because it takes account only of team members' subjective views and fails to attempt to measure the final outputs from a project. Moreover, the numbers which appear in Table 8.4 and Table 8.5 conceal the inherent subjectivity and falsely suggest objectivity. It may also be more difficult to apply where the schemes being compared are fundamentally different and consensus harder to achieve on the relative weights. As will be seen in the next chapter, there are powerful ways of measuring non-market outputs which are very relevant to the public sector.

Key points of chapter

1. Within the public sector, there are different approaches to defining capital expenditure and depreciation.
2. The capital programme is an important aspect of multi-year project planning.
3. Project generation and selection is a multi-year project planning.
4. Projection of net RCCE to first full year is essential.
5. Much current practice ignores outputs; desiderata ranking represents a subjective way of dealing with this problem.

8.6 Summary

This chapter first considered the different methods of defining capital expenditure in the public sector and the general absence of a depreciation provision. However, in both local authorities and the National Health Service, policies are changing.

This chapter has examined an essentially finance-based approach to project appraisal. It has stressed that the capital investment decision should be made in a framework of specific objectives and long-term strategy. A capital programme is the major form of expression of an overall plan for the development of a public sector organization's activities and services. The chapter has stressed that the capital programme and the associated revenue effects form an essential part of the planning process of the organization.

The process takes place in stages and is also affected by the time horizon of government funding and grants and the public sector planning process which can be subject to significant changes. Political expediency and the imbalance of capital and revenue funds can also play a major part in the public sector. These factors do not negate the value of planning but they make it more difficult and, in a sense, more essential in that the organization must know what it is attempting to achieve in order to measure how significantly it has failed to achieve its stated objectives.

The chapter has also indicated how a capital programme may be prepared, and how the details of the revenue consequences are obtained. Finally, it has examined an approach by which non-financial factors can also be brought into the analysis.

Exhibit 8.1

This exhibit contains a brief case study which illustrates the estimation of capital payments and net revenue effects as discussed earlier.

A public sector organization requires to expand, and, possibly, centralize its office accommodation. It is considering three proposals; either to extend existing offices, to erect a purpose-built office in a run-down part of the city or to rent space in a commercial development in the city centre. Each of the last two options would permit the centralization of office accommodation and management.

The current offices are spread on four sites, three of which are owned by the organization with one being rented. The owned premises are debt free and currently stand in the balance sheet at their cost prices of £80 000, £70 000 and £30 000, while the annual rent of the existing office is £12 500 on a five-year lease, payable annually in advance and subject to review at the beginning of year three when it is expected to double. Average yearly running costs of current premises amount to £185 000 but there are additional costs of £87 500 per year resulting from travelling expenses, postage etc., consequent upon the split-site operation. Unless new accommodation is obtained an extension will be constructed in year four at an estimated cost of £200 000; this will add a further £20 000 to running costs (excluding debt charges) in a full year; it will be occupied at the start of the fourth quarter of year four with the bulk of the capital expenditure taking place during the first half of year four.

A purpose-built office is estimated to cost £8m; it will take three years to build with capital payments phased as follows:

| Year 1: 40%; | Year 2: 40%; | Year 3: 20% |

Work will commence in June of year one and it is expected to be completed by October of year three.

One-off relocation costs will amount to £150 000 in year three. Running costs for the new offices will amount to £50 000 per annum from the start of January of year three when the premises will be fully occupied.

The three existing offices will be sold immediately staff move to the new offices; sale proceeds are expected to be 15 times their total book value. The proceeds are to be used in redemption of long-term outstanding debt in October of year four.

Rental of centralized office space would amount to £0.65m per year subject to annual rent review, expected to result in rent increases of 15% per annum. One-off relocation costs are expected to amount to £200 000. Running costs will amount to £71 000 per year from the date of occupation, which is identical to the purpose-built option. The sale of the existing buildings is assumed to proceed as with the purpose-built option.

In the event of the existing rented accommodation being vacated before the end of the five-year period, a penalty of three months' rent is payable in addition to the rental for the year in which the accommodation is vacated.

Information on current borrowing rates is as follows:

temporary   9.75%
long-term   11.25%.

The organization uses the equal instalment of principal method of repayment and has approval to fund all the necessary capital expenditure by borrowing over 40 years. Principal repayments are made half-way through each year and commence in the year following that in which the borrowing takes place.

The building of new offices has gained initial outline approval and stands in the capital programme of the organization. However, the harsher financial climate has led to a request for a detailed project appraisal of all three options. For this the organization requires the preparation of capital and revenue estimates for each of the three options over a period of five years.

Solution

| | Year | | | | | |
	1 £000	2 £000	3 £000	4 £000	5 £000	Total £000
Capital costs						
Extension				200		200
Construction	3200	3200	1600			8000
Revenue costs						
Extension						
Running costs:						
Existing	272.5	272.5	272.5	272.5	272.5	
New				5	20	
Rent	12.5	12.5	25	25	25	
Financing costs:						
Principal					5	
Interest				16.875	22.5	
Totals	285	285	297.5	319.375	345	
Construction of new offices						
Running costs:						
Existing	272.5	272.5	204.375			
New			12.5	50	50	
Rent	12.5	12.5	25			
Penalty			6.25			
Relocation			150			
Financing costs:						
Principal		80	160	200	200	
Interest	150	535.5	837	861.75	839.25	
Totals	435	900.5	1395.125	1111.75	1089.25	

Less income:						
Interest				151.875	303.75	
Totals	0	0	0151.875	303.75		
Net revenue effect	435	900.5	1395.125	959.875	785.5	
Rent of new offices						
Running costs:						
Existing	272.5	272.5	204.375			
New			17.75	71	71	
Rent – old	12.5	12.5	25			
Penalty			6.25			
Rent – new			162.5	674.375	775.531	
Relocation			200			
Totals		285	285	615.875	745.375	846.531
Less income:						
Interest				151.875	303.75	
Totals	0	0	0	151.875	303.75	
Net revenue effect	285	285	615.875	593.5	542.781	

Notes:

1. *Running costs*

Extension:	Year 4	One quarter's occupation of the extension giving 25% of £20 000, the full-year cost.
Construction:	Year 4	Existing offices are occupied for nine months giving 75% of £272 500, the full-year cost. New offices are occupied for three months giving 25% of £50 000, the full-year cost.
Rent:	Year 4	Existing offices are occupied for nine months giving 75% of £272 500, the full-year cost. New offices are occupied for three months giving 25% of £71 000, the full-year cost.

2. *Financing charge calculations*

Extensions

Year 4: £200 000 advanced in the first half of year 4, on average, the money was outstanding for nine months. Thus, interest charged is £200 000 × 0.75 × 11.25% = £16 875.

Year 5: £200 000 × 11.25%.

Construction of new offices

	Year				
	1	2	3	4	5
	£000	£000	£000	£000	£000
Principal b/fwd	0	3200	6320	7760	7560
Borrowed in year	3200	3200	1600		
Repaid year		–80	–160	–200	–200
Principal c/fwd	3200	6320	7760	7560	7360

Interest:

Year 1: £3200K × 5/12 × 11.25% = £150 000.
£3200K was advanced over the ten-month period from June to March, so the average time that advances were outstanding was five months.

Year 2: (£3200K + £3200K × ½) – (½ × £80K) × 11.25% = £535 500.
The year 1 advance of £3200K outstanding for the whole of the year.
The year 2 advance of £3200K is made evenly over the year, so the average time for which the advance is outstanding is six months.
The year 2 repayment of £80 000 (1/40 of £3200K) is made mid-way through the year and so represents a reduction in interest for just six months.

Year 3: (£6320K + (£1600K × ¾)) – (½ × £160K) × 11.25% = £837 000.
The balance b/fwd of £6320 is outstanding for the whole of the year.
The year 3 advance of £1600K is made in the first half of year 3, so the average time for which the advance is outstanding is nine months.
The year 3 repayment of £160 000 (1/40 of £6400K) is made mid-way through the year and so represents a reduction in interest for just six months.

Year 4: (£7760K – (½ × £200K)) × 11.25% = £861.750.
The repayment of principal is 1/40 of £8 millions borrowed.

Year 5: (£7560K – (½ × £200K)) × 11.25% = £839.250.

3. *Investment of capital receipts*

Year 4: Proceeds £180 000 × 15 = £2 700 000

Interest savings:
Year 4: £2 700 000 × (6 months) × 11.25% = £151 875

Year 5: £2 700 000 × 11.25% = £303 750

Questions

8.1 List the benefits of capital programmes.

8.2 Explain one way of taking account of the non-financial aspect of capital schemes.

8.3 A local authority is carrying out an appraisal of a new leisure centre. The following information is available:

	[£]
Estimated annual costs:	
Premises costs	14 000
Employees – Manager	16 500
– Centre assistants	32 000
CDTSS	5 500
Supplies and services	11 800
Estimated annual revenue:	
Sports hall	19 800
Squash courts	17 700
Equipment hire	3 500
Hire of hall (for functions)	2 500
Estimated capital costs:	
Land and construction	545 000

All capital costs are being financed by a loan at 10%. The loan is repayable over 20 years in equal instalments of principal.

Required

Set out the estimated revenue consequences of the scheme in the first full year of operation.

8.4 A county council has 400 places in homes for the elderly. Demand for places exceeded supply in 19X0/X1 by 200 places. This shortfall in places is expected to increase by 50% by the end of the next five years.

In addition one 156-bed home built in 1930 is scheduled to be closed in 19X2/X3. The home has an annual net revenue cost of £320 000 and a disposal value of £600 000.

The council has established a policy to eliminate the shortfall in places by 19X5.

Average income per resident place is £1700 per annum.

It has been decided that only two types of new home will be provided as a matter of policy. These are 40-bed homes and 75-bed homes.

Cost information on the two types of home is as follows:

	40-bed home £	75-bed home £
Capital costs	900 000	1 460 000
Gross revenue costs (including financing costs)	300 000	500 000

The social services committee has been allocated £9 million capital and £1 950 000 additional revenue resources for the provision of new homes in the period 19X1/19X5.

Required

Detail the main conclusions from this information for inclusion in a financial report on the provision of homes for the elderly.

8.5 In the current period of economic restraint your organization has decided that only one of three proposed projects can be started.

You are required to:

(a) Prepare a statement of the annual costs of each project from the following information.

(b) Discuss the limitations of this method of project appraisal.

		£
Project A	Construction	200 000
	Equipment	60 000
	Furniture	45 000
	Premises	15 000
	Other running expenses	5 000
	Employees	25 000
Project B	Construction	300 000
	Furniture	5 000
	Equipment	25 000
	Employees	30 000
	Premises	10 000
	Other running expenses	14 000
Project C	Employees	60 000
	Other running expenses	30 000
	Premises	5 000

Notes:

(i) Construction costs and professional fees are amortized over 40 years, equipment over ten years, and furniture over five years.

(ii) Annuity factors are: 0.1129 on 40 years
0.1706 on 10 years
0.2714 on 5 years.

(iii) Professional fees are to be charged at 10% of construction costs.

(iv) £500 of furniture and £10 000 of equipment included in these figures for Project A refers to annual replacements.

(v) A charge is to be made for administration at 5% of annual expenditure exclusive of amortization.

8.6 The following schemes are included in the draft 19X8/X9 capital programme of a service of a local authority.

Scheme	Total £000	19X7/X8 Revised £000	19X8/X9 £000	19X9/X0 £000	19X0/X1 £000	Scheme opens
		Programme of capital expenditure				
Teign Phase 1	150	28	–	–	–	Sept–8
Clyst Vale	230	80	–	–	–	Jan–9
Collompton	160	120	10	–	–	May–9
Ashburton	300	180	100	20	–	Sept–9
Teign Phase 2	400	20	300	80	–	Oct–9
Great Torrington	50	–	20	30	–	June–9
Teignmouth	100	–	75	25	–	June–9
Dawlish	200	–	25	100	75	Sept–0
Holsworthy	40	–	–	40	–	May–0
Tiverton	500	–	–	–	300	Sept–1

Other information available to you:

1. *Financing*

As much of the capital programme as possible is to be financed from internal sources. It is expected that £50 000 will be set aside annually for revenue contributions to capital outlay. Capital receipts of £160 000 are expected for 19X7/X8 and £200 000 in 19X8/X9.

If it is necessary to borrow to finance the schemes they will all be financed over 60 years with the exception of:

Great Torrington	all expenditure	20 years
Teign Phase 2	£200 000 in 19X8/X9	5 years
Holsworthy	all expenditure	5 years

Interest charges are 12.5% and advances are made once a year, at the end of the year. Interest is payable as soon as the money is advanced, principal repayments start at the end of the first year.

2. *Revenue costs other than financing costs*

Running costs in a full year (in addition to financing charges):

Scheme:	£000
Teign Phase 1	60
Clyst Vale	65
Collompton	80
Ashburton	65
Teign Phase 2	50
Great Torrington	–
Teignmouth	100
Dawlish	55
Holsworthy	–
Tiverton	120

3. *Capital expenditure allocations*

The capital expenditure allocation for 19X7/X8 is £380 000. The authority is allowed to supplement this with 30% of capital receipts. The authority may also carry forward the previous year's allocation or anticipate the next year's allocation subject to the total of these being not more than 10% of the enhanced capital expenditure allocation. Capital spending in 19X6/X7 anticipated the 19X7/X8 allocation by £20 000. The capital expenditure allocation for 19X8/X9 has been announced as £360 000. It seems reasonable to assume that the capital expenditure allocation for future years will be even lower. The authority intends to conform to the capital spending regulations.

4. *Priority for schemes*

Council policy dictates that first priority should be given to continuing schemes. This means that the scheme will be allowed to go ahead but not necessarily with the original phasing of expenditure. New schemes are prioritized with a ranking of 1 to 3. Priority 1 is given to schemes that must start in the year. Priorities 2 and 3 are for schemes that may be put back into the next year with Priority 2 being preferred to start over Priority 3.

The priority of the schemes that start after 19X7/X8 are as follows:

Great Torrington	2
Teignmouth	1
Dawlish	2
Holsworthy	3
Tiverton	1

Required

(a) Prepare a revised capital programme for the service for the year 19X8/X9 to include detailed financing for each scheme in the programme and a full-year revenue cost for the scheme when completed. Changes made to the draft capital programme must conform to the polices stated in the question. (8 marks)

(b) Show the impact of the changes made in the capital programme for 19X8/X9 on the capital budgets for future years. (2 marks)

(c) As the accountant appointed to produce the accounts of the service, write a memorandum to the borough treasurer to accompany the revised capital programme for 19X8/X9. This should explain the reasons for changes made and justify each change made to the draft budget. (10 marks)
(Total 20 marks)

8.7 A large comprehensive school has a local sports centre on the same site; both are financed by the same metropolitan authority. Currently, all the heating for the sports centre is supplied from the main boiler house based in the school. This arrangement has been criticized by the authority's energy efficiency officer because the school boiler and heating system have to be activated at weekends and during school holidays. It has also been suggested that, during summer when hot water only is required, there is excessive heat loss in the transmission of hot water between the buildings.

The energy efficiency office has proposed two alternative schemes:

(a) The first scheme involves the installation of electric water heaters in the sports centre at a capital cost of £5000. These would require virtually no maintenance but should be replaced every five years. Likely consumption is 5500 therms annually, estimated on the basis of current hot water consumption. Heating would continue to be generated by the school.

(b) The second scheme involves the installation of a gas boiler to satisfy both hot water requirements and to provide space heating when the school system is not in use. The gas boiler would be plumbed directly into the existing system and would incur capital expenditure of £20 000. The estimated consumption would be 12 000 therms annually. Annual maintenance charges under a contract are expected to last for seven years.

Other relevant information is as follows:

(i) Current and estimated thermal demands on the comprehensive school system by the sports centre is as follows:

		Thermal consumption (per annum)
	Current system	28 000
Option (a)	Electric heaters	16 900
Option (b)	Gas boiler	7 600

(ii) The school caretaker is currently paid an allowance of £1000 per annum for boiler lighting during the vacation. This service would not be required if option (b) was adopted.

(iii) The school heating system is oil fired and the boiler is expected to last for at least another seven years.

(iv) Contract prices negotiated for each of the four fuels used in the authority are as follows:

	Per therm (pence)
Coal	41.0
Electricity	52.1
Gas	42.6
Oil	44.1

Estimated increases in contract prices for the foreseeable future are 5% per annum for all fuels. However, it is considered that both gas and oil are more vulnerable to fluctuations in prices than the other two fuels.

(v) Both schemes can be accommodated within the capital programme for 19X8/X9.

(vi) It is proposed that in each case financing will be effected by an advance from the authority's loans fund, repayable by equal instalments of principal over five years. The current loans fund rate is 9%.

(vii) The authority's policy on loans fund advances is to charge a half-year's interest in the year of advance. Principal repayments are made at the end of each financial year, commencing in the year in which the advance is made.

(viii) Current market rates of interest are as follows:

Period of loan	Rate of interest
1 year	9%
5 years	10%
10 years	11%

(ix) The sports centre has displayed a consistent growth in use over recent years.

(x) The energy efficiency working party has asked the treasurer to present a report on the financial implications of each option.

Required

Draft a report on behalf of the treasurer to the energy efficiency working party recommending the action that should be undertaken. (24 marks)

9 Project appraisal

Key learning objectives

After reading this chapter you should be able to:

1. Understand the concept of the time value of money and why future benefits should be discounted to the present time for assessment.
2. Be able to deal with inflation in the capital investment decision-making process.
3. Discuss the applicability of cost-benefit analysis to the public sector.

The previous chapter pointed out that the distinction between capital and revenue expenditure is essentially one that can be based on time. Revenue expenditure is that expenditure on current goods and services the benefits of which are consumed within the present time period, that is the conventional time period of the annual revenue statement. Capital expenditure normally results in expenditure in the framework of the annual time period of the revenue statement but in exchange for the receipt of benefits in future time periods and their annual revenue statements. The essence of this chapter is to use the concept of time and its impact on monetary flows as a basis for the development of a sound framework of investment appraisal in the public sector. The chapter will also consider the technique of cost-benefit analysis which has been developed in the public sector in an attempt to facilitate the finding of better solutions to the problem of resource allocation in the absence of the market mechanism. In order to develop student understanding a number of detailed exhibits are obtained within the chapter. These exhibits gradually grow in complexity to ensure student understanding and detailed coverage of this complex topic.

9.1 Discounted cash flow

The objectives of the discounted cash flow model of investment appraisal are to evaluate the net financial benefit of individual projects and to enable an informed financial comparison to be performed between projects. These projects may have different lives and consequently different returns or the same life but differing returns.

The model recognizes that the use of funds has an opportunity cost by the application of a rate of interest to discount future cash flows. If, for example, an individual were offered £100 now or £100 in a year's time the rational individual would accept the £100 today as he could invest it and receive more than a £100 in one year's time as a result of the action of the rate of interest. If, however, the after-tax rate of interest was 10% and the sum offered in one year's time was £110 then the individual would be indifferent between two sums. Finally, if the after-tax rate of interest was 8% but the offer of £110 in the year's time still stood then the rational investor would wait one year as £110 receivable in a year's time is worth £101.86 today, as this is the sum that will amount to £110 one year hence when invested at 8%. Effectively, it can be seen that, by discounting the future sum by the rate of interest, it is possible to compare the two cash flows and make a rational investment decision. This essentially very simple, but powerful, technique forms the conceptual basis for a wide range of investment decisions and will be applied in this chapter. It should be pointed out that the technique is concerned with the action of the rate of interest and not the effect of inflation on the value of the sums involved. The effect of inflation in the investment decision is dealt with later in the chapter.

The interest rate used in the discounting process is known as the 'hurdle' or 'cut-off' rate, in that, for a project to be successful, the future benefits when discounted by the cost of capital must exceed the discounted cost associated with the project. The discount rate is thus the required minimum rate of return for a project.

The timing and nature of cash flows

It is a convention for simplicity to assume that cash flows occur only at the beginning or end of a year. Clearly, this is unrealistic given the nature of projects and, while it is possible to overcome this objection by more complex analysis, which may be appropriate in certain circumstances, in the majority of cases the results obtained from year-end calculations are adequate.

It is also essential to appreciate that the emphasis in discounted cash flow calculations is on cash flow. There is no place in the technique for the use of accounting concepts such as depreciation. This is because depreciation is an accounting method used to apportion costs to a relevant accounting period over the life of an asset and as such is a bookkeeping entry with no associated cash flow. The cash flows used should also be the incremental cash flows, that is the cash flows which occur as a direct result of undertaking the proposal. It follows from this that any costs already invested in the project at the time that a new investment decision is needed should be treated as sunk costs and similarly ignored except for any salvage or other escape values. Any operating costs estimated to be saved, for example, through installation of a new machine, should be treated as the equivalent of a cash receipt in the analysis. The use of the technique is demonstrated in Exhibit 9.1.

Exhibit 9.1 illustrates the decision rules for the organization. Net Present Value (NPV) represents the excess of the present value of future cash inflows over the present value of cash outflows. The project had a positive NPV and thus the organization could consider the proposal for inclusion in the capital programme. If the calculation had revealed that the project had a negative NPV then the proposal would be rejected on financial grounds.

Exhibit 9.1

A public sector organization operates a joinery workshop and is considering buying a new forming machine at a cost of £4000. The machine is estimated to last five years with zero scrap value. It is estimated that the new machine will achieve savings of £1200 in the first three years of operation and £800 in the last two years as maintenance cost increase. The organization has stated the required rate of return is 10%. Should the organization undertake the investment in the new machinery?

Timing of cash flow	Cash flow	10% discount factor	Discounted cash flow
	£		£
Year 1	1 200	0.909	1 091
Year 2	1 200	0.826	991
Year 3	1 200	0.751	901
Year 4	800	0.683	546
Year 5	800	0.621	497
			4 026
Year 0 (i.e. today)	4 000	1	(4 000)
Net present value (NPV)			26

The proposal has been appraised using the discounted cash flow method. The discount rate is 10% and factors were obtained from the table in the appendix at the end of this book. The discount factor for any sums spent today (i.e. year 0) is £1; quite simply, £1 spent now is worth exactly £1. The incremental savings in operating costs have been treated as the cash flows of the project.

The project has a positive NPV: the discounted savings exceed the discounted costs at 10% and, as such, would prove acceptable to the organization, unless, of course, any competing projects give a higher NPV. It could now go forward for consideration for inclusion in the capital programme.

Internal rate of return

An alternative discounting technique to NPV is termed the internal rate of return (IRR). The technique involves an iterative search for the rate of interest which equates the discounted value of cash inflows and cash outflows; calculation is not a problem, not least because most spreadsheet packages incorporate a function to calculate a project's IRR. The resulting IRR is then compared with the appropriate interest rate facing the organization; an IRR in excess of the rate of interest must indicate that the project has a positive NPV at that rate of interest and vice versa. Surveys have indicated that it is very popular with businessmen within the private sector, and, in most cases, it leads to the same conclusions as NPV. However, the IRR does have certain drawbacks and, in certain cases, gives an incorrect decision; such drawbacks are well documented and the reader is referred to, for example, Drury (2000).

The decision rules under IRR are:

1. IRR greater than cost or capital – consider the project for inclusion in the capital programme.
2. IRR less than cost of capital – reject the project.

9.2 Ranking projects

The previous chapter indicated how projects might be ranked using a desiderata table to consider non-financial aspects. We now examine the problem of ranking projects, in financial terms only, when investment funds are constrained.

It was stated earlier that if a project has a positive NPV then it can be considered for inclusion in the capital programme. Almost inevitably, however, the investment requirement of acceptable projects is likely to exceed the funds which are available for investment. Almost certainly, the capital programme for an individual service will be restricted and available funds will need to be rationed. Consequently, it is necessary to rank schemes to identify priorities. This is done by the calculation of a 'profitability index' and is simply computed by dividing the present value of the surplus cash inflows by the initial investment. This procedure will only apply to those projects which have a positive cash flow. The greater the value of the index the higher the priority that should be given to the scheme. However, it is insufficient to look at each scheme in isolation; careful analysis should be made of the sum available and possible combinations of projects should be studied to obtain the best NPV for the organization as a whole in order to use the limited resources to the maximum effect.

9.3 Risk and uncertainty

As the process of project appraisal necessarily involves dealing with the future there will be a degree of risk attached to many projections. Therefore, it is essential that consideration be given to these risks; this will be of particular importance to the competitive public sector as in a competitive situation a poor investment decision could have a serious impact. However, it should be remembered that if all possible states of nature were considered, the decision maker would be overwhelmed with information.

A number of options are available in dealing with risk:

1. *Standard deviation and probability distribution.* Calculate the standard deviation and probability distribution of the cash flows associated with the project to obtain a measure of the likely risk associated with the possible outcomes.
2. *Simulation techniques.* Undertake simulation using a technique such as Monte Carlo analysis where each factor affecting the investment decision is examined and random numbers used to generate an estimated NPV, probability distribution and standard deviation for the project.
3. *Sensitivity analysis.* Carry out sensitivity analysis by a systematic analysis of the effects of varying the values assumed for certain variables on the overall result of the proposal. Clearly, by this process it would be possible to identify those factors to which the project is most at risk. If the project does, subsequently, go ahead these factors would be the key statistics to monitor.
4. *Risk premium.* Incorporate a risk premium into the discount rate; this involves increasing the discount rate by a specific percentage so as to reflect risk. The higher the discount rate the lower will be the expected NPV and thus a measure can be achieved of the project's sensitivity to risk with the more marginal projects being

rejected. The choice of the risk premium would clearly be crucial to this process. Unfortunately, the choice of premium is largely arbitrary, but it has been used within the NHS to appraise 'risky' projects which have been subject to a discount rate 2% higher than for low risk projects.

5. *Limited time horizons.* Limit the time horizon of the appraisal; this is likely to hit benefits more severely than costs as conventional projects are characterized by high cash outflows in the early years in return for future benefits. This procedure is quite arbitrary as would be any decision to inflate costs and/or reduce income.

9.4 The cost of capital

In the simple example given in Exhibit 9.1, the rate of interest or discount rate was specified as 10%, but considerable debate exists as to the choice of the appropriate discount rate in the public sector. In the private sector the cost of capital of a company can be found using the capital asset pricing model (see, for example, Van Horne, 1988) which uses a basic assumption of profit maximization in its construction. In the public sector no equivalent model is available and a number of possible discount rates are possible. However, there are two main approaches to the solution of this problem.

1. *Social opportunity cost rate.* Insofar as funds used for a public sector project come ultimately from the private sector it can be argued that they have displaced either current consumption or investment by private individuals and businesses. To the extent that private sector investment is displaced, the concept of a social opportunity cost rate has been developed. This is defined as the marginal pre-tax rate of return in the private sector, i.e. the rate of return which the funds would have yielded for society, abstracting from externalities, had they not been commandeered by the public sector. One obvious difficulty is defining the private sector return.

2. *Social time preferences rate.* To the extent private consumption is displaced it is argued that the social time preference rate is the relevant concept. This is defined as the after-tax rate of return required by society to induce it to sacrifice present consumption for the promise of future consumption as generated by the investment. The social time preference rate will depend, among others, on factors such as the age structure of the population, which will change over time, expectations about the growth in prosperity and the general level of prosperity, etc. There is an obvious discrepancy between the social time preference rate and the social opportunity cost rate as one is before tax and the other is after tax.

The Treasury's approach has been to use the concept of the social opportunity cost rate and then exclude inflation from the resulting rate of interest. This rate is known as the test discount rate and is currently 6% for services such as the NHS. As it is a real rate it removes the need to take account of inflation from the discounting process and, as such, removes one complication from an already complicated process. The problem of inflation is a real one, however, and it is discussed more fully later in the next section. The rate of return for nationalized industries was first set at 5% in 1978 but in the light of returns made in the private sector the government announced in April 1989 that it had increased this rate to 8%. This was intended to ensure that the industries made what the government regarded as an appropriate return on the resources invested and that resources were not diverted from areas where they could be used more effectively.

For institutions such as local government, which have day-to-day access to money markets, there is the possibility of using market interest rates as the cost of capital. These market rates include assumptions about future inflation and as such, if they are used, then the cost and income cash flows in the appraisal should include anticipated assumptions about the level of future inflation. Where a combination of sources of finance is used, a local authority would calculate a weighted cost of funds. Local authorities also calculate internal rates on their consolidated loans funds, but these rates are based on the average historic cost of debt. They also calculate notional interest rates on their capital funds, but these are based purely on internal financing and transfer pricing decisions and may have no relationship with the market rate. There is no justification for using either the consolidated loans fund rate or the capital fund rate in the appraisal exercise as they do not represent the opportunity cost of funds.

9.5 Inflation

If a real discount rate such as the test discount rate is used, then costs and income in future years should be expressed in real terms (i.e. base year prices) and thus exclude the effects of general inflation. If, however, the relative price of different inputs is expected to change, the real price of the inputs will not remain constant. Relative price changes must therefore be considered. Historically, for example, the relative price effect has been particularly important with regard to labour costs given the high percentage of the revenue budget which is consumed by salaries and wages in the public sector. To leave out such a significant factor as pay inflation would weaken the results of the appraisal exercise.

Exhibit 9.2 illustrates three distinct approaches to the problem of inflation.

Exhibit 9.2

A water business has identified that its diversified local stores depots are experiencing difficulty in meeting the demands of its repairs and maintenance division. A study carried out by a firm of consultants has revealed two ways of effecting improvements:

1. *Taking on additional employees at the stores.* This would result in increases in wage costs of £250 000 per annum in the first year (inclusive of employers' National Insurance and superannuation contributions); such costs are expected to increase by 2% in excess of the rate of general price inflation.
2. *Purchasing stores handling equipment.* This would require an immediate payment of £780 000 and annual maintenance and operating charges of £40 000, increasing in line with general inflation. The equipment is expected to have a five-year life.

General price inflation (measured by the retail price index) is expected to continue at the rate of 5% per annum for the foreseeable future. The company can currently raise finance at 16%. Appraisal is to be carried out over a five-year period.

The calculations illustrate the three alternative methods of accounting for inflation in the capital budgeting process. Method 1 has ignored the specific inflation of 2% above the retail price index and as such is not recommended. Methods 2 and 3 are both acceptable with method 3 being further developed later in this chapter. Technically the Fischer formula should have been applied to arrive at the real rate of interest. This can be calculated by 1.16/1.05 and is 10.5%. The actual effect on the calculations, however, is so small that it can be ignored.

Method 1

Year	Labour				Machinery, etc.	
	CF	11% factor	PV		CF	PV
0					−780	−780
1	−250				−40	
2	−250				−40	
3	−250	3.695	−923.75		−40	−147.8
4	−250				−40	
5	−250				−40	
NPV			−923.75			−927.8

Method 2

Year	Labour				Machinery, etc.	
	+ 7% p.a. CF	16% factor	PV		+ 5% p.a. CF	PV
0		1			−780	−780
1	−250	0.862	−215.5		−40	−34.48
2	−267.5	0.743	−198.753		−42	−31.206
3	−286.225	0.641	−183.470		−44.1	−28.2681
4	−306.261	0.552	−169.056		−46.305	−25.5604
5	−327.699	0.476	−155.985		−48.6203	−23.1432
NPV			−922.763			−922.658

Method 3

Year	Labour				Machinery, etc.	
	+ 2% p.a. CF	11% factor	PV		CF	PV
0		1			−780	−780
1	−250	0.901	−225.25		−40	−36.04
2	−255	0.812	−207.06		−40	−32.48
3	−260.1	0.731	−190.133		−40	−29.24
4	−265.3	0.658	−174.567		−40	−26.32
5	−270.6	0.594	−160.736		−40	−23.76
NPV			−957.747			−927.84

1. Use a real discount rate, and project cash flows in base year prices, accepting the weakness as outlined.
2. Use a money rate of interest and project cash flows in the money prices estimated for future years.
3. Use a real discount rate and take account of relative inflation.

9.6 Other techniques of investment appraisal

Before turning to a detailed examination of cost-benefit analysis a brief examination will be made of two other techniques used in the private sector.

Payback

This is a simple method of investment appraisal and is frequently used in the private sector. The technique compares the length of time that a project takes to recover its original investment from its net cash flow and then compares this with a laid-down decision rule. If the project fails to pay for itself within, say, a decision rule of two years the project would be rejected. The method can be adjusted to take account of the time value of money but is deficient in its narrow concentration on the payback period. Its only possible use suggested in the public sector is for those competition services which are experiencing cash flow problems as this type of organization would face increased interest charges.

Accounting rate of return

The technique uses the average accounting profit made by an investment divided by the average investment cost, which will depend on the depreciation method used. The method makes no use of the time value of money, considers financial accounting flows rather than cash and has little to commend it, even in the private sector.

9.7 Cost-benefit analysis

Cost-benefit analysis (CBA) is concerned with economic choice and has as its objective the provision of assistance to decision makers in their choice concerning the use of scarce resources. It has been defined as follows:

> A practical way of assessing the desirability of projects where it is important to take a long view (in the sense of looking at repercussions in the future, as well as nearer future) and a wide view (in the sense of allowing for side effects of many kinds on many persons, industries, regions, etc.), i.e. it implies the enumeration and evaluation of all the relevant costs and benefits. (Prest and Turvey, 1965, pp.685–705)

In the private sector, operating within the market mechanism, the goal of the organization is seen as profit maximization and is thus purely a financial objective. The firm would only consider private costs and benefits in its investment decisions, selecting only those schemes which are within its ability to fund ranked by their contribution to its welfare (i.e. profit). The problem for the public sector is that the market mechanism does not operate for many of its goods and services yet society is faced with major questions when it is considering its use of resources: Is the scheme worthwhile? Are the relative merits of scheme A greater than scheme B? When should a programme be implemented to achieve optimal timing? What scale of operation should be adopted? CBA has been developed to help with these types of decisions.

Intangible items and valuation

CBA attempts to place a value not on only the direct costs of particular programme (e.g. the construction costs of a new road) but also the more intangible benefits that may occur as a result of completing the project (e.g. time savings) or intangible costs (e.g. noise). It is clearly with these more intangible benefits and costs that difficulties of valuation occur although, as will be seen, the direct costs also have their own particular difficulties in this area as well. It should also be remembered that definitive answers will not always be provided by CBA but, to the extent that additional information is provided to decision makers, it will aid choice concerning complex decisions on resource allocation in the public sector.

In the public sector we are dealing with a wide range of decisions on the potential use of resources. At the heart of government policy will be decisions on the allocation of resources to defence, health, education, etc. Clearly, these allocation decisions will be based on political expediency and the political objectives and priorities of the party in power. At the other end of the scale will be day-to-day decisions on, for example, financing, including decisions such as whether or not to lease or borrow money in order to acquire new plant and machinery. This type of resource utilization decision would be one performed using a comparison of cash flows and an appropriate discount rate as discussed earlier. In between these two extremes, we have a large range of decisions for which the technique of CBA has the potential to make a major contribution and it is with these areas that subsequent sections are concerned.

The problem of valuation in CBA

There is a need to examine each item and identify its economic cost to the community. In an attempt to ascribe value to costs and benefits the economist will first resort to market prices, but in some cases market prices may fail to reflect true values due to the presence of market distortions, while in others a relevant market may just not exist, as in the case of environmental factors. In a situation of market imperfections the economist will resort to shadow prices which are simply the values more appropriate for the purpose of economic calculations than the existing price. Certain gains or losses to the project can be valued at zero since, for the economy as a whole, they represent transfer payments, while costs for, say, labour, for example, which would otherwise remain unemployed would be valued at opportunity cost and not at wages actually paid. Two difficulties will, however, be referred to:

1. The shadow price of a particular input, due to interrelationships between commodities, may well require the shadow price of other inputs to be amended but the difficulty is that data on the complex dependency may not exist.
2. The task of measurement may be so difficult as to make the data so unreliable that the base for the exercise becomes questionable.

In practice, therefore, given that the information requirements are such that the fullest information is difficult to achieve, market prices are typically used. It has been pointed out, however, by some economists that observed market prices may be as reliable a measure of economic value as the efforts to derive shadow prices.

As has just been demonstrated, problems exist in the valuation of costs and benefits even where market prices exist. In CBA, however, there is also a need to value those items for which no market exits. Examples include savings in travel time if a new transport system were to be developed, plus the possible reductions in deaths and injuries giving benefits to the economy and the potential loss or gain to the environment if the scheme goes ahead. One approach has been to develop surrogate prices where an attempt is made to derive a cost that consumers would be prepared to pay – to save travelling time for example. Improvements in transport systems are normally expected to reduce the severity and frequency of accidents. A number of measures have been developed to measure the costs of avoided deaths and injuries. These include a measure of avoided costs, where a measure is made of the income and output not foregone as a result of the system improvement; an examination of defensive expenditure, where a study is made of the past expenditure by society on road safety or the amounts individuals were prepared to pay in terms of insurance cover; or finally by reference to the amount that would be paid for a reduction in the probability of death or injury by reference to indifference curves for a population of individuals. Finally, of considerable concern given today's 'green movement' is the effect of any proposal on the environment.

Clearly this is a difficult area but contingency valuation may have a role to play. Basically, under this proposal, the population is asked directly how much it is prepared to pay for the environment and how much compensation they would require for the loss of the amenity if they were denied. One of the difficulties with this approach is that consumers are being made to measure something which is not as yet within their experience, as they are effectively considering their future reaction to possible extra noise and pollution.

The application of cost-benefit analysis to a road transport scheme

In examining the possibility of building a new road scheme it is necessary to identify the costs and benefits associated with the scheme and these are now set out:

Costs	*Benefits*
1. Opportunity cost of physical resources	1. Savings in travel time
2. Construction costs	2. Reductions in vehicle operating costs
3. Maintenance	3. Reduction in accident cost
4. Environmental costs	4. Other benefits – reduced stress and discomfort

The relative importance of each item will obviously vary between schemes. In terms of valuation, items 1–4 on the cost side of the equation are reasonably easy to value, subject to the discussion on shadow prices earlier. The environmental effect is more difficult but could be considered in terms of the possible effect on crop yields by the examination of historic data and attempts could also be made to estimate health damage as a result of consulting medical opinion. The Roskill Inquiry into the third London airport made an attempt to value the social cost of the loss of historic churches by reference to their fire insurance value. This process was held up to ridicule and probably detracted from the Committee's work in measuring the physical distributional effect of noise on the area if the airport were to be built.

In an examination of the benefits associated with a road or any public transport scheme the major objective of the scheme is probably time saving. Indeed in such schemes as the construction of the M1 motorway and the Victoria Line it was the time saving which was the major benefit of the proposals. Two categories of time can be identified. These are work and leisure time and therefore the question has to be addressed as to what value should be given to these savings. The conventional approach is to measure the value of work time in terms of the average gross salary for the type of work time saved plus an additional sum for extra costs associated with the costs of employing labour (e.g. National Insurance and pension costs). This of course assumes that the time saved can be converted directly into additional output. The problems of valuing non-work time (commuting and leisure) are, however, more difficult as no equivalent market price in terms of direct wage rates exist. For the value of non-work time it is necessary to impute values from choices which people make regarding the use of time (the behaviour observation method) or to use a questionnaire or other experiments to derive a value (the contingent valuation method). The Ministry of Transport has suggested a standard figure of 25% of the national average gross hourly rate as a measure of commuting time but there are obvious difficulties in the application of one figure in a range of differing situations. The Department's figures are also restricted to commuting time and do not cover leisure travel.

With a new road it would be hoped that savings could be generated by the reduction in vehicle operating costs as wear and tear on vehicles is reduced. However, it is necessary to consider the distinction between generated and non-generated traffic. While data are available in respect of vehicle operating costs it is the level of traffic that it is difficult to estimate. Generally, the larger the generated or extra traffic, the greater will be the effect on the original estimated time savings of the scheme. The M25 indicates that generated traffic will have a major impact on the success or failure of a scheme; in this particular case, additional generated traffic may actually reduce (or even eliminate) total time savings!

The question of accident costs has already been touched upon earlier. The physical costs of treatment, for example, will be available from health authorities and in the M1 study costs were input for accident savings in terms of loss of output, medical expenses, property damage and administration costs. However, the authors of the study admitted the difficulties of placing a monetary value on death itself and personal distress. Some writers have suggested the use of court awards but inevitably there will always be disagreement on the value of this element of the cost-benefit equation. Finally there is a need to consider the value of such benefits as reduced stress and strain on drivers and passengers if congestion can be reduced. It can be argued, however, that such factors are related to time in that time pressures cause stress and discomfort. This factor might therefore be included in the general framework of time valuation.

Summary of cost-benefit analysis

It can be seen from the previous statements that there are considerable difficulties in the application of cost-benefit analysis. The method does, however, require a systematic analysis of a problem and its potential solutions. It focuses on the important issue in any project appraisal and is based on focuses on techniques consistent with economic principles including the discounting of future monetary flows. Decision makers are being called on to exercise judgement with imperfect knowledge but partial or approximate information is better than no information at all. In each step assumptions have been made but, given the earlier discussion on probability, all investment decisions inevitably entail risk and the public sector cannot be protected from a fact of life.

9.8 Cost-effectiveness analysis

This technique has been developed in an attempt to overcome the difficulties of gathering and valuing information in a complete CBA exercise. Cost-effectiveness analysis identifies all costs and benefits but concentrates on measuring the measurable and provides a description of the non-quantifiable factors only. The technique, therefore, does not provide an absolute measure of the value of the project. In the field of housing and inner-city renewal the provision of a given standard of accommodation at minimal cost could be the subject of a cost-effectiveness exercise. The exercises may thus be considered to be more realistic than a full cost-benefit exercise as no attempt has been made to measure the unmeasurable.

A form of cost-effectiveness analysis is the technique of option appraisal as developed in the health service, although it has the potential for application in the public sector in general. Option appraisal can be defined as a method of project appraisal which systematically informs the decision maker of all the advantages and disadvantages of the practical alternatives for achieving an objective by providing all relevant information. It is a process of informing rather than actually determining the decision. On some occasions option appraisal will change the decision makers' mind about the best way of deploying resources while on others it will merely confirm that solutions arrived at intuitively are correct. It is a team approach in that it is multidisciplinary and inevitably involves value judgements.

The steps in optional appraisal are:

1. *Identify the strategic planning context* as this will put any proposals for change in the context of the overall organization's goals and objectives.
2. *Set the objectives, constraints and performance criteria* for the proposed changes.
3. *Formulate options,* this should include doing nothing as this will provide a reference point to assess how successfully the options considered meet the current service problems.
4. *Evaluate options,* this involves a preliminary sift to eliminate options which are not practical in that they fail to satisfy step (2). For remaining options:
   (a) prepare a detailed description of each option giving full background;
   (b) assess benefits describing and quantifying where possible the effectiveness of each option in satisfying the objective of the scheme;
   (c) assess revenue and capital costs;
   (d) access discount to take account of the timing of cost flows;
   (e) assess any significant costs and benefits in the wide non-organizational context;
   (f) carry out sensitivity analysis to assess the relative importance of particular assumptions to the options under consideration.
5. *Select the preferred option.*
6. *Monitor results.*

The organizational environment in which appraisal takes place is clearly important and this point lends support to the accusation that appraisals can be used for political purposes to advance a case or protect an organization from outside interference rather than for purely evaluation reasons (McAlister, 1990, p.49). Clearly, in a political environment the political consequences of any decision cannot be ignored but the technique of option appraisal has the potential to bring all relevant factors to the attention of the decision maker and thus inform him/her of the full consequences of any decision.

In summary option appraisal has the potential to provide:

1. a disciplined approach to ensure that all relevant factors are considered in a multidisciplinary framework before a decision is reached;

2. a mechanism to ensure that all feasible alternative methods of meeting an objective are considered;

3. a framework to marshal the arguments for and against potential solutions;

4. the opportunity to take account of risk and uncertainty in the decision-making process;

5. full information to decision makers on the consequences of the choice of a particular option.

6. after the decision has been taken, a basis to monitor progress in achieving the original objective(s) set.

The application of the technique is now demonstrated in Exhibit 9.3 in relation to a proposed capital project by a central government department, and also draws on the 'desiderata' principles demonstrated in Chapter 8 on capital budgeting.

Exhibit 9.3

A government department is considering developing new office accommodation and has assembled an appropriate team to examine in full the alternatives available to it (the options). The department currently operates on a split site in two office buildings in the heart of a town centre in the South East of England. Only one of these sites has adequate land to build additional offices although the remaining site could be redeveloped by internal modernization of the current office layout and the addition of an extra floor on top of the present structure. The only other alternative is the purchase of land and the building of new office accommodation on the outskirts of the town. Relocation to other parts of the United Kingdom is not possible due to the work of the department. It is also not possible to do nothing as the work of the department is suffering from the split site and the public is seriously dissatisfied with the service resulting in political pressure to act.

In summary the options are thus:

1. develop existing site by the utilization of surplus land for new offices (site A);
2. modernize present offices and add new floor to existing structure (site B);
3. purchase new site and use sale proceeds of selling sites A and B to reduce capital costs;
4. relocate – impractical;
5. do nothing – operationally and politically unacceptable.

It is first necessary to cost the feasible alternatives:

	Land £000	Building costs £000	Annual revenue cost £000	NPV
Option 1		2 300	750	13 321
Option 2		2 000	680	11 998
Option 3	300	2 200	670	12 038

Notes:
1.   The discount rate is 6% with the life of the buildings estimated at 5 years (i.e. cumulative discount factor year 51 at 6% is 15.813).

2. Building costs are spread over one year with payment assumed at the end of year one (i.e. discount factor 0.943).
3. The annual revenue costs of the buildings once complete (i.e. cumulative discount factor 15.813 − 0.943) = 14.87.
4. Capital cost after income from sale of other sites. It is assumed that the sites are sold for £530 000 in one year's time. The total capital cost of the land is estimated at £800 000 payable up front. (Total capital cost = £800 000 × 1 − (£530 000 × 0.943) = £300 210.)

On the basis of this financial appraisal option 2 is the cheapest and would appear to be the one that should be adopted. There is a need, however, to consider the other benefits that would occur. At this stage the team might draw up the desiderata matrix shown in the table below. (It will be noted that this desiderata exercise is presented differently from that in Chapter 8. This is to indicate that alternative formats are available.)

Clearly in this exhibit the weights given to each of the criteria plus the criteria themselves will be those identified by the team. It can be seen that while option 2 is the cheapest it scores badly on the non-financial appraisal. Option 1 is the most expensive but scores well on the non-financial appraisal. Option 3 costs marginally more than 2 but is significantly better in terms of its effectiveness. On the basis of this appraisal option 3 should be chosen subject to detailed tenders to ensure the original cost estimates were realistic.

All options can be subjected to sensitivity analysis to test the strength of the assumptions on which they are based and to recognize the uncertainty of capital investment.

Desiderata table for option appraisal exercise

Criteria	Weights	Option 1	Option 2	Option 3
Lack of disruption to existing workload	10	7	3	9
Car parking	5	3	2	5
Access to public transport	5	4	4	3
Suitability for future expansion	10	7	1	8
Staff perceptions	5	3	2	3
Total benefits		190	80	225

Key points of chapter

1. The importance of considering the time value of money in the capital investment decision has been stressed.
2. The problem of inflation was discussed and illustrated.
3. The potential for cost-benefit analysis was explored.
4. The value of option appraisal in the public sector was explored.

9.9 Summary

This chapter has examined techniques which take account of the time value of money in project appraisal. It also developed economic concepts of investment appraisal in the calculation of the cost of capital and the development of cost-benefit analysis. The difficulties of the cost-benefit approach were discussed but the conclusion reached was that the technique is of considerable value in public sector investment appraisal. Cost-effectiveness analysis was also examined but it was pointed out that this technique is less ambitious than CBA but can make a valuable contribution to the capital investment decision-making process.

Exhibit 9.4

Chilly County Council is considering installing a new central heating system in one of its older offices. As part of its long-term plan this office will be sold in three years' time on 31/12/X3. The authority believes that installing the central heating system will make the building easier to sell and add £100 000 to the final selling price. Three systems are regarded as feasible and the estimated capital costs of each are set out here:

	£
Gas	170 000
Oil	150 000
Solid fuel	140 000

Annual fuel costs are dependent on the severity of the winter each year and the rate of increase in fuel price. At the prices expected to be in force during 19X1 the annual fuel costs are estimated at:

	Severe winter £	Mild winter £
Gas	40 000	24 000
Oil	53 000	37 000
Solid fuel	45 000	36 000

The authority estimates that in each year there is a 70% chance of a severe winter and a 30% chance of a mild winter. The chance of a mild or severe winter in any year is considered to be independent of the chance of a mild or severe winter in the previous year.

Fuel prices are expected during 19X2 and 19X3 to increase by either 8% (probability equal to 0.4) or 10% (probability equal to 0.6%). Whichever rate of increase applies in 19X2 will be repeated the following year. Maintenance costs (payable at the end of year) are expected to be:

	£
Gas	2 500
Oil	2 000
Solid fuel	10 000 (in 19X2)

Maintenance costs are fixed.

There is no difference in performance between the systems.

The authority uses the monetary cost of capital as its hurdle rate. This rate is currently 12%.

Which system should be purchased by the authority?

The following solution uses expected value to calculate risk, and expresses project costs in monetary terms, permitting discounting using the monetary cost of capital.

Gas heating

Expected value of fuel costs, based upon the probabilities of a mild (0.3) or severe (0.7) winter:

$$= (0.7 \times £40\,000) + (0.3 \times £24\,000)$$
$$= £35\,200$$

Annual fuel costs

Year	12% discount factor	8% inflation Cash flow £	PV £	10% inflation Cash flow £	PV £
1	0.893	35 200	31 433	35 200	31 433
2	0.797	38 016	30 298	38 720	30 860
3	0.712	41 057	29 234	42 592	30 326
			£90 965		£92 619

Expected value of discounted fuel costs, allowing for probabilities of 8% inflation (0.4) and 10% inflation (0.6): (0.4 × £90 965) + (0.6 × £92 619)

	£
Expected value	91 960
Capital costs	170 000
Maintenance (£2000 per annum for 3 years)	6 005
= £2500 × 2.402	
NPV of gas option	£–267 965

Oil heating

Expected value of fuel costs, based upon the probabilities of a mild (0.3) or severe (0.7) winter:

$$= (0.7 \times £53\,000) + (0.3 \times £37\,000)$$
$$= 48\,200$$

Annual fuel costs

Year	12% discount factor	8% inflation Cash flow £	PV £	10% inflation Cash flow £	PV £
1	0.893	48 200	43 043	48 200	43 043
2	0.797	52 056	41 489	53 020	42 257
3	0.712	56 220	40 029	58 322	41 525
			£124 561		£126 825

Expected value of discounted fuel costs, allowing for probabilities of 8% inflation (0.4) and 10% inflation (0.6): (0.4 × £124 561) + (0.6 × £126 825).

	£
Expected value	125 920
Capital costs	150 000
Maintenance (£2 000 per annum for 3 years)	4 804
= £2 000 × 2.402	
NPV of oil option	£280 724

Solid fuel heating

Expected value of fuel costs, based upon the probabilities of a mild (0.3) or severe (0.7) winter:

$$= (0.7 \times £45\ 000) + (0.3 \times £36\ 000)$$
$$= £42\ 300$$

Annual fuel costs

Year	12% discount factor	8% inflation		10% inflation	
		Cash flow £	PV £	Cash flow £	PV £
1	0.893	42 300	37 774	42 300	37 774
2	0.797	45 684	36 410	46 530	37 084
3	0.712	49 339	35 129	51 183	36 442
			£109 313		£111 300

Expected value of discounted fuel costs, allowing for probabilities of 8% inflation (0.4) and 10% inflation (0.6): (0.4 × £109 313) + (0.6 × £111 300)

	£
Expected value	110 505
Capital costs	140 000
Maintenance (£10 000 in 2 years time)	7 970
= £10 000 × 0.797	
NPV of solid fuel option	£258 475

Based on these calculations, the solid fuel option has the lowest NPV of costs and on financial grounds would appear to be the favoured option. It also requires less capital investment than the other two options, which may be important if there are severe constraints on capital expenditure.

The main limitations on this type of analysis are that the expected value will never occur and we are ignoring the decision maker's attitude to risk. A possible alternative would be to attempt to redefine the problem in terms of utility but clearly this is difficult ground to read. A decision must be made and therefore we have to take into account uncertainty whatever decision-making technique is used and there is inevitable compromise. The comparison between the three systems must also take into account both financial and so-called non-financial factors. A selection of these are now set out:

1. How reliable are the estimates of cost, the probabilities of fuel price inflation and the chances of a mild or severe winter?
2. Is there a legal obligation to install a new system?

3. While the increase in the selling price has been ignored since it is common to all three systems the question must arise as to the validity of this assumption due to the possible views of potential buyers.
4. There is no mention of storage problems or extra employees to check deliveries of the appropriate systems.
5. Gas may be an environmentally cleaner fuel.

Exhibit 9.5

A town centre is heavily congested with road traffic. It has been suggested that a bypass be constructed to relieve the congestion.

The projected road will be 2.5 miles long and will require a capital cost of £0.3 million per mile and annual maintenance costs of £12 000 per mile. The projected route is via rich agricultural land which was acquired by the Department of Transport in anticipation of the road scheme being built for £0.5m some five years ago. In its present use it yields crops worth £60 000 per year. The new road will result in higher noise levels and houses will require to be soundproofed at a cost ranging between £2500 and £3500 each. One hundred houses are affected.

It is predicted that there is a:

    0.2 probability of 1.5 million journeys per year
    0.5 probability of 2.0 million journeys per year
    0.3 probability of 3.0 million journeys per year

along the new road.

In each case approximately 40% of the journeys will compromise generated traffic and 50% of the journeys will be for leisure purposes. The average mileage saved per journey will be 1.2 miles and the average time saved will be 12 minutes per journey.

It is expected that there will be a reduction in accidents from 30 per year to 14 year:

	Fatal	Serious	Minor
Town centre route	2	6	22
Bypass	2	8	4

During construction of the bypass there will be considerable delays to users of the existing route.

Notes:

1. Generated traffic is weighted 0.5 of existing traffic. This is to reflect the impact that generated vehicles currently using other routes will have on traffic flow. The case of the M25 might suggest that generated traffic be treated as a cost due to its potential to remove the benefits of time savings and increase operating costs.
2. Time savings are to be valued as follows:

Work time	£2.25 per hour
Leisure time	£1.00

3. Recent court awards for loss of life range from £50 000 to £250 000, and for serious accidents from £5000 to £85 000.

4. Hospital statistics reveal that the cost per case is £1500 for serious accidents and £80 for minor accidents.
5. The project is to be appraised using the test discount rate of 6%.
6. The project is to be evaluated over a 30-year time horizon.
7. Vehicle operating costs amount to £0.10 per mile.

Should the bypass be built?

The problem examines the role that CBA can play in a decision-making situation. The following calculation illustrates how the costs and benefits of the scheme can be calculated once the difficult conceptual issues of valuation have been addressed.

Years		Cost £000	Discount factor	NPV £000
Costs:				
0	Construction costs	750.00	1.00	750.00
1–30	Maintenance	30.00	13.76	412.80
1–30	Land–opportunity cost	60.00	13.76	825.60
0	Soundproofing	300.00	1.00	300.00
1–30	Serious injuries	90.00	13.76	123.84
1–30	Additional hospital costs	3.00	13.76	41.28
	Total costs			2 453.52
Benefits:				
1–30	Time saved	577.50	13.76	7 870.72
1–30	Vehicle operating costs	198.00	13.76	2 906.11
1–30	Minor accidents	1.44	13.76	19.81
Total benefits				10 796.94
Net benefits				8 343.12

The discount factor of 13.76 was taken from annuity tables for 6%. The incremental changes resulting from building the road were used as appropriate. Where a range of values was given, as for soundproofing, the average value was calculated. The number of journeys undertaken is based on the expected value calculated by multiplying the probability factor by the expected number of journeys associated with that factor and taking the sum of the three resultant figures (i.e. 2.2. million). This was then multiplied by the anticipated number of generated journeys (0.4). The balance of 60% is the number of non-generated journeys. This results in generated journeys of 880 000 and non-generated journeys of 1 320 000; 50% of each of these journeys are for work and 50% are for leisure. It is now possible to calculate the time factor saving (12/60) at the appropriate rate for work (£2.25) and leisure (£1.00) and to take account of note 1 on the weighting of generated journeys. A similar calculation was then undertaken for operating cost savings using the appropriate distance saved and note 7.

Questions

9.1 (a) Indicate briefly why discounted cash flow techniques are used in the public sector.

(b) Following a review by the fire prevention officer the chief building works manager has recently presented an adverse report on an operational building in your public sector organization. To bring the existing building up to standard would cost capital expenditure of £90 000 next year, and extra maintenance expenditure of £15 000 in each of the next three years, commencing next year. Alternatively if the building were replaced after those three years there would be no need for capital expenditure, and additional maintenance expenditure of only £4000 in each of those three years would be required.

The management board suggests that it would be more economic to replace the building as, because of the nature of the building, staffing and running costs are also high.

The figures are as follows:

Annual cost	Existing building £000	Replacement building £000
Staffing	130	96
Running costs	42	26
	172	122
Income	51	51
	121	71

The cost of building and furnishing a new building on an adjacent site owned by the organization would be £630 000, spread evenly over the next three years. The present building could be sold for £40 000.

The chief accountant asks you to:

(i) Assess whether it would be economic over a 20-year period to replace the building on the basis of these costs (assuming a discount rate of 6% in real terms).

(ii) Indicate the other factors to be taken into account by the organization in considering whether to go ahead with the proposal.

9.2 (a) Discuss the view that payback is a more appropriate investment appraisal technique than net present value for public sector organizations, since liquidity is of critical importance.

(b) Metroland County Ambulance Service is considering changing from petrol to liquefied petroleum gas (LPG) as the primary fuel for its ambulance fleet of 208 vehicles. Some of the costs and benefits involved with the change have been identified, allowing a preliminary evaluation of the financial viability of the proposal to be made. All costs and benefits are at November 1987 prices and a 5% discount rate is normally used in appraisals.

Capital costs so far established can be categorized as vehicle conversion costs, bulk installation costs and training costs.

Vehicle conversion costs have been calculated as averaging £540 per vehicle. It is assumed that 40 vehicles will be converted now, payment being made immediately, then 100 vehicles during the first year, payment to be made at the end of the year, and the remaining vehicles during the second year, with payment at the end of the year. From then on there will be no need for conversion, and no additional costs, as replacement ambulances will be fitted to run on LPG.

Bulk installation costs arise from the need for bulk storage tanks to contain LPG. It will be necessary to purchase 21 tanks, all of which are initially presumed to be of a two-tonne size. The cost of each tank and its installation is estimated at £7650. Purchase will be phased over seven years with payment assumed to be made at the beginning of each year.

Training costs arise from the need to retrain maintenance staff and operational staff who number 520. For maintenance staff it is assumed that the retraining programme will cost £2200, payable immediately. It is estimated that on average £10 will be incurred on training for each member of the operational staff, with the training programme taking two years. Assume that the payment is made in two halves, at the end of the first and second years.

Revenue costs involve maintenance and insurance costs per year for the tanks of £25 per tank, and additional maintenance for each vehicle of £12 per year, both payable at the end of the year.

The financial benefit of LPG is its price advantage over petrol. Given the size of deliveries and quantities likely to be required for the fleet, it is estimated that LPG would produce a saving of 4p per litre, for a range of consumption between 1.15 million and 1.35 million litres per annum when all the vehicles have been covered. It has been decided to assess the change to LPG over a ten-year period.

9.3 Midlands Airport Authority is considering the construction of a new airport terminal building to handle international passenger traffic.

The following estimates of the most likely increase in passenger movements and cost data have been derived from the preliminary feasability study, just completed by consultants at a cost of £100 000:

(i)   The increase in international passenger movements is anticipated to be 3m per annum.
(ii) It would be necessary to spend £2m immediately on infrastructure before construction of the terminal could commence.
(iii) The estimated capital development cost of the terminal building is £52m. The construction period is anticipated to be two years. Payments would be phased and £26m would be paid at the end of the two years.
(iv) Expected annual running costs are:

Fixed costs   £4 million
Variable costs   £10 per passenger movement

(v)   Competitive considerations suggest that landing fees should be fixed at £12 per passenger movement. In addition, each passenger will generate £2 average net income from duty-free sales.
(vi) Advances in air travel technology indicate that the useful life of the terminal building could be as short as 18 years.
(vii) Capital can be readily obtained at a cost of 10% per annum.

Required

(a) You are required to prepare a report to the Board of the Authority indicating whether the construction of the new terminal building is likely to be worthwhile. Your report should include an assessment of the sensitivity of the proposals to the annual level of passenger movements. (15 marks)

(b) What are the limitations of using the information given for assessing the desirability of the airport extension from the viewpoint of society as a whole. What other factors should be taken into consideration and to what extent can they be quantified in financial terms? (5 marks)

(Total 20 marks)

9.4 Your council is concerned at the substantial amounts paid in car allowances for the reimbursement of officers who use their own vehicles for the provision of services and wishes to investigate alternative methods of provision. The objective of this exercise is to provide a comprehensive report on the most cost-effective alternative method(s) for the provision of car transport for its employees with high car mileage.

Option 1 considers contract leasing for the hire of 37 vehicles at a rental of £120 per month whatever the mileage. Maintenance costs are included in the agreement.

Option 2 considers operating a vehicle fleet financed from the renewal and repairs fund. Ford Escorts and Fiestas are selected and the average cost per vehicle is £4550; initial outlay from the R & R fund will be made this year. Annual repayments of principal are to be made over three years and the cost of internal finance is 12%. Residual value at the end of year 3 is £67 340.

Option 3 is the finance leasing option. A lease for the purchase of 37 vehicles totals £188 520. Annual repayments are made evenly over three years. A commission of 0.5% of capital expenditure is normally charged at the beginning of the agreement. The residual value of the vehicles is £67 340 less 5% paid to the lessor at the end of the third year.

To make valid comparison maintenance costs must be taken into account. One local garage has expressed an interest in contract maintenance and has quoted £20 per month per vehicle as an indication of their charges. In their quotation they say a 7% inflation factor must be built into the figures and payment made yearly in advance.

(a) Calculate which of the three options is the most cost effective. It is suggested that a discount factor of 7% should be built into the calculations. Base your calculations on a fleet of 37 vehicles.

(b) Although discounting procedures are a recommended method of investment appraisal many organizations use the simple payback method of evaluation. Why should this be the case and what are the disadvantages of payback?

Year	Discount factor 7%
0	1.0000
1	0.9346
2	0.8734
3	0.8163

9.5 The National Mining Corporation extracts and sells coal using open-cast mining methods. This involves three major operations:

(a) First, the removal and setting aside of the topsoil covering the coal to be excavated.
(b) Second, the extraction, preparation and sale of the minerals.
(c) Finally, the restoration of the site by filling in the excavation and replacing the topsoil with general restoration to at least the same condition as before the operation commenced.

The corporation owns a site and is faced with two possible alternatives for the use of the site. These are:

1. To sell the site immediately for £350 000.
2. To develop the site for mining purposes.

If alternative 2 is adopted the following data will need to be considered:

Physical data

Volume of topsoil	2 500 000 cubic metres
Coal in site	1 500 000 tonnes
Extraction rate	300 000 tonnes per annum

Cost data
Equipment costs £800 000 (paid at end of first year)
Topsoil removal by private contractor £1.30 per cubic metre
Mining costs £8.00 per tonne
Restoration £1 250 000 (paid at end of seventh year)

Income
Mineral sales £15.00 per tonne

Other data
Equipment will be sold at the end of year seven at 10% of the original cost. The value of the restored site at the end of the seventh year is estimated at £450 000.

The corporation uses a 20% discount rate as its cost of capital.

The payments to the private contractor are spread evenly over the first 12 months of the scheme.

Required

Advise the corporation as to which of the two alternatives it should follow in a report to the Management Board, including any non-financial factors they might consider.

Ignore inflation.

Discount factors

Year 1	0.833
Year 2	0.694
Year 3	0.579
Year 4	0.482
Year 5	0.402
Year 6	0.335
Year 7	0.279

9.6 Deptford Health Authority is planning to change its geriatric care service. The proposals of the Geriatric Health Care Planning Committee (composed of medical staff) are set out in the following paper which has been presented directly to the Area Management Team.

Extract from Geriatric Care Paper to Management Team

The Geriatric Health Care Planning Committee has considered the need to improve services to the elderly given the increasing trend towards a more elderly population. It is considered three alternatives exist:

1. to build a new specialist unit (Scheme A);
2. to convert part of an existing hospital (Scheme B);
3. to improve the current units and also to offer wider ranging care in the community to prevent admission to hospital. The Revenue Allocation would be increased each year by £5000 over the current allocation for each of the next ten years (Scheme B).

After due consideration the Committee has decided to recommend the adoption of Scheme A as on the Cost Statement set out as it is the only scheme that will pay for itself in ten years (i.e. the period of the current planning cycle).

Cost Statement

		Schemes	
	A	B	C
	£000	£000	£000
Capital cost	1 050	700	
Additional revenue			
Running cost	–	–	50
	1 050	700	50
Income from sale of redundant property	(60)	(40)	–
Net reduction in annual revenue costs			
£100 000 p.a.	(1 000)	–	–
£63 000 p.a.		(630)	
Total income/savings	(1 060)	(670)	–
Surplus	10	–	–
Deficit	–	30	50

The Report has only just been sighted by the Area Treasurer who is to attend the Management Team meeting and he has asked you for your comments on the proposals.

The following additional information is available to you:

(i)   The life of the buildings is as follows

Scheme A   60 years (annuity factor 0.1201)
Scheme B   30 years (annuity factor 0.1241)

(You should assume that loan repayments are due to begin at the end of the first year on schemes A and B, the capital works taking one year to complete.)

(ii) The reduction in administration costs are achieved in the first year after the completion of the capital works, this is the same year as the increased revenue funding would commence for scheme C.

(iii) The income from the sale of property is received in the third year after completion of the capital works. The figures have been confirmed by independent valuers.

(iv) Present value tables for £1 receivable at the end of each year at 12% are:

1	0.89	6	0.51
2	0.80	7	0.45
3	0.71	8	0.40
4	0.64	9	0.36
5	0.57	10	0.32

Prepare a report to your Treasurer commenting on the appraisal performed by the Geriatric Care Committee, identifying which solution in your view should be adopted and including any other factors which you consider important.

9.7 A town centre is heavily congested with road traffic. It has been suggested that a bypass be constructed to relieve the congestion.

The projected road will be three miles long and will require a capital cost of £0.5 million per mile and annual maintenance costs of £25 000 per mile. The projected route is via rich agricultural land which was acquired by the Department of Transport some five years ago in anticipation of the road scheme being built for £0.5m. In its present use it yields crops worth £160 000 per year. The new road will result in higher noise levels and houses will require to be soundproofed at a cost ranging between £2500 and £3500 each. One hundred houses are affected.

It is predicted that there is a:

0.1 probability of 1.5 million journeys per year
0.5 probability of 2.0 million journeys per year
0.4 probability of 3.0 million journeys per year

along the new road. In each case approximately 30% of the journeys will comprise generated traffic and 40% of the journeys will be for leisure purposes. The average mileage saved per journey will be 2.2 miles and the average time saved will be 20 minutes per journey.

It is expected that there will be a reduction in accidents from 30 per cent to 14 per year:

	Fatal	Serious	Minor
Town centre route	2	6	22
Bypass	2	8	4

During construction of the bypass there will be considerable delays to users of the existing route.

Notes:
1. Generated traffic is weighted 0.2 of existing traffic.
2. Time savings are valued as follows:

Work time   £2.25 per hour
Leisure time £1.00

3. Recent court awards for loss of life range from £50 000 to £250 000, and for serious accidents from £5000 to £85 000.
4. Hospital statistics reveal that the cost per case is £1500 for serious accidents and £80 for minor accidents.
5. The project is to be appraised using the test discount rate of 6%. The appropriate factor is 13.76.
6. The project is to be evaluated over a thirty-year time horizon.
7. Vehicle operating costs amount to £0.14 per mile.

Required

Prepare a report for the Ministry of Transport advising whether or not the bypass should be built.

9.8 Aqua Water utility is to provide a water supply to part of a new town development comprising partially of industrial units and partially of domestic dwellings. The following information is available to you:

1. Land acquisition costs amount to £145 000 and will be incurred at the commencement of the project.
2. Construction costs of laying the supply are £110 000 and will be incurred 50% at the commencement of the scheme and the balance one year later.
3. A pumping station will operate from the beginning of year 2. Annual costs of maintenance are estimated at £33 000 per annum and will increase by 10% from the beginning of year 3 and the beginning of each year thereafter.
4. When developed the area will comprise:
   (a) 3000 dwellings of which 1000 will be completed by the start of year 2 and the remaining 2000 by the start of year 3. Each property will yield an income of £25 per annum increasing by 10% per annum from the start of year 4 and from the beginning of each year thereafter (assume all properties occupied on completion).
   (b) The industrial estate will consume water at the rate of 2.5 million gallons from the commencement of year 3, 4 million gallons from the commencement of year 4 and 10 million gallons per annum thereafter. This will be charged for at the rate of 0.3p per gallon for the whole period under review.

Required

(i) The water utility uses a 7-year time cycle in calculating the returns on capital projects. You are required to calculate the net present value of the project using discount rates of 10% and 20%. Indicate the approximate internal rate of return.
(ii) What other factors should be considered by the utility? Present the results in report form to the Management Board of the utility.

10 The audit of public organizations

Key learning objectives

After reading this chapter you should be able to:

1. Understand the development of auditing in the public sector.
2. Contrast the increased importance of value for money auditing today with the decline of emphasis on stewardship auditing in the public sector.
3. Explain what is meant by the term value for money and discuss the difficulties of achieving value for money in the public sector.
4. List the audit processes necessary for achieving value for money.
5. Understand the concepts of best value and benchmarking.

Highly important to accountability in the public sector is the function exercised by the external audit of public sector organizations and today's increased demand for value for money appraisal placed upon it. This chapter examines the development of audit in the public sector and its changing role over time. It then turns to examine the role that value for money audit exercises contribute in the current role played by the auditor. External audit in the public sector is performed by the National Audit Office (NAO) for government departments and other *ad hoc* bodies such as the Arts Council which are financed by central government and by the Audit Commission for local government and the National Health Service, the Commission having taken over this duty from the Department of Health. The private sector audits on the 'true and fair view' basis those nationalized industries that remain in the public sector under the original Acts which established them. It should, however, not be forgotten that as important as the role of the external auditor is, a vital role is also played by internal audit. Increasingly the internal audit section is being required to undertake value for money assignments and it can be seen that pressures on the external auditor are reflected in the demands placed on internal audit staff. The opportunity has also been taken in this chapter to develop a number of exhibits which apply what might seem to be theoretical issues in a practical context. This effectively concludes what has been a theme of this book – the development of student understanding of complex financial management issues in the challenging environment of the public sector.

10.1 The audit of central government

The National Audit Office was established by the National Audit Act 1983 which represented the first major amendment to the role of the central government auditor since the statutory changes of 1921. The 1921 Act had itself only modified the original Exchequer and Audit Department Act of 1866. The Act of 1866 provided for the appointment of the Comptroller and Auditor General (C and AG) and the appointment of staff to carry out the statutory duties of the examination, certification and reporting on government department accounts. Under the 1866 Act the audit was to be a 100% check of the transactions of government departments but this was amended in 1921 to allow test checking. The 1921 Act also provided for the preparation and audit of trading accounts and the extension of powers to examine the revenue accounts of government. The C and AG's full title is the 'Comptroller General of the Receipt and Issue of Her Majesty's Exchequer and Auditor General of Public Accounts'. This rather long title covers two main functions:

1. As Comptroller General he is responsible for the issue of public funds to appropriate bodies.
2. As Auditor General he is required to certify the accounts, carry out value for money studies and report on these matters to parliament.

In practice these matters are referred to the Public Accounts Committee which was established in 1861 and by tradition is chaired by a leading member of the opposition. The Committee has a maximum of 15 members but, again by tradition, does not question the policy of the government and tends not therefore to divide on party lines. An example of the work of the Public Accounts Committee can be found in its report on the recent developments on community care. It expressed doubts about the level of financial controls exercised over joint financing schemes by the Department of Health and was also critical of the differences in planning timescales between health authorities and local authorities. It is interesting to note that this was the Committee's second report into this area only to discover similar problems.

By the early 1980s pressure had built up such that a review of the functions of the C and AG was called for. Underlying this pressure were greater demands for accountability, not in the traditional narrow stewardship sense for the proper use of resources, but rather for a wider interpretation of stewardship to include economy, efficiency and effectiveness in the use of resources provided. The result of this pressure was the passing of the 1983 National Audit Act which established a National Audit Office and a Public Accounts Commission to strengthen independence. Prior to this the Treasury had significant influence over the C and AG in that it could direct the area and nature of his work. Traditionally the Treasury had supplied from its ranks the C and AG, it audited the accounts of the Exchequer and Audit Department and it exerted influence over the level of remuneration and conditions of service of staff. The Act also provided for a discretionary power to undertake examinations of the economy, efficiency and effectiveness with which departments used resources.

The most recent piece of legislation to affect the role of the Comptroller and Auditor General is the Government Resources and Accounts Act 2000. The reasons given for the Act in the background documentation for the original bill are a desire to enable the introduction of resource account budgeting and to modernize the operation of the Exchequer and Audit Department Acts. Under section 6 the audit certificate is required to state that in the auditor's opinion the accounts show:

1. a true and fair view;
2. that money provided by parliament has been expended for the purposes intended;
3. that the financial transactions covered by the accounts are in accordance with the relevant authority that governs them.

Under Section 11 the C and AG is to audit the whole of government accounts and to certify and issue a report on them. The section also requires the Treasury to lay the accounts, together with the auditor's report, before the House of Commons.

As an example of the qualification of the financial accounts of a government body it was reported in *Accountancy Age* (January 2001, p.3) that the NAO had qualified the accounts of the Ordnance Survey (OS). The decision was based on the failure of the OS to value the National Topographic Database which should have been capitalized under FRS15. This omission had the effect of distorting the return on capital employed. In addition *Public Finance and Accountancy* (February 2001, p.8) points out that in auditing the resource accounts for the Welsh Assembly the NAO report was 'scathing' in its criticisms. These criticisms included the failure to carry out basic accounting controls such as bank reconciliations and consequently exposed the Assembly to the risk of fraud.

The C and AG is independent of the Executive as is shown by the following:

1. The appointment is made by the Queen and he can only be dismissed by a vote of both houses of parliament. Advice for the appointment is given by the prime minister after discussion with the chairman of the Public Accounts Committee.
2. The salary for the post is paid from the Consolidated Fund.
3. The C and AG decides his own objectives within the statutory framework and the extent to which those objectives will be carried out.
4. The C and AG sets and appoints the number and conditions of service of his staff.

The powers of the C and AG are not, however, all embracing in that there is no power to disallow expenditure and give legal rulings; there is no right of access to the accounts of public corporations or local authorities; he cannot 'follow public money wherever it goes' as there is no right of access to any other than government accounts; he cannot question policy; and finally maladministration affecting individual members of the public is a matter for the Ombudsman.

In central government there are numerous internal audit sections which have been given a stimulus by such events as the development of the Financial Management Initiative and the publication of 'Improving Management in Government: The Next Steps'. During this period internal audit has moved from a regularity function to being integrated within the drive to promote economy, efficiency and effectiveness. The stronger these internal audit sectors are the more the C and AG will be able to place reliance on their work.

The importance of value for money auditing undertaken by the C and AG is illustrated by his report on the *Ministry of Defence: Major Projects Report 2000* (National Audit Office, 2000a). This report covers 20 defence equipment projects and suggests that the ministry is exercising better cost control than previously over defence projects but that the control of completion times remains a problem. The report discovered, for example, that:

1. Forecasted costs of projects were 0.2% (£78 million) lower than in the previous year but still 5.7% (£2.4 billion) higher in total than the main investment approval.
2. The average project delay is getting longer with consequent 'knock-on' effects on defence capability (e.g. the delay in the Brimstone Missile project required the purchase of an alternative missile as a stop gap).

3. Delays in the completion of projects had led to capability shortfalls in 13 projects.

4. The Ministry of Defence expects to meet 98% of the customer's key requirements.

In respect of the Millennium Dome project (National Audit Office, 2000b) the auditor recognized that opening the project on time was a major achievement but was highly critical of the organizational arrangements, the highly ambitious visitor numbers and the failure to establish sufficiently robust financial management systems and controls. The lack of controls over projects are mirrored in a report in the *Sunday Times* on a HM Customs operation that went badly wrong and potentially appears to have cost the taxpayer up to £2 billion (11 February 2001, p.19).

In February 2001 Lord Sharman reported on his review of central government audit. If the government accepts the recommendations of this report the NAO will be given a 'right to roam' in that it will be able to trail through a range of public and private sector bodies to examine how public money has been spent. The report also suggests a three-tiered approach to corporate governance with audit committees, independently chaired and consisting mostly of independent members and stronger and well-resourced internal audit. Both these functions to be backed by the external audit. A different role for the public accounts committee is also envisaged in that it should hold an annual hearing to examine themes across government such as risk taking, fraud and corporate governance. Interestingly the report also suggests that the NAO should be resourced to brief departmental select committees on key financial matters without drawing the C and AG into policy matters. The report suggests also that 25% of the resources available for financial audit work should be subject to competition. The C and AG has additionally proposed that the NAO be subject to regular inspection for the quality of its work.

10.2 The health service

The health service was audited by auditors appointed by the Secretary of State for Health but under new legislation this work has been taken over by the Audit Commission (from 1 September 1990 under Statutory Instrument 1990/1329). The powers of the external auditors are now contained in three Acts of parliament; the National Health Service Act 1977, the Local Government Finance Act 1982 and the National Health Service and Community Care Act 1990. The National Health Service and Community Care Act 1990 made provision for the following changes to the Local Government Finance Act 1982:

1. The name of the Commission was changed to the Audit Commission for Local Authorities and the National Health Service in England and Wales. Membership of the Commission increased from 15 to 20 members (s. 11).
2. The Commission is responsible for the appointment of auditors of the health service but need not by law consult with the component bodies of the health service (s. 13).
3. The Commission is to prepare a Code of Audit Practice for the health service (s. 14).
4. The Auditors must satisfy themselves that the accounts comply with directions issued under the NHS Act and that value for money is achieved (s. 15).
5. Gives auditors the right of access to documents held by GP fundholders (s. 16).
6. There is no right of question of the auditor or inspection and objection to the accounts. Powers on illegal expenditure prohibition orders and surcharge do not apply (ss. 17, 19, 20 and 24). Under s. 20 (3) the auditor must report immediately to the Secretary of State where unlawful expenditure may occur.

Under the former system the audit system was an in-house service which reported directly to the minister of health. Essentially this procedure could be summarized as an examination of the systems of accounting and control and an assessment of their effectiveness, the undertaking of studies on the economy, efficiency and effectiveness of procedures and the verification of assets and liabilities. There was a close relationship between the centre (i.e. the Department of Health) and the individual health authorities and the concept of independence could be questioned. Also, as the audit was not conducted by the Comptroller and Auditor General, there was no direct accountability to parliament.

In 1987 it was announced that in addition to the Audit Directorate use would be made of the private sector to carry out the statutory audit. The National Audit Office is responsible for examining and certifying the summarized accounts of the health authorities but they relied on the role of the Directorate in performing this task. The National Audit Office does, however, attempt to monitor the quality of the audit undertaken and has access if necessary to the books and records of all health authorities, the Department of Health, the Welsh Assembly and Scottish Parliament. Internal audit in the NHS has been criticized and has been given low priority in the past. Some health authorities have privatized their internal audit services. Recent examples of value for money work undertaken by the Department of Health's auditors include enquiries into central sterile supplies departments and energy use. The National Audit Office has also undertaken value for money studies on a rolling programme using a sampling approach to select authorities, and, for example, in its report 'Management of the Family Practitioner Service' found a wide variation in the quality of information available to the service.

In 1998 the Local Government Act 1982 and the National Health Service and Community Care Act were consolidated into the Audit Commission Act 1998.

10.3 Local government

Local government has a long tradition of audit. The earliest known reference is dated 1430 when an audit was conducted into the application of monies to build a town wall. Modern audit in the form of the district audit was established by the Poor Law Amendment Act 1844, but the system, as the Act implies, only related to the Poor Law. The history of local government audit is one, however, in which the district auditor gradually gained more influence over the accounts of local government until the abolition of the service and the establishment of the Audit Commission in 1982. In its earliest days the district audit was primarily a stewardship audit but this did not prevent value for money questions from raising their head. The case of *Roberts* vs. *Hopwood* (1925) AC 578 is a case in point. (For a fuller discussion on the development of the district audit see Coombs and Edwards, 1990.)

By 1979 the government was becoming increasingly concerned about the effectiveness of the audit of local government, in particular the lack of detailed economy, efficiency and effectiveness studies. Indeed this concern was not only confined to the government as, in 1976, the Layfield Commission had recommended the appointment of an independent auditor with the same status as the C and AG. The result of this concern was that in 1982 the Local Government Finance Act established the Audit Commission. The role of the Commission from 1 April 1983 included the duties of:

1. appointing auditors to local authorities either from their own staff or the professional firms;

2. fixing the level of fees for audits;
3. preparing and maintaining an audit code of practice;
4. retaining the previous duties of auditors with regard to financial and regularity audit with specific reference to illegality and wilful misconduct. With the passing of the Local Government Act 1988 auditors gained new powers to apply for the judicial review of possible unlawful actions by authorities or to issue a prohibition order;
5. ensuring auditors satisfy themselves that adequate arrangements are made for 'securing economy, efficiency and effectiveness' in the discharge of functions by authorities.

The local government elector has a right of inspection of the accounts including a right to make copies of most information. The Freedom of Information Act 1985 also aids the local elector by greater publicity of material. The local government elector also has the right of objection to the accounts and may appeal to the auditor if any matter is considered to be illegal. On application to the courts by the auditor the sum may be declared illegal and the sum recovered from the individual.

The chief financial officer (the responsible officer) of a local authority has a statutory obligation to make proper arrangements for the conduct of a local authority's financial activities (Local Government Act 1972, ss. 151). This has normally meant that an in-house internal audit section has been established as the accounts and audit regulations stipulate the need for the responsible officer to provide an adequate internal audit (the Audit Commission verify that this duty has been properly discharged). It should be pointed out, however, that this function does not have to be provided internally only that the function must be adequate. It is often stated that the internal audit section is the 'eyes and ears' of the chief financial officer although clearly there is the potential for conflict with service officers and the function is not independent of his own department. The main advantage to the external auditor is that a strong active internal audit section will reduce workload. This should help keep the external audit fees lower than they might otherwise have been as relevant information is exchanged sufficient to maximize audit performance.

A number of public sector organizations, including local government, have market tested the provision of services such as internal audit in advance of compulsory competitive tendering. Others have established service level agreements between internal audit sections and client departments. Both these steps represent a major challenge to internal audit as, under the first, there is the potential for the loss of the in-house function and, under the second, the need to perform to agreed standards as set out in the internal contract. In addition, a further threat to the future of the internal audit department/section is the reduction in audit activity as services leave the control of the organization. In local government, for example, the loss of colleges of higher education in local government, resulted in lower income and a consequent inability of the section, unless replacement work was generated, to support existing staff numbers. Internal audit therefore faces numerous challenges while, service managers, will need increasingly to appreciate the role that internal audit performs in order to achieve high standards in terms of the service they need and demand.

The major steps that internal audit must take to prepare for competitive tendering or to prepare a realistic service level agreement are:

1. to establish the level of work necessary to achieve the basic statutory obligations of the director of finance and agree the level of service required by the organization in terms of those areas regarded as non-mandatory;

2. to build up a long-term plan for the future of internal audit based on a risk index. A rolling plan for a three-year period is probably the minimum necessary;
3. to establish quality standards with clients to ensure that the client is fully conversant with the role and function of internal audit;
4. to cost all activities such as accommodation and computer services and in any tender situation ensure that all non-audit costs are excluded and that there are no costs attributable to the client function;
5. to prepare a business plan which, during the process of preparation, fully identifies the strengths, opportunities, threats and weaknesses of the section. Appropriate action should be taken to build on the strengths, exploit the opportunities and overcome the threats and weaknesses identified;
6. to establish systems to advise the client on the costs of audit work to date, feedback systems to ensure audit reports are followed up and quality is maintained and to monitor progress against the business plan.

Internal auditors may find that the marketing is part of the departmental/sectional strategy as new opportunities are identified in the business planning process. Clients can then be targeted as they may not be fully aware of what the service has to offer (Jones, 1993, p.15).

Service managers need to be aware of the range of audit activity. While financial probity is a major function, the internal audit 'toolkit' includes systems development work, value for money activities, performance review, consultancy and possibly training. In deciding which services to accept service managers should be fully aware of the costs of these services and the quality required. In negotiating a service level agreement for internal audit services the service manager could consider, for example, the inclusion of the following:

1. extent of agreed duties;
2. the hourly rate to be charged for a particular service and the agreed maximum number of hours;
3. the level and basis of charges for additional work and the authorization procedure necessary for that work to be carried out;
4. the quality standard to be achieved;
5. response times;
6. redress procedures for work which is below standard and possible access to audit staff timesheets;
7. reporting practices;
8. timing of invoices and payment procedures.

A number of internal audit sections have adopted quality British Standard BS5750 (Connor, 1993, pp.10–12) as a means of ensuring customer satisfaction and competitive edge. BS5750 provides a quality assurance system possibly as part of a total quality management system. The basic objective of operating such a system is to develop a clear understanding of the necessity to provide clients with a high quality service, increase customer satisfaction, have greater control over operating costs due to the constant drive to improve quality and uniformity of working practice.

As mentioned earlier the Audit Commission Act 1998 consolidated previous legislation. Accordingly the external auditor of both a local authority and health authority has to be satisfied that:

1. accounts are prepared in accordance with the relevant regulations and all other statutory provisions applicable to the accounts;

2. proper accounting practice has been observed in compiling the accounts;
3. the body being audited has made proper arrangements for securing economy, efficiency and effectiveness in the use of resources;
4. if required to publish performance indicators proper arrangements have been made for the collecting, recording and publishing of such information.

In addition the auditor has to comply with the Audit Code of Practice as currently in force and also to consider whether or not to issue any report which the public interest dictates should be issued (see Exhibit 5.1 Hackney BC). The power of surcharge has now been removed (Local Government Act 2000) and replaced by an advisory power (Sec 90/91).

10.4 Best value

The Local Government Act 1999 subjects most local authorities to the concept of best value or more accurately the desire to continuously improve the exercise of all functions undertaken by the authority. The objective is ensure local authorities seek continuously to improve by developing a culture in which challenge, consultation, comparing and competing are the accepted way of conducting business (see Table 10.1). Second, the Act also provided for the abolition of a number of previous acts which had required local authorities to submit specified activities to compulsory competitive tendering replacing it with best value. Section II of the Act gives powers to the Secretary of State to intervene where it is considered a local authority's budget is excessive and to take appropriate action.

The spirit of these provisions in respect of best value and compulsory competitive tendering has subsequently been extended to the Health Service while other organizations such as social housing providers are also subject to the best value regime.

Table 10.1   The concepts of best value

Challenge	Compare	Consult	Compete
Why is the service provided? What would happen if it were not provided? What are the service objectives? Does it meet statutory objectives?	Informed comparison through: • best value indicators • Audit Commission performance indicators • local indicators Set quality targets in line with top 25% of local authorities Set cost and efficiency targets Welsh local authorities have established over 100 benchmarking clubs to compare performance and process	To include: • actual and potential service users • local citizens and taxpayers • employees and trade unions • local business and other partners This process can take place through surveys, referenda, focus groups, web sites, public meetings, citizens panels etc.	Authorities to ensure that fair competition is an option Competition to be approached with an open mind Key issue is that approach to the provision of a service which delivers best value to stakeholders Authorities to set out reasons for either accepting or rejecting competition in a transparent and auditable way

(*Source:* Adapted from National Assembly for Wales, 2000)

Best value principles were originally published in 1997 and developed in two green papers aimed at modernizing local government in England and Wales. Responsibility for the audit of best value performance and the public reporting thereon lies with the Audit Commission and is aimed at verifying the integrity of the best value process and confirming the comparability of any performance information.

The principles of best value excluding those relevant to external audit (covered earlier) are:

1. the setting of performance targets to achieve not only economy and efficiency but effectiveness and quality;
2. the application of best value to a wider range of services than simply those which had been subject to CCT;
3. a duty of best value is owed to all stakeholders and not only as customers and taxpayers;
4. central government continuing to set the framework for service provision;
5. designing an appropriate form of intervention where best value has failed;
6. both national and local targets being built on performance information which is relevant to managers;
7. a provision for government intervention where best value has failed;
8. competition continuing as an important tool of best value and is to be a feature of performance plans;
9. no presumption that the private sector should undertake services;
10. detailed targets should be set with regard to national targets and performance indicators and targets set by the Audit Commission.

Linked with best value is the concept of benchmarking. This is a means of concentrating on improving business practices by learning and applying best practice from other organizations. It is about discovering more about the way in which the organization works and judging how improvements can be made. There needs to be a desire to integrate the process of benchmarking into the planning cycle or it is suggested that it can become an expensive academic exercise. There is also a need to be imaginative as traditionally the public sector has compared itself with other public sector organizations which can limit the value of the potential benefits of the exercise.

Part of the process of achieving best value is the publication of performance plans. The purposes of these plans include:

1. setting out the authority's strategic objectives;
2. reporting on current performance against stated objectives and targets with comparisons with other authorities and service providers;
3. reporting on key results of best value reviews and to announce future planned reviews;
4. identifying targets for all services on an annual and longer term basis;
5. commenting on the means of achieving targets including relevant capital investment decisions and procedural changes.

Every performance plan is subject to audit by the authority's external auditor.

10.5 The public corporations

The nationalized industries are audited by the private sector under the provision of the original nationalization acts and, as such, are subject to the 'true and fair' view concept.

The accounts of these industries therefore are prepared on the lines of best commercial practice as set out in the Companies Act 1989, the relevant Statements of Standard Accounting Practice and any advisory pronouncements of the professional accounting bodies.

10.6 Value for money auditing

The earlier sections of this chapter have shown the increasing importance of value for money auditing in the public sector for the role of the external auditor. This role is not only confined to the external auditor, however, as in its Statements on Internal Audit Practice in the Public Sector CIPFA identifies the following responsibilities of reviewing, appraising and reporting for internal audit:

1. the soundness, adequacy and application of internal controls;
2. the extent to which the organization's assets and interests are accounted for and safeguarded from losses of all kinds arising from:
   (a) fraud and other offences;
   (b) waste, extravagance and inefficient administration, poor value for money or other cause;
3. the suitability and reliability of financial and other management data developed within the organization.

(*Source:* CIPFA, 1979)

It can be seen that item 2 (b) specifically refers to value for money, but sound systems of internal control also imply that adequate steps be taken within the organization to achieve it.

As outlined in Chapter 1 the achievement of value for money is no longer seen as a virtue but a necessity for public sector managers. It must be pointed out, therefore, that the search for value for money is not confined to either internal or external auditors but should permeate through the organization. This section of the text should thus be seen in this wider context and consequently develops general concepts which can be applied by both auditors and managers in their attempts to achieve the better use of limited resources. As previously explained, value for money has come to be associated with the three Es – economy, efficiency, and effectiveness.

It must be emphasized that no value for money exercise can be considered to be complete unless it has considered all three elements. The main problem is obviously with effectiveness due to the great difficulty in expressing and quantifying the often multiple goals and objectives of many public sector organizations and activities. It must also be pointed out that it is not the duty of the auditor to question policy. It it his duty to consider the effects of policy and to examine arrangements by which policy decisions are reached. The government has recently announced that in any future examination of the Health Service the Audit Commission will examine the effect of ministerial policy decisions on value for money. To this end the auditor will need to consider whether:

1. objectives have been set for the policy to achieve;
2. all relevant data were considered in arriving at the decision, including the examination of any feasible alternatives;
3. there is any conflict between policy objectives;
4. there is a monitoring and review procedure.

10.7 Sources of value for money studies

Policy areas for review are identified in a number of ways. These include:

1. *Comparative statistics.* The Audit Commission has identified similar authorities by devising expenditure profiles and using multiple regression techniques. CIPFA also publishes comparative statistics for various services and these may provide a guide to overspending. These statistics are only indicators and need to be treated with caution. In the case of the CIPFA statistics differences in accounting treatment may explain even significant variations.
2. *General audit activities.* In carrying out normal audit activities the auditors may identify waste and extravagance. This may then be investigated as resources permit.
3. *Special studies.* Each year specific target areas may be identified for study as is the case with the Audit Commission. Past studies include rent arrears, central purchasing and vehicle maintenance. If this policy is adopted then the appropriate man days must be set aside in the audit plan.
4. *Miscellaneous.* Includes specific requests from departments, direction by elected members and information from professional journals, e.g. the results of investigations in similar public sector bodies.

Clearly there is a need to build these factors into the audit strategic plan, whether for the internal or external auditor. Figure 10.1 sets out a possible procedure for this.

As each year proceeds the auditor will be able to examine the action taken on any previous recommendations and build any appropriate action into his ongoing plan. In devising and amending the plan on value for money work the audit should take into account the activity of complementary parties to avoid duplication of effort (for example, the work of an organization and methods unit).

In carrying these out studies, however, hindsight should not be seen as a virtue. Decisions should be judged on the information available at the time the decision was made. The actual studies can be broken down into two categories. Single-loop learning studies where the goal of the policy is not questioned but the method of achieving the

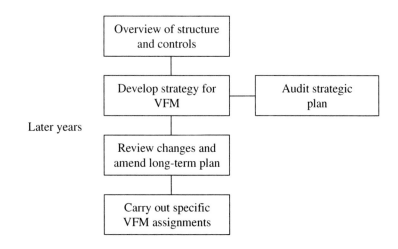

Figure 10.1 Incorporating VFM studies in the overall audit plan

goal is examined, and double-loop learning exercises where the policy goal itself is questioned and if necessary changes as a result of the outcome of the exercise.

10.8 Undertaking a value for money study

In carrying out a successful value for money assignment it is essential, as with all audit activity, that sound planning take place. Detailed planning begins with a thorough examination of the area to be examined. This would include the need to:

1. obtain past audit reports on the area to be examined;
2. check policy decisions to identify if policy objectives have been set and how their effectiveness is to be measured;
3. examine the efficiency yardsticks for appropriateness;
4. review the allocation of overheads to the activity under scrutiny;
5. establish the level of delegation to managers and their relationship to the existing department structure;
6. establish the current level of activity;
7. review the budget and budget control procedures within the activity.

Clearly the preceding is background work and the list is by no means exhaustive. Having established the necessary information the next step is then to set the audit objectives and to identify the appropriate level of staff and the man days to be committed to the study. It almost goes without saying that there will be a need to monitor progress to prevent drift.

The next stage is the conduct of the exercise. It must be remembered that the Auditor is dealing with people who traditionally have associated audit as a checking function and may have difficulty adjusting to the new demands placed on them by audit staff. One way of overcoming resistance may be to make all concerned fully aware of the benefits of the exercise – communication can break down barriers. Where there is a need for the agreement of the client department in undertaking the exercise the appointment of a coordinating officer may help alleviate problems quickly. Where a sensitive issue is being examined the choice of staff in the planning stage may be crucial to success. Clearly these staff must be properly briefed and must fully understand the nature of the task in hand and their part in it. The importance of good working papers cannot be overemphasized as is the cross-checking of material facts, as any factual errors in reports will distract from a generally sound exercise, especially in a politically sensitive area.

In carrying out the study various investigatory techniques will be used. These include:

1. Input-based reviews where the resources devoted to a particular activity are expressed in terms of the output of that activity (for example, the cost per mile of street cleaned). There is a danger here, however, that least cost is seen as giving value for money when all we have is an expenditure measure which says nothing about quality of service.
2. System-based reviews where the concentration is on the systems and procedures of the organization. This might include how marketing strategies for leisure centres are developed and reviewed with specific reference to pricing policy.
3. Comparison with the private sector where data are available.
4. Internal comparison as with those organizations having various divisions set up on a regional basis. It will be possible to compare between regions and adjust for price and cost differentials.
5. Output measurement by the use of trained specialists as with incentive bonus schemes and the use of work study techniques.

Table 10.2 provides a guide to fact finding, recording and interpreting information gained in carrying out this exercise.

Table 10.2 Guide to carrying out a value for money exercise

1. Begin by planning the exercise properly. Identify specific goals and objectives avoiding any inbuilt bias that the area covered by the investigation fails to provide value for money.
2. Establish proper systems to record the facts. In order to form a reasoned judgement these will provide a basis for any conclusions and recommendations.
3. Ensure that a structured approach is adopted to the collection of facts in order that all relevant information is gathered and that there is a detailed understanding of the reasons for the current system. Any pilot study should be consulted to verify that the results are consistent or otherwise.
4. In obtaining information use all the skills available to the auditor. These should include the use of Internal Control Questionnaires (ICQs), interviews, analysis of the underlying accounting and non-financial records and observations of procedures.
5. Flowchart systems if information is not available and identify weaknesses.
6. At interviews make interviewee aware, as far is reasonable, of the nature of the exercise and try to establish enthusiasm for the task in hand. Attempt to interview with list of points and ensure that all are covered.
7. Review results of interviews and data collection to identify any missing factors. Consider the implications for the study of statements which may have been made but which were 'off the record'.
8. Divide conclusions into factual matters and those resting on opinion. Ensure that there is no error of fact as the higher the strategic value of the report the greater the probability that political capital will be made to embarrass the auditor.
9. Base recommendations on content of the report. Ensure that any recommendations represent a practical solution to the problem in hand.

10.9 Effectiveness auditing

It has already been pointed out that the great difficulty for the auditor in carrying out value for money studies lies in the area of effectiveness. It will be noted that under best value there is also a requirement to judge quality of service which compounds this difficulty even more. The problem for the auditor, however, is that parliament and public sector organizations expect that these criteria will be measured. It is also probably true to state that surveys on vehicle maintenance and the collection of rent arrears are bound up more with economy and efficiency than the major question of the effectiveness of a policy on, say, homelessness. Clearly, the major reviews that can be undertaken are fraught with political difficulty and definition problems with regard to objectives. There is also the problem of the difficulty of measuring inputs. For example, direct inputs such as money can be measured for the education service but quasi-inputs such as parental support also play a part.

There is also the question as to whether or not the output of the education system rests solely, for example, with examination results or does it include wider objectives and, if so, what are they and how do you measure them? In this type of situation it will be necessary for some form of consensus to be reached with management and policy makers if the auditor is to attempt to measure value for money. Clearly, in any policy decision the decision makers must have had an objective in mind. It is defining this objective which is the challenge to the auditor and subsequently relating the output of the decision to it. On the positive aspect of effectiveness auditing there are many value for money studies which can be carried out without major debate. Examples would include refuse disposal and the effectiveness of an incentive bonus scheme. The problem for the auditor is that these are not necessarily at the strategic level of policy making and as such as auditor is not providing a positive contribution at the highest level.

Key points of chapter

1. There is an increased emphasis on economy, efficiency and effectiveness in all areas of auditing in the public sector.
2. The role that both internal and external auditors have to play in seeking economy, efficiency and effectiveness was explored.
3. The challenging nature of this work was examined with specific reference to the measurement of effectiveness.

10.10 Summary

This chapter has examined the evolution of the external audit in the public sector and pointed out the increasing importance of the search for economy, efficiency and effectiveness in its role. It has also stressed that internal audit has a vital role to play in this process and suggested that this role may expand as 'agencies', for example, develop in the provision of central government functions. The section on value for money indicates that the difficult area for the auditor in terms of value for money auditing lies in evaluating effectiveness but that this problem must be solved if a contribution is to be made at the strategic policy level. The exhibits attempt to illustrate the challenge that faces the auditor in carrying out an actual assignment and draw together concepts from earlier chapters of the text.

Exhibit 10.1

Tayside University is investigating its refectory service and has requested a value for money audit be undertaken of the service to students. The refectory is of the self-service type offering a choice of several meals at various counters. There is a separate buffet bar in the refectory with its own till. Customers collect their meals at the service counters and pay at centralized tills prior to the consumption of meals. There is limited competition to the University's service in the area.

Identify the major items that would be considered in undertaking a VFM study of the refectory.

The first step would be to identify the objective of providing the service as clearly any set profit margin will have implications throughout the exercise. There is, of course, the option of closing the refectory and this may be a possibility if alternative facilities were available to staff and students. It might then be considered desirable solely to operate a small cafeteria system to meet residual demand. If this were a school meals exercise there would be a need to consider statutory implications such as a possible duty to provide free meals. All feasible options would need to be costed and this provides a link with much of the previous text.

It is possible in the university refectory exercise to identify five key areas for detailed examination. These are:

1. provisions;
2. staff costs;
3. overheads and administration;
4. revenue generation;
5. management.

Each of these areas is now examined in turn to indicate the type of factors that would be considered.

Provisions

Clearly there will be a need to examine the manner in which items are purchased, stored and issued. Competitive tendering should be undertaken on all major purchases with appropriate contracts negotiated. Storage areas should be adequate to cope with quantities consumed and to provide conditions conductive to storing the commodities involved. Security should be adequate for the risks involved. Menu and portion controls should be in operation and comparative unit cost exercises should be undertaken. Quality of meals should be investigated as this will have an impact on consumption of meals. The level of waste should be monitored and the possibility of sale for agricultural use considered.

Staff costs

Staff are normally the major cost in any public sector operation and as such the area needs detailed examination. Clearly appropriate rates of pay should be paid which may be laid down in national agreements, but consideration can be given to flexible local arrangements subject to union negotiation. Working arrangements should be flexible, possibly to include a core staff available at peak demand periods with casuals employed as appropriate. Investigate labour-saving devices such as the purchase of ready-prepared vegetables, cook-chill meals (although this may need a significant capital investment unless shared facilities are used with another organization) and the use of microwaves. Investigate workload, for example number of meals prepared per cook. Investigate till operation procedures to ensure sufficient staff are on duty to avoid creating a queue and deterring return custom. Investigate the number of supervisors in relation to direct employees and compare with available standard data and trends over time. Examine cleaning staff to consider competitive tendering. Examine method of cleaning as 'flow' cleaning is more efficient than floorspace allocation. (In the public sector it is a common practice to allocate cleaners a floor to clean on which they undertaken all cleaning duties. In the private sector the alternative is for one cleaner to start with, say, emptying bins and for another cleaner to follow behind undertaking another cleaning task. The flow of work is thus not interrupted.) It might be possible for this service to be put out to competitive tender, in which case it is essential to put it in sound economic shape if it is considered desirable that an in-house bid be successful.

Overheads and administration

Some overheads may be allocated to the refectory on an arbitrary basis and, as such, will need examination. This review would include factors such as whether or not such services are necessary. This would include the need to consider the contribution that administrative staff make to the service and whether such services can be provided in an alternative manner.

Revenue generation

It is obvious that pricing and marketing strategies must be examined and it is here that the objectives set for the refectory will play a major role. Careful consideration has to be given to the choice on offer. Do the several counters, for example, include a vegetarian dish? Check prices of the competition, and if different meals are on offer which could be produced by the refectory, investigate the feasibility of production. Increased take-up means increased contribution. Students should be aware of what is on offer so undertake a client survey to obtain their views on improvements. Consider a 'no smoking' policy and its implications for patronage.

Management

There is a need to strengthen commercial management which implies delegating responsibility to ensure greater accountability. This may also imply additional rewards being paid for enterprise. If this policy is adopted the financial information system must be geared to meet the needs of managers with appropriate time periods for production and level of aggregation. Margins on meals would need to be identified and monitored.

Exhibit 10.2

One of the major considerations in any stores exercise is whether or not the store/s is/are really needed for the smooth and efficient running of the organization. The existence of local suppliers willing to deliver on call could reduce or eliminate the need to hold items in stock as a store results in capital being tied up in goods rather than being available for investment. The exercise should therefore have the mutually exclusive options of stores or no stores in mind in considering the alternatives. There is also an intermediate stage where only emergency items are held.

The main items to be examined in considering the stores managed by the organization will be the systems and procedures operated by the stores and their physical properties. The following sections identify a selection of relevant questions to which answers will need to be sought.

Systems and procedures

1. Are maximum and minimum stock levels clearly identified for each item and reviewed at appropriate periods?
2. Are economic order quantities identified and reviewed at appropriate periods?
3. Is there an adequate system for emergency orders and are goods ordered and received by different persons?
4. Is there a proper procedure for the issue of goods on authorized requisitions?
5. Are inventory procedures adequate?

6. Does the coding system provide adequate information?
7. Are computer stores records received promptly in the store and do they identify slow-moving stock?
8. Are operational and financial procedures defined in writing and stores managers and other appropriate staff aware of their responsibilities? Does senior management take an active interest in the stores at least to the minimum extent of requiring an annual summary of performance to be prepared and acted upon?
9. Do procedures exist to monitor major changes in operational needs such that the stores are able to respond quickly?

Physical properties

1. Is security adequate for the value of items retained at the stores?
2. Is the location appropriate to the demands placed on the stores and for deliveries?
3. Is the stores layout appropriate for the materials stored there? Does it facilitate stock checking?
4. Is stock deterioration prevented?
5. Is there adequate storage of scrap materials returned from jobs appropriate to the value of that material?

Finally, the auditor will be keen to examine all available statistics, including stock turnover ratios, number of requisitions handled per storeman, number of times stock-outs have occurred and slow-moving stock to see if a smaller store could be used if these items were removed. It will also be necessary to examine stores overhead costs to judge their reasonableness.

Exhibit 10.3

As marketing and proper pricing policies are becoming increasingly important to the public sector this final exhibit examines the major areas in this field with which a value for money study would be concerned. Typical areas to be examined might be:

1. the extent to which pricing policy is constrained by government. An income register should be kept which details at a minimum all charges, the extent of statutory control and the date of last review;
2. whether all charges reflect the organization's policies and are set on the fullest information of costs;
3. that an analysis is carried out of the effect of different pricing policies with reference to demand changes;
4. whether pricing policies reflect seasonal variations, peak demand periods etc.;
5. if no charges are set for service, that this policy is regularly reviewed and decision makers were fully aware of the implications of this policy when making the decision to provide the free service.

Questions

10.1 The director of social services of a large county council in a socially deprived area is concerned to achieve value for money in the provision of the home help service to the elderly. He has directed you to examine the service with this objective in mind. Prepare a report for the director of social services explaining what you understand by the term value for money and the main areas you would examine.

10.2 You are employed as team leader of the management audit team for the Clueless Health Authority. The following information gives a summary of the costs of providing the hospital meals service together with comparative costs for a similar authority. A member of the authority has gained access to the figures and requested that a VFM study be undertaken. Suggest explanations for the differences and suggest ways of improving the VFM of your hospital meals service by analysis of the major variables.

	Clueless HA		'X' HA	
	Total cost £m	Unit cost p	Total cost £m	Unit cost p
Provisions	2.0	23	1.89	21
Kitchen staff	3.4	38	3.06	34
Supervision	0.7	8	0.81	9
Administrative staff	0.4	5	0.54	6
Overheads	1.3	14	0.9	10
Gross expenditure	7.8	88	7.2	80
Income from meals	2.8	32	3.6	40
Notional income duty meals*	1.7	19	1.26	14
Net cost of service	3.3	37	2.34	26

*Notional income duty meals is the value of free meals issues to staff while on duty shifts.

10.3 Compare and contrast the roles that the internal and external auditor play in achieving economy, efficiency and effectiveness in the provision of a public sector organization's services.

10.4 What do you understand by the terms economy, efficiency and effectiveness? Outline the difficulties experienced by the value for money auditor in measuring these three elements. Illustrate your answer with practical examples.

10.5 How are auditors able to assist management in attaining value for money in meeting the growing need to allocate scarce resources among the many demands placed on public sector organizations?

10.6 Under the 1936 Public Health Act amended by the Control of Pollution Act 1974, it is the statutory duty of Mid-Norton Borough Council to collect refuse from domestic and commercial premises and transport it to the Eastham County Council landfill waste disposal site.

Mid-Norton's gross expenditure on refuse collection during 19X4/X5 was £860 000 (see following table) and 28 800 tonnes of refuse were collected. The Borough Council are empowered to charge for trade refuse and it has been the Council's policy to levy a flat-rate charge of £3 for commercial premises for the last three years: this yielded income of £21 000 in 19X9/X0

	Mid-Norton BC: Waste collection service expenditure actuals 19X5/X6–19X9/X0				
	19X5/X6 £000	19X6/X7 £000	19X7/X8 £000	19X8/X9 £000	19X9/X0 £000
Employees	292	401	472	574	628
Running expenses	81	91	109	114	117
Debt charges	17	18	49	92	115
Gross expenditure	390	510	630	780	860
Income	15	17	19	20	21
Net expenditure	375	493	611	760	839
Tonnes (000)	27	27.6	28.1	28.6	28.8

The method of operation is the collection of bins by the 'task and finish' system: as soon as the task of work is complete the employees are free to leave. With the expansion of the UK motorway programme, Mid-Norton is becoming a growth area. Over the past five years there has been a steady increase in the population, coupled with a rapid development of light commercial industries and an expanding shopping centre.

Between 19X5 and 19X9 this has resulted in refuse tonnage increasing from 27 000 to 28 800 tonnes. In addition, there has been a change in the composition of refuse with decreasing quantities of heavy solid fuel waste and increasing quantities of more bulky plastic and paper packaging material. The trend over the last four years has been to increase both the weight and volume of waste, leading to increasing use by householders of larger 3.25 cu. ft. bins replacing the old 2.5 cu. ft. bins, and by a significant number of households now having two bins.

Faced with this increasing pressure on the waste disposal service at a time when the Authority was also under pressure to restrict spending, the Council decided in 19–6 to introduce an incentive bonus scheme in order to increase the productivity of the waste disposal service.

A firm of management consultants were brought in to review operations and measure the workload. Their conclusions (see the following appendix) indicated that a bonus scheme was viable after an initial two-year lead-in period. (NB: The Authority has a long-term 'no redundancy' arrangement with the trade union.) A measured day work (stint) bonus scheme was implemented on 1 April 19X6, on completion of a 'stint' or 'task' of work resulting in a flat rate of 25% bonus on basic wages.

Recent developments

The changing density of refuse, together with advances in technology, has had an effect on the design of refuse collection vehicles and over the three years 19X6 to 19X8 Mid-Norton have replaced their fleet of 18 vehicles with 15 larger vehicles. These have filling and compacting mechanisms which operate with automatically closing hoppers and are capable of high ratios of refuse compaction.

The external auditors submitted a report to the Council in 19X9/X0 about the adverse trend in Mid-Norton's expenditure in comparison with authorities in the same family group and national statistics (see following table).

National statistics – waste collection service

	19X5/X6	19X6/X7	19X7/X8	19X8/X9
Gross expenditure per tonne	15.5	18.0	21.7	24.0
Net expenditure per tonne	14.8	16.7	20.0	22.0

Required

As the Management Auditor of Mid-Norton Borough Council, prepare a formal report for the Authority, analyzing the performance of the Council's refuse collection service, explaining possible reasons for this performance, and making practical recommendations on how the efficiency on the service may be improved.

(40 marks)

Appendix

Reference period data for proposed productivity scheme in the Mid-Norton refuse collection service

Prepared by: Anon & Partners, Consultants
Date: 31 December 19X6

	Actual		Expected Estimated				
	19X3/X4	X4/X5	X5/X6	X6/X7	X7/X8	X8/X9	X9/X0
Annual tonnage (000)	23	25	27	29	30	32	34
Density (cu. yds per tonne)	7.7	7.8	7.9	8.1	8.2	8.3	8.3
Bulk (000 cu. yds)	177	195	213	235	246	266	282
Index of bulk	83	92	100	110	116	125	132
No. of operatives	65	70	75	75	75	75	75
No. of vehicles	16	17	18	18	18	18	18

A flat-rate bonus of 25% to all operatives from 19X6/X7 would result in a net loss for the Authority during the first two-year lead-in period. However, in 19X8/X9 the Authority would break even and from 19X9/X0 onwards the quantity/bulk of refuse collected will increase by more than the 25% bonus payment and the Authority will gain by not recruiting any more additional operatives.

10.7 Compact City Health Authority serves a population of 400 000 and operates an in-house building and maintenance service to its 19 hospital locations.

Builders and engineers in the authority are based at ten of the 19 hospitals and from their bases they also carry out maintenance work in the remaining nine hospitals, community health centres, clinics and ambulance stations.

There are currently separate stores for building and engineering supplies at each of the ten hospital bases which are controlled by ten storekeepers at a total staff cost of £62 000 p.a. The value of issues of building and engineering materials is £950 000 p.a. As each store only employs one storekeeper the building foreman and engineers have tended to be involved in the day-to-day operation of the stores.

The last audit of these stores was undertaken two years ago, but recent preliminary audit investigations have revealed the following:

1. the past two years' year-end stock levels were £450 000 and £550 000;
2. stores reordering is based on visual inspection of bins or racks;
3. order quantities are based on estimates of future usage by the builder or engineer concerned;
4. the accounting system is based on the 'end-user' charges whereby materials are charged directly to the ultimate end-user and held in stock until they request it;
5. monthly management information is provided only on total stock balances and total expenditure for each of the ten stores.

You are a principal internal auditor in Compact and you have been requested by your Chief Internal Auditor to the following task:

Prepare a draft report for the general management team of Compact proposing a value for money investigation into the building and engineering stores.

Your proposal should include:

(i) The objective of the investigation.
(ii) An outline of the process which you intend to follow to achieve this objective.
(iii) An initial analysis of the weak areas of the present stores system which your future investigation will be focused on.

11 Case studies

11.1 Service level agreement – ambulance service

The Darwen Ambulance Service serves a population of approximately 300 000 in a semi-rural district of the United Kingdom covering an area of 1800 square miles. The ambulance service is, at present, a directly managed service under the control of the district health authority, it employs 130 staff, has 50 ambulances and 12 ambulance stations. The service delivers both an emergency and a non-emergency transport service to patients. The total expenditure of the service for the last financial year was £8m. Following the enactment of the NHS and Community Care Act 1990 the ambulance service operates on a purchaser and provider split. The ambulance service acts as the provider of services and bills its expenditure on the provision of the service directly to the district health authority.

An emergency service is delivered by a block contract with the district health authority and is recovered on a full cost basis. In the last financial year the emergency service achieved its financial target of breakeven. At the end of the last financial year, however, the non-emergency service was under-recovered on its block contract against the original budget by £95 000. This service must be provided on the basis of clinical need under statutory obligations. The service is demand led and at present is provided on request to hospitals, doctors and so on. The costs of the non-emergency transport operation were intended to be recovered under the block contract based on a flat rate call-out fee to each user. This fee covered call-outs over the whole of the service's geographical area but inadequate information on cost and estimated demand caused the under-recovery mentioned.

GPs and directly managed units are unconcerned regarding the overspend. The financial target of the ambulance service for the non-emergency transport service is breakeven point. The NHS trust hospitals in the district have negotiated contracts with private ambulance services for non-emergency transport for the next three years despite a bid by Darwen Ambulance Services. While the service, clearly, knows who its clients are there is also little or no monitoring of the quality of service, both users of that service and the ambulance service itself. A number of patients have, however complained about late arrival of ambulances, cancellation (often at very short notice) of the service and a poor standard of cleanliness in some of the older vehicles in the fleet.

The ambulance service is considering setting itself up with trust status but, as a first step, wishes to establish a service level agreement with each of its non-emergency clients. The financial objective of this process is that all costs will be recovered from clients on an equitable basis.

Tasks

Outline how you would undertake the exercise of establishing a service level agreement with clients concentrating on the manner in which you would identify the full cost of the non-emergency ambulance service and what costs you should include.

1. What problems do you think you might encounter?
2. Discuss the alternative ways in which you might charge users for the service.
3. What advantages and disadvantages do you see in introducing a system of service level agreements?
4. Outline the main features you would expect to see in any service level agreement for the ambulance service.

11.2 The Ministry of Supply

The Ministry of Supply is a central government ministry which has numerous stores throughout the United Kingdom distributing a wide range of products to other government departments. Stores vary in size with a number of medium-sized central town developments and approximately 20 smaller sub-depot stores nationwide. It has also, as part of its expansion programme, planned a number of large-scale developments which will enable it to rationalize some of its stores expanding some and closing others.

The stores operate within a largely decentralized decision-making structure but retain a number of head office functions for such activities as finance, legal and personnel. Head office is also responsible for high level strategic decisions such as new stores and other matters where a corporate centralist view is required. Store managers, however, have a considerable amount of autonomy over the hiring and firing of local staff, store layout and even some discretion over the purchase of items for stocking in their stores. The stores operate as an executive agency and are required to make a 6% return on the current cost of assets (defined in the *Government Accounting Manual* as stocks and fixed assets) at their current value in use (i.e. in their present state and condition).

The main agency offices are, naturally, in London where the senior ministerial and administrative management decisions are made. Board meetings are also held in London.

There are, however, a number of distributed administrative sites at other locations within the UK. A number of these sites are dedicated to specific functions, for example, the Agency's information technology functions are in the main concentrated in these distributed sites. The distributed sites have an appropriate section head at the central office. The distributed sites were established to serve specific stores and as such were built to meet the specific needs of their users although not all stores are necessarily close to their administrative centre.

The cost of all these administrative units is charged to a central overhead account and then apportioned to stores. The apportionment method is the same irrespective of the size of store and is applied to all stores. These charges are accumulated during the course of the year and one adjustment to transfer these costs to stores is made at the end of the year when the total actual cost is known. This procedure was adopted 'in order to arrive at the true cost of stores' (as quoted in the Agency's financial procedures manual), so that the net surplus for each outlet after central charges can be calculated. Net surplus is one of the Agency's key performance indicators and is used, for example, to identify potential store closures. Store managers are provided with an estimate of their store's likely total for central support costs at the start of the year as this would represent a commitment against their store budget.

The cost of the central support (including distributed administrative sites) in the last year (19X9/X0) was as follows:

Category of expense	Original estimate (per budget)	Revised* estimate probable (calculated at month 9)	Actual cost at year end	Number of staff (estimate compared to actual)	
	£	£	£	E	A
Financial advice	900 000	960 000	990 000	23	28
Computer services	850 000	846 000	840 000	20	19
Legal	100 000	100 000	105 000	7	7
Personnel	50 000	55 000	56 000	6	6
Corporate functions	1 750 000	1 760 000	1 750 000	22	21

*This figure is calculated at month 9 as a projection of the likely budget spend.

The costs for the central office were £3 000 000 (19X7/X8) and £2 800 000 (19X8/X9).

The system for recharging the cost of the distributed offices is initially to accumulate their costs at head office in London by category of function (computer services, finance, etc.).

At head office each section head (e.g. personnel, legal, etc.) completes a time sheet for the time spent on each store in his/her section for the year just past (including the distributed centres) although in practice a detailed revision only takes place every three years. The time sheets are collected by activity (e.g. finance) as no costs are collected by cost centre (e.g. specific stores) as these do not exist. Each store is charged at the end of the budget year with a single cost representing its allocation of central office costs however that cost is made up. No previous notification of actual costs are given to store managers during the year although such costs are treated as controllable by store managers. These costs appear as one line in the managers' financial statement.

It should be noted that at no time do the store managers have any say in the level of central support costs or the functions that these sections carry out.

In addition to central overheads all car allowance costs for the Agency are collected centrally. In the last three financial years car allowance expenditure has risen from £350 000 to £850 000. The Agency has 110 essential user employees in central departments, distributed administrative centres and the stores. Included in this figure are the ten senior directors of the Agency. These costs are again recharged at the end of the year. This recharge is direct to the stores with no allocation to overhead departments first. The recharge is based on the percentage that an individual store's issues represent of total stores' issues. Mileage costs are monitored monthly in the finance department but store managers are unaware of the total costs of mileage that they will receive at the end of the financial year until that date is reached. Claim forms for mileage are sent directly to the central finance function by staff effectively bypassing store managers who thus have no sight of mileage claims. The only information on the claim form is the name of the claimant and the total monthly mileage the individual is claiming. Where an individual claims subsistence expenses (lunches etc.) in relation to any journey an additional note is attached to the mileage claim form as to the sum involved and reclaimed. These sums are charged as part of the general car allowance recharge.

Appointment to a position as an essential car user is decided by the store manager in the case of employees at stores while central administration and distributed administration centres essential user designation is decided by the appropriate head (e.g. head of finance, head of IT etc.). The Agency's board decides the policy on the classification of board members as essential or casual user but all board members are essential users.

The Agency's definitions are:

- Essential users are those individuals within the Agency who must provide their own car as its use is vital to their duties.
- Casual users need access to their own vehicle on an occasional basis in undertaking their duties.

The current mileage rates payable by the Agency are as follows:

Engine size	<1100cc	1100–1350cc	1351–1500cc	>1500cc
Essential user				
Lump sum	£2 000	£2 500	£3 000	£4 500
Miles per annum				
Per mile<15 000	35p	37p	40p	50p
Per mile>15 000	12p	13p	14p	16p
Casual user				
0 to 5 000	45p	47p	48p	50p
5 001 to 9 000	35p	36p	40p	45p
9 001 to 15 000	25p	27p	30p	35p
after 15 000	12p	13p	14p	16p

Tasks

From a financial management perspective analyze the information given and produce a report for the chief executive of the Agency on your findings together with any recommendations for change you consider appropriate.

This report should include:

1. An identification of what is wrong (if anything) with the Agency's system relating to the recharging of central support services and car allowances.
2. An outline of any alternatives that you think are available to the current system.
3. A discussion of the advantages and disadvantages of the main alternatives that you think are available.
4. An outline of the main features you would expect to see for each of the alternatives.
5. Clear and concise recommendations.

11.3 Central administration charges finance section

Hopeless District Council treasurer's department recharges for services it provides on the basis of a central holding account. All costs of the treasurer's department are charged to this account. These costs include all salaries and salary-related overheads, travelling and subsistence allowances and office accommodation expenses. At the end of the financial year all the costs held on the treasurer's department's central administration holding account are charged to the various service committees of the authority and other holding accounts both capital and revenue.

The functions provided by the department are accountancy, internal audit, council tax and national non-domestic rates (business rates), housing benefits, general revenue collection and corporate management. The cost of the treasurer's department for the last financial year is set out here:

Treasurer's department costs 19X9/X0

Category of expense	Original estimate	Revised estimate	Actual	No. of staff
	£	£	£	
Accountancy	420 150	425 000	425 500	25
Audit	295 000	297 000	297 250	16
Council tax/business rate	415 000	415 000	412 000	28
Housing benefits	400 000	405 000	403 000	25
Revenue collection	250 000	255 000	253 250	20
Corporate management	130 000	130 000	130 000	4
	1 910 150	1 927 000	1 921 000	118
Travel allowances	159 000	145 000	140 000	
Accommodation costs	500 000	500 000	525 000	
Total cost	2 569 150	2 572 000	2 586 000	118

Salary costs of the treasurer's departments for the previous three years, beginning with the last financial year, were £1 814 000, £1 707 760 and £1 535 180. Employee numbers starting with the previous financial year, were 105, 101 and 100 respectively.

To establish the costs to be recharged to departments each member of staff completes a time sheet to show the amount of time spent on each activity by service department. These time sheets are completed by activity (e.g. accountancy) as no costs are collected by cost centre (for example, housing accountancy team) as they do not exist. At the end of the financial year these completed time sheets are then used as the basis for the recharge. The budget for recharges is based on last year's time sheet allocation uprated for inflation. Travel expenses and accommodation costs are allocated to service departments on the basis of the percentage of total direct service department salaries that each individual service department represents. These costs are allocated at the end of the financial year with no previous notification to chief officers. They are, however, treated as outside the service manager's control. In addition, as these costs form part of the global recharge of central administration costs, the service manager has no easy way of separating the cost of financial services from other central services, for example legal services.

Matters regarding the charging of central finance costs (and in reality other central services) came to a head following the complaints of the direct services manager. She feels that the addition of £90 000 in the previous financial year to her budget to pay for the treasurer's costs was totally unjustifiable. This cost represented an addition of 5% of the original total budget of the DSO and was totally unexpected. She believes this is not justifiable as she has to meet competitive pressures and such figures could make the difference between profit and loss. She feels finance and other central services are 'feather-bedded', being divorced from the real world and could do with a dose of competition. Of particular concern to her is that the current year is expected to be very difficult for the DSO and the budget could not absorb a similar increase. No accurate estimate of the level of charges likely to be imposed is yet available for the current year despite the fact that it is now January.

The recent announcement of the possible extension of competitive tendering to the treasurer's department (granting the DSO manager's wish) has also meant that the current system of recharging appears to be indefensible in the immediate future.

Tasks

1. Identify what you consider to be the advantages and disadvantages of the current system of recharging the treasurer's administration costs.
2. Consider what other system of charging for financial services might be introduced, what information you would require to appraise the alternatives and how you might go about introducing an alternative system.
3. Outline the advantages and disadvantages of any alternatives you consider viable.
4. Consider the non-financial implications of any proposed change.

11.4 Vehicle replacement

The Highways Department of the Covert Country Council has spent the sums of money disclosed by the following table in financing its vehicle replacement policy over the last five years.

Comparison of planned expenditure on vehicle replacement with actual expenditure 19X5/6 to 19X9/0

	19X5/6 £	19X6/7 £	19X7/8 £	19X8/9 £	19X9/0 £
Capital estimate	600 000	500 000	550 000	400 000	350 000
Actual expenditure	580 000	650 000	750 000	200 000	150 000
	(20 000)	50 000	200 000	(200 000)	(200 000)
Cutbacks				200 000	200 000
Capital virements transfers (to)		40 000	195 000		
from revenue	(20 000)	10 000	5 000		
	(20 000)	50 000	200 000	(200 000)	(200 000)

Due to the anticipated high level of demand for capital finance in 19X4/5 no provision for replacement vehicles was made in that year. The fleet size is 150 vehicles.

In October prior to the new financial year a capital allocation is normally made to cover the cost of vehicle replacement in the next financial year. It is set on the basis of what can be afforded with no account taken of the actual physical condition of the vehicles. Some vehicles are purchased from revenue. The amount of money available from this source is dependent on the hourly rate charged to jobs to recover vehicle operating costs achieving a surplus. A surplus arises if more hours are worked than estimated or running costs are lower than anticipated. Any deficit on operating cost recovery is carried forward into the next financial year. Vehicle operating hours for this calculation are based on each vehicle being available for 1200 productive hours in any one year. On purchase an estimate is made of the anticipated useful life of the vehicle but no commitment to replace is implied at that time. The fleet is thus larger than is probably required in order to have spare vehicles to cover for the downtime of vehicles under repair.

The total estimated cost of replacing the fleet is over £5m and with the increased pressure on financial resources the authority recognizes that it is increasingly important that capital assets are managed effectively. The fleet is, however, in a generally poor condition with many vehicles requiring major repairs or renewal. It is estimated that a sum of £450 000 is needed immediately to bring the fleet into an efficient operating condition. The authority recognizes the crisis situation and wishes to consider a number of ways of financing the fleet. The alternatives identified by the management accountant for the authority include establishing a renewals and repairs fund, borrowing, leasing and funding from revenue.

Tasks

1. Identify the type of replacement policy adopted by the authority from the information given.
2. Outline the advantages and disadvantages of such a policy. What alternatives are available?
3. Outline the major features of the alternative methods of financing that the authority has identified.
4. The management accountant has obtained a number of quotations for the alternative methods of funding available. These are:

Leasing	Borrowing
Primary period	
3 years £380 per £1000 in advance	Rate of interest 10%
4 years £320 per £1000 in advance	Equal instalment of principal
5 years £280 per £1000 in advance	Repayable at the end of each year
8 years £255 per £1000 in advance	

The breakdown of the capital requirement for new vehicles is:

	£
3-year finance	100 000
4-year finance	50 000
5-year finance	150 000
8-year finance	150 000
Total finance needed	450 000

Calculate the cost of the alternative methods of funding and compare. Which would you advise?

11.5 Computer recharges

The computer section of the Glamwent Health Authority employs 20 full-time staff and costs £903 000 a year to operate. At present the costs of running the section are apportioned to user departments on an annual basis. There is no interim billing and no analysis of the charge is provided to users. The recharge to users takes place some three months into the next financial year and thus users have difficulty incorporating these charges into their budget plant. Computer charges for the last three years are as follows:

	19X9/0 £	19X8/9 £	19X7/8 £
Finance section	210 000	190 000	195 000
Legal services	90 000	100 100	85 000
Estates	175 000	170 000	160 000
Medical and dental	190 000	195 000	198 000
Nursing	75 000	75 000	75 000
Catering	50 000	55 000	48 000
Pharmacy	15 000	14 000	13 000
Physiotherapy	8 000	7 500	7 000
Other	90 000	81 000	75 000
	903 000	887 600	856 000

Costs are apportioned to departments on the basis of the number of times the department has accessed the central mainframe computer. In addition there is an element of 'manager's discretion' whereby costs are reallocated between users to reduce the cost to certain users.

The computer department is organized into four teams under the computer manager. These teams are development services (five staff), computer operators (six staff), support staff (four staff) and data preparation staff (four staff). Staff do not complete time sheets for any category of work. No external work to the authority is performed by the section although it is felt that there is some spare capacity. The work done by the teams is broadly as follows:

System development is carried out at the request of departments either to improve existing systems or design new systems. Much of this work recently has been designing a new financial information system in conjunction with the finance department. Computer operators are concerned with the maintenance and operation of the mainframe computer.

Data preparation is the section concerned with inputting the relevant information into the mainframe. There is no distributed data input. Remote terminals are only allowed read-only facilities.

Computer support is an advice unit. The increasing use of remote terminals has meant an increase in workload. The section also runs a number of short courses in basic computing. Demand for these courses is rising as more staff seek to become computer literate in, for example, spreadsheet packages.

The costs for the last financial year are broken down into the following categories:

	£
Machines – Maintenance	80 000
– Lease	18 000
Support staff	120 000
Operators	100 000
Support	140 000
Development	95 000
Applications software	68 000
Consumables	40 000
Purchase of PCs and printers	80 000
Total cost	903 000

The authority is concerned about the cost of the computer section and the lack of accountability and is considering the possibility of contracting out the work. It wishes first, however, to put the in-house operation right and is examining four possibilities:

1. retain the current system of apportionment as it stands;
2. retain the present system of apportionment but improve the basis of apportionment;
3. adopt a non-commercial basis for charging aiming only to break even;
4. charge users on a normal commercial basis with a set target for the section to achieve.

Tasks

Identify the advantages and disadvantages of the alternatives open to the health authority.

Consider:

1. How you would improve the system of apportionment.
2. What methods exist for recharging the computer section on commercial lines and how you would carry out this exercise.
3. Whether full commercial charging is appropriate for the section.
4. What recommendation you would make.

11.6 Falling school rolls

Clueless County Council is responsible for the management of 40 secondary schools. The total budgeted expenditure of these schools in 19X8/X9 is £80m. The county is primarily industrial although this industry is concentrated in the southern part of the county. The northern half of the county is primarily a commuter area but with a high percentage of agricultural land and strong village communities. This part of the country also has a large elderly population. No schools within the county have, to date, opted out of local authority control.

Concern has been expressed both within the authority and externally at the number of surplus places that exist within the county's secondary schools. In 19X8/X9 there are an estimated 5000 surplus places with a projected rise to 7500 surplus places over the next four years. The Department of Education is calling for the removal of 70% of these surplus places by the end of the four years. In addition the Audit Commission is known to be concerned at the potential waste of resources.

In their last audit report the Audit Commission identified the cost of surplus places as £0.75m for the financial year 19X7/X8. This figure was based on 4500 surplus places and related to premises cost per comprehensive school place. In addition to external pressures the authority has to cope with the problems of formula-based funding where school budgets are based primarily on a calculation in which a major component is the number of pupils on roll. As school rolls are projected to fall this will clearly place additional pressure on resources. In addition another component of the authority's formula is floor area of schools. This means that the authority will effectively be funding inefficiency unless it takes action on surplus places.

The education service is arranged on a district basis and the following table shows the cost per district based on premises costs only for 19X8/X9:

District cost	District A £	District B £	District C £	District D £
Premises cost	900 000	850 000	825 000	1 025 000
School capacity	5 500	5 750	6 500	7 100
Premises cost per place	163	147	126	144
Surplus places	1 100	1 450	900	1 550
Cost of surplus places	179 300	213 150	113 400	223 200

A number of options have been identified by the authority to deal with the problem. These are:

1. the closure of certain schools with possible amalgamation. Premises could then either be sold or mothballed;
2. closure of one or more schools and the building of new purpose-built units;
3. closure and mothballing of part of a school;
4. removal of temporary mobile classrooms;
5. establishing of sixth form colleges as all current secondary schools have retained their sixth form, and making the necessary adjustments outlined in points 1 to 4.

Tasks

1. Outline what you consider to be the major financial implications for Clueless in implementing a policy of reducing surplus places under each of the alternatives given.
2. Consider how you might calculate the costs associated with these alternatives identifying clearly the basis for the calculation of any costs identified.
3. Identify the non-financial implications of the policy of reducing surplus places.
4. How might you take account of these factors in any options you identify as being feasible?

11.7 Capital financing policy

Drift County Council is considering reviewing its capital financing policy. Capital expenditure amounts to £50m in the current financial year (19X9/X0). Capital expenditure in each of the next three years is planned at £60m, £65m and £70m respectively. Revenue expenditure in the current year is planned at £300m of which capital charges represents £20m. This compares with actual revenue expenditure in the previous financial year of £290m and capital charges of £7.4m. The authority feels politically that expenditure on its capital programme is essential due to the high level of social deprivation within the authority's area. In previous years it also had a history of failing to achieve its planned capital expenditure programme and there now exists political pressure to ensure that this does not happen again. It would also like to finance as large a capital programme as possible as there are many priority schemes which are not included in the capital expenditure plans as set out. The authority would fund these schemes if it has the resources to do so.

Actual capital expenditure over the last five years has been financed as follows:

	Value of capital exp. £m	Revenue £	Borrowing £	Financed by Leasing £	Grants* £
19X4/X5	45 (48)	9	28	6	2
19X5/X6	50 (55)	12	25	8	5
19X6/X7	42 (41)	13	20	6	3
19X7/X8	40 (46)	12	18	7	3
19X8/X9	35 (38)	10	17	5	3

(Figures in brackets represent the original planned levels of capital expenditure for the years shown.)

*External grants were largely from the European Community's Regional Development Fund.

The authority's policy has been to invest capital receipts and earn interest on this balance.

External borrowing is limited by the annual credit approvals set by central government. While these are difficult to predict the authority anticipates credit approvals of £35m for 19X9/X0 and £37m, £40m and £38m for each of the next three years. The level of grants for capital expenditure is also seen as falling to £1m per annum for the current year and each of the next three years due to a change in EC rules. The authority in setting its original capital spending plans was hoping to make greater use of external borrowing in order to finance its expenditure plans.

Tasks

1. Discuss the legal constraints under which the local authority must operate its capital financing policy.
2. From the information given comment on the capital financing policy adopted by the authority to date and the strengths and weaknesses of that policy.
3. What objectives would you set for a capital financing strategy?
4. What advice would you give to the authority in planning how it will finance its proposed capital expenditure programme?

11.8 NHS case costing

Under the NHS and Community Care Act 1990 provider units in the NHS were required to enter into contracts for services with their own health authority, other health authorities and general practitioner fundholders for the provision of health care. Trauma (i.e. injury or wound) and orthopaedic services at the Getwell Hospital (currently a non-trust hospital) are charged out under this system on the basis of the average cost per case. The current cost of these services are £15m per annum. The typical patient can be classified into in-patients (5000 per annum), out-patients (35 000 per annum) and day patients (500 per annum). It is estimated that in-patients cost £9m, out-patients £5m and day patients £1m. Management is particularly concerned with the cost and recovery of in patient services due to the high level of expenditure and the complexity of the surgery involved.

The trauma and orthopaedic unit has 90 beds and occupies a complete wing of the hospital. Contracts have been entered into with the 'parent' health authority, three other health authorities and two GP fundholders. The following costs have been calculated for in-patient services in the current year:

	£
Direct patient costs	7 250 000
General overheads	1 750 000

Direct patient costs represent the following:

Nursing	–	charged directly to the trauma ward.
Medical staff	–	charged directly to specialty but costs are split over in-patients, out-patients and day cases. This allocation takes place on the basis of doctor workload returns completed at the end of each month. This split is based simply on the number of patients treated in each category.
Dressings	–	charged on the basis of actual use.
Drugs	–	recharged by the hospital pharmacy on an estimate of use by each specialty in the hospital at the end of the financial year.
Other specialties	–	based on the estimated time spent dealing with cases referred by trauma.
Surgical supplies theatre	–	actual cost (e.g. of replacement hip joints). Costs are apportioned on the average amount of theatre time devoted to the specialty.

Pathology/radiology — apportioned on the basis of the number of tests carried out for the specialty.

General overheads are apportioned as follows:

Catering — apportioned to the specialty on the number of in-patient days.

Laundry/linen — as catering.

Building costs — repairs, heating, maintenance etc. are allocated on the basis of floor area.

Other costs — administration, training, general management, etc. are apportioned on the basis of in-patient days.

Capital charges — the capital charges are based on the value of the buildings and equipment. The total capital charges are spread over specialties by the number of in-patient days.

Non-emergency ambulances — based on number of patients using the service.

The contract price was then based on the total costs allocated to the specialty for the current year calculated by the methods divided by the anticipated case load. This resulted in a single flat-rate charge for all patients regardless of the complexity of any single operation.

Tasks

1. Identify what you believe is wrong (if anything) with the present system of charging for trauma and orthopaedic services.
2. Taking each of the methods of allocating costs set out earlier comment on the suitability of each method of allocating both direct and indirect costs.
3. What changes would you propose?
4. Consider what alternative exist for the pricing of trauma services.

11.9 Private Finance Initiative

The City of Karibya Health Trust is currently examining the options for financing a new health centre in a large suburb in the north-west of the city. The existing health centre at Park Way was built over 40 years ago and is built on land owned by the city council. The increase in population in the district means that it can no longer meet local demand at an appropriate level of service. Additionally, the electrical wiring requires replacing. Recent legislation requires health centres in Karibya to have their own car parking facilities. There is insufficient room for car parking at the current site.

The Trust has found a greenfield location for a new health centre in the more rural outskirts of the suburb. The area is near some new housing developments and is large enough to accommodate a modern purpose-built health centre and a large car park.

Actual and estimated costs have been obtained as follows:

Actual annual premises costs of the Park Way Health Centre

		£
Running costs		40 000
Depreciation		1 000
Total		41 000

The estimated costs of acquiring the land, building the Health Centre and car park and equipping the centre are estimated to total £750 000. The estimated running costs will amount to £42 000 excluding depreciation. The annual revenue costs if the centre is constructed and owned by the Trust will also include depreciation of approximately £38 000 per year. The centre will also increase the asset base on which the Trust's required return of 6% is calculated.

The Health Trust has an external financial limit of £5m and it has spare capacity to accommodate the financing of the project. However, the Karibya Health Executive insists that private sector financing initiatives also be investigated. The Karibyan system of evaluating PFI proposals requires a Public Sector Comparator to be compared with the PFI proposal.

Karibyan Health Investors (KHI) has a track record of funding health schemes in Karibya and has made a PFI proposal for the project as follows:

1. KHI would acquire the land, build the centre and car park and equip the centre.
2. KHI would have ownership of the centre.
3. KHI would manage the property, initially over a 20-year period. This would include responsibility for maintenance, repair, cleaning, insurance and re-equipping in accordance with a programme established by KHI.
4. KHI would charge the Health Trust £95 000 per year for 20 years.

In making an evaluation of the two alternative methods of finance, the rules specify that:

- Both financing approaches are discounted at 6% in real terms.
- The annual revenue consequences of both options are compared.

Tasks

1. Carry out an appraisal of both methods of providing the Health Centre.
2. List the issues that would need to be examined from a value for money perspective.
3. PFI is about risk transfer. Might this proposal increase some elements of risk for the Health Trust?
4. What advice would you give having considered the financial and non-financial issues?

11.10 An occupational health unit

A health authority currently administers an occupational health unit. The unit has a budget of £300 000 and employs the following staff:

1   consultant
1   senior medical officer

4 nursing officers
3 other nursing staff
6 administrative and clerical staff

The unit is based in three locations: a hospital in the south of the area, a hospital in the north of the authority about 25 miles distant and at a large county council.

The work undertaken falls into three main areas of activity, pre-employment examinations, medical examinations (primarily for long-term sickness assessment and for drivers of public carrying vehicles) and immunization services. In recent years the unit has also reacted to an increasing volume of tests on VDU operatives and work is also increasing due to health and safety at work legislation. The client base includes health authority staff, the county council, two district councils and various companies.

It is planned that the unit will become a self-financing entity from 1 April, 20X1 and it will need to cover its costs from the income which it is able to generate.

It is June 19X9. The accounts for the unit for the previous financial year have just been made available. They demonstrate that the unit has underspent its staffing and non-staffing budgets by £20 000 largely because a nurse vacancy was left unfilled for nine months.

Investigation reveals that a variety of costs are not currently charged to the unit. These include cost apportionments from the pathology and radiology departments, capital charges, energy costs, postal costs, telecommunication costs and the health authority's charges for financial services. These are estimated to amount to £112 000 in the current financial year. If these costs are charged, the unit spends considerably in excess of budget.

Services are not costed in any systematic way by the authority. Prices for services are set by the consultant occupational health physician. A comparison of the unit's current prices currently charged with the BMA-recommended fees for the specific services reveals that prices are between 20–40% below the recommended levels. However, a recent audit exercise has revealed that if all costs were taken into consideration then prices would need to be 20% in excess of the BMA figures. The audit investigation also came up with the following conclusions:

1. Cost of inputs suggest uneconomic practice: salaries are high because of high grade clinical staff.
2. Non-productive time is high; to some extent this is due to the split-site operation.
3. There is often a duplication of work and roles, especially in the administration of the unit.
4. Work done for some local authorities in the area and the fire service is carried out well below current cost.
5. The in-house service to the County Council is the result of an agreement dating back to when the service was in part provided by the local authority sector. The County Council receives 400 free sessions per annum (a session is defined as 3.5 hours of a doctor's time) and pays for any service over and above this level at the prices charged by the authority.

The Unit is preparing a business plan as part of its preparation for the environment within which it will operate from 1 April 20X1. As the first stage in the preparation of the business plan the Unit is identifying its strengths, weaknesses, opportunities and threats (SWOT analysis).

Required

Assist in the preparation of the SWOT analysis by the Occupational Health Unit.

11.11 Blood collection service

A regional blood collection service is responsible for collecting, processing and distributing all blood and blood products required by the district health authorities and hospital trusts within the region. Its annual collection cost is about £2.8 million.

The centre of operations is in the more densely populated south-eastern part of the region. In the area surrounding the centre of operations, blood is collected using daily visits to establishments where blood donation is taking place (generally work places, local halls or by means of the mobile collection service). The blood from outlying areas is collected by 'tours', whereby staff stay away from home in hotel accommodation for several days. All blood is shipped back to the centre for processing on a daily basis. Good road communications are essential and they are generally excellent between the regional centre and the outlying areas.

The regional blood collection service has an agreed collection target annually which is specified in its business plan. In order to achieve this target:

1. There is an annual planning cycle and most blood collection sessions are organized four months in advance. Each visit is preceded by support work which has access to a database holding information for each location, detailing donors, staffing requirement, transport requirement and any overnight accommodation requirement.
2. Total care of the donor has the highest priority during the blood donation process. This is ensured by the training of all staff, whose performance is carefully monitored by nursing staff and by team leaders. (Nursing staff are drawn from local hospitals.) Each donor on a local list is requested to contribute about every six months.

The blood collection service is currently faced with a number of challenges:

1. First, it is faced with an annual cost improvement target and in the current year this amounts to 2.3%.
2. Second, its market is becoming increasingly competitive and its customers are becoming increasingly demanding about the prices charged for blood as they themselves come under increasing cost pressure.
3. Third, the demands for blood are increasing but it is having to make increasingly effective use of donors in order to maintain blood supplies at past levels. There are a variety of reasons for this last challenge; generally, only 50% of a local donor list turn up to sessions and this has been declining; annually about 10% of donors leave the local lists; and an increasing number of donation attendances provide below normal levels of donation because of weakness resulting from a poor diet.

There are six donor teams in operation with, on average, ten people in each team: a team leader, six donor attendants, a receptionist, medical officer and driver. There is also cover provided for other staff for sickness, emergencies and annual leave. There is always a medical officer present at each session to ensure that there is medical cover in the event of any problems. The teams work four weeks at collection sessions and one week in the regional centre which is used for leave purposes (due to the high number of hours worked while on duty) and for training.

Tours themselves tend to be organized on a yearly basis to ensure a fair distribution to each team. There are usually no tours in December or January because of the difficulties of finding hotel accommodation. On average four of the teams are on tour at any one time. Tours are, of course, a far more expensive way of collecting blood than daily visits; the average cost of collection per donation is £17.31 for tours and £11.96 for daily visits.

Managers of the collection service are currently reviewing the cost-effectiveness of the service with particular reference to outlying areas. A small multidisciplinary group has been formed to address the problem and they have come up with two additional options for the service:

1. The collection in outlying areas could be provided by the establishment of a few locally based and recruited collection teams. All team members would reside in the area and operate from a local base to provide the blood collection service, Blood would be transported back to the regional centre on a daily basis.
2. The new area teams could come under regional management or they could operate local management, undertaking all planning, recruitment and collection activities.

You are a key member of the multidisciplinary team.

Tasks

1. List the primary financial costs and savings associated with the options to be examined.
2. Produce a list of non-financial desiderata that can be used in the appraisal. Justify your selection of desiderata.

11.12 The bridge

A county council is responsible for a toll bridge which crosses an estuary in an outlying but well-populated area of the county. The bridge was constructed some ten years ago and its eventual capital cost was well over budget. Since opening it has made a loss; furthermore, it does not cover the annual interest charge on the construction of the bridge so that the initial loan is being increased by the amounts of unpaid interest. The county council itself is not in a position to subsidize the bridge and the accumulated revenue deficit is projected to increase by £100 000 per annum to £1.2m within ten years.

Approximately 40% of the costs are staffing and 60% are capital related. In five years time there will be a bridge-strengthening programme which will cost £750 000. It is planned to fund this expenditure by borrowing.

The council has increased tolls above the rate of inflation in recent years and there has been some downturn in traffic as compared with ten years ago but this may reflect the relative economic decline of the country rather than the impact of the price increases. No attempt has been made to measure price sensitivity. The bridge saves a ten-mile round trip and it currently charges £2 to cars for each single journey. This toll was increased by 40p six months ago. There are other tolls for motorcycles, lorries and coaches. The Council gives a discount for pre-payment and a booklet of ten tickets may be purchased for £18.

There are some internal control problems as well. The bridge is a four-lane construction and there are two ticket collectors at each end of the bridge, one for each lane and each pair is supervised by an inspector. There are three shifts per day. There is also a bridge manager. The supervision by inspectors is occasioned by the collection system. Different classes of users pay different rates, as already indicated, and different coloured tickets are available for this purpose. There is an underroad counter but this is incapable of discriminating between classes of vehicles. There is no way of ensuring that each user pays, or pays the correct amount or receives the correctly coloured ticket. Hence the inspectors are required.

Finally there is strong political pressure from the area in which the bridge is located and this pressure is directed against the increase of toll prices.

Tasks

Examine how the council may resolve the problem of the deficit from the bridge.

11.13   The manager's dilemma

Debbie Davies is the manager of a social services department in a local authority based in the south-east of Wales. She is under considerable pressure in her job to perform to increasingly tight targets which are both financial and non financial. Caseloads per member of staff have increased over the last five years so that each of her social service officers is now handling on average 5% more cases than five years ago with 10% fewer resources. Front line staff numbers have also been reduced although administration staff have not suffered so much given the increased demands of the central government and the local authority itself for monitoring information on quality and performance and the need to meet critical dates for the return of this information.

Debbie has to manage her budget within strict cash limits within a budget process, which is primarily incremental. This takes the form of a 'bid' for resources to the local authority and swingeing cuts are often introduced into this bid for resources. These cuts are frequently introduced into the budget process late in the planning cycle. This has led to the development of the view among her members of staff that social services are not regarded as a core service in the fight against social need. Heavy emphasis is placed on comparative unit costs with other local authority social services in measuring performance and frequently critical reports come back to the authority based on the Audit Commission analysis of these figures (particularly regarding unit cost per case of all front line services such as homes for the elderly/child care costs etc.).

The annual budgetary bid for resources (excluding central services – see later) is prepared by Debbie and her team although none of her staff is professionally qualified and all have learnt their financial skills over time and through experience. Each year's budget is stand-alone and is not produced within any long-term financial framework. The budget figures produced are forwarded to the centre for decision as just discussed but Debbie is not involved in this process once the figures have been forwarded to the finance department and agreed by full council, the figures returned are frequently changed out of all recognition from those submitted. The feedback of the budget to Debbie is to provide a total cash limit figure but this is then broken down over individual subjective heads such as employees, premises, transport etc. These individual subjective heads represent authorizations to spend. When Debbie complains to the central finance department that this is grossly unfair she is told that there are proper channels for raising concerns over the final budget allocation. Debbie is not aware of the existence of these channels but feels that such channels would have no effect were she to use them.

In the next financial year Debbie will be facing for the first time additional capital charges for the assets used to deliver her services. These charges will be based on the current value of her assets in their present age and condition. These include social services homes, a significant number of vehicles and some surplus land. She understands that there will be a depreciation charge plus an additional charge for something called the cost of capital. She has no idea what this means but understands that these charges will increase the budgeted expenditure for Social Services. She is not aware of the implications but fears that such a charge will result in additional charges for services in a politically sensitive area.

Financial targets are imposed, based on the allocated budget figures and Debbie is expected to achieve these figures. The primary financial control is through the budget allocation which is a cash-limited figure. As already stated, individual budget heads represent authority to spend but the history of the service is one in which there will be overspends on certain heads and underspending on others. The budget in general, however, has historically been balanced with actual spending equalling the cash limit. In the last financial year (19X9/X0) Debbie actually deliberately underspent as she was promised a carry-forward of any underspendings up to a value of 10% of the budget to the next financial year. She was, however, disappointed as, due to the financial position of the authority (low balances), she lost this money.

It is now approaching the end of the financial year (19X9/X0). Debbie has overspent on a number of budget heads but is underspending on others so that the budget will balance in terms of planned total expenditure. Debbie has a reserve list of items on which she has plans to spend if there is any danger of an underspend against the budget in total. These items primarily are new IT facilities that can be delivered promptly by external suppliers even if orders cannot be raised until late in March. Under the authority's rules all items have to be delivered prior to 31 March if they are to count against this year's budget.

Monitoring information is supplied by the central finance department and consists of large computer printouts produced weekly. They contain considerable information broken down by subjective head of expenditure. The information provided is cash based and lists total cash expenditure to the date of the printout. Information provided rarely agrees with Social Service staff perception of the financial situation. As a result, Debbie keeps an informal record of her expenditure and as such never looks at the computer printout.

At the end of the financial year central charges are added to the final spending printout. Central charges are built into the original budget by the finance section after Debbie has submitted her original figures for the estimated cost of the service. These charges cover finance, legal, personnel and central administrative support. The charges for central services are regarded as controllable by Debbie. The system for charging, so far as Debbie can work out, is based on actual time spent on the service by central support staff. To establish the costs to be recharged to the service each member of the central staff completes a time sheet to show the amount of time spent on each of the direct service departments. The time sheets are completed by activity (for example, personnel) as no costs are collected by cost centre (for example, recruitment within personnel) and added together at the end of the year to amount to 100% of total time spent on all activities. If Social Services have used 10% of total central support time it will receive 10% of the total cost of that central service. All central costs are recharged to direct service departments.

In practice, time sheets are completed by all staff every three years. These then form the basis of the actual recharge although if it is judged that there has been a significant increase in time spent on any particular activity for a service department, such as social services, an adjustment will be made to the annual recharge for that department. These charges appear in Debbie's final spending figures without any prior notification that they are to appear and are shown as one figure so that it is not possible to identify specific overhead charges for specific central services. It is rumoured that central charges will be some 10% higher than the original notified budget. This figure is primarily the result of the finance department failing to control costs.

Debbie has done some 'digging' and in relation to the treasurer's department it has been discovered that all costs are charged to a central holding account before the system as described operates. These costs include all salaries and salary-related overheads, travel and subsistence and office accommodation expenses. The functions provided by the treasurer's department are accountancy, internal audit, income collection, housing benefits, treasury management and corporate management (financial control and advice).

The following information has come into Debbie's possession for the financial year 19X9/X0.

Category of expense	Original estimate £	Probable expenditure £	Estimated staff	Probable staff
Accountancy	1 000 000	950 000	40	39
Audit	850 000	850 000	30	30
Income collection	1 250 000	1 350 000	45	50
Housing benefits	500 000	750 000	25	40
Treasury management	50 000	45 000	1	1
Corporate management	500 000	600 000	10	12
Total	4 150 000	4 545 000	151	172

The last three financial years show a rise from £3 800 000 actual expenditure to the probable of £4 545 000 given here.

Capital investment in the service is subject to a separate budget for which the service makes an annual bid. Any capital expenditure approved is paid for from central funds in the year in which it occurs and consequently there are no debt charges to be met in the annual revenue budget. Debbie ensures that she always spends her capital money and has done quite well out of the bid system over the last five years (much to her surprise). She is planning another bid for 19X0/X1 as she feels she must bid or her service will lose out in future years.

Tasks

You have been asked to act as an external consultant to investigate this situation within Social Services. Prepare a report for the Chief Executive in which you:

1. Identify what problems you feel exist in the scenario set out in the case.
2. Suggest solutions you feel are relevant to the problems discussed under point 1.
3. Fully explore the features and the advantages and disadvantages of any proposed solutions you have identified under point 2.
4. Make positive recommendations on what you consider to be the best course of action to solve the problems you have identified.

11.14 University budgeting: Colingbourne Metropolitan University

Colingbourne Metropolitan University (CMU) is a modern university that was formed in 1992. It is based in the south-west of the Kingdom of Karibya. It provides a wide range of undergraduate and post-graduate courses and has achieved awards for teaching and research excellence in the majority of the subjects offered by the University.

The University is situated on a suburban campus with excellent road and rail links. The teaching blocks, halls of residence, the library, the sports centre and the administrative buildings are all located on the single campus.

The University has a 'flat' management structure with relatively few levels of management. Each academic school and administrative department is managed by a head of school (or department) who reports directly to a triumvirate of Vice Chancellor, and his two most senior assistants, the Deputy Chancellor and the Pro Chancellor; these three top managers are referred collectively to as the Directorate and they are supported by 20 other staff. All school and departmental managers meet weekly under the chairmanship of the Deputy Chancellor. Additionally, there are a series of policy formulation and reporting meetings held throughout the academic year under the chairmanship of one of the Directorate.

The academic schools are as follows:

Business

Social Science

Humanities

Law

Applied Science

Science and Medicine.

The administrative departments are:

Registry

Finance

Student Services

Residential Services and the Directorate.

The University's accounting year runs from 1 August to 31 July. The annual planning cycle starts on 1 November when the financial plans for each school are developed. These plans must be completed by the following 31 January at which point they are submitted to the Deputy Chancellor whose office summarizes and reviews these plans for presentations at the annual departmental plans reviews towards the end of February in each year.

Within each school there are two senior staff who assist the head of school. They are the associate head (academic) and the associate head (resources). The former deals with all course-related issues such as teaching, field boards, scheme boards and examination boards. The latter deals with all resource issues including staff recruitment and budgetary issues affecting the school. You are Associate Head (Resources) of the Business School. It is November and you are currently involved in preparing the School's financial plan for the next accounting year.

Income is derived from two sources: tuition fees payable by students and funding per student received from the Department of Education. Currently, each EU student pays £1000 per year and the DoE funding per full-time student amounts to £2200 per year. Non-EU students pay £5500 per year; there is no DoE funding of non-EU students.

Currently, there is significant resource pressure within the University system and the budget for next year will require an overall efficiency gain; the University sector has been making such efficiency gains in each of the last seven years. The required efficiency gain for the next accounting year is made up as follows:

	%
Income	
Student tuition fees	no change
DoE funding per EU student	−0.2
Expenditure	
Inflationary increase in costs	+1.4
Overall efficiency gain required	+1.6

Each school is required to at least break even. Budgeting for a loss is not permitted. The draft budget for next year will take as its starting point the budget for the current year.

The preparation of the school's financial plan includes the completion of a budgetary pro forma; the completed budgetary pro forma for the current year is appended in the following.

Inspection of the completed budget reveals that:

- The academic schools generate all income.
- The costs of the administrative departments and the Directorate are regarded as overheads.
- Overheads are apportioned to each academic school by 'topslicing' income as follows: EU student income (fees and DoE funding) is topsliced with a rate of 30%. Non-EU students (fees only) are topsliced with a rate of 40%.
- Work undertaken for other academic schools is termed 'servicing' and the workflows between schools result in transfer payments based on the number of students taught. The Business School earns a net £500 000 from its servicing activities. This income is also topsliced at 30%.
- The balance is available to the School to fund its staff and non-staff budgets.

As Associate Head (Resources), you are aware of several issues as you begin the process of preparing the financial plan for next year:

1. For next year the School will be charged 'rent' on its use of rooms within the University. This is estimated to amount to £50 000. There will be no commensurate reduction in the topslicing percentages.

2. The non-EU students are from the Far East and in order to continue to recruit these students, the School has budgeted to spend approximately £30 000 from its non-staff budget on marketing in the Far East this year. It is planned that the expenditure, at its higher inflated level, will continue next year.
3. Inflation will affect both staff and non-staff budgets equally.
4. The servicing work carried out by the Business School next year is expected to be below the level of the current year. After taking account of the slight reduction in DoE funding as well, it is estimated that servicing will net £475 000 next year.
5. This year there are 350 EU students in the first year of their courses, 400 in the second year and 375 in the final year. Next year it is expected that 400 EU students will be recruited to the first year. In the current year there are 50 non-EU students but the number of such students is expected to fall by 10% next year.
6. Any surplus left at the end of the accounting year is shared equally between the School and the Directorate. The School's share of any surplus will not be subject to topslicing next year. For the current year, income and expenditure are in line with budget and it is currently estimated that the end of year surplus for the School will be approximately £25 000.

Your Head of School has required you to do the following:

1. Complete the draft budget for next year taking account of this year's budget and the information presented here.
2. Prepare a report examining how the school can balance its budget for next year.
3. Provide for your Head of School a briefing note summarizing the weaknesses of the University's budgetary system, indicating how it can be improved.

The Business School: budget statement

		Current year budget	
Tuition income		£	£
EU			
Paid by students	(Note 1)	1 125 000	
Paid by DoE	(Note 2)	2 475 000	3 600 000
Non-EU: Paid by students	(Note 3)		275 000
Net servicing inflow			500 000
Totals			4 375 000
Less			
Retention at 30%	(Note 4)	1 230 000	
Retention at 40%	(Note 5)	110 000	1 340 000
Allocated to Business School after retention		3 035 000	
Surplus b/fwd.			0
Planned costs			
Staff costs		2 530 500	
Non-staff costs		480 000	3 010 500
Planned School surplus			24 500

Notes:
1. 1125 students * £1000
2. 1125 students * £2200
3. 50 students * £5500
4. 30% * (£3 600 000 + £500 000)
5. 40% * £275 000

11.15 University budgeting: The University of Shangri-La

The new University of Shangri-La is situated in the centre of a busy medium-sized town on the south coast of England close to the seafront. It attracts students from a wide geographical area but increasingly with student fees and loans more of its students come from the local area. The town itself relies for its trade on general tourism, the University, business travellers and conferences with very little industry although the area is not regarded as economically deprived.

The University owns and runs a Conference Centre. The Centre was established to make a contribution to University funds. It relies for its business on academic conferences, in-house university conferences/events (such as providing the venue for the graduation ceremony buffet) or additional passing trade as a result of major conferences being held at other venues in the town. In addition the Conference Centre takes in visitors particularly over the summer season when students have returned home although when it has spare capacity members of the public frequently stay during term time. Reception is on the ground floor (including the bar and restaurant area) and it has 220 en-suite rooms (40 with sea view) on floors one to four and the conference facility on the ground floor. The conference facility consists of six large rooms, one of which doubles as a banquet suite and three syndicate rooms for use as necessary. The various conference rooms also have bar facilities available if required. Wedding parties frequently use the restaurant area for wedding receptions as the grounds of the Conference Centre are known for their beauty. The Centre is also hired out for dinner dances which are occasionally promoted by the Centre. The Centre is also the regular monthly meeting venue for the local Rotary Club. Rooms are sold on a 'room only' basis to visiting non-conference guests although breakfast is available at extra cost. This charge is some 30% below equivalent hotel accommodation charges in the town. The Conference Centre is well equipped and if it were a hotel would be classed as four or possibly five star.

The Centre is managed under four divisions: Rooms Division, Restaurant Division, the Conference Division and the Bar Division. These four divisions form the basis for financial reporting with each division headed by a manager who is responsible for day-to-day management. This includes all aspects of budgeting and budgetary control. The Conference Centre's administration office provides the financial figures. The Conference Division, the Rooms Division and Restaurant are broadly funded by an apportionment of the fee income received from each conference delegate. The bar is funded from cash sales. Income from individual guests, for example overnight visitors, is taken directly to the facilities used.

As part of the University, the University's Directorate are closely involved in decision making and expect monthly team meetings with divisional managers on general management issues concerning the running of the Centre. Quarterly management accounts are provided, although no qualified accountant is employed at the Conference Centre. All administrative support functions of the Conference Centre are concentrated in a general office and the costs of the office are allocated to the divisions quarterly. The University charges a flat-rate administrative charge for any services it provides. This is negotiated prior to the start of the financial year and adjusted at the end of the financial year which is 1 August to 31 July. It has been known to vary considerably from that agreed at the start of the year.

Mid-December, January and early February represent the slow season. The peak period has traditionally been March to November. Conferences provide the main business except July to September. The school holiday months from the middle of July to early September represent the period when the Conference Centre would expect to be fully booked with families who find it significantly cheaper than local hotels. The families are also entitled to use the University's sports facilities. As stated this period is a slack time for the conference trade although they do occasionally take place. A trend in recent years, however, has been noted in that more UK residents are taking holidays abroad and that rooms are becoming increasingly hard to fill even in the traditionally busy periods. In addition the English Tourist Board has been less successful in attracting overseas visitors to the UK and to the Shangri-La's area in particular.

As a result of a feared downturn in revenue for the restaurant a special report for the Conference Centre for the month ending 31 March was requested. These results were distributed at the May management team meeting where concern was expressed at the loss that has occurred in the restaurant. As outlined earlier the restaurant is funded by a contribution from each delegate taken out of the conference fee plus individual payments from guests who use the restaurant during their stay. At the same meeting another paper was brought to the team which suggested that a cost of capital charge and depreciation should be introduced given the value of the building. Depreciation is estimated at £25 000 per year while the value of the building is put at £2 500 000. The cost of capital charge would be based on 6%.

A number of ideas were raised in the brainstorming session that took place when the figures were made available although, inevitably, no conclusions could be reached given the nature of the meeting and the short time to consider the results. These ideas included:

1. Raising prices in the restaurant to be recharged to conference delegates and guests.
2. Closing the restaurant during the quietest months of the year.
3. Reducing prices in the restaurant.

The results for the last month ending 31 March are as follows:

Shangri-La University Conference Centre financial results for the month ending 31 March (by division)

Rooms Division	Budget £	Actual £
Income		
Room revenue	92 000	83 000
Expenses		
Chambermaids	25 000	27 000
Supplies to rooms	4 000	3 700
Linen	1 000	1 250
Building allocation	50 000	49 250
Administration allocation	5 500	4 750
Other	1 250	1 400
	86 750	87 350
Divisional profit (loss)	5 250	4 350
Percentage occupancy (%)	60	54
Average room rate (per night)	50	52

Restaurant Division	Budget £	Actual £
Income		
Food sales	60 500	45 425
Wine and beers	30 150	24 825
	90 650	70 250
Expenses		
Cost of sales – food	14 520	10 902
Cost of sales – drinks	10 050	8 192
Waitress wages [1]	12 065	10 095
Supplies	18 130	14 050
Managers' salary	5 000	5 000
Dish washing [1]	1 906	1 702
Building allocation	19 000	19 000
Administration	4 250	4 250
	84 921	73 191
Divisional profit (loss)	5 729	(2 941)
Volume	3 020	2 510
Sales price/unit	£30	£28

[1] Includes £3000 fixed costs for waitresses and £1000 fixed costs for dishwashing

Bars	Budget	Actual
Income		
Liquor sales	60 150	62 000
Expenses		
Cost of sales	14 436	14 880
Bar wages	5 200	5 200
Supplies	9 020	9 300
Managers' salary	3 250	3 250
Building allocation	10 000	10 000
Administration	3 250	3 250
	45 156	45 880
Divisional profit (loss)	14 994	16 120

Conference Division	Budget	Actual
Income		
Conference income	41 500	44,000
Expenses		
Miscellaneous costs	4 150	4 400
Managers' salary	5 000	5 000
Building allocation	3 250	3 250
Administration	7 150	7 150
	19 550	19 800
Divisional Profit (Loss)	21 950	24 200
Conferences planned/held	20	25

Tasks

The University's Directorate has now called for a special report into the financial results of the restaurant and has asked you as a management accountant to prepare this report.
Using the information in the case:

1. Consider what contribution management accounting can make to the scenario set out in the case.
2. Advise management what financial information it needs to be able to make a decision on the issues being discussed. Why does it need any specific information you have identified?
3. Provide this information to the hotel management.
4. What non-financial information would aid management in their decision and how would it help?
5. Comment on the value of the financial information that is produced at present.
6. What changes in the format of financial reporting would you make (if any) and why?

Your answer should initially be in the form of a written report but you have been asked to prepare a summary of the report for presentation at a special meeting which has been called for next week.

Appendix

Present value of 1

Year	1	2	3	4	5	6	7	8	9	10
					Rate of interest %					
0	1.0000	1.0000	1.0000	1.0000	1.0000	1.0000	1.0000	1.0000	1.0000	1.0000
1	0.9901	0.9804	0.9709	0.9615	0.9524	0.9434	0.9346	0.9259	0.9174	0.9091
2	0.9803	0.9612	0.9426	0.9246	0.9070	0.8900	0.8734	0.8573	0.8417	0.8264
3	0.9706	0.9423	0.9151	0.8890	0.8638	0.8396	0.8163	0.7938	0.7722	0.7513
4	0.9601	0.9238	0.8885	0.8548	0.8227	0.7921	0.7629	0.7350	0.7084	0.6830
5	0.9515	0.9057	0.8626	0.8219	0.7835	0.7473	0.7130	0.6806	0.6499	0.6209
6	0.9420	0.8880	0.8375	0.7903	0.7462	0.7050	0.6663	0.6302	0.5963	0.5645
7	0.9327	0.8706	0.8131	0.7599	0.7107	0.6651	0.6227	0.5835	0.5470	0.5132
8	0.9235	0.8535	0.7894	0.7307	0.6768	0.6274	0.5820	0.5403	0.5019	0.4665
9	0.9143	0.8368	0.7664	0.7026	0.6446	0.5919	0.5439	0.5002	0.4604	0.4241
10	0.9053	0.8203	0.7441	0.6756	0.6139	0.5584	0.5083	0.4632	0.4224	0.3855
11	0.8963	0.8043	0.7224	0.6496	0.5847	0.5268	0.4751	0.4289	0.3875	0.3505
12	0.8874	0.7885	0.7014	0.6246	0.5568	0.4970	0.4440	0.3971	0.3555	0.3186
13	0.8787	0.7730	0.6810	0.6006	0.5303	0.4688	0.4150	0.3677	0.3262	0.2897
14	0.8700	0.7579	0.6611	0.5775	0.5051	0.4423	0.3878	0.3405	0.2992	0.2633
15	0.8613	0.7430	0.6419	0.5553	0.4810	0.4173	0.3624	0.3152	0.2745	0.2394
16	0.8528	0.7284	0.6232	0.5339	0.4581	0.3936	0.3387	0.2919	0.2519	0.2176
17	0.8444	0.7142	0.6050	0.5134	0.4363	0.3714	0.3166	0.2703	0.2311	0.1978
18	0.8360	0.7002	0.5874	0.4936	0.4155	0.3503	0.2959	0.2502	0.2120	0.1799
19	0.8277	0.6864	0.5703	0.4746	0.3957	0.3305	0.2765	0.2317	0.1945	0.1635
20	0.8195	0.6730	0.5537	0.4564	0.3769	0.3118	0.2584	0.2145	0.1784	0.1486
21	0.8114	0.6598	0.5375	0.4388	0.3589	0.2942	0.2415	0.1987	0.1637	0.1351
22	0.8034	0.6468	0.5219	0.4220	0.3418	0.2775	0.2257	0.1839	0.1502	0.1228
23	0.7954	0.6342	0.5067	0.4057	0.3256	0.2618	0.2109	0.1703	0.1378	0.1117
24	0.7876	0.6217	0.4919	0.3901	0.3101	0.2470	0.1971	0.1577	0.1264	0.1015
25	0.7798	0.6095	0.4776	0.3751	0.2953	0.2330	0.1842	0.1460	0.1160	0.0923
26	0.7720	0.5976	0.4637	0.3607	0.2812	0.2198	0.1722	0.1352	0.1064	0.0839
27	0.7644	0.5859	0.4502	0.3468	0.2678	0.2074	0.1609	0.1252	0.0976	0.0763
28	0.7568	0.5744	0.4371	0.3335	0.2551	0.1956	0.1504	0.1159	0.0895	0.0693
29	0.7493	0.5631	0.4243	0.3207	0.2429	0.1846	0.1406	0.1073	0.0822	0.0630
30	0.7419	0.5521	0.4120	0.3083	0.2314	0.1741	0.1314	0.0994	0.0754	0.0573
31	0.7346	0.5412	0.4000	0.2965	0.2204	0.1643	0.1228	0.0920	0.0691	0.0521
32	0.7273	0.5306	0.3883	0.2851	0.2099	0.1550	0.1147	0.0852	0.0634	0.0474
33	0.7201	0.5202	0.3770	0.2741	0.1999	0.1462	0.1072	0.0789	0.0582	0.0431
34	0.7130	0.5100	0.3660	0.2636	0.1904	0.1379	0.1002	0.0730	0.0534	0.0391
35	0.7509	0.5000	0.3554	0.2534	0.1813	0.1301	0.0937	0.0676	0.0490	0.0356
36	0.6989	0.4902	0.3450	0.2437	0.1727	0.1227	0.0875	0.0626	0.0449	0.0323
37	0.6920	0.4806	0.3350	0.2343	0.1644	0.1158	0.0818	0.0580	0.0412	0.0294
38	0.6852	0.4712	0.3252	0.2253	0.1566	0.1092	0.0765	0.0537	0.0378	0.0267
39	0.6784	0.4619	0.3158	0.2166	0.1491	0.1031	0.0715	0.0497	0.0347	0.0243
40	0.6717	0.4529	0.3066	0.2083	0.1420	0.0972	0.0668	0.0460	0.0318	0.0221
41	0.6650	0.4440	0.2976	0.2003	0.1353	0.0917	0.0624	0.0426	0.0292	0.0201
42	0.6854	0.4353	0.2890	0.1926	0.1288	0.0865	0.0583	0.0395	0.0268	0.0183
43	0.6519	0.4268	0.2805	0.1852	0.1227	0.0816	0.0545	0.0365	0.0246	0.0166
44	0.6454	0.4184	0.2724	0.1780	0.1169	0.0770	0.0509	0.0338	0.0226	0.0151
45	0.6391	0.4102	0.2644	0.1712	0.1113	0.0727	0.0476	0.0313	0.0207	0.0137
46	0.6327	0.4022	0.2567	0.1646	0.1060	0.0685	0.0445	0.0290	0.0190	0.0125
47	0.6265	0.3943	0.2493	0.1583	0.1009	0.0647	0.0416	0.0269	0.0174	0.0113
48	0.6203	0.3865	0.2420	0.1522	0.0961	0.0610	0.0389	0.0249	0.0160	0.0103
49	0.6141	0.3790	0.2350	0.1463	0.0916	0.0575	0.0363	0.0230	0.0147	0.0094
50	0.6080	0.3715	0.2281	0.1407	0.0872	0.0543	0.0339	0.0213	0.0134	0.0085

					Rate of interest %					
	11	12	13	14	15	16	17	18	19	20
Year										
0	1.0000	1.0000	1.0000	1.0000	1.0000	1.0000	1.0000	1.0000	1.0000	1.0000
1	0.9009	0.8929	0.8850	0.8772	0.8696	0.8621	0.8547	0.8475	0.8403	0.8333
2	0.8116	0.7972	0.7831	0.7695	0.7561	0.7432	0.7305	0.7182	0.7062	0.6944
3	0.7312	0.7188	0.6931	0.6750	0.6575	0.6407	0.6244	0.6086	0.5934	0.5787
4	0.6587	0.6355	0.6133	0.5921	0.5718	0.5523	0.5337	0.5158	0.4987	0.4823
5	0.5935	0.5674	0.5428	0.5194	0.4972	0.4761	0.4561	0.4371	0.4190	0.4019
6	0.5346	0.5066	0.4803	0.4556	0.4323	0.4104	0.3898	0.3704	0.3521	0.3349
7	0.4817	0.4523	0.4251	0.3996	0.3759	0.3538	0.3332	0.3139	0.2959	0.2791
8	0.4339	0.4039	0.3762	0.3506	0.3269	0.3050	0.2848	0.2660	0.2487	0.2326
9	0.3909	0.3606	0.3329	0.3075	0.2843	0.2630	0.2434	0.2255	0.2090	0.1938
10	0.3522	0.3220	0.2946	0.2697	0.2472	0.2267	0.2080	0.1911	0.1756	0.1615
11	0.3173	0.2875	0.2607	0.2366	0.2149	0.1954	0.1778	0.1619	0.1476	0.1346
12	0.2858	0.2567	0.2307	0.2076	0.1869	0.1685	0.1520	0.1372	0.1240	0.1122
13	0.2575	0.2292	0.2042	0.1821	0.1625	0.1452	0.1299	0.1163	0.1042	0.0935
14	0.2320	0.2046	0.1807	0.1597	0.1413	0.1252	0.1110	0.0985	0.0876	0.0779
15	0.2090	0.1827	0.1599	0.1401	0.1299	0.1079	0.0949	0.0835	0.0736	0.0649
16	0.1883	0.1631	0.1415	0.1229	0.1069	0.0930	0.0811	0.0708	0.0618	0.0541
17	0.1696	0.1456	0.1252	0.1078	0.0929	0.0802	0.0693	0.0600	0.0520	0.0451
18	0.1528	0.1300	0.1108	0.0946	0.0808	0.0691	0.0592	0.0508	0.0437	0.0376
19	0.1377	0.1161	0.0981	0.0829	0.0703	0.0596	0.0506	0.0431	0.0367	0.0313
20	0.1240	0.1037	0.0868	0.0728	0.0611	0.0514	0.0433	0.0365	0.0308	0.0261
21	0.1117	0.0926	0.0768	0.0638	0.0531	0.0443	0.0370	0.0309	0.0259	0.0217
22	0.1007	0.0826	0.0680	0.0560	0.0462	0.0382	0.0316	0.0262	0.0218	0.0181
23	0.0907	0.0738	0.0601	0.0491	0.0402	0.0329	0.0270	0.0222	0.0183	0.0151
24	0.0817	0.0659	0.0532	0.0431	0.0349	0.0284	0.0231	0.0188	0.0154	0.0126
25	0.0736	0.0588	0.0471	0.0378	0.0304	0.0245	0.0197	0.0160	0.0129	0.0105
26	0.0663	0.0525	0.0417	0.0331	0.0264	0.0211	0.0169	0.0135	0.0109	0.0087
27	0.0597	0.0469	0.0369	0.0291	0.0230	0.0182	0.0144	0.0115	0.0091	0.0073
28	0.0538	0.0419	0.0326	0.0255	0.0200	0.0157	0.0123	0.0097	0.0077	0.0061
29	0.0485	0.0374	0.0289	0.0224	0.0174	0.0135	0.0105	0.0082	0.0064	0.0051
30	0.0437	0.0334	0.0256	0.0196	0.0151	0.0116	0.0090	0.0070	0.0054	0.0042
31	0.0394	0.0298	0.0226	0.0172	0.0131	0.0100	0.0077	0.0059	0.0046	0.0035
32	0.0355	0.0266	0.0200	0.0151	0.0114	0.0087	0.0066	0.0050	0.0038	0.0029
33	0.0319	0.0238	0.0177	0.0132	0.0099	0.0075	0.0056	0.0042	0.0032	0.0024
34	0.0288	0.0212	0.0157	0.0116	0.0086	0.0064	0.0045	0.0036	0.0027	0.0020
35	0.0259	0.0189	0.0139	0.0102	0.0075	0.0055	0.0041	0.0030	0.0023	0.0017
36	0.0234	0.0169	0.0123	0.0089	0.0065	0.0048	0.0035	0.0026	0.0019	0.0014
37	0.0210	0.0151	0.0109	0.0078	0.0057	0.0041	0.0030	0.0022	0.0016	0.0012
38	0.0190	0.0135	0.0096	0.0069	0.0049	0.0036	0.0026	0.0019	0.0013	0.0010
39	0.0171	0.0120	0.0085	0.0060	0.0043	0.0031	0.0022	0.0016	0.0011	0.0008
40	0.0154	0.0107	0.0075	0.0053	0.0037	0.0026	0.0019	0.0013	0.0010	0.0007
41	0.0139	0.0096	0.0067	0.0046	0.0032	0.0023	0.0016	0.0011	0.0008	0.0006
42	0.0125	0.0086	0.0059	0.0041	0.0028	0.0020	0.0014	0.0010	0.0007	0.0005
43	0.0112	0.0076	0.0052	0.0036	0.0025	0.0017	0.0012	0.0008	0.0006	0.0004
44	0.0101	0.0068	0.0046	0.0031	0.0021	0.0015	0.0010	0.0007	0.0005	0.0003
45	0.0091	0.0061	0.0041	0.0027	0.0019	0.0013	0.0009	0.0006	0.0004	0.0003
46	0.0082	0.0054	0.0036	0.0024	0.0016	0.0011	0.0007	0.0005	0.0003	0.0002
47	0.0074	0.0049	0.0032	0.0021	0.0014	0.0009	0.0006	0.0004	0.0003	0.0002
48	0.0067	0.0043	0.0028	0.0019	0.0012	0.0008	0.0005	0.0004	0.0002	0.0002
49	0.0060	0.0039	0.0025	0.0016	0.0011	0.0007	0.0005	0.0003	0.0002	0.0001
50	0.0054	0.0035	0.0022	0.0014	0.0009	0.0006	0.0004	0.0003	0.0002	0.0001

References and further reading

Anthony, P. (1993) 'Healthcare resource groups in the NHS: a measure of success', *Public Finance and Accountancy*, 23 April, pp.8–10.

Argyris, C. (1953) 'Human problems with budgets', *Harvard Business Review*, 31, 1, pp.97–110.

Armstrong, C. (1992) 'Base budgeting: a modified approach', *Public Finance and Accountancy*, 10 July, pp.13–15.

Armstrong, W. (1980) *Budgetary Reform in the United Kingdom*, Oxford: Oxford University Press.

Atkinson, M. (2000) 'Can Gordon resist the pull of the crowd?', *Public Finance*, 7 July, pp.18–20.

Barnett, J. (1982) *Inside the Treasury*, London: André Deutsch.

Boyfield, K. (1992) 'Private sector funding of public sector infrastructure', *Public Money and Management*, 12, 2, pp.41–6.

British Waterways (1999) Annual Report and Accounts, 1998/99.

Budgetary Reform (1992) Cm 1867, London: HMSO.

Buttery, R. and Simpson, R. (1989) *Audit in the Public Sector*, 2nd edn, London: Woodhead Faulker.

Capon, B. (1992) 'The inevitability of the internal trading market', *Public Finance and Accountancy*, 8 May, pp.16–18.

Cardiff City Council (2000) Annual Report and Accounts, March 2000.

Cargill, R. (1991) 'Investing surplus funds', *Public Finance and Accountancy*, 13 December, pp.10–12.

Caulfield, I. and Schultz, J. (1989) *Planning for Change: Strategic Planning in Local Government*, London: Longman.

Chartered Institute of Management Accountancy (1987) *Management Accounting Official Terminology of the CIMA*, London: CIMA.

CIPFA (Chartered Institute of Public Finance and Accountancy) (1971) *Programme Budgeting – the Approach*, London: CIPFA.

CIPFA (Chartered Institute of Public Finance and Accountancy) (1979) *Statements on Internal Audit*, London: CIPFA.

CIPFA (Chartered Institute of Public Finance and Accountancy) (1990) *Financial Information System: Vol. 4, Budgetary Processes*, London: CIPFA.

CIPFA (Chartered Institute of Public Finance and Accountancy) (1991a) *The Management of Overheads in Local Authorities*, London: CIPFA.

CIPFA (Chartered Institute of Public Finance and Accountancy) (1991b) *Service Level Agreements: A Compendium*, London: CIPFA.

CIPFA (Chartered Institute of Public Finance and Accountancy) (1995) *Accounting for Overheads in Great Britain*, London: CIPFA.

CIPFA (Chartered Institute of Public Finance and Accountancy) (2000) *Further and Higher Education Newsletter*, December, London: CIPFA.

CIPFA (Chartered Institute of Public Finance and Accountancy) *Financial Information Service*, various volumes. Regularly updated manual.

Citizen's Charter (1991) 'Raising the Standard', Cm 1599, London: HMSO.

Citizen's Charter (1992) 'First Report', Cm 2101, London: HMSO.

Connor, S. (1993) 'Accounting for quality in audit', *Public Finance and Accountancy*, 23 July, pp.10–12.

Coombs, H.M. and Edwards, J.R. (1990) 'The evolution of the district audit', *Financial Accountability and Management*, 6, 3.

Coombs, H.M. and Edwards, J.R. (1996) *Accounting Innovation in Municipal Corporations*, New York: Garland.

Coombs, H.M. and Evans, A. (2000) 'Managing central support services through service level agreements', *The Government Accountants Journal*, 49, 1, pp.54–9.

Coombs, H.M., Hobbs, D. and Jenkins, D.E. (2000) 'Management accounting for the millennium and beyond', in *Simulation and Gaming Research Yearbook* (Saunders, S. and Smalley, N. (eds)), vol. 8, London: Kogan Page.

Cooper, R. and Kaplan, R.S. (1988) 'Measure costs right: make the right decisions', *Harvard Business Review*, September/October, pp.96–103.

Cowan, N. (1993) 'Marketing for survival', *Public Finance and Accountancy*, 28 May, pp.8–9.

Department of Health (1989) 'Working for Patients', London: HMSO.

Department of Environment, Transport and the Regions (2000) 'Modernising Local Government: A Green Paper', available from: http://www.detr.gov.uk/greenpap/part4.htm

DHSS (1982) 'Investment Appraisal in the Public Sector', NHS(82)34, London: DHSS.

Dixon, R. (1991) 'Local management of schools', *Public Money and Management*, 11, 3, pp.47–52.

Dopson, S. (1993) 'Are agencies an act of faith? The experience of HMSO', *Public Money and Management*, 13, 2, pp.17–24.

Drury, C. (2000) *Management and Cost Accounting*, 5th edn, London: Thomson Learning.

Edwards, P. (1992) 'Formula funding: three years on', *Public Finance and Accountancy*, 6 March, pp.27–8.

Efficiency Unit (1988) 'Improving Management in Government: The Next Steps', London: HMSO.

Efficiency Unit (1991) 'Making the Most of Next Steps, Report to the Prime Minister', London: HMSO.

Giddings, P. (1991) 'Cash management: joining forces with the specialists', *Public Finance and Accountancy*, 25 October, pp.14–15.

Gray, M. (1992) 'Business planning', *Public Finance and Accountancy*, 10 April, pp.12–14.

Hardcastle, A. (1990) 'Financial accountability and reporting in central government', *Public Money and Management*, 10, 1, pp.23–8.

Haring, P. (1993) 'Restructuring debt', *Public Finance and Accountancy*, 22 January, pp.14–15.

Henderson, J. (1984) *Appraising Options*, Health Economics Research Unit, Aberdeen University.

Henley, D., Likierman, A., Perrin, J., Evans, M., Lapsley, I. and Whiteoak, J. (1992) *Public Sector Financial Accounting and Control*, 4th edn, London: Chapman & Hall.

Hennessy, P. (1989) *Whitehall*, London: Secker & Warburg.

HM Government (1976) 'Cash Limits on Public Expenditures', Cm 6440, London: HMSO.

HM Government (1978) 'The Nationalised Industries', Cm 7131, London: HMSO.

HM Government (1988) 'A New Public Expenditure Planning Total', Cm 441, London: HMSO.

HM Government (1989) 'Public Expenditure Management', London: HMSO.

HM Government (1990) 'The Government's Expenditure Plans', Cm 1021, London: HMSO.

HM Government (1992) 'Autumn Statement', Cm 2096, London: HMSO.

HM Government (1994) 'Better Accounting for the Taxpayers' Money, The Government's Proposals', Cm 2626, London: HMSO.

HM Government (1998a) 'NHS Modern and Dependable', Cm 3807, London: HMSO.

HM Government (1998b) 'Report of the Independent Inquiry into Inequalities in Health' (Acheson Report), London: HMSO.

HM Government (1998c) 'Stability and Investment for the Long Term', Cm 3978, London: HMSO.

HM Government (1998d) 'Public Services for the Future, Modernisation Reform, Accountability', Cm 4181, London: HMSO.

HM Government (1999a) 'Public Expenditure Statistical Analysis', Cm 4201, London: The Stationery Office.

HM Government (1999b) 'Explanatory Notes to Local Government Act 1999', London: The Stationery Office.

HM Government (2000a) 'Spending review 2000, Prudent for a Purpose', Cm 4807, London: The Stationery Office.

HM Government (2000b) 'Public Expenditure Statistical Analysis', Cm 4601, London: The Stationery Office.

HM Government (2000c) '2000 Spending Review: Public Service Agreements', Cm 4808, London: The Stationery Office.

Horngren, C.T. (1987) *Cost Accounting: A Managerial Approach*, 6th edn, Englewood Cliffs, NJ: Prentice Hall.

Jacobs, K. and Smith-Bowers, B. (2000) 'Catch 22 for rent collection', *Public Finance*, 24 March, pp.24–5.

Jones, R. (1993) 'Customers, financial services and the competitive edge', *Public Finance and Accountancy*, 4 June, pp.14–15.

Jones, R. and Pendlebury, M. (2000) *Public Sector Accounting*, 5th edn, London: Pearson Education.

Jones, T. and Prowle, M. (1988) *Health Service Finance: An Introduction*, 2nd edn, London: Certified Accountant Educational Trust.

Kelly, J. (2000) 'Changing the meaning of time', *Public Finance*, 31 March, p.34.

Kemp, P. (1990) 'Can the civil service adapt to managing by contract?', *Public Money and Management*, 10, 3, pp.25–32.

Knights, A. (1991) 'Investing within a framework', *Public Finance and Accountancy*, December, pp.12–14.

Korner, E. (1984) 'Report of the Steering Group on Health Service Information', London: HMSO.

Lapsley, I. (1986a) 'Investment appraisal in UK non-trading organisations', *Financial Accountability and Management*, 2, 2, pp.135–51.

Lapsley, I. (1986b) 'Investment appraisal in public sector organisations', *Management Accounting*, June, pp.28–31.

Lapsley, I. and Llewellyn, S. (1993) 'Costing care packages: dilemmas and difficulties', *Public Money and Management*, 13, 3, pp.15–17.

Likierman, A. (1988) *Public Expenditure: Who Really Controls It and How*, London: Penguin.

Masters, S. (1993) 'Financial management in the NHS', *Public Money and Management*, 13, 1, p.4.

McAlister, D. (1990) 'Option appraisal: turning an art into a science', *Public Money and Management*, 10, 4, pp.27–34.

McHugh, J. (2000a) 'Final attempt to close Hackney's black hole', *Public Finance*, 3 November, p.13.

McHugh, J. (2000b) 'Hackney pleads for help', *Public Finance*, 10 November, p.6.

Miller, A. (2000) 'New fears for finance staff jobs at the BBC', *Accountancy Age*, p.1227 July.

Monmouthshire County Council (2000) Annual Reports and Accounts, March 2000.

Morgan, T. and Weaver, M. (1993) 'Budget making – is there a better way', *Public Finance and Accountancy*, 11 June, pp. 51–6.

Morley, D. (1992) 'The Citizen's Charter and a 21st-century vision', *Public Money and Management*, 12, 1, p.6.

National Assembly for Wales (2000) 'Local Government Best Value: Guidance to Local Authorities in Wales', Circular 14/2000.

National Audit Office (1986a) *The Financial Management Initiative*, London: HMSO.

National Audit Office (1986b) 'The Rayner Scrutiny Programmes 1979–1983', HC 322, London: HMSO.

National Audit Office (2000a) 'Ministry of Defence: Major Projects Report 2000', HC 970 1999/2000, London: The Stationery Office.

National Audit Office (2000b), 'The Millennium Dome', HC 936 1999/2000, London: The Stationery Office.

Parkes, J. (1988) *Capital Accounting: The Way Forward*, London: CIPFA.

Pendlebury, M. (ed.) (1989) *Management Accounting in the Public Sector*, London: Heinemann.

Pendlebury, M.W. (1985) *Management Accounting in Local Government: A Research Study*, London: The Institute of Cost and Management Accountants.

Perrin, J. (1988) *Resource Management in the NHS*, London: Chapman & Hall.

Phyrr, P. (1970) 'Zero-based budgeting', *Harvard Business Review*, 43, 12, pp.111–21.

Plowden Report (1961) 'The Control of Public Expenditure', Cm 1432, London: HMSO.

Post Office (2000) Annual Report and Accounts 1999–2000.

Preddy, B. (1993) 'Performance targets for managing cash', *Public Finance and Accountancy*, 9 April, pp.13–14.

Prest, A.R. and Turvey, R. (1965) 'Cost benefit analysis: a survey', *Economic Journal*, LXXXV, 300, pp.685–705.

Public Accounts Committee (1976–77) 'Cash Limits', 3rd Report, HC 274, London: HMSO.

Public Accounts Committee (1986–87) 'Financial Reporting to Parliament', 8th Report, HC 383, London: HMSO.

Public Finance (2000) 'Tuition fees hailed a great success', 11 February, p.16.

Puxty, A.G. and Dodds, J.C. (1988) *Financial Management Method and Meaning*, London: Chapman & Hall.

Queen Victoria NHS Trust (1998) Financial Report, 1997/98.

Robinson, R. (1991) 'Health expenditure: recent trends and prospects for the 1990s', *Public Money and Management*, 11, 4, pp.19–24.

Rutherford, B.A. (1983) *Financial Reporting in the Public Sector*, London: Butterworth.

Simon, H.A. (1953) *Administrative Behaviour*, London: Macmillan.

Simon, H.A. (1959) 'Theories and decision making in economics and behavioural science', *American Economic Review*, XLIX, June, pp.253–83.

Sugden, R. and Williams, A. (1978) *The Principles of Practical Cost Benefit Analysis*, Oxford: Oxford University Press.

Thain, C. and Wright, M. (1990) 'Haggling in Mr Clarke's Turkish Bazaar', *Public Money and Management*, 4, pp.51–6.

Thompson, P. (2000) 'Brixton breaks the mould', *Public Finance*, 14 July, pp.22–23.

Treasury and Civil Service Committee (1982) 'Efficiency and Effectiveness in the Civil Service', Cm 8616, London: HMSO.

Treasury and Civil Service Committee (1991) 'The Next Steps Initiative', 7th Report session 1990–91, HC 496, London: HMSO.

Treasury and Civil Service Committee (1992) 'Banking Supervision and BCCL Role of Local Authorities and Money Brokers', London: HMSO.

Van Horne, J.C. (1986) *Financial Management and Policy*, 6th edn, Englewood Cliffs, NJ: Prentice Hall.

Walker, D. (1993) 'A Private Style at the Heart of Whitehall',

Ward, S. (2000) 'Market testing ends for NHS', *Public Finance*, 6 October, p.15.

While, R. (1993) 'How to live with SSAs', *Public Finance and Accountancy*, 25 June, pp.20–2.

Wildavsky, A. (1974) *The Politics of the Budgetary Process*, 2nd edn, Boston: Little Brown.

Wilson, John (ed) (1998) *Financial Management for the Public Services*, Buckingham: Open University Press.

Index